An Introduction to the Advanced Theory of Nonparametric Econometrics

Interest in nonparametric methodology has grown considerably over the past few decades, stemming in part from vast improvements in computer hardware and the availability of new software that allows practitioners to take full advantage of these numerically intensive methods. This book is written for advanced undergraduate students, intermediate graduate students, and faculty, and provides a complete teaching and learning course at a more accessible level of theoretical rigor than Racine's earlier book co-authored with Qi Li, Nonparametric Econometrics: Theory and Practice (2007). The open source R platform for statistical computing and graphics is used throughout in conjunction with the R package np. Recent developments in reproducible research is emphasized throughout with appendices devoted to helping the reader get up to speed with R, R Markdown, TeX and Git.

Jeffrey S. Racine is Professor in the Department of Economics and Professor in the Graduate Program in Statistics in the Department of Mathematics and Statistics at McMaster University, Canada. He holds the Senator William McMaster Chair in Econometrics and is a Fellow of the Journal of Econometrics. He is co-author of Nonparametric Econometrics: Theory and Practice (2007). He has published extensively in his field and has co-authored the R packages np and crs that are available on the Comprehensive R Archive Network (CRAN).

An Introduction to the Advanced Theory of Nonparametric Econometrics

A Replicable Approach Using R

JEFFREY S. RACINE

McMaster University, Ontario

CAMBRIDGE
UNIVERSITY PRESS

University Printing House, Cambridge CB2 8BS, United Kingdom

One Liberty Plaza, 20th Floor, New York, NY 10006, USA

477 Williamstown Road, Port Melbourne, VIC 3207, Australia

314–321, 3rd Floor, Plot 3, Splendor Forum, Jasola District Centre, New Delhi – 110025, India

79 Anson Road, #06–04/06, Singapore 079906

Cambridge University Press is part of the University of Cambridge.

It furthers the University's mission by disseminating knowledge in the pursuit of education, learning, and research at the highest international levels of excellence.

www.cambridge.org
Information on this title: www.cambridge.org/9781108483407
DOI: 10.1017/9781108649841

First published 2019

Printed in the United States of America by Sheridan Books, Inc.

A catalogue record for this publication is available from the British Library.

ISBN 978-1-108-48340-7 Hardback

Contents

List of Tables

List of Figures

Preface

In the early 20th century, the pioneering statistician Sir R. A. Fisher (1890-1962) set in motion what is known today as the *classical parametric Fisherian* approach by casting statistical estimation as a problem involving a *finite* number of parameters. However, parametric models provide only an approximation to the underlying data generating process and may therefore be biased and inconsistent. Models that seek to describe the data generating process in a statistically consistent manner are more involved, since the unknown components in such models are functions that fully characterize the underlying joint distribution of a data sample. *Nonparametric* methods are suitable for the estimation of an unknown function that belongs to a very broadly defined class of functions, and in this context, the number of parameters involved is said to be of *infinite* dimension. Although the complexity of nonparametric estimators often exceeds that of their more rigid parametric counterparts, they offer practitioners alternative approaches that can reveal features present in a data sample that might otherwise remain undetected.

Interest in nonparametric methodology has grown considerably over the past few decades, stemming in part from vast improvements in computer hardware and the availability of new software that allows practitioners to take full advantage of these numerically intensive methods. The earliest work on nonparametric *kernel* estimation of *probability density functions* dates back to the early 1950s (Fix and Hodges, 1951), on kernel estimation of *regression functions* to the 1960s (Watson, 1964), and on kernel estimation of *probability mass functions* to the 1970s (Aitchison and Aitken, 1976). There exist a variety of books that are devoted to nonparametric estimation and inference, although most of them appear to have been written with an audience of advanced graduate students and researchers in mind, and their focus is often on one very specific aspect of the field (e.g., density estimation). A list of notable contributions would include

- Prakasa Rao (1983; Prakasa Rao, 2014) (devoted to large sample properties of various nonparametric estimators)
- Devroye and Györfi (1985) (devoted to the L_1 approach to nonparametric estimation)

- Silverman (1986) (devoted to density estimation and related topics)
- Härdle (1990) (devoted to applied nonparametric regression)
- Scott (1992) (devoted to density estimation and high-dimensional visualization)
- Wand and Jones (1995) (devoted to an accessible treatment of kernel density estimation and regression)
- Fan and Gijbels (1996) (devoted to local polynomial estimation)
- Simonoff (1996) (devoted to smooth density estimation, regression, and ordered categorical data)
- Bowman and Azzalini (1997) (devoted to the application of kernel methods in S-plus)
- Hart (1997) (devoted to nonparametric smoothing and lack-of-fit tests)
- Bosq (1998) (devoted to the theory of kernel methods for dependent data)
- Horowitz (1998) (devoted to semiparametric econometric methods)
- Pagan and Ullah (1999) (first broad treatment of nonparametric econometrics)
- Fan and Yao (2003) (devoted to time series modeling)
- Yatchew (2003) (devoted to applied semiparametric methods using a differencing technique)
- Ruppert et al. (2003) (devoted to semiparametric modeling)
- Härdle et al. (2004) (devoted to nonparametric and semiparametric modeling)
- Wasserman (2006) (devoted to brief accounts of many modern topics in nonparametric inference)
- Li and Racine (2007) (devoted to nonparametric and semiparametric modeling with an emphasis on categorical covariates)
- Tsybakov (2009) (devoted to construction of optimal estimators, minimax optimality and adaptivity)
- Ahamada and Flachaire (2010) (devoted to an accessible introduction to nonparametric and semiparametric econometrics)
- Henderson and Parmeter (2015) (devoted to an accessible treatment of nonparametric econometrics)
- Politis (2015) (devoted to a transformation-based approach to model free inference)
- Hansen (2018) (devoted to econometrics but with chapters for kernel regression and density estimation)

In Li and Racine (2007), our aim was to provide a rigorous and comprehensive treatment of nonparametric econometric methodology, with an emphasis on mixed categorical and continuous data settings, intended for advanced graduate students and researchers looking to keep abreast of this rapidly growing field. The accompanying R (R Core Team, 2018) package, titled np, (Hayfield and Racine, 2008) was intended to facilitate the implementation in applied research settings of many of the methods that we discussed. We are grateful for the constructive criticism and helpful feedback that we have received about these projects, and we owe an enormous debt to the scores of researchers whose work made them possible.

In this book, we are aiming our attention squarely at advanced undergraduate students, intermediate graduate students, and faculty who wish to explore this exciting field, although not necessarily at the level of theoretical rigour that was found in our previous treatment. We take a more *organic* approach than existing treatments of the subject, and present a unique sequence of topics that are not collectively found elsewhere. We begin with a simple estimator that is standard fare in introductory statistics courses, namely the sample proportion, which is a nonsmooth nonparametric estimator of an unknown probability. This serves as preliminary motivation for the progressive introduction of kernel-smoothing, density estimation, conditional density estimation, and the estimation of more general conditional moments such as the conditional mean (regression), variance, and related objects. Proof concepts are illustrated *once* when each unique case is first encountered, whereas proofs that are of a similar nature to those already treated are either relegated to exercises or accompanied by citation info so that the interested reader may find them in existing treatments. Our approach emphasizes the plug-in principle that is the essence of most nonparametric methods. This involves identifying a fundamental statistical object (e.g., a conditional mean), expressing the object in terms of unknown density or distribution functions, and then plugging in *smooth* and *consistent* estimates of these unknowns. Special attention is also given to smoothing parameter selection and to the statistical properties of the estimator that results.

Our treatment of nonparametric estimation evolves along the lines of what one might encounter in an introductory statistics course, closely following the conventional sequence of topics. That convention is to first introduce discrete probability (i.e., mass) functions in Chapter 1 and then proceed to the study of continuous probability density functions in Chapter 2. However, one chapter that is conspicuously absent from introductory courses is a chapter on probability distributions with mixed discrete and continuous features (such problems are known to be "parametrically awkward" (Aitchison and Aitken, 1976, page 419)). In a nonparametric framework, modeling such objects isn't awkward at all, and hence we fill this gap in Chapter 3 with a treatment of mixed discrete and continuous probability density functions and their cumulative counterparts. Moreover, it will be seen that we can subsequently tackle in a seamless manner *any* statistical object that is defined over mixed discrete and continuous data. Along the way, we will also cover nonparametric estimation of smooth quantile functions and copula functions. We then consolidate and fix notation by means of a parsimonious representation of the mixed-data multivariate product kernel. This then allows us to plunge into a range of methods for estimation and inference including nonparametric regression, nonparametric modeling of volatility, as well as methods for stationary time series.

We assess *pointwise* and *global* estimation error via the mean square and integrated (summed) mean square error, respectively. The pointwise error of estimation at a given point x is the difference between an estimate of the statistical object of interest and the object itself. For instance, we might compute the difference between the empirical CDF $F_n(x)$ and the unknown CDF $F(x)$. Pointwise error is a simple measure that is useful for the construction of confidence intervals. The *integrated* mean square error (or the *summed* mean square error in the context of discrete support random variables) measures the overall error of estimation and is useful as a criterion for bandwidth selection. *Uniform* error is another metric that is computed as the maximal difference between the estimate and the object, i.e., $\sup_x |F_n(x) - F(x)|$. It is typically approached using empirical process theory (Prakasa Rao, 2014). Uniform error is useful for placing bounds on other types of error and establishing *simultaneous* or uniform confidence bands. In this book, we consider only the first two types of error (pointwise and global) and direct the reader whose interest lies in uniform error to other more advanced treatments.

We emphasize how kernel estimators can be interpreted as *shrinkage* estimators (Stein, 1956), as demonstrated in Kiefer and Racine (2009) and Kiefer and Racine (2017). From this perspective, the local constant, local linear, and other variants of local polynomial kernel estimators can be improved; for a broad class of data-generating processes (the class of *analytic* functions), these estimators are able to achieve the rate of convergence that is associated with correctly specified parametric models. Theoretical underpinnings for this result, which is achieved through joint selection of the polynomial degree and bandwidth vectors, can be found in Hall and Racine (2015). Although this approach requires a solution to a mixed-integer problem, its implementation is now feasible in R, and this represents an exciting advance in the area of local polynomial estimation of statistical objects. The interpretation of kernel methods as shrinkage estimators is underscored wherever appropriate in each chapter. Simulations and practical exercises reveal that the performance of this estimator may be superior to that of alternative approaches that are based on ad hoc selection of the polynomial order. Our perspective on kernel estimators, as seen through the lens of shrinkage estimators, is quite novel and, to the best of our knowledge, is not found elsewhere.

The computational run time of various routines in the R package np (Hayfield and Racine, 2008) can be reduced through their ability to exploit the power of multiple processors (see the R package npRmpi) and through their incorporation of algorithmic enhancements such as the use of trees. That being said, kernel methods are computationally intensive relative to many of their parametric peers; however, patience in this regard often pays dividends.

R code for all examples in this book is sourced from an R Markdown script and can be studied and modified by readers (this document is composed in R Markdown and uses R bookdown extensions (https://bookdown.org/yihui/bookdown) (Xie, 2017)). Each chapter ends with a *Practitioner's Corner* that provides a set of commented examples in R that can be refined by the reader to suit their needs. A solutions manual is available to instructors along with LaTeX *Beamer* PDF formatted slides authored in R Markdown that can be modified and tailored to an instructor's needs.

In this book, we derive results only for the *notationally parsimonious* case involving univariate data (or univariate conditioning/conditioned variables). Where appropriate, we present results for the multivariate case and draw attention to the salient differences between the two; however, for a thorough theoretical treatment of the multivariate cases, we simply direct the interested readers to Li and Racine (2007) and other sources. It is our conjecture that essentially all of the intuition underlying nonparametric kernel methods can be distilled from the univariate case, at least from the theoretical perspective. However, from the applied perspective, we impose no such limitations, and emphasize cases involving multivariate (and often mixed multivariate) data throughout.

We also touch upon a number of practical aspects of nonparametric kernel methods such as *kernel carpentry* (i.e., the construction of kernel functions with certain useful properties), and provide empirical examples to illustrate these concepts. We encourage the use of tools that facilitate reproducible research.

This book would not exist without the legacy (and ongoing) contributions of an incredibly talented global network of academics harbouring a wide array of research interests in the field of nonparametric statistics and econometrics. If you are reading this and have contributed to this exciting field, please take a virtual bow and accept our heartfelt thanks.

I would like to thank an abbreviated cast of characters, without whom this project would not exist. Qi Li, a co-author on a range of projects, has been an ongoing source of guidance, support, and encouragement. Tristen Hayfield and Zhenghua Nie, co-authors on the R packages np and crs, respectively, have helped craft user-friendly and computationally efficient implementations of the procedures that are detailed in this book. Nick Kiefer, a co-author, was the first to open my eyes to the interpretation of kernel estimators as shrinkage estimators. Peter Hall, a co-author whose acumen, friendship, and wisdom are sorely missed, made enduring contributions to the field and left a rich legacy that will surely last for generations. I would also like to thank but not implicate John Kealey, a former Ph.D. student who painstakingly pored through this book and polished its many rough edges, along with the students and faculty who attended a graduate course at McMaster University in the Fall of 2017 and who reported numerous typos in early drafts of this book (Alyssa, Anthony, Camille, Francis, James, Joaquin, Karen, Mark, Richard, Yuyan, and Zvezdomir). And last but certainly not least, I am indebted to my wife Jennifer and son Adam, who endured far too many months of my seven-day-a-week obsession with this project.

This book is dedicated to the memory of our kind, gentle, generous, and irreplaceable colleague, Peter Gavin Hall AO FAA FRS (November 21, 1951—January 9, 2016), an Australian researcher who worked in the areas of probability theory and mathematical statistics. Peter was described by the American Statistical Association as one of the most influential and prolific theoretical statisticians in the history of the field. It is fitting that The School of Mathematics and Statistics Building at The University of Melbourne was renamed the Peter Hall Building in his honour on December 9, 2016.

Glossary of Notation

Object	Brief Definition
$\beta(x)$	marginal effects function (derivative or finite difference of $g(x)$)
$\hat{\beta}(x)$	kernel smoothed marginal effects function (derivative or finite difference of $\hat{g}(x)$)
$C(u_x, u_y)$	bivariate copula function
$f(x)$	probability density function
$\hat{f}(x)$	kernel smoothed probability density function
$f(y|x)$	conditional probability density function
$\hat{f}(y|x)$	kernel smoothed conditional probability density function
$F(x)$	cumulative distribution function
$F_n(x)$	empirical cumulative distribution function
$\hat{F}(x)$	kernel smoothed cumulative distribution function
$F(y|x)$	cumulative conditional distribution function
$\hat{F}(y|x)$	kernel smoothed cumulative conditional distribution function
γ	vector of bandwidths and smoothing parameters for q continuous, r unordered, and s ordered covariates
$G((x - X_i)/h)$	continuous support univariate cumulative probability density kernel function
$G_\gamma(X_i, x)$	mixed-data multivariate cumulative probability density kernel function
$g(x)$	conditional mean function
$\hat{g}(x)$	kernel smoothed conditional mean function
h	bandwidth for continuous covariate
$K((x - X_i)/h)$	continuous support univariate probability density kernel function
$K_\gamma(X_i, x)$	mixed-data multivariate probability density kernel function
λ	smoothing parameter for discrete covariate

Object	Brief Definition
$l(X_i, x, \lambda)$	unordered discrete support univariate probability mass kernel function
$L(X_i, x, \lambda)$	ordered discrete support univariate probability mass kernel function
$\mathcal{L}(X_i, x, \lambda)$	ordered discrete support univariate cumulative probability mass kernel function
$M(x)$	conditional mode function
$\hat{M}(x)$	kernel smoothed conditional mode function
$p(x)$	probability mass function
$p_n(x)$	empirical probability mass function (sample proportion)
$\hat{p}(x)$	kernel smoothed probability mass function
q_τ	unconditional quantile function (inverse CDF)
$\hat{q}_\tau$	kernel smoothed unconditional quantile function
$q_\tau(x)$	conditional quantile function (inverse conditional CDF)
$\hat{q}_\tau(x)$	kernel smoothed conditional quantile function

Part I

Probability Functions, Probability Density Functions, and Their Cumulative Counterparts

Chapter 1

Discrete Probability and Cumulative Probability Functions

> While being shown a house to buy, Garp and his wife Helen witness a single-engine plane, presumably suffering catastrophic mechanical failure, plowing right into the side of the house. Garp takes this as a good sign – "The odds of another plane hitting this house are astronomical!" – and agrees right then and there to buy the house. (John Irving, *The World According to Garp*).

1.1 Overview

The first random variable typically encountered by students of basic statistics is known as a *discrete* random variable, after which they proceed to study *continuous* random variables. Discrete random variables do not always receive as much attention as continuous random variables receive, but in a nonparametric framework, the importance of their study should not be understated. Whether the discrete random variable is the number of times a single-engine plane crashes into a home or whether option "a", "b", or "c" was selected by a respondent on a questionnaire, it plays a fundamental role in statistical analysis.

A discrete random variable is one that can take on a *countable* number of values. They come in many different flavours and go by a variety of names including *nominal* (*unordered*) and *ordinal* (*ordered*) categorical variables. Examples would include the number of heads in three tosses of a coin where the random variable takes on the values $\{0, 1, 2, 3\}$, or an individual's employment status being classified as either "employed" or "unemployed" (i.e., an *unordered* categorical variable), or a response to a survey question recorded as one of "a", "b", or "c" where "a" indicates "most preferred" and

3

"c" "least preferred" (i.e., an *ordered* categorical variable). Their defining features are that their support[1] is *discrete*, repeated values in a random sample are to be expected, and *counting* the number of sample realizations for a particular outcome is a sensible thing to do.

Although the probability function for a discrete support random variable plays a key role in statistical inference, in applied settings this function is generally unknown and must be estimated. There are three approaches we might entertain when estimating the unknown probability function for a discrete random variable:

    i. Presume a parametric family (e.g., binomial) and estimate under this presumption.

    ii. Use the (nonsmooth) sample proportions.

    iii. Use a kernel-smoothed approach.

The first two are standard fare and are routinely taught in introductory courses on data analysis. The third, however, is likely far less familiar. One drawback with the first approach is that if the parametric family we have assumed is not compatible with the underlying data generating process (DGP), then the resulting estimates can be statistically *biased* and *inconsistent*. One drawback with the second approach is that, even though it is *unbiased* and *consistent*, there may be very few realizations of a particular outcome in the sample at hand, and hence the sample proportion for such an outcome will be highly variable.[2] The third approach introduces some finite sample bias by smoothing the sample proportions in a particular manner,[3] but this smoothing also reduces finite sample variance. The estimator that uses kernel smoothing is *asymptotically unbiased* and *consistent*, and may therefore exhibit better finite sample performance than either of its peers.

One of the benefits of beginning the study of nonparametric methods with kernel-smoothed estimators of probability functions is that, at least for the unordered case, there is no need for the type of approximation that is required when studying the kernel-smoothed estimators of density functions, which we will do in Chapter 2. We obtain simple and exact expressions for quantities such as the bias and variance of the estimator, its *summed* mean square error, and optimal smoothing parameters, among others. And for a special ordered case, we are introduced to an approximation technique that is widely used when studying kernel-smoothed estimators of density functions (this appears as an exercise). Another benefit is that when we migrate to the mixed-data case (i.e., datasets containing a mix of continuous

---

[1]By *support* we simply mean the *sample space* or set of all possible outcomes, i.e., it is the set of all outcomes whose probability (or probability density that we study in Chapter 2) is strictly positive.

[2]See Simonoff (1996) who proposes the use of discrete support kernel functions for smoothing sparse contingency tables.

[3]Essentially it *shrinks* the sample proportions in the direction of the discrete uniform distribution.

and discrete support random variables) the powerful potential uncovered by smoothing discrete support random variables in the manner outlined below will be revealed.

1.2   Parametric Probability Function Estimation

Suppose that we were interested in modeling a univariate probability function for some discrete random variable X. Furthermore, without loss of generality,[4] assume that $X \in \mathcal{D} = \{0, 1, \ldots, c-1\}$ where c is the number of outcomes taken on by X, and assume that $\{X_1, X_2, \ldots, X_n\}$ represents n independent random draws from the probability distribution $p(x)$. We denote the probability function $p(x) = \Pr(X = x)$, $x \in \mathcal{D}$, $0 \leq p(x) \leq 1$, $\sum_{x \in \mathcal{D}} p(x) = 1$ (the last two are necessary conditions for *proper* probabilities). In general, $p(x)$ is unknown and must be estimated.

Suppose that we took a parametric approach towards modeling the unknown probability function $p(x)$. The parametric approach would presume a parametric distribution for the unknown $p(x)$.[5] By way of illustration, we might presume that the data were generated from the binomial distribution given by

$$p(x; \pi) = \binom{n}{x} \pi^x (1 - \pi)^{n-x},$$

where n is the number of trials, π the probability of a *success* on each trial, and $\binom{n}{x} = n!/((n-x)!x!)$ with $x! = x \times (x-1) \times (x-2) \times \cdots \times 1$ and $0! \equiv 1$. We shall make use of this parametric model in the following illustrative example.

Example 1.1. Boy-Girl Ratio in Families (Adapted from Berry and Lindgren (1990), page 563).

> Occasionally, we hear parents remark something along the lines of "we have three boys and wanted a girl so thought we would try again", which begs the question of whether the sex of successive children in a family is akin to a coin toss, i.e., whether it behaves like a sequence of independent *Bernoulli* trials with the probability π of having a boy and $1 - \pi$ of having a girl. If so, the number of boys in a family of given size is binomially distributed, and we can compute the probability of obtaining x boys in a family of 8 children under this presumption where $x \in \mathcal{D} = \{0, 1, 2, \ldots, 8\}$. In a random sample of $n = 1,000$ families having eight children, there were 4,040 boys so our estimate of π is $\hat{\pi} = 4,040/8,000 =$

---

[4]The generality is that here we assume X is integer-valued, but it could just as easily be the characters "a" and "b".

[5]Common distributions for discrete random variables include the hypergeometric, Poisson, binomial, and negative binomial, by way of example.

Table 1.1: Boy-girl ratio in families. The null probability is $p_0(x) = \binom{8}{x}0.505^x(1-0.505)^{8-x}$ and the expected frequency is $e_x = 1,000 \times p_0(x)$.

x	Null Probability	Expected Frequency	Observed Frequency
0	0.0036	3.6	10
1	0.0294	29.4	34
2	0.1050	105.0	111
3	0.2143	214.3	215
4	0.2733	273.3	239
5	0.2231	223.1	227
6	0.1138	113.8	115
7	0.0332	33.2	34
8	0.0042	4.2	15

0.505. We compute the expected number of families with $x = 0, 1, \ldots, 8$ boys (i.e., $1,000 \times p_0(x)$ where $p_0(x)$ is the *null* probability if the sex of successive children in a family behave like independent Bernoulli trials). Our null is therefore $H_0: p(x) = \binom{8}{x}0.505^x(1-0.505)^{8-x}$ for all $x \in \mathcal{D} = \{0, 1, \ldots, 8\}$ versus the alternative that it is some other discrete distribution. The results presented in Table 1.1 summarize the observed frequencies as well as the probabilities and frequencies under the null that the number of children of a given sex is binomially distributed.

We can use the χ^2 goodness-of-fit procedure[6] to test the null that the data were generated by the binomial distribution. To measure how close the observed frequencies are to the expected frequencies, we calculate the statistic $\chi^2_\nu = \sum_{j=1}^c (o_j - e_j)^2/e_j$ where o_j and e_j denote observed and expected frequencies under the null, respectively. For our data, the statistic is $\chi^2 = 44.24$. The degrees of freedom here is $\nu = 7$ and equals the number of outcomes ($c = 9$) minus 1 minus the number of estimated parameters (we estimated one parameter, $\hat{\pi} = 0.505$). The critical value at the 5% level of significance is $\chi^2_{1-0.05,7} = 14.07$. The P-value is $1.92e - 07$, which is extremely strong evidence against the null, and we would therefore reject the null that the data were generated by a binomial distribution at all conventional levels of significance.

Table 1.1 and Figure 1.1 reveal that the binomial distribution

---

[6]Tests for goodness-of-fit are used to determine whether a set of data is consistent with a proposed model.

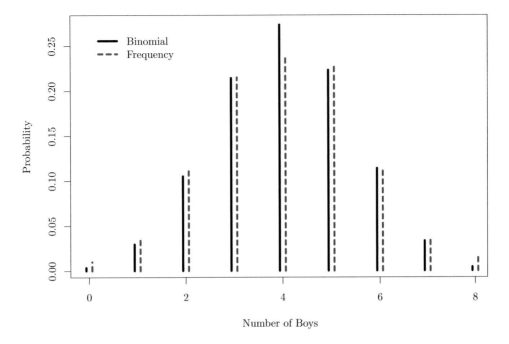

Figure 1.1: Parametric (binomial) versus nonsmooth nonparametric (sample proportion) probability estimates for the number of boys in families with eight children.

predicts more families with equal numbers of boys and girls and fewer families having all boys or all girls than is supported by the data.[7] The dice are stacked against you if you think that "trying again" behaves just like an independent coin toss. The results from the goodness-of-fit test conclusively reject this parametric model for the unknown probability distribution $p(x)$.

This example highlights the dilemma faced by practitioners who wish to model unknown discrete probability distributions. We can always *presume* a functional form for the underlying parametric model and estimate probabilities under this presumption. However, if we entertain the possibility that the parametric model might be misspecified, we would naturally test for correct specification of the presumed parametric model (e.g., test for correct specification of the binomial distribution as we did above). If the parametric model is rejected (as was the case above), then we return to where we began, having ruled out perhaps one of a number of potential parametric distributions. Furthermore, repeatedly testing alternative parametric specifications opens the *pre-test* can of worms, a fact that is often conveniently ignored by practitioners.

[7]Figure 1.1 compares the binomial probabilities with the *frequency* estimator of the probabilities defined in Section 1.3 below.

Against this backdrop, we might instead consider a nonparametric approach, and we shall consider two popular methods. The first is the familiar *frequency* estimator that was used in the illustrative example above (i.e., the *sample proportion*, which computes the *relative frequency* of occurrence and is a *nonparametric nonsmooth* approach). The second is a kernel[8] estimator that smooths a discrete support random variable in a particular manner (i.e., a *nonparametric kernel-smoothed* approach). We now turn our attention to the nonsmooth frequency estimator of the unknown probability function $p(x)$.

1.3   Nonsmooth Probability Function Estimation

All readers will no doubt be aware of an extremely popular nonparametric estimator of unknown probabilities, namely the *sample proportion* $p_n(x)$ defined below, which we refer to as the *nonsmooth* or *frequency* estimator. Students of introductory statistics know that this estimator is unbiased (i.e., $\operatorname{E} p_n(x) = p(x)$) and has variance $p(x)(1 - p(x))/n$. It will be instructive to derive these results because familiarity with this proof concept will lend transparency to the proof for the kernel-smoothed approach that we consider afterwards.

Let $X \in \mathcal{D} = \{0, 1, \ldots, c - 1\}$ be a discrete random variable having finite support. Suppose that we have a sample of n independent random draws from the probability distribution $p(x)$, denoted $\{X_1, X_2, \ldots, X_n\}$. The univariate frequency estimator of $p(x)$ is the familiar sample proportion given by

$$p_n(x) = \frac{\#X_i \text{ equal to } x}{n}$$

$$= \frac{1}{n} \sum_{i=1}^{n} \mathbf{1}(X_i = x),$$

where "$\#X_i$ equal to x" is simply the number of sample realizations equal to any particular outcome x and where $\mathbf{1}(\cdot)$ is an *indicator function* defined by

$$\mathbf{1}(X_i = x) = \begin{cases} 1 & \text{if } X_i = x \\ 0 & \text{otherwise.} \end{cases}$$

This indicator function is for *counting* and is limited to conducting a binary operation, *equal* or *not equal*. Hence the expression $n^{-1} \sum_{i=1}^{n} \mathbf{1}(X_i = x)$ simply considers each member of the sample of n observations $\{X_1, X_2, \ldots, X_n\}$, assigns to each the value 1 if it equals the particular outcome x and 0 otherwise, adds up all of the 1s and divides by the number of observations n. In the end, this is simply the sample proportion of observations equal to x.

---

[8]The term *kernel* simply refers to the use of weight functions having particular properties.

Recall that the *expected value* of a discrete random variable is obtained by multiplying each element of the outcome space $\mathcal{D}$ by its probability of occurrence and taking the sum thereof, while the expected value of some *function* of a discrete random variable is obtained by multiplying the function evaluated at each element of the outcome space by its probability of occurrence and taking the sum thereof. The expected value of $p_n(x)$ is therefore given by

$$
\begin{aligned}
\mathrm{E}\, p_n(x) &= \frac{1}{n} \sum_{i=1}^{n} \mathrm{E}\, \mathbf{1}(X_i = x) \\
&= \mathrm{E}\, \mathbf{1}(X_1 = x) \\
&= \sum_{t \in \mathcal{D}} \mathbf{1}(t = x) p(t) \\
&= \mathbf{1}(x = x) p(x) + \sum_{t \in \mathcal{D}, t \neq x} \mathbf{1}(t = x) p(t) \\
&= 1 \times p(x) + \sum_{t \in \mathcal{D}, t \neq x} 0 \times p(t) \\
&= p(x),
\end{aligned}
$$

where the second line follows from the identical distribution assumption (i.e., under identical distributions $\mathrm{E}\, \mathbf{1}(X_1 = x) = \mathrm{E}\, \mathbf{1}(X_2 = x) = \cdots = \mathrm{E}\, \mathbf{1}(X_n = x)$, so $\sum_{i=1}^{n} \mathrm{E}\, \mathbf{1}(X_i = x) = \sum_{i=1}^{n} \mathrm{E}\, \mathbf{1}(X_1 = x) = n \times \mathrm{E}\, \mathbf{1}(X_1 = x)$), and the third line follows from the definition of the expected value of a function of a discrete random variable described above. Moving from the third to the sixth line, note that $t = x$ for only one value of $t \in \mathcal{D}$ (e.g., suppose $x = 2$, although x could be any outcome that we might consider). Hence $\mathbf{1}(t = x)$ equals 1 for $t = x$ and $\mathbf{1}(t = x) p(t) = 1 \times p(x) = p(x)$ for $t = x$, while $\mathbf{1}(t = x) p(t) = 0 \times p(t) = 0$ for the remaining outcomes in $\mathcal{D}$ (i.e., all $t \in \mathcal{D}$ for which $t \neq x$). Since $\mathrm{E}\, p_n(x) = p(x)$, this estimator is clearly *unbiased* (i.e., $\mathrm{Bias}\, p_n(x) = \mathrm{E}\, p_n(x) - p(x) = 0$).

The variance of $p_n(x)$ is given by

$$
\begin{aligned}
\mathrm{Var}\, p_n(x) &= \mathrm{E}\left((p_n(x) - \mathrm{E}\, p_n(x))^2 \right) \\
&= \mathrm{E}\left(\left(\frac{1}{n} \sum_{i=1}^{n} (\mathbf{1}(X_i = x) - \mathrm{E}\, \mathbf{1}(X_i = x)) \right)^2 \right) \\
&= \frac{1}{n^2} \left(\sum_{i=1}^{n} \mathrm{E}\, \eta_i^2 + \sum_{i} \sum_{j, i \neq j} \mathrm{E}\, \eta_i \eta_j \right) \\
&= \frac{1}{n} \mathrm{E}\left(\mathbf{1}(X_1 = x) - \mathrm{E}\, \mathbf{1}(X_1 = x) \right)^2 \\
&= \frac{1}{n} \left(\mathrm{E}\, \mathbf{1}^2(X_1 = x) - (\mathrm{E}\, \mathbf{1}(X_1 = x))^2 \right)
\end{aligned}
$$

$$= \frac{1}{n} \left(\mathrm{E}\,\mathbf{1}(X_1 = x) - (\mathrm{E}\,\mathbf{1}(X_1 = x))^2 \right)$$

$$= \frac{1}{n} \left(p(x) - p(x)^2 \right)$$

$$= \frac{p(x)(1 - p(x))}{n},$$

where $\eta_i = \mathbf{1}(X_i = x) - \mathrm{E}\,\mathbf{1}(X_i = x)$, $\mathbf{1}^2(\cdot) = \mathbf{1}(\cdot)$, $\mathrm{E}\,\eta_i\eta_j = 0$ for $i \neq j$ since we assumed i.i.d. draws (*independent and identically distributed*), and $\mathrm{E}\,\mathbf{1}(X_1 = x) = p(x)$ from the previous derivation. To go from line three to line four note that the second term in brackets is 0 since, for i.i.d. draws, $\mathrm{E}\,\eta_i\eta_j = 0$ when $i \neq j$, and note that $\sum_{i=1}^n \mathrm{E}\,\eta_i^2 = n\,\mathrm{E}\,\eta_1^2 = n\,\mathrm{E}\left(\mathbf{1}(X_1 = x) - \mathrm{E}\,\mathbf{1}(X_1 = x)\right)^2$ since $\mathrm{E}\,\eta_1^2$ is a constant. To go from line four to line five recall that $\mathrm{E}\left((\hat{\theta} - \mathrm{E}\,\hat{\theta})^2\right)$ $= \mathrm{E}\left(\hat{\theta}^2 - 2\hat{\theta}\,\mathrm{E}\,\hat{\theta} + (\mathrm{E}\,\hat{\theta})^2\right) = \mathrm{E}\,\hat{\theta}^2 - 2\,\mathrm{E}\,\hat{\theta}\,\mathrm{E}\,\hat{\theta} + (\mathrm{E}\,\hat{\theta})^2 = \mathrm{E}\,\hat{\theta}^2 - 2(\mathrm{E}\,\hat{\theta})^2 + (\mathrm{E}\,\hat{\theta})^2$ $= \mathrm{E}\,\hat{\theta}^2 - (\mathrm{E}\,\hat{\theta})^2$ for any estimator $\hat{\theta}$.

The mean square error (MSE) criterion is perhaps the most important criterion used to evaluate the performance of an estimator $\hat{\theta}$ of some population characteristic θ. The MSE reflects the *bias, precision* (i.e., variance), and overall *accuracy* in statistical estimation as a function of the sample size, and is defined as $\mathrm{E}\left((\hat{\theta} - \theta)^2\right)$. Recalling that the MSE of an estimator can be expressed as its variance plus the square of its bias, the MSE of $p_n(x)$ is given by

$$\mathrm{MSE}\, p_n(x) = \mathrm{Var}\, p_n(x) + (\mathrm{Bias}\, p_n(x))^2$$

$$= \frac{p(x)(1 - p(x))}{n} + 0^2$$

$$= \frac{p(x)(1 - p(x))}{n}.$$

This is of *large order of magnitude* $O(n^{-1})$ and small order $o(1)$. Hence its *root MSE* (i.e., $\sqrt{\mathrm{MSE}}$) is of $O\left(n^{-1/2}\right)$ and $o(1)$, which is the familiar rate of convergence typically associated with *correctly specified* parametric models. In other words, it is *root-n-consistent* (note that an incorrectly specified parametric model has a bias term that never vanishes, hence such estimators are *inconsistent*).[9]

This tells us that this estimator is of large order in probability $O_p(n^{-1/2})$ and small order in probability $o_p(1)$, i.e.,

$$p_n(x) - p(x) = O_p\left(n^{-1/2}\right) = o_p(1)$$

(see Appendix A for an overview of orders of magnitude and probability).

---

[9] MSE is measured in units of X *squared*, while $\sqrt{\mathrm{MSE}}$ is measured in the same units as X - either can be reported. To say that an estimator has MSE of $O(n^{-1})$ simply means that the MSE is proportional to $1/n$ (MSE is non-stochastic).

Moreover, we can deploy the Lindeberg-Levy[10] central limit theorem (CLT) to obtain the asymptotic sampling distribution of this estimator, which is given by:

$$\sqrt{n}\left(p_n(x) - p(x)\right) \overset{d}{\to} N\left(0, p(x)(1 - p(x))\right).$$

That is, $p_n(x)$ has an asymptotic normal sampling distribution. In summary, we have demonstrated that the sample proportion $p_n(x)$ is unbiased, has variance $p(x)(1 - p(x))/n$, and has a limit normal distribution and a $\sqrt{n}$ rate of convergence. These results establish the foundations for inference concerning the unknown $p(x)$ based on $p_n(x)$, which includes the construction of confidence bands and hypothesis testing. We will need to derive similar results for the kernel-smoothed counterpart to $p_n(x)$, so hopefully this exercise has provided the necessary background to follow the slightly more involved proofs that appear in the next section.

1.4   Smooth Kernel Probability Function Estimation

Below we shall consider *smooth* kernel methods for estimating probability functions. These methods require that the practitioner specify a *kernel function* and a *smoothing parameter* (also called a *bandwidth* in the density estimation context). It can be shown that the kernel function plays a relatively minor role, whereas the selection of the smoothing parameter is crucially important. The kernel function need only satisfy the conditions under which the estimated probabilities are *proper* (i.e., sum to one over the support and be non-negative). The smoothing parameter will depend on unknown quantities, and we will see that there exist a variety of *data-driven* approaches for its selection, each having known statistical properties. We can derive *optimal* smoothing parameters and even *optimal* kernel functions for a given loss function such as square error loss. As noted above, there are two types of discrete random variables, unordered (in R these are cast using `factor()`) and ordered (in R these are cast using `ordered()`). Corresponding

---

[10]The Lindeberg-Levy CLT is straightforward to apply and it simply tells us that $\sqrt{n}(n^{-1}\sum_{i=1}^n Z_i) \overset{d}{\to} N(0, \sigma^2)$ ($\overset{d}{\to}$ denotes *convergence in distribution*), provided that Z_i is i.i.d. $(0, \sigma^2)$. If we let $Z_i = \mathbf{1}(X_i = x) - p(x)$ and let σ^2 be n times the variance of $p_n(x)$, i.e., $p(x)(1 - p(x))$, and assume that we observe n independent random draws $\{X_1, X_2 \dots, X_n\}$, then we see that $\sqrt{n}(n^{-1}\sum_{i=1}^n Z_i) = \sqrt{n}(p_n(x) - p(x))$ which obviously has mean 0 and variance $p(x)(1 - p(x))$. Hence the conditions required for this CLT to hold are satisfied, and therefore $\sqrt{n}\left(p_n(x) - p(x)\right) \overset{d}{\to} N\left(0, p(x)(1 - p(x))\right)$. Intuitively, this simply tells us that averages of i.i.d. random variables have limit normal distributions regardless of the underlying distribution of the data. Clearly $p_n(x) = n^{-1}\sum_{i=1}^n \mathbf{1}(X_i = x)$ is an average of i.i.d. indicator functions when the X_i are themselves i.i.d. See White (1984) page 62 for further details on the Lindeberg-Levy CLT.

to these data types, we consider two types of kernel functions, namely those appropriate for unordered data types and those appropriate for ordered ones. We begin with the unordered case which is the simpler of the two. In what follows, we simply replace the indicator function that appeared earlier in the expression for $p_n(x)$ with a kernel function such as the unordered kernel function $L(X_i, x, \lambda)$, which is defined below. We will denote the resulting estimator by $\hat{p}(x)$ to distinguish it from $p_n(x)$.

1.4.1   Estimator Properties for Unordered Categorical Variables and Kernels

Let $X \in \mathcal{D}$, $c \geq 2$, be an unordered discrete random variable having a countable support. For instance, the support $\mathcal{D}$ could be the set of Canadian provincial and territorial capitals {*Charlottetown, Edmonton, Fredericton, Halifax, Iqaluit, ...*}. The essence of an unordered variable is that each outcome in the support $\mathcal{D}$ represents an attribute or label, and nothing more. That is, for an individual, an element of $\mathcal{D}$ is either present or absent (you either live in Charlottetown or you don't), and the ordering of the outcomes is arbitrary and irrelevant.

The univariate kernel estimator of $p(x)$ is given by

$$\hat{p}(x) = \frac{1}{n} \sum_{i=1}^{n} L(X_i, x, \lambda),$$

where $L(\cdot)$ is a kernel function (Aitchison and Aitken, 1976) defined by

$$L(X_i, x, \lambda) = \begin{cases} 1 - \lambda & \text{if } X_i = x \\ \lambda/(c-1) & \text{otherwise,} \end{cases}$$

and where $\lambda \in [0, (c-1)/c]$.[11] We could also express this kernel function as

$$L(X_i, x, \lambda) = (1 - \lambda)^{\mathbf{1}(X_i = x)} \left(\lambda/(c-1) \right)^{1 - \mathbf{1}(X_i = x)}.$$

Like its indicator function counterpart, this weight function is for *counting* and conducts a binary operation only, *equal* or *not equal*. Unlike the indicator function that assigns weights 1 or 0, this weight function can assign weights ≤ 1 when $X_i = x$ and ≥ 0 when $X_i \neq x$.

This kernel function possesses a number of desirable properties. First, it sums to 1 over $x \in \mathcal{D}$ and is non-negative, rendering the estimator $\hat{p}(x)$ proper. Second, when $\lambda = 0$, it becomes the indicator function $\mathbf{1}(X_i = x)$, which implies that $\hat{p}(x) = p_n(x)$ when $\lambda = 0$. Third, when $\lambda = (c-1)/c$, it can easily be shown that $\hat{p}(x) = 1/c$ for all $x \in \mathcal{D}$, which delivers the

---

[11] Note that this is a variation of the kernel function used by Aitchison and Aitken (1976), page 419. We redefine their λ to be $1 - \lambda$, since our $\lambda \to 0$ as $n \to \infty$ seems more natural than their $\lambda \to (c-1)/c$ as $n \to \infty$.

rectangular (i.e., *discrete uniform*) distribution. Since the value of λ can have a marked impact on the resulting estimate, its selection must be taken seriously, and we discuss this important issue in Section 1.4.2. First, we establish the bias and variance of $\hat{p}(x)$.

Assume that $\{X_1, X_2, \ldots, X_n\}$ represents n independent random draws from the probability distribution $p(x)$. The expected value of $\hat{p}(x)$ is given by

$$
\begin{aligned}
\mathrm{E}\,\hat{p}(x) &= \frac{1}{n} \sum_{i=1}^{n} \mathrm{E}\,L(X_i, x, \lambda) \\
&= \mathrm{E}\,L(X_1, x, \lambda) \\
&= \sum_{t \in \mathcal{D}} L(t, x, \lambda) p(t) \\
&= (1 - \lambda) p(x) + \frac{\lambda}{c - 1} \sum_{t \in \mathcal{D}, t \neq x} p(t) \\
&= p(x) + \lambda \left(\frac{1}{c - 1} \sum_{t \in \mathcal{D}, t \neq x} p(t) - p(x) \right) \\
&= p(x) + \lambda \left(\frac{1}{c - 1} (1 - p(x)) - p(x) \right) \\
&= p(x) + \lambda \left(\frac{1 - cp(x)}{c - 1} \right) \\
&= p(x) + \lambda \Lambda_1 \\
&= p(x) + O(\lambda),
\end{aligned}
$$

and when moving from line five to six note that $\sum_{t \in \mathcal{D}, t \neq x} p(t) = \sum_{t \in \mathcal{D}} p(t) - p(x)$, and that $\sum_{t \in \mathcal{D}} p(t) = 1$.

This estimator is biased for $\lambda > 0$ (the bias being $\mathrm{E}\,\hat{p}(x) - p(x) = \lambda \Lambda_1$, which can be positive or negative), and hence $|\operatorname{Bias} \hat{p}(x)| \geq |\operatorname{Bias} p_n(x)| = 0$. The exception to this occurs when $p(x)$ has a discrete uniform (*rectangular*) distribution, in which case $p(x) = 1/c$, $1 - cp(x) = 0$, and $\Lambda_1 = 0$ for *any* $\lambda \in [0, (c - 1)/c]$.

The variance of $\hat{p}(x)$ is given by

$$
\begin{aligned}
\operatorname{Var} \hat{p}(x) &= \mathrm{E}\left((\hat{p}(x) - \mathrm{E}\,\hat{p}(x))^2 \right) \\
&= \mathrm{E}\left(\left(\frac{1}{n} \sum_{i=1}^{n} (L(X_i, x, \lambda) - \mathrm{E}\,L(X_i, x, \lambda)) \right)^2 \right) \\
&= \frac{1}{n^2} \left(\sum_{i=1}^{n} \mathrm{E}\,\eta_i^2 + \sum_{i} \sum_{j, i \neq j} \mathrm{E}\,\eta_i \eta_j \right) \\
&= \frac{1}{n} \mathrm{E}\left(L(X_1, x, \lambda) - \mathrm{E}\,L(X_1, x, \lambda) \right)^2
\end{aligned}
$$

$$= \frac{1}{n}\left(\operatorname{E}L^2(X_1, x, \lambda) - (\operatorname{E}L(X_1, x, \lambda))^2\right).$$

Note that

$$\operatorname{E}L^2(X_1, x, \lambda) = \sum_{t \in \mathcal{D}} L^2(t, x, \lambda)p(t)$$

$$= (1-\lambda)^2 p(x) + \left(\frac{\lambda}{c-1}\right)^2 \sum_{t \in \mathcal{D}, t \neq x} p(t)$$

$$= p(x) - 2\lambda p(x) + \lambda^2 \left(\left(\frac{1}{c-1}\right)^2 \sum_{t \in \mathcal{D}, t \neq x} p(t) + p(x)\right)$$

$$= p(x) - 2\lambda p(x) + \lambda^2 \left(\left(\frac{1}{c-1}\right)^2 (1 - p(x)) + p(x)\right)$$

$$= p(x) - 2\lambda p(x) + \lambda^2 \left(\frac{1 + c^2 p(x) - 2cp(x)}{(c-1)^2}\right)$$

$$= p(x) - 2\lambda p(x) + \lambda^2 \Lambda_2.$$

We therefore obtain the variance, given by

$$\operatorname{Var}\hat{p}(x) = \frac{1}{n}\left(\operatorname{E}L^2(X_1, x, \lambda) - (\operatorname{E}L(X_1, x, \lambda))^2\right)$$

$$= \frac{1}{n}\left(p(x) - 2\lambda p(x) + \lambda^2\Lambda_2 - (p(x) + \lambda\Lambda_1)^2\right)$$

$$= \frac{1}{n}\left(p(x) - 2\lambda p(x) + \lambda^2\Lambda_2 - p(x)^2 - 2\lambda p(x)\Lambda_1 - \lambda^2\Lambda_1^2\right)$$

$$= \frac{1}{n}\left(p(x) - p(x)^2 - 2\lambda p(x)(1 + \Lambda_1) + \lambda^2(\Lambda_2 - \Lambda_1^2)\right)$$

$$= \frac{p(x)(1 - p(x))}{n} - \frac{2\lambda}{n}\Lambda_3 + \frac{\lambda^2}{n}(\Lambda_2 - \Lambda_1^2)$$

$$= \frac{p(x)(1 - p(x))}{n} + O\left(\frac{\lambda}{n}\right) + O\left(\frac{\lambda^2}{n}\right),$$

which can be seen to be

$$\frac{p(x)(1 - p(x))}{n}\left(1 - \lambda\frac{c}{(c-1)}\right)^2,$$

which tells us that $-\frac{2\lambda}{n}\Lambda_3 + \frac{\lambda^2}{n}(\Lambda_2 - \Lambda_1^2) \leq 0$ (see the simplifications detailed below).

Therefore, since $\lambda \in [0, (c-1)/c]$, it follows that $0 \leq 1 - \lambda c/(c-1) \leq 1$, and so we can see that $\operatorname{Var}\hat{p}(x) \leq \operatorname{Var}p_n(x) = p(x)(1-p(x))/n$. Furthermore, $\operatorname{Var}\hat{p}(x) = 0$ when $\lambda = (c-1)/c$, its upper bound value, while $\operatorname{Var}\hat{p}(x) = \operatorname{Var}p_n(x)$ when $\lambda = 0$.

The following simplifications arise in the context of the unordered Aitchison and Aitken kernel estimator and were used to obtain the variance formula provided above.

  i. Note that

$$\Lambda_2 - \Lambda_1^2 = \left(\frac{1 + c^2 p(x) - 2cp(x)}{(c-1)^2} \right) - \left(\frac{1 - cp(x)}{c-1} \right)^2$$

$$= \left(\frac{1 + c^2 p(x) - 2cp(x) - 1 - c^2 p^2(x) + 2cp(x)}{(c-1)^2} \right)$$

$$= \frac{c^2 p(x)(1 - p(x))}{(c-1)^2}.$$

  ii. Note that

$$\Lambda_3 = p(x)(1 + \Lambda_1)$$

$$= p(x) \left(1 + \left(\frac{1 - cp(x)}{c-1} \right) \right)$$

$$= \frac{cp(x)(1 - p(x))}{(c-1)}.$$

  iii. Note that

$$-\frac{2\lambda}{n}\Lambda_3 + \frac{\lambda^2}{n}(\Lambda_2 - \Lambda_1^2) = -2\lambda \frac{c}{(c-1)} \frac{p(x)(1 - p(x))}{n}$$

$$+ \lambda^2 \frac{c^2}{(c-1)^2} \frac{p(x)(1 - p(x))}{n}.$$

  iv. Therefore,

$$\mathrm{Var}\,\hat{p}(x) = \frac{p(x)(1 - p(x))}{n} - \frac{2\lambda}{n}\Lambda_3 + \frac{\lambda^2}{n}(\Lambda_2 - \Lambda_1^2)$$

$$= \frac{p(x)(1 - p(x))}{n} \left(1 - 2\lambda \frac{c}{(c-1)} + \lambda^2 \frac{c^2}{(c-1)^2} \right)$$

$$= \frac{p(x)(1 - p(x))}{n} \left(1 - \lambda \frac{c}{(c-1)} \right)^2.$$

It is easy to see from the results above that, in general, the *larger* the smoothing parameter λ, the *larger* the bias and the *smaller* the variance. This *bias-variance trade-off* is common to all kernel smoothing procedures. If we consider square error loss, then the smoothing parameter might be chosen to optimize this trade-off. One popular approach is to consider the MSE, expressed as the sum of the variance and the *square* of the bias, and to minimize this with respect to the smoothing parameter. This is a useful exercise because it not only tells us the optimal value of the smoothing parameter, but also establishes the *rate of convergence* of the resulting estimator *when the optimal smoothing parameter is used.*

1.4.2 The SMSE-Optimal Smoothing Parameter and Rate of Convergence

In order to select an appropriate value for the smoothing parameter λ in applied settings, we need to rely on a statistical criterion that measures estimator performance. The popular MSE criterion given by $\mathrm{E}\left((\hat{p}(x) - p(x))^2\right)$ is a natural candidate that we could optimize with respect to λ if we were interested in obtaining an MSE-optimal estimator for *some* particular $x \in \mathcal{D}$. In general, we are interested in a criterion tailored to *all* $x \in \mathcal{D}$; hence we ought to adopt a *global* measure of performance. One popular measure is the *summed* MSE (SMSE), which aggregates the MSE over the set of all outcomes $\mathcal{D}$. Obviously, smaller MSE and SMSE values are preferred.

For the estimator $\hat{p}(x)$, the MSE and SMSE are given by

$$\mathrm{MSE}\,\hat{p}(x) = \mathrm{Var}\,\hat{p}(x) + (\mathrm{Bias}\,\hat{p}(x))^2$$
$$= \frac{p(x)(1 - p(x))}{n} - \frac{2\lambda}{n}\Lambda_3 + \frac{\lambda^2}{n}(\Lambda_2 - \Lambda_1^2) + \lambda^2\Lambda_1^2,$$

and

$$\mathrm{SMSE}\,\hat{p}(x) = \sum_{x \in \mathcal{D}} \mathrm{MSE}\,\hat{p}(x)$$
$$= \sum_{x \in \mathcal{D}} \frac{p(x)(1 - p(x))}{n} - \frac{2\lambda}{n}\sum_{x \in \mathcal{D}}\Lambda_3 + \frac{\lambda^2}{n}\sum_{x \in \mathcal{D}}(\Lambda_2 - \Lambda_1^2)$$
$$+ \lambda^2\sum_{x \in \mathcal{D}}\Lambda_1^2.$$

The SMSE-optimal smoothing parameter λ_{opt} is that which minimizes the SMSE criterion, thereby satisfying the necessary first order condition for a minimum. Noting that the first derivative with respect to λ is given by

$$\frac{d\,\mathrm{SMSE}}{d\lambda} = -\frac{2}{n}\sum_{x \in \mathcal{D}}\Lambda_3 + 2\frac{\lambda}{n}\sum_{x \in \mathcal{D}}(\Lambda_2 - \Lambda_1^2) + 2\lambda\sum_{x \in \mathcal{D}}\Lambda_1^2,$$

the value that equates this expression to zero is given by

$$\lambda_{opt} = \left(\frac{\sum_{x \in \mathcal{D}}\Lambda_3}{\sum_{x \in \mathcal{D}}(\Lambda_2 - \Lambda_1^2) + n\sum_{x \in \mathcal{D}}\Lambda_1^2}\right)$$

$$= O\left(\frac{1}{n}\right).$$

The reader can establish whether or not the necessary second order condition for a minimum is satisfied. Note that because $\sum_{x \in \mathcal{D}} \Lambda_3$, $\sum_{x \in \mathcal{D}}(\Lambda_2 - \Lambda_1^2)$, and $\sum_{x \in \mathcal{D}} \Lambda_1^2$ are constants that depend only on the underlying DGP, the presence of n multiplying $\sum_{x \in \mathcal{D}} \Lambda_1^2$ in the denominator renders this expression of order $O(n^{-1})$.

Note that the MSE and SMSE expressions based on the *optimal* smoothing parameter are of order $O(n^{-1})$. To see this, observe that since $\lambda_{opt} \propto 1/n$, then the terms in the MSE and SMSE expressions that involve λ/n, λ^2, and λ^2/n are of order $O(n^{-2})$, $O(n^{-2})$, and $O(n^{-3})$, respectively, and therefore vanish more quickly as $n \to \infty$ (i.e., are of *smaller order*) than the leading term, $p(x)(1 - p(x))/n$, which is of order $O(n^{-1})$.

A *plug-in* smoothing parameter selector would be particularly easy to implement, as it simply involves replacing the unknown $p(x)$ in Λ_1, Λ_2, and Λ_3 with their frequency-based counterpart $p_n(x)$. Thus, the *plug-in* smoothing parameter is the optimal smoothing parameter with $p_n(x)$ replacing the unknown $p(x)$. Note that for Aitchison and Aitken's unordered kernel function, we can express the terms in λ_{opt} as

$$\sum_{x \in \mathcal{D}} \Lambda_3 = \frac{c}{(c-1)} \sum_{x \in \mathcal{D}} p(x)(1 - p(x)),$$

$$\sum_{x \in \mathcal{D}} (\Lambda_2 - \Lambda_1^2) = \frac{c^2}{(c-1)^2} \sum_{x \in \mathcal{D}} p(x)(1 - p(x)),$$

$$n \sum_{x \in \mathcal{D}} \Lambda_1^2 = n \sum_{x \in \mathcal{D}} \left(\frac{1 - cp(x)}{c-1}\right)^2.$$

Hence we observe that $\lambda_{opt} \to 0$ as $n \to \infty$ for non-uniform X (i.e., for $p(x) \neq 1/c$ so that $\Lambda_1 \neq 0$). Note that, for uniform X (i.e., $p(x) = 1/c$), $\Lambda_1 = 0$ and

$$\lambda_{opt} = \frac{\sum_{x \in \mathcal{D}} \Lambda_3}{\sum_{x \in \mathcal{D}} \Lambda_2}$$

$$= \frac{c-1}{c}$$

for *any* n. This is the maximum value that λ may assume, and for which $\text{Var}\, \hat{p}(x) = 0$.

Other methods for selecting the smoothing parameter include likelihood cross-validation, which has been addressed by Aitchison and Aitken (1976) (page 415), and least squares cross-validation, which has been examined by Ouyang et al. (2006) and extended to the mixed-data setting by Li and Racine (2003). We will defer digging into likelihood and least squares cross-validation methods until we study density estimation in Chapter 2.

Since $\lambda_{opt} \propto n^{-1}$, using this rate of convergence for λ, we can obtain

$$\hat{p}(x) - p(x) = O_p(n^{-1/2}) = o_p(1).$$

Therefore, this estimator has the same rate of convergence as a correctly specified parametric model.

1.4.3   Asymptotic Normality

By the Liapounov CLT (we defer the study of this CLT until Chapter 2; see White (1984) page 112), it can readily be shown that when using the SMSE-optimal smoothing parameter,

$$\sqrt{n}\,(\hat{p}(x) - p(x)) \overset{d}{\to} N\,(0, p(x)(1 - p(x))).$$

Therefore, $\hat{p}(x)$ has the same asymptotic distribution as $p_n(x)$, which stands to reason since $\lambda_{opt} \to 0$ as $n \to \infty$ and hence $\hat{p}(x) \to p_n(x)$ asymptotically provided that this condition holds. Bias $\hat{p}(x)$ is an $O(\lambda)$ term particular to this estimator, and it vanishes asymptotically when using λ_{opt}.

In summary, we have demonstrated that the smooth kernel estimator $\hat{p}(x)$ of $p(x)$ for an *unordered* random variable is biased in finite samples (the bias vanishes asymptotically when using λ_{opt}), but that $\text{Var}\,\hat{p}(x) \leq \text{Var}\,p_n(x)$ (its nonsmooth counterpart) for any $\lambda < (c-1)/c$. We have also shown that $\hat{p}(x)$ has a limit normal distribution and a $\sqrt{n}$ rate of convergence when using λ_{opt}. Furthermore, there always exists a smoothing parameter λ for which $\text{MSE}\,\hat{p}(x) \leq \text{MSE}\,p_n(x)$ (this is left as an exercise). These results establish the foundations for inference concerning the unknown $p(x)$ based on $\hat{p}(x)$, which includes the construction of confidence bands and hypothesis testing.

1.4.4   Kernel Estimation and Shrinkage

In statistics, a *shrinkage* estimator is one that is pulled away from a *raw* estimate and *shrunk* towards some fixed value. Through this process, a raw estimate can be improved in terms of its MSE. One general result in the shrinkage literature is that many standard estimators can be improved in MSE terms by shrinking them towards some fixed value. The new estimator will depend on a parameter that can be specified so as to minimize the MSE of the new estimate. For this value of the parameter, the new estimate will have a smaller MSE than the raw one, and has thus been improved. This is often achieved by transforming an *unbiased* raw estimate into an improved *biased* one, and is typically encountered in Bayesian settings.

A *Stein effect* (Stein, 1956) occurs when $c > 2$ objects are estimated simultaneously and there exist *combined* estimators that are more accurate on average (i.e., they have lower expected MSE) than any method that handles the objects separately. The nonsmooth nonparametric estimators $p_n(x)$,

$x \in \mathcal{D}$, are in effect separate estimates, whereas the smooth nonparametric estimator of $p(x)$ is a *combined* estimator when $\lambda > 0$ since it gives positive weight to observations for which $t \neq x$. It is easily seen that $\hat{p}(x) = p_n(x)$ when $\lambda = 0$, while as $\lambda \rightarrow (c-1)/c$, its upper bound, $\hat{p}(x) \rightarrow 1/c$, which is the discrete uniform distribution. So, when $\lambda > 0$, the smooth kernel estimator is pulled away from the raw estimate $p_n(x)$ and shrunk towards the discrete uniform distribution. Although it is biased, it has lower expected MSE than $p_n(x)$ for some $\lambda \in [0, (c-1)/c]$, which is a very appealing feature. Verification of this result is left as an exercise (see Kiefer and Racine (2009) for a theoretical treatment when estimating a multivariate mean vector using discrete support unordered kernel functions).

Example 1.2. Mother's Religion in India.

> In this example, we consider a mother's religion (an *unordered* categorical variable) taken from the Demographic and Health Survey on childhood nutrition in India (http://www.econ.uiuc.edu/~roger/research/bandaids/india.Rda). This variable has a discrete unordered support $\mathcal{D} = \{christian, hindu, muslim, other, sikh\}$. Figure 1.2 presents the empirical estimate $p_n(x)$ and the unordered kernel estimate $\hat{p}(x)$ for a range of smoothing parameter values. When $\lambda = 0$, the empirical and kernel estimates coincide, while as $\lambda \rightarrow (c-1)/c$, the kernel estimator becomes less peaked. When $\lambda = (c-1)/c$, it becomes the discrete uniform distribution, $\hat{p}(x) = 1/c$, where $c = 5$ is the number of outcomes.

1.4.5 Estimator Properties for Ordered Categorical Variables and Kernels

When the discrete random variable X is ordered, we adopt a kernel function that is capable of reflecting this fact. An *ordered kernel function* tends to assign greater weight to neighbouring values of x than to values lying farther away.[12] Supposing that X can assume c different *ordered* values, e.g., $X \in \mathcal{D} = \{0, 1, \dots, c-1\}$, Aitchison and Aitken (1976) (page 419) suggest using the kernel function given by

$$l(X_i, x, \lambda) = \binom{c}{|x - X_i|} \lambda^{|x-X_i|}(1 - \lambda)^{c-|x-X_i|},$$

where $0 \leq |x - X_i| \leq c$ and where

$$\binom{c}{|x - X_i|} = c! / \left(|x - X_i|!(c - |x - X_i|)! \right).$$

---

[12]The unordered kernel function places a binary *counting* weight on each observation, one when $X_i = x$ and one when $X_i \neq x$, but it cannot assess distance.

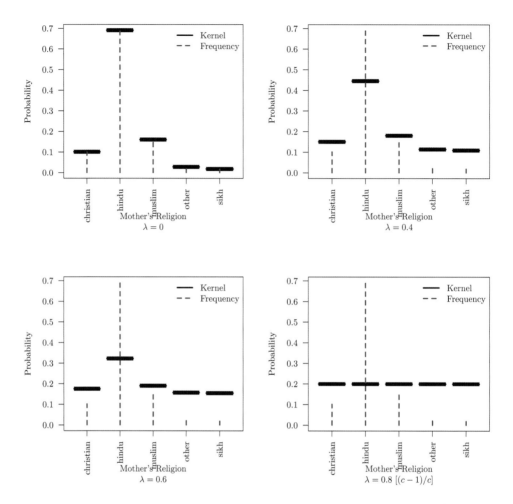

Figure 1.2: Unordered kernel versus nonsmooth nonparametric (sample proportion) probability estimates for mother's religion taken from the Demographic and Health Survey on childhood nutrition in India for a variety of smoothing parameters. Note how, as λ increases, the kernel estimator shrinks towards the discrete uniform distribution $p(x) = 1/c = 0.2$ ($c = 5$).

Note the similarity of this kernel function and the binomial distribution, where λ, c, and $|x - X_i|$ are the respective analogues of π, n, and x. It turns out that this kernel function is lacking in an important property, namely the ability to assign equal weight to all outcomes for some value of the smoothing parameter (there is no value of π for which the binomial probability function is *flat* for $c > 2$). Aitchison and Aitken's unordered kernel function possesses this important property since for $\lambda = (c-1)/c$, the unordered kernel function is $1/c$ for all $x \in \mathcal{D}$. However, this property is absent in its ordered counterpart. Other ordered kernel functions have been proposed, such as that of Wang and van Ryzin (1981), but one of its limitations is its presumption that the number of outcomes increases with the sample size, which may not be the case for the data at hand. Furthermore, existing kernel functions can exhibit undesirable behaviour when there are *gaps* in the support of a discrete random variable. See also Chu et al. (2017), who propose a discrete Epanechnikov kernel function, and Harfouche et al. (2017), who propose a multiplicative bias-corrected discrete support kernel function. There is, however, no smoothing parameter for which the former is the discrete uniform, and it also presumes no gaps exist, while the variance of the latter estimator can be higher than the variance of its peers. It turns out that constructing a bounded support discrete kernel function that is capable of applying uniform weight, adaptable to *gaps*, and *proper* simply requires some *kernel carpentry*.

Consider instead the following ordered kernel function:

$$l(X_i, x, \lambda) = \frac{\lambda^{d_{xi}}}{\Lambda_i},$$

where $0 \leq \lambda \leq 1$, $d_{xi} = |x - X_i|$, and the normalizing factor $\Lambda_i = \sum_{x \in \mathcal{D}} \lambda^{d_{xi}}$ (*not* a constant) is tailored to the particular value of $X_i \in \mathcal{D}$.[13] A non-constant normalizing factor is necessary when c, the cardinality of $\mathcal{D}$, is finite and exceeds 2 because the d_{xi} differ depending on where X_i lies in the order (there are always c d_{xi} values, but they differ across the X_i). For example, let $c = 3$, $\mathcal{D} = \{0, 1, \ldots, c - 1\} = \{0, 1, 2\}$, and let $\{X_1, X_2, X_3\} = \{0, 1, 2\}$ denote the ordered sample space. Consider the d_{xi} when $X_i = 0$ and $x \in \{0, 1, 2\}$. When $X_i = 0$, we observe that $d_{xi} = \{|0 - X_i|, |1 - X_i|, |2 - X_i|\} = \{|0 - 0|, |1 - 0|, |2 - 0|\} = \{0, 1, 2\}$, and when $X_i = 1$, we see that $d_{xi} = \{|0 - 1|, |1 - 1|, |2 - 1|\} = \{1, 0, 1\}$, etc. If $\lambda = 0.25$, then the normalizing factors would be $(\Lambda_1, \Lambda_2, \Lambda_3) = (1.3125, 1.5, 1.3125)$. Thus, for finite $\mathcal{D}$, $c > 2$, and $0 < \lambda < 1$, there is no unique normalizing constant Λ for which the kernel function will sum to 1 for all $x \in \mathcal{D}$. We observe that Λ_i *automatically* adjusts to where X_i lies in the order *and* adapts to the presence of non-consecutive outcomes such as $\mathcal{D} = \{0, 3, 8\}$. Furthermore, the ratio $\lambda^{d_{xi}}/\Lambda_i$ is well-defined since, for $\lambda = 0$, $\Lambda_i = 1$ (i.e., $\Lambda_i = \sum_{x \in \mathcal{D}} \lambda^{d_{xi}} = 0^0 + 0^1 \cdots = 1$) and $l(X_i, x, \lambda) = \mathbf{1}(X_i = x)$, while for $\lambda = 1$, this kernel function applies weight $1/c$ to all observations since $\Lambda_i = c$ (i.e., $\Lambda_i = \sum_{x \in \mathcal{D}} \lambda^{d_{xi}} = 1^0 + 1^1 \cdots = c$) and $l(X_i, x, \lambda) = 1/c$. Finally, for any X_i, this kernel function sums to 1 over the $x \in \mathcal{D}$ for *any* value of $\lambda \in [0, 1]$, and hence its use will render the associated estimator *proper*. This ordered kernel function possesses all of the desirable features of its unordered counterpart outlined in Section 1.4.1. However, unlike its unordered counterpart which conducts a binary *counting*

---

[13]Note that we can express $\Lambda_i = \sum_{x \in \mathcal{D}} \lambda^{d_{xi}}$ as $1 + \sum_{x \in \mathcal{D}, x \neq X_i} \lambda^{d_{xi}} = 1 + \Lambda_{-i}$ since $d_{xi} = 0$ when $x = X_i$ and $\lambda^0 = 1$ for all λ. For proofs we could therefore write $l(X_i, x, \lambda) = \frac{\lambda^{d_{xi}}}{1 + \Lambda_{-i}}$ which admits the expansion $l(X_i, x, \lambda) = \lambda^{d_{xi}}(1 - \Lambda_{-i} + \Lambda_{-i}^2 - \ldots)$ providing $|\Lambda_{-i}| < 1$. Since the optimal λ will be of $O(1/n) = o(1)$, this is an innocuous assumption.

operation, this kernel function conducts a *measuring* operation and considers the *distance* from any particular outcome to all other outcomes in the sample space. See Racine et al. (2017) for further details.

Without loss of generality, let $X \in \mathcal{D} = \{0, 1, \ldots, c-1\}$, $c \geq 2$, be an ordered discrete random variable having finite support. The univariate kernel estimator of $p(x)$ is given by

$$\hat{p}(x) = \frac{1}{n} \sum_{i=1}^{n} l(X_i, x, \lambda).$$

Results that are analogous to those established previously for the unordered case can be obtained for the ordered case using similar proofs. However, due to the increased complexity of the kernel function when $c > 2$, the proofs are somewhat lengthier, and hence some of these derivations are left as exercises. Regardless, as in the unordered case, $\lambda_{opt} \propto n^{-1}$, and we can show that

$$\hat{p}(x) - p(x) = O_p(n^{-1/2}) = o_p(1).$$

Moreover, by the Liapounov CLT, it can be shown that

$$\sqrt{n}(\hat{p}(x) - p(x)) \overset{d}{\to} N(0, p(x)(1 - p(x)))$$

provided that $\lambda = o_p(n^{-1/2})$. The derivation of these results is left as an exercise.

Example 1.3. Boy-Girl Ratio in Families (Adapted from Berry and Lindgren (1990), page 563).

> Figure 1.3 presents the nonsmooth frequency estimate $p_n(x)$ and the ordered kernel estimate $\hat{p}(x)$ for a range of smoothing parameter values for the boy-girl data considered earlier. The number of boys in families with eight children is an example of an *ordered* discrete random variable. When $\lambda = 0$, the frequency and kernel estimates coincide. As $\lambda \to 1$, the kernel estimator becomes less peaked and when $\lambda = 1$, it becomes the discrete uniform distribution, $\hat{p}(x) = 1/c = 0.111$, where $c = 9$ is the number of outcomes.

Smoothing parameter selection proceeds in exactly the same manner as for the unordered case.

1.5   Nonsmooth Cumulative Probability Function Estimation

Suppose that we are interested in modeling a univariate cumulative probability function for some discrete random variable X. Without loss of generality,

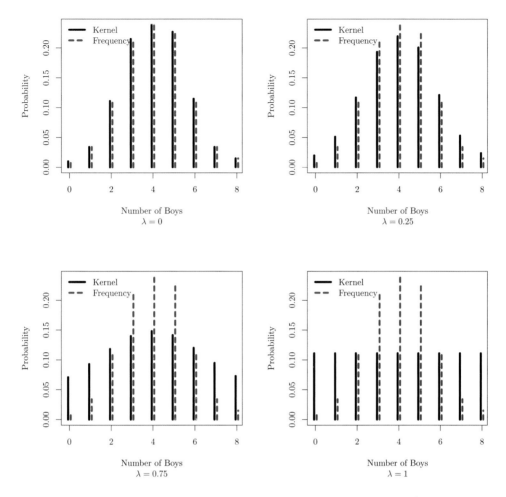

Figure 1.3: Ordered kernel versus nonsmooth nonparametric (sample proportion) probability estimates for the boy-girl ratio data using a variety of smoothing parameters. Note how, as λ increases, the kernel estimator shrinks towards the discrete uniform distribution $p(x) = 1/c = 0.11$ ($c = 9$).

suppose that $X \in \mathcal{D} = \{0, 1, \ldots, c - 1\}$, where c is the number of outcomes taken on by X, and that $\{X_1, X_2, \ldots, X_n\}$ represents n independent random draws from the probability distribution $p(x)$. For $x \in \mathcal{D}$, we denote the cumulative probability function $F(x) = \Pr(X \leq x) = \sum_{t \leq x} p(t)$, where $0 \leq F(x) \leq 1$, $F(-\infty) = 0$, and $F(\infty) = 1$. In general, $F(x)$ is unknown and must be estimated. We might consider parametric estimation of $F(x)$ but, with the pitfalls of the parametric approach that were outlined earlier being equally applicable here, we shall move directly to the nonsmooth nonparametric estimator, denoted by $F_n(x)$.

The univariate frequency estimator of $F(x)$ is commonly called the *em-*

pirical cumulative distribution function (ECDF) and is given by[14]

$$F_n(x) = \frac{\#X_i \leq x}{n}$$

$$= \frac{1}{n} \sum_{i=1}^{n} \mathbf{1}(X_i \leq x),$$

where $\mathbf{1}(\cdot)$ is an indicator function defined by

$$\mathbf{1}(X_i \leq x) = \begin{cases} 1 & \text{if } X_i \leq x \\ 0 & \text{otherwise.} \end{cases}$$

Note that, unlike the indicator function used for $p_n(x)$ which was binary and used for *counting* only, the indicator function above requires that the $x \in \mathcal{D}$ can be *ordered* (i.e., that the $\leq$ operator can be applied). If the variable was, say, country of birth (an unordered categorical variable), we could use the binary comparison $X_i = x$, but any attempt to apply the operator $\leq$ would be senseless and would fail.[15] Therefore, when you construct the ECDF, you must be modeling the behaviour of a random variable that is endowed with a natural order.

Presuming i.i.d. draws, the expected value of $F_n(x)$ is given by

$$\mathrm{E}\, F_n(x) = \frac{1}{n} \sum_{i=1}^{n} \mathrm{E}\, \mathbf{1}(X_i \leq x)$$

$$= \mathrm{E}\, \mathbf{1}(X_1 \leq x)$$

$$= \sum_{t \in \mathcal{D}} \mathbf{1}(t \leq x) p(t)$$

$$= \sum_{t \leq x} 1 \times p(t) + \sum_{t > x} 0 \times p(t)$$

$$= \sum_{t \leq x} p(t)$$

$$= F(x),$$

hence this estimator is unbiased.

Presuming i.i.d. draws, the variance of $F_n(x)$ is given by

$$\mathrm{Var}\, F_n(x) = \mathrm{E}\left((F_n(x) - \mathrm{E}\, F_n(x))^2 \right)$$

$$= \mathrm{E}\left(\left(\frac{1}{n} \sum_{i=1}^{n} (\mathbf{1}(X_i \leq x) - \mathrm{E}\, \mathbf{1}(X_i \leq x)) \right)^2 \right)$$

---

[14]Unlike the nonsmooth estimator for $p(x)$ (discrete X) and the nonsmooth estimator for $f(x)$ (continuous X) outlined in Chapter 2, the ECDF is the same for both discrete and continuous support random variables.

[15]Of course, you could order countries by land mass, population, etc., but that would use information extraneous to the variable itself.

$$= \frac{1}{n^2} \left(\sum_{i=1}^{n} \mathrm{E}\,\eta_i^2 + \sum_i \sum_{j, i \neq j} \mathrm{E}\,\eta_i \eta_j \right)$$

$$= \frac{1}{n} \mathrm{E} \left(\mathbf{1}(X_1 \leq x) - \mathrm{E}\,\mathbf{1}(X_1 \leq x) \right)^2$$

$$= \frac{1}{n} \left(\mathrm{E}\,\mathbf{1}^2(X_1 \leq x) - (\mathrm{E}\,\mathbf{1}(X_1 \leq x))^2 \right)$$

$$= \frac{1}{n} \left(\mathrm{E}\,\mathbf{1}(X_1 \leq x) - (\mathrm{E}\,\mathbf{1}(X_1 \leq x))^2 \right)$$

$$= \frac{1}{n} \left(F(x) - (F(x))^2 \right)$$

$$= \frac{F(x)(1 - F(x))}{n},$$

where $\eta_i = \mathbf{1}(X_i \leq x) - \mathrm{E}\,\mathbf{1}(X_i \leq x)$ and where we used the facts that $\mathbf{1}^2(\cdot) = \mathbf{1}(\cdot)$, $\mathrm{E}\,\eta_i \eta_j = 0$ for $i \neq j$ for i.i.d. draws, and $\mathrm{E}\,\mathbf{1}(X_1 \leq x) = F(x)$.

Hence,

$$\mathrm{MSE}\,F_n(x) = \frac{F(x)(1 - F(x))}{n}$$

$$= O\left(\frac{1}{n}\right),$$

which implies that

$$F_n(x) - F(x) = O_p\left(n^{-1/2}\right) = o_p(1).$$

Moreover, by the Lindeberg-Levy CLT, we can obtain

$$\sqrt{n}\left(F_n(x) - F(x)\right) \xrightarrow{d} N\left(0, F(x)(1 - F(x))\right).$$

In summary, we have demonstrated that the ECDF $F_n(x)$ is unbiased, has variance $F(x)(1 - F(x))/n$, and has a limit normal distribution and a $\sqrt{n}$ rate of convergence. These results establish the foundations for inference concerning the unknown $F(x)$ based on $F_n(x)$, which includes the construction of confidence bands and hypothesis testing. We will need to derive similar results for the kernel-smoothed counterpart to $F_n(x)$, so hopefully this exercise has provided the background that will enable the reader to follow the slightly more involved proofs in the next section.

1.6 Smooth Kernel Cumulative Probability Function Estimation

Unlike the case where we considered smooth estimates of the probability function $p(x)$ that could apply to either unordered or ordered discrete random variables, here we limit our attention to the ordered case. The reason for this is simple: $F(x) = \Pr(X \leq x)$ is predicated on being able to order realizations of the random variable and compare them via the $\leq$ operator. This stands in contrast to $p(x)$, which only entailed comparison based on the equality relation (i.e., $\mathbf{1}(X = x)$ is a binary indicator of the presence/absence of an attribute). Some might protest and attempt to use the unordered kernel function for this purpose, defining the cumulative probability in terms of sums of the estimated probability functions $\hat{p}(x)$, where the x have been arranged in some arbitrary order. However, this would have to rely on information that is extraneous to the unordered kernel function and to the data which admit no such ordering (recall that unordered kernel functions are binary operators and can do nothing more than determine whether two values are *equal* or *unequal*). If we are to rely on the data and kernel function only, then we *must* rely on ordered data types and kernel functions that are predicated on the weak inequality relation $\leq$. That is, we must move beyond counting and instead make use of kernel functions that measure *distance*.

The univariate kernel estimator of $F(x)$ is given by

$$\hat{F}(x) = \frac{1}{n} \sum_{i=1}^{n} \mathcal{L}(X_i, x, \lambda),$$

where the ordered kernel is defined by

$$\mathcal{L}(X_i, x, \lambda) = \sum_{z \in \mathcal{D}, z \leq x} \frac{\lambda^{d_{zi}}}{\Lambda_i},$$

and where $0 \leq \lambda \leq 1$, $d_{zi} = |z - X_i|$, and the normalizing factor $\Lambda_i = \sum_{z \in \mathcal{D}} \lambda^{d_{zi}}$ is tailored to the particular placement of $X_i \in \mathcal{D}$. When $\lambda = 0$, it can be seen that $\mathcal{L}(X_i, x, \lambda) = \mathbf{1}(X_i \leq x) = \sum_{z \in \mathcal{D}, z \leq x} \mathbf{1}(X_i = z)$.[16] Intuitively, if $\lambda \to 0$ as $n \to \infty$, then $\hat{F}(x) \to F_n(x)$ and the two estimators will have the same asymptotic properties.

Let $d_{zt} = |z - t|$, $d_{zx} = |z - x|$, $\Lambda_t = \sum_{z \in \mathcal{D}} \lambda^{d_{zt}}$, and $\Lambda_x = \sum_{z \in \mathcal{D}} \lambda^{d_{zx}}$, and for notational simplicity, always presume that $z \in \mathcal{D}$ and $t \in \mathcal{D}$.

It can be shown that the expected value of $\hat{F}(x)$ is given by

$$\begin{aligned} \mathrm{E}\,\hat{F}(x) &= \mathrm{E}\,\mathcal{L}(X_1, x, \lambda) \\ &= F(x) + O(\lambda) + \mathcal{R}, \end{aligned}$$

where $\mathcal{R}$ is a remainder term.

The variance can be shown to be

$$\mathrm{Var}\,\hat{F}(x) = \frac{1}{n} \left(\mathrm{E}\,\mathcal{L}^2(X_1, x, \lambda) - (\mathrm{E}\,\mathcal{L}(X_1, x, \lambda))^2 \right)$$

---

[16]To see this, note that $d_{zi} = 0$ when $z = X_i$, and if $\lambda = 0$, then $l(X_i, z, 0) = \lambda^{d_{zi}}/\Lambda_i = 0^0/(0^0 + 0^1 + \dots) = 1$ when $z = X_i$ and 0 otherwise. So, for any X_i and $z \leq x$, $l(X_i, z, 0)$ will equal 1 if X_i equals any value $z \leq x$ and zero otherwise. Hence $\mathcal{L}(X_i, x, \lambda) = \mathbf{1}(X_i \leq x) = \sum_{z \in \mathcal{D}, z \leq x} \mathbf{1}(X_i = z)$ when $\lambda = 0$.

$$= \frac{F(x)(1 - F(x))}{n} + O\left(\frac{\lambda}{n}\right) + O\left(\frac{\lambda^2}{n}\right) + \mathcal{R}.$$

Furthermore, presuming that $\lambda \to 0$ as $n \to \infty$ at its optimal rate (i.e., $\lambda = o(n^{-1})$), then by the Liapounov CLT, we can obtain

$$\sqrt{n}\left(\hat{F}(x) - F(x)\right) \xrightarrow{d} N\left(0, F(x)(1 - F(x))\right).$$

In summary, the kernel estimator $\hat{F}(x)$ is biased in finite samples (the bias vanishes asymptotically), has variance $F(x)(1 - F(x))/n$, and has a limit normal distribution and a $\sqrt{n}$ rate of convergence. Furthermore, there always exists a smoothing parameter λ for which MSE $\hat{F}(x) \leq$ MSE $F_n(x)$. These results establish the foundations for inference concerning the unknown $F(x)$ based on $\hat{F}(x)$, which includes the construction of confidence bands and hypothesis testing.

Example 1.4. Boy-Girl Ratio in Families (Adapted from Berry and Lindgren (1990), page 563).

> Figure 1.4 presents the empirical estimate $F_n(x)$ and the ordered kernel estimate $\hat{F}(x)$ for a range of smoothing parameter values. When $\lambda = 0$, the empirical and kernel estimates coincide, while as $\lambda \to 1$, the kernel estimator approaches the discrete uniform cumulative distribution which is linear.

Smoothing parameter selection proceeds in exactly the same manner as for $\hat{p}(x)$, and will not be discussed any further at this juncture (we will have much more to say on this matter after we cover the material in Chapter 2).

1.7   The Multivariate Extension

The extension of the above results to the multivariate setting is quite straightforward and, with minor modification, each of the estimators outlined above has a natural multivariate counterpart. For the univariate kernel-smoothed estimators outlined above, this modification involves the use of what are known as *product kernel functions*. When modeling the probability function $p(x)$ in a multivariate discrete variable setting, we could encounter a combination of both unordered and ordered variables (here x is a vector but clearly $p(x)$ is a scalar). Suppose that we have r unordered variables and s ordered variables. The product kernel function for estimating the joint probability function would be given by

$$\prod_{j=1}^{r} L(X_{ij}^u, x_j^u, \lambda_j^u) \prod_{j=1}^{s} l(X_{ij}^o, x_j^o, \lambda_j^o)$$

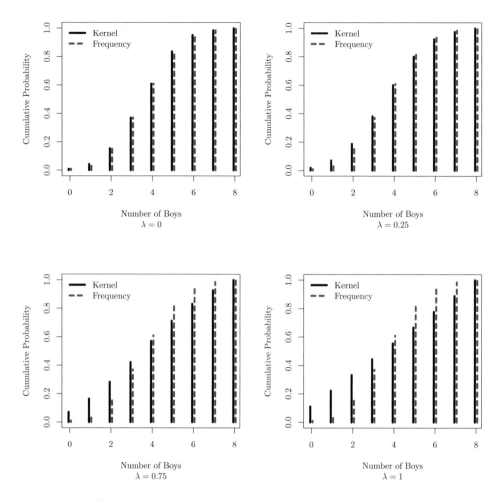

Figure 1.4: Ordered kernel versus nonsmooth nonparametric (cumulative sample proportion) cumulative probability estimates for the number of boys in families with eight children for a variety of smoothing parameters.

and the resulting estimator would be

$$\hat{p}(x) = \frac{1}{n} \sum_{i=1}^{n} \prod_{j=1}^{r} L(X_{ij}^{u}, x_{j}^{u}, \lambda_{j}^{u}) \prod_{j=1}^{s} l(X_{ij}^{o}, x_{j}^{o}, \lambda_{j}^{o}),$$

where the superscripts ^{u} and ^{o} and the functions $L(\cdot)$ and $l(\cdot)$ serve to distinguish the unordered and ordered variables and kernel functions, respectively. Note that x is an $(r + s)$-dimensional vector consisting of r unordered and s ordered variables, and that each variable has its own smoothing parameter. Note also that when using the R package np, if you first cast your *discrete* variables according to their type using the operators `factor()` and `ordered()`, then the appropriate kernel functions are automatically applied with no further input required from the user.[17]

If instead we were modeling the cumulative probability function $F(x)$ which, the reader will recall, is only defined for ordered data types, then the resulting estimator would be

$$\hat{F}(x) = \frac{1}{n} \sum_{i=1}^{n} \prod_{j=1}^{s} \mathcal{L}(X_{ij}^{o}, x_{j}^{o}, \lambda_{j}^{o}).$$

Both of these estimators are biased in finite samples but less variable than their empirical nonsmooth counterparts. Providing that $\max_{1 \le j \le r} \lambda_{j}^{u} \to 0$ and $\max_{1 \le j \le s} \lambda_{j}^{o} \to 0$ as $n \to \infty$, they retain the rates of convergence of their univariate counterparts and are once again characterized by asymptotically normal distributions. The leading bias term for $\hat{p}(x)$ is of order $O(\sum_{j=1}^{r} \lambda_{j}^{u} + \sum_{j=1}^{s} \lambda_{j}^{o})$, while that for $\hat{F}(x)$ is of order $O(\sum_{j=1}^{s} \lambda_{j}^{o})$. The leading variance terms are identical to those established for their univariate counterparts, and again we can obtain the results

$$\sqrt{n} \left(\hat{p}(x) - p(x) \right) \overset{d}{\to} N \left(0, p(x)(1 - p(x)) \right)$$

and

$$\sqrt{n} \left(\hat{F}(x) - F(x) \right) \overset{d}{\to} N \left(0, F(x)(1 - F(x)) \right).$$

In summary, the smooth kernel estimators of $p(x)$ and $F(x)$ for multivariate x are biased in finite samples (their respective biases vanish asymptotically provided that $\max_{1 \le j \le r} \lambda_{j}^{u} \to 0$ and $\max_{1 \le j \le s} \lambda_{j}^{o} \to 0$ as $n \to \infty$), but their respective variances are less than or equal to that of their nonsmooth nonparametric counterparts. Furthermore, there always exist vectors of smoothing parameters λ for which MSE $\hat{p}(x) \le$ MSE $p_n(x)$ and MSE $\hat{F}(x) \le$ MSE $F_n(x)$. Finally, the estimators exhibit a $\sqrt{n}$ rate of convergence, regardless of the dimensionality of x.

Smoothing parameter selection proceeds in the same manner as in the univariate cases, with the modification that there is now a vector of smoothing parameters that needs to be selected (we will have much more to say on this matter after we cover the material in Chapter 2).

1.8 Practitioner's Corner

1.8.1 Estimating Probability Functions in R

In R, there exist a range of parametric probability functions that we might invoke (see, e.g., `?dbinom` where in R, a question mark before a command pulls up its help file). For instance, if we wish to compute the probabilities

---

[17] The default data type in R is `numeric()`, which is treated as *continuous* by functions in the np package.

$\Pr(X = x)$ for $x = \{0, 1, 2\}$ when the discrete random variable X is binomially distributed with $n = 2$ trials and a probability of success on each trial of $\pi = 0.4$, we could run the following commands in R (note that `0:2` computes the sequence of integers from 0 to 2):

```
x <- 0:2
dbinom(x,2,0.4)
## [1] 0.36 0.48 0.16
```

To compute the cumulative probability, we can use `pbinom()`:

```
pbinom(x,2,0.4)
## [1] 0.36 0.84 1.00
```

If we had a random sample of size 100, $\{X_1, X_2, \ldots, X_{100}\}$, drawn from the same binomial distribution that was used above and we wanted to compute the *sample proportions* $p_n(x)$ (i.e., the nonsmooth nonparametric estimates of $p(x)$), we could use the functions `table()` and `prop.table()` as follows (the seed is set so that we get the same random draw each time we run this example):

```
set.seed(42)
X <- sort(rbinom(100,2,0.4))
prop.table(table(X))
## X
##    0    1    2
## 0.33 0.49 0.18
```

Take heed of the fact that R is *case sensitive*. Hence the objects `x` and `X` in the previous two code chunks are *not* the same object.

If we wanted the cumulative sample proportions $F_n(x)$ (i.e., the ECDF), we could invoke the function `cumsum()` or the function `ecdf()`:

```
cumsum(prop.table(table(X)))
##    0    1    2
## 0.33 0.82 1.00
Fn <- ecdf(X)
Fn(0:2)
## [1] 0.33 0.82 1.00
```

One powerful aspect of the R programming environment is that we can easily write our own custom functions via a call to `function()`. Suppose we wanted to create an unordered kernel function and then compute the smooth probabilities for some random sample $\{X_1, X_2, \ldots\}$, such as the one generated above.[18] We might construct the following kernel function and kernel probability estimator function to compute $\hat{p}(x)$ which we defined earlier:

```
unordered.kernel <- function(X,x,lambda) {
    ## X is a vector of sample realizations, x a point at which we wish to
```

---

[18] By way of illustration, we are using the unordered kernel function on a random variable that is in fact ordered (i.e., the binomial is ordered). There is nothing wrong with doing this, as we still get consistent estimates of the underlying probabilities.

```
    ## construct a probability estimate, and lambda a smoothing parameter
    ## (note that length(unique(X)) determines the number of unique outcomes
    ## in the sample space, which we called `c' above)
    ifelse(X==x,1-lambda,lambda/(length(unique(X))-1))
}
kernel.probability <- function(X,lambda) {
    ## D is the ordered empirical support (empirical sample space)
    D <- sort(unique(X))
    ## p.hat is a vector for storing the probability estimates
    p.hat <- numeric()
    ## For each unique outcome in the ordered sample space, compute the
    ## kernel probability estimate
    for(i in 1:length(D)) p.hat[i] <- mean(unordered.kernel(X,D[i],lambda))
    ## Return a list with the sorted sample space and the corresponding
    ## kernel probability estimates
    list(X=D,P=p.hat)
}
```

In the code chunk above, X is a vector of sample realizations and x is a member of the outcome space $\mathcal{D}$ for which we wish to compute the kernel-smoothed probability. The first function that we defined above computes $L(X_i, x, \lambda)$ for $i = 1, 2, \ldots, n$ and returns a vector with elements $1 - \lambda$ when $X_i = x$ and $\lambda/(c-1)$ when $X_i \neq x$. The second function computes $\hat{p}(x) = n^{-1} \sum_{i=1}^{n} L(X_i, x, \lambda)$ for $x \in \mathcal{D} = \{0, 1, \ldots, c-1\}$. When $\lambda = 0$, the second function will return the sample proportions (i.e., the nonsmooth nonparametric probability estimates):

```
kernel.probability(X,0)
## $X
## [1] 0 1 2
##
## $P
## [1] 0.33 0.49 0.18
```

When $\lambda = (c-1)/c = 2/3$ for this example, the second function will return the discrete uniform probabilities $1/3$:

```
kernel.probability(X,2/3)
## $X
## [1] 0 1 2
##
## $P
## [1] 0.3333 0.3333 0.3333
```

We could accomplish the same thing using the **npudens()** function from the R package np. Before attempting these commands, you must first install the np package via `install.packages("np")` and then load the package via `library(np)`. We would typically pre-cast our vector of sample realizations X as a factor (unordered) via `factor()` and then invoke **npudens()** with our specification of the kernel function type and the value of the smoothing parameter (note that ~X is simply the R *formula* interface for specifying the list of variables present in the (joint) probability):

```
## Cast X as a factor (unordered)
X <- factor(X)
model <- npudens(~X,ukertype="aitchisonaitken",bws=0)
summary(model)
##
## Density Data: 100 training points, in 1 variable(s)
##                 X
## Bandwidth(s): 0
##
## Bandwidth Type: Fixed
## Log Likelihood: -102.4
##
## Unordered Categorical Kernel Type: Aitchison and Aitken
## No. Unordered Categorical Vars.: 1
unique(fitted(model))
## [1] 0.33 0.49 0.18

model <- npudens(~X,ukertype="aitchisonaitken",bws=2/3)
summary(model)
##
## Density Data: 100 training points, in 1 variable(s)
##                     X
## Bandwidth(s): 0.6667
##
## Bandwidth Type: Fixed
## Log Likelihood: -109.9
##
## Unordered Categorical Kernel Type: Aitchison and Aitken
## No. Unordered Categorical Vars.: 1
c(unique(fitted(model)[X==0]),
  unique(fitted(model)[X==1]),
  unique(fitted(model)[X==2]))
## [1] 0.3333 0.3333 0.3333
```

Note that the R expression `fitted(model)` uses the generic R function `fitted()` to return a vector of length $n = 100$ that corresponds to the vector of sample realizations X. Therefore, the last line returns the three probability estimates for x = $\{0, 1, 2\}$, just like the R function `kernel.probability()` that we constructed above.

If we want to obtain data-driven smoothing parameters via the method of likelihood cross-validation that will be introduced in Chapter 2, then we can call the function `npudensbw()`. Alternatively, we can simply drop the `bws=` argument in the call to `npudens()` which will cause it to invoke the function `npudensbw()` using any arguments provided to `npudens()` (the default is likelihood cross-validation, i.e., `bwmethod="cv.ml"`):

```
bw <- npudensbw(~X,ukertype="aitchisonaitken",bwmethod="cv.ml")
summary(bw)
##
## Data (100 observations, 1 variable(s)):
##
## Bandwidth Selection Method: Maximum Likelihood Cross-Validation
```

```
## Formula: ~X
## Bandwidth Type: Fixed
## Objective Function Value: -104.3 (achieved on multistart 1)
##
## Var. Name: X Bandwidth: 0.09268 Lambda Max: 0.6667
##
## Unordered Categorical Kernel Type: Aitchison and Aitken
## No. Unordered Categorical Vars.: 1
## Estimation Time: 0.003 seconds
model <- npudens(~X,ukertype="aitchisonaitken",bwmethod="cv.ml")
summary(model)
##
## Density Data: 100 training points, in 1 variable(s)
##                             X
## Bandwidth(s): 0.09268
##
## Bandwidth Type: Fixed
## Log Likelihood: -102.6
##
## Unordered Categorical Kernel Type: Aitchison and Aitken
## No. Unordered Categorical Vars.: 1
```

In the summary of the smoothing parameter object bw (i.e., summary(bw)), the objective function value is the maximized value of the *delete-one* cross-validation function that occurs at the optimal λ (see Chapter 2). This differs from the full-sample log-likelihood function that is reported by summary(model).

A range of R *interrogator* functions, including fitted(), predict(), summary(), plot() and so on, can be used on objects of class npdensity (note that plot() calls npplot() - see ?npplot for details):

```
class(model)
## [1] "npdensity"
## Construct 95% pointwise nonparametric bootstrap confidence bands
## then plot the smooth probability estimates and their bootstrap CIs
plot(model,plot.errors.method="bootstrap",plot.errors.type="quantiles")
```

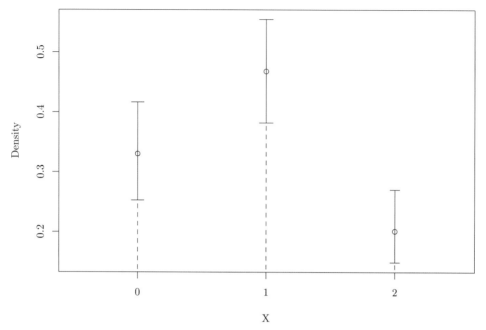

For cumulative probability functions, we can invoke the np package functions `npudistbw()` and `npudist()` for smoothing parameter selection and estimation of $F(x)$, respectively. This can be carried out in a similar manner to how we previously invoked `npudensbw()` and `npudens()` to obtain smoothing parameters and to compute $\hat{p}(x)$, respectively (the smoothing parameter selection methods and the kernel function options will naturally differ though).

1.8.2   A Monte Carlo Comparison of Probability Estimators

Sometimes practitioners would like to compare the *finite sample* performance of two or more estimators rather than rely solely on their asymptotic distributions. This is because it is not uncommon for competing estimators' asymptotic distributions to coincide, which might suggest that the estimators are equivalent even though, in applied finite sample settings, one may clearly outperform the other on SMSE grounds. For instance, the asymptotic distributions of $p_n(x)$ and $\hat{p}(x)$ are identical since the optimal smoothing parameter $\lambda = o(1)$ vanishes asymptotically, which implies $p_n(x) = \lim_{\lambda \to 0} \hat{p}(x)$. Therefore, based on their asymptotic distributions alone, we might be indifferent as to which of these two nonparametric estimators, nonsmooth or smooth, to use in finite sample settings. But the Stein effect suggests that $\hat{p}(x)$ dominates $p_n(x)$ for some SMSE-optimal smoothing parameter λ if $c > 2$ (the latter is therefore said to be *inadmissible*), and we have shown that theoretically, there *always* exists a λ for which SMSE $\hat{p}(x) \leq$ SMSE $p_n(x)$. Meanwhile, $\hat{p}(x)$ can dominate a misspecified parametric model but never a correctly specified one.

A finite sample comparison of two or more estimators can be carried out by means of a *Monte Carlo* simulation. These types of simulations rely on random number generators, much like the games of chance that are played in the world famous Monte Carlo Casino located in the principality of Monaco, hence the name *Monte Carlo* simulation. Below, we will run two Monte Carlo simulations that are designed to assess the finite sample performance of three probability estimators, namely the parametric $p(x; \pi)$, the nonparametric nonsmooth $p_n(x)$, and the nonparametric smooth $\hat{p}(x)$. In the first simulation, the practitioner correctly guesses the parametric form of the DGP, while in the second simulation, their guess is incorrect. We generate $M = 1000$ Monte Carlo replications (i.e., random samples), and for each replication we compute the three estimators and their respective sample SMSEs. We can compute their sample SMSEs because we *know* $p(x)$ from the DGP that we ourselves have defined, so that $\widehat{\text{SMSE}}\hat{p}(x) = \sum_{x \in \mathcal{D}} (\hat{p}(x) - p(x))^2$, etc. We then compare the finite sample distributions of the estimators' $M = 1000$ sample SMSEs by summarizing them in tables and figures.

Correct Parametric Specification

We simulate data from a binomial DGP $p(x) = p(x; \pi)$, and compare a correctly specified parametric binomial probability function $p(x; \hat{\pi})$, where we have estimated π, with the nonsmooth nonparametric estimator $p_n(x)$, the kernel smoothed estimator with data-driven smoothing parameters $\hat{p}(x)_{ml}$, and the kernel smoothed estimator with fixed smoothing parameters $\lambda = 1/10, 1/2$, and $3/4$ (the latter value of λ being the upper bound $(c-1)/c$ where $c = 4$ since $\mathcal{D} = \{0, 1, 2, 3\}$). Note that $\hat{p}(x) = p_n(x)$ when $\lambda = 0$. We draw $M = 1000$ samples, each of size $n = 100$, from the DGP $p(x; \pi) = \binom{3}{x} 0.5^x (1 - 0.5)^{3-x}$ (3 Bernoulli trials with a probability of success on each trial $\pi = 0.5$) and estimate each model. Note that this is the situation that some practitioners *falsely* believe to *always* be the case, i.e., that any parametric model they scribble down is *correctly specified*. Naturally, if this was the case, their estimator would *always* have the *lowest* MSE and SMSE among the class of all estimators. But any parametric misspecification will induce bias that *never vanishes*, which gives rise to inconsistent estimation. On the other hand, the nonsmooth and smooth estimators are always consistent. Note that in this simulation, the performance of the smooth nonparametric kernel estimator $\hat{p}(x)$ is similar to that of the nonsmooth nonparametric estimator $p_n(x)$ because the data-driven method for smoothing parameter selection imposes limited smoothing for this DGP, which is appropriate. Results are summarized in Table 1.2 and Figure 1.5, while Figure 1.6 presents the three estimates for a single Monte Carlo replication.

```
## Set seed for replicability
set.seed(42)
## Sample size and number of Monte Carlo replications
```

```
n <- 100
M <- 1000
## Vectors for storage
rsmse.p.binomial <- numeric()
rsmse.p.n <- numeric()
rsmse.p.hat.lambda.1 <- numeric()
rsmse.p.hat.lambda.5 <- numeric()
rsmse.p.hat.lambda.75 <- numeric()
rsmse.p.hat.cv.ml <- numeric()
lambda.cv.ml <- numeric()
for(m in 1:M) {
    ## Generate X from a binomial so the binomial is in fact correctly
    ## specified
    X <- rbinom(n,3,.5)
    p <- dbinom(0:3,3,.5)
    ## Empirical sample space
    D <- sort(unique(X))
    ## Binomial
    n.trial <- length(D)-1
    pi.hat <- mean(X)/n.trial
    p.binom <- dbinom(D,n.trial,pi.hat)
    ## Empirical
    p.n <- fitted(npudens(tdat=factor(X),edat=factor(D),bws=0))
    ## Kernel, lambda=0.1,.5,.75 (upper bound for this case)
    p.lambda.1 <- fitted(npudens(tdat=factor(X),edat=factor(D),bws=.1))
    p.lambda.5 <- fitted(npudens(tdat=factor(X),edat=factor(D),bws=.5))
    p.lambda.75 <- fitted(npudens(tdat=factor(X),edat=factor(D),bws=.75))
    ## Likelihood cross-validated smoothing parameter (default)
    model <- npudens(tdat=factor(X),edat=factor(D))
    lambda.cv.ml[m] <- model$bws$bw
    p.hat.cv.ml <- fitted(model)
    ## Root summed mean square error
    rsmse.p.binomial[m] <- sqrt(sum((p.binom-p)^2))
    rsmse.p.n[m] <- sqrt(sum((p.n-p)^2))
    rsmse.p.hat.lambda.1[m] <- sqrt(sum((p.lambda.1-p)^2))
    rsmse.p.hat.lambda.5[m] <- sqrt(sum((p.lambda.5-p)^2))
    rsmse.p.hat.lambda.75[m] <- sqrt(sum((p.lambda.75-p)^2))
    rsmse.p.hat.cv.ml[m] <- sqrt(sum((p.hat.cv.ml-p)^2))
}
## Data frame with vectors of RSMSE for each estimator
rsmse <- data.frame(binom=rsmse.p.binomial,
                    p.n=rsmse.p.n,
                    p.hat.ml=rsmse.p.hat.cv.ml,
                    p.hat.1=rsmse.p.hat.lambda.1,
                    p.hat.5=rsmse.p.hat.lambda.5,
                    p.hat.75=rsmse.p.hat.lambda.75)

## tikzDevice labels for column names
rsmse.names <- c("$p(x;\\hat\\pi)$",
                "$p_n(x)$",
                "$\\hat p(x)_{ml}$",
                "$\\hat p(x)_{\\lambda=0.1}$",
                "$\\hat p(x)_{\\lambda=0.5}$",
```

Table 1.2: Root SMSE summaries when the parametric model is correctly specified.

	$p(x; \hat{\pi})$	$p_n(x)$	$\hat{p}(x)_{ml}$	$\hat{p}(x)_{\lambda=0.1}$	$\hat{p}(x)_{\lambda=0.5}$	$\hat{p}(x)_{\lambda=0.75}$
Min.	0.0000	0.0100	0.0014	0.0073	0.1283	0.25
1st Qu.	0.0150	0.0539	0.0537	0.0502	0.1585	0.25
Median	0.0300	0.0728	0.0736	0.0707	0.1684	0.25
Mean	0.0356	0.0761	0.0780	0.0737	0.1691	0.25
3rd Qu.	0.0500	0.0943	0.0982	0.0925	0.1795	0.25
Max.	0.1307	0.2335	0.2103	0.2051	0.2140	0.25

```
                    "$\\hat p(x)_{\\lambda=0.75}$")
knitr::kable(apply(rsmse,2,summary),col.names = rsmse.names,
        caption="Root SMSE summaries when the parametric model is
                correctly specified.",
        escape=FALSE,
        booktabs=TRUE,
        linesep="",
        digits=4)

boxplot(rsmse,notch=TRUE,outline=FALSE,ylab="RSMSE",names=rsmse.names,las=2)
```

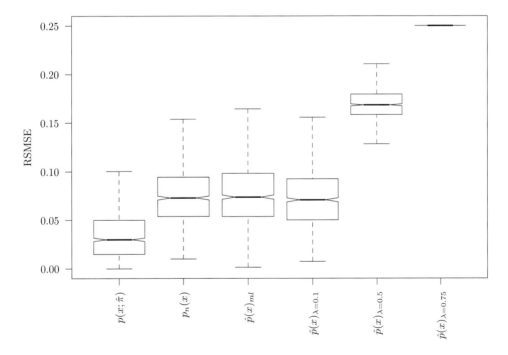

Figure 1.5: Boxplots of the root SMSEs when the parametric model is correctly specified.

```
## Plot true probabilities, binomial, and cross-validated kernel smoothed
## probabilities for one sample (last run in MC simulation)
plot(D,p,
     ylim=c(0,0.5),
     ylab="Probability",
     xlab="$X$",
     type="h",
     lwd=2,
     xaxt="n")
axis(1, at=0:3, labels=0:3)
points(D-0.04,p.binom,type="h",lty=2,col=2,lwd=2)
points(D+0.04,p.hat.cv.ml,type="h",lty=3,col=3,lwd=3)
legend("topleft",c("$p(x)$ (DGP)",
                   "$p(x;\\pi)$ (parametric binomial)",
                   "$\\hat p(x)$ (nonparametric smooth)"),
       lty=1:3,
       col=1:3,
       lwd=rep(2,3),
       bty="n")
```

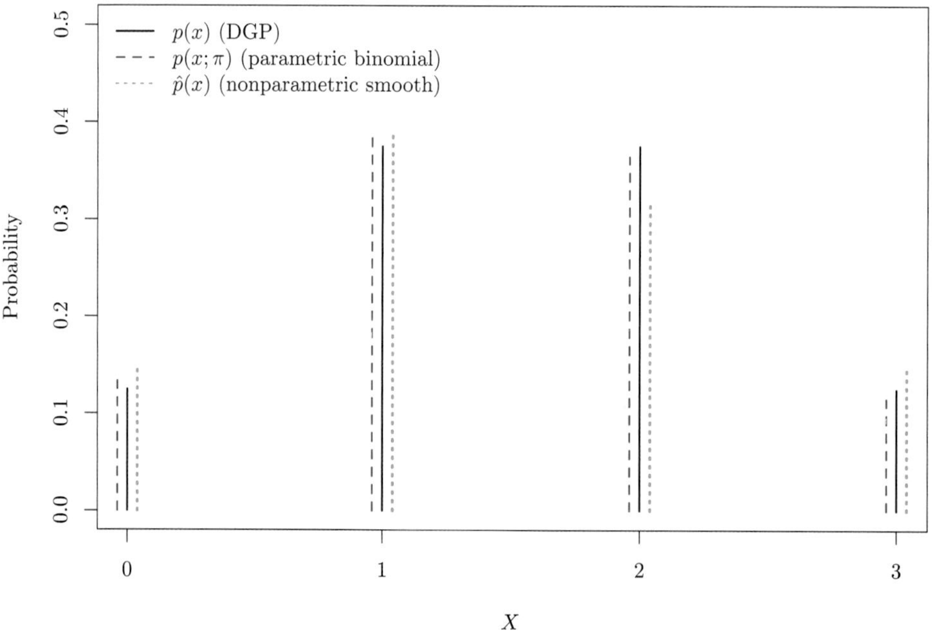

Figure 1.6: Probability estimates for parametric and kernel smoothed methods for one draw from the underlying DGP when the parametric model is correctly specified ($\lambda_{ml} = 0.10$).

Incorrect Parametric Specification

We simulate data from the discrete uniform distribution, $p(x) = 1/c = 1/4$, and compare an incorrectly specified parametric binomial probability function

$p(x; \hat{\pi})$, where we have estimated π, with the nonsmooth nonparametric estimator $p_n(x)$, the kernel-smoothed estimator with data-driven smoothing parameters $\hat{p}(x)_{ml}$, and the kernel-smoothed estimator with fixed smoothing parameters $\lambda = 1/10, 1/2$, and $3/4$ (the latter value of λ being the upper bound $(c-1)/c$ where $c = 4$ since $\mathcal{D} = \{0, 1, 2, 3\}$). The bias present in the misspecified binomial model is readily apparent, while the data-driven nonparametric kernel estimator $\hat{p}(x)_{ml}$ is the best performer of $p(x; \hat{\pi})$, $p_n(x)$, and $\hat{p}(x)_{ml}$. Note that the nonparametric kernel estimator $\hat{p}(x)$ performs better than the nonsmooth estimator $p_n(x)$ in this simulation because the data-driven method for smoothing parameter selection imposes a substantial amount of smoothing for this DGP, which is appropriate. Hence there is a large reduction in variance, which leads to a fall in root SMSE relative to the nonsmooth estimator. Results are summarized in Table 1.3 and Figure 1.7, while Figure 1.8 presents the estimates for a single Monte Carlo replication.

```
## Set seed for replicability
set.seed(42)
## Sample size and number of Monte Carlo replications
n <- 100
M <- 1000
## Vectors for storage
rsmse.p.binomial <- numeric()
rsmse.p.n <- numeric()
rsmse.p.hat.lambda.1 <- numeric()
rsmse.p.hat.lambda.5 <- numeric()
rsmse.p.hat.lambda.75 <- numeric()
rsmse.p.hat.cv.ml <- numeric()
lambda.cv.ml <- numeric()
for(m in 1:M) {
    ## Generate X from the discrete uniform, generate true
    ## probabilities for ordered sample space
    p <- rep(0.25,4)
    X <- sample(0:3,n,p,replace=TRUE)
    ## Empirical sample space
    D <- sort(unique(X))
    ## Binomial
    n.trial <- length(D)-1
    pi.hat <- mean(X)/n.trial
    p.binom <- dbinom(D,n.trial,pi.hat)
    ## Empirical
    p.n <- fitted(npudens(tdat=factor(X),edat=factor(D),bws=0))
    ## Kernel, lambda=0.1,.5,.75 (upper bound for this case)
    p.lambda.1 <- fitted(npudens(tdat=factor(X),edat=factor(D),bws=.1))
    p.lambda.5 <- fitted(npudens(tdat=factor(X),edat=factor(D),bws=.5))
    p.lambda.75 <- fitted(npudens(tdat=factor(X),edat=factor(D),bws=.75))
    ## Likelihood cross-validated smoothing parameter (default)
    model <- npudens(tdat=factor(X),edat=factor(D))
    lambda.cv.ml[m] <- model$bws$bw
    p.hat.cv.ml <- fitted(model)
    ## Root summed mean square error
    rsmse.p.binomial[m] <- sqrt(sum((p.binom-p)^2))
```

Table 1.3: Root SMSE summaries when the parametric model is incorrectly specified.

	$p(x;\hat\pi)$	$p_n(x)$	$\hat p(x)_{ml}$	$\hat p(x)_{\lambda=0.1}$	$\hat p(x)_{\lambda=0.5}$	$\hat p(x)_{\lambda=0.75}$
Min.	0.2500	0.0141	0.0000	0.0123	0.0047	0
1st Qu.	0.2503	0.0561	0.0000	0.0486	0.0187	0
Median	0.2511	0.0787	0.0000	0.0682	0.0262	0
Mean	0.2522	0.0801	0.0173	0.0694	0.0267	0
3rd Qu.	0.2528	0.1010	0.0267	0.0875	0.0337	0
Max.	0.2746	0.2093	0.1602	0.1814	0.0698	0

```
    rsmse.p.n[m] <- sqrt(sum((p.n-p)^2))
    rsmse.p.hat.lambda.1[m] <- sqrt(sum((p.lambda.1-p)^2))
    rsmse.p.hat.lambda.5[m] <- sqrt(sum((p.lambda.5-p)^2))
    rsmse.p.hat.lambda.75[m] <- sqrt(sum((p.lambda.75-p)^2))
    rsmse.p.hat.cv.ml[m] <- sqrt(sum((p.hat.cv.ml-p)^2))
}
## Data frame with vectors of RSMSE for each estimator
rsmse <- data.frame(binom=rsmse.p.binomial,
                    p.n=rsmse.p.n,
                    p.hat.ml=rsmse.p.hat.cv.ml,
                    p.hat.1=rsmse.p.hat.lambda.1,
                    p.hat.5=rsmse.p.hat.lambda.5,
                    p.hat.75=rsmse.p.hat.lambda.75)

## tikzDevice labels for column names
rsmse.names <- c("$p(x;\\hat\\pi)$",
                 "$p_n(x)$",
                 "$\\hat p(x)_{ml}$",
                 "$\\hat p(x)_{\\lambda=0.1}$",
                 "$\\hat p(x)_{\\lambda=0.5}$",
                 "$\\hat p(x)_{\\lambda=0.75}$")
knitr::kable(apply(rsmse,2,summary),col.names = rsmse.names,
             caption="Root SMSE summaries when the parametric model is
                      incorrectly specified.",
             escape=FALSE,
             booktabs=TRUE,
             linesep="",
             digits=4)

boxplot(rsmse,notch=TRUE,outline=FALSE,ylab="RSMSE",names=rsmse.names,las=2)

## Plot true probabilities, binomial, and cross-validated kernel smoothed
## probabilities for one sample (last run in MC simulation)
plot(D,p,
     ylim=c(0,0.5),
     ylab="Probability",
     xlab="$X$",
     type="h",
     lwd=2,
```

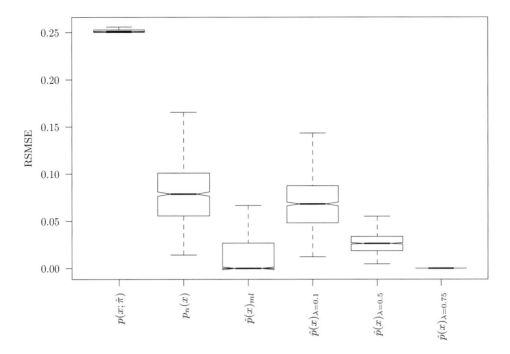

Figure 1.7: Boxplots of the root SMSEs when the parametric model is incorrectly specified.

```
        xaxt="n")
axis(1, at=0:3, labels=0:3)
points(D-0.04,p.binom,type="h",lty=2,col=2,lwd=2)
points(D+0.04,p.hat.cv.ml,type="h",lty=3,col=3,lwd=3)
legend("topleft",c("$p(x)$ (DGP)",
                   "$p(x;\\pi)$ (parametric binomial)",
                   "$\\hat p(x)$ (nonparametric smooth)"),
       lty=1:3,
       col=1:3,
       lwd=rep(2,3),
       bty="n")
```

Discussion

An estimator based on a correctly specified parametric model is sometimes called an *oracle*[19] estimator. These simulations highlight the fact that misspecified parametric models are inconsistent due to the presence of a bias term that will never vanish. In contrast, their nonsmooth and smooth nonparametric counterparts are consistent. If a parametric model is correctly specified, then naturally it cannot be beat. Under this scenario, the para-

---

[19]In classical antiquity, an *oracle* was a priest or priestess acting as a medium through whom advice or prophecy was sought from the gods.

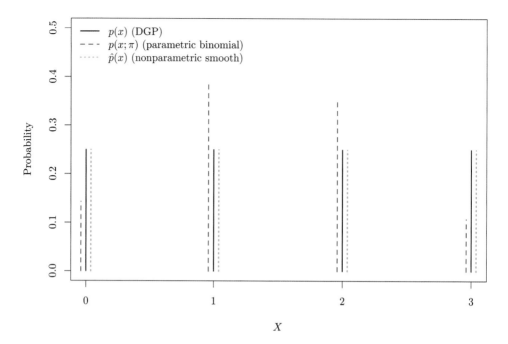

Figure 1.8: Probability estimates for parametric and kernel smoothed methods for one draw from the underlying DGP when the parametric model is incorrectly specified ($\lambda_{ml} = 0.75$).

metric, smooth, and nonsmooth estimators will all be consistent, but the correctly specified parametric model will be the most efficient in small sample settings because it uses information that is not available to its nonparametric counterparts. Each of $p_n(x)$ and $\hat{p}(x)$ are root-n consistent (i.e., their RMSEs are of $O(1/\sqrt{n})$), whereas misspecified parametric models are sometimes described as "$N^{-1/2}$-inconsistent" (Robinson, 1988, page 933) since, although their variance does indeed fall and is of $O(1/n)$, their bias is of $O(1)$ and does not disappear as n increases. Hence the MSE cannot fall below a squared bias term that is ever present, which is why such estimators are not consistent. This can be seen in Table 1.3, where for this particular example, the MSE for the misspecified binomial model is bounded below by 0.25 (the root SMSE is given by `sqrt(sum((dbinom(0:3,3,.5)-rep(1/4,4))^2)) = 0.25`). If the reader wishes to assess consistency, these examples can be re-run with the sample size doubled from $n = 100$ to $n = 200$. The reader will observe that, when n is doubled, the root SMSE for $p_n(x)$ and $\hat{p}(x)$ falls, while that for the misspecified parametric model never falls below 0.25.

The astute reader may have noticed that in the second simulation, the ad hoc kernel estimator with the upper bound smoothing parameter value of $\lambda = 0.75$ has a root SMSE of zero. This stems from a particular feature of the kernel estimator when the DGP is the discrete uniform (i.e., $p(x) = 1/c$, here $c = 4$). In this case, the bias term when using Aitchison and Aitken's unordered kernel function is $\lambda\Lambda_1 = \lambda(1 - cp(x))/(c-1) = 0$ for *any* λ. The SMSE will therefore achieve its lowest value when λ is selected to minimize variance, which occurs when $\lambda = (c-1)/c = 0.75$ for this example where the variance is 0. Interestingly, the data-driven estimator $\hat{p}(x)_{ml}$ has a median root SMSE of 0 because likelihood cross-validation tends to correctly select a value of λ that lies near its upper bound. However, it has the added advantage that it does not require any assumptions about the underlying distribution, which is a very powerful property. The only *caveat* is that this property will manifest itself only if there exists a smoothing parameter for which $\hat{p}(x) = 1/c$ (the discrete uniform distribution), which may require some kernel carpentry.

Problem Set

1. Demonstrate that the unordered kernel estimator of $p(x)$ that uses Aitchison and Aitken's unordered kernel function is *proper* (i.e., it is non-negative and it sums to one over all $x \in \{0, 1, \ldots, c-1\}$).

2. Consider the unordered kernel estimator of $p(x)$ that uses Aitchison and Aitken's unordered kernel function.
   i. Express the MSE of $\hat{p}(x)$ in terms of the MSE of $p_n(x)$ and the constants Λ_1, Λ_2, and Λ_3 that were defined in the previous chapter.
   ii. A comparison of the finite sample performance of $\hat{p}(x)$ and that of $p_n(x)$ revolves around the magnitudes of Λ_1, Λ_2, and $\Lambda_3 = p(x)(1 + \Lambda_1)$. Suppose that X has a discrete uniform distribution (i.e., $p(x) = 1/c$ for all $x \in \mathcal{D}$). Express $\mathrm{MSE}\,\hat{p}(x) - \mathrm{MSE}\,p_n(x)$ in terms of n, c, and λ and determine its sign for *any* λ.

3. Consider the probability function $p(x)$ for the unordered discrete random variable $X \in \mathcal{D} = \{0, 1, \ldots, c-1\}$, where $c \geq 2$ represents the number of unique outcomes. Let $\{X_i\}_{i=1}^n$ represent i.i.d. draws from a distribution with unknown $p(x)$. The kernel estimator of $p(x)$ is given by

$$\hat{p}(x) = \frac{1}{n} \sum_{i=1}^{n} L(X_i, x, \lambda),$$

   where $L(\cdot)$ is an unordered kernel function defined by

$$L(X_i, x, \lambda) = \begin{cases} 1 & \text{if } X_i = x \\ \lambda & \text{otherwise,} \end{cases}$$

   and where $\lambda \in [0, 1]$.
   i. Derive the bias of this estimator.
   ii. Derive the variance of this estimator.
   iii. Using the SMSE as your criterion, derive the optimal smoothing parameter for this estimator.
   iv. Is this estimator a proper probability function estimator? You must clearly explain and support your answer.

4. Consider an *ordered* random variable with discrete support, $X \in \mathcal{D} = \{0, 1\}$, so that the number of outcomes is $c = 2$. Consider the kernel

estimator of $p(x) = \Pr(X = x)$ defined by

$$\hat{p}(x) = \frac{1}{n} \sum_{i=1}^{n} l(X_i, x, \lambda),$$

where $l(\cdot)$ is an *ordered* kernel function defined by

$$l(X_i, x, \lambda) = \lambda^{d_{xi}} / \Lambda_{xi},$$

where $0 \le \lambda \le 1$, $d_{xi} = |x - X_i|$, and the normalizing factor $\Lambda_{xi} = \sum_{x \in \mathcal{D}} \lambda^{d_{xi}}$ is tailored to the particular value of $X_i \in \mathcal{D}$.
Presume that you have n independent random draws $\{X_1, X_2, \ldots, X_n\}$ from the probability distribution $p(x)$.

i. How many values can this kernel assume? What is the value of the kernel when $X_i = x$? How about when $X_i \ne x$? Is distance taken into account?

ii. Derive the bias of this estimator and show that the *leading* bias term is of $O(\lambda)$, which mirrors the result for the unordered case.[20] Presume that $0 \le \lambda < 1$ so that, at a certain point in the proof, you can express $1/(1+\lambda)$ as the infinite series $1 - \lambda + \lambda^2 - \lambda^3 + \ldots$ (hint: first get to the point where you have $E\hat{p}(x) = p(x) + \ldots$ and where you have collected the terms involving $\lambda/(1 + \lambda)$, then use this approximation so that you can write $\lambda/(1+\lambda) = \lambda - \lambda^2 + \lambda^3 - \ldots$).

iii. Derive the variance of this estimator up to terms of order $O(\lambda^2)$.

iv. What are the MSE and the SMSE of this estimator? You may leave your expression in terms of Λ_1, Λ_2, and Λ_3 without simplifying any further.

v. What is the optimal smoothing parameter? You may leave your expression in terms of Λ_1, Λ_2, and Λ_3 without simplifying any further.

5. Code up a Monte Carlo simulation that compares the SMSE performance of $p_n(x)$ and $\hat{p}(x)$, where the latter uses Aitchison and Aitken's unordered kernel function with three alternatively chosen smoothing parameters:

i. The SMSE-optimal λ that uses the *true* (unknown in general) probabilities

ii. The SMSE-optimal λ that uses plug-in estimates $p_n(x)$ of the probabilities

iii. The likelihood cross-validated λ

Run two simulations – one where the probabilities differ substantially across the $x \in \mathcal{D}$ and another where they are the discrete uniform $p(x) = 1/c$. Conduct $M = 1000$ Monte Carlo replications and consider

---

[20]This will involve approximations that are similar to those we will encounter when we consider kernel-smoothed density estimation, so it will serve you well in what is to come.

the following probabilities and methods for generating the random samples:

```
## Use one or the other (i.e., comment one out)
## Probabilities differ
p <- c(0.07, 0.13, 0.20, 0.27, 0.33)
## Discrete uniform
p <- c(0.20, 0.20, 0.20, 0.20, 0.20)
## Generate a random sample on the support {0,1,...,c-1}
c <- length(p)
X <- sample(0:(c-1),n,replace=TRUE,prob=p)
```

For each replication, compute the SMSE via, e.g.,

```
sum((kernel.probability(X,lambda.mse.opt(p))$P-p)^2)
```

where `lambda.mse.opt(p)` is a function that you have created that accepts a vector of probabilities p and returns λ_{opt} using the formula that we derived. Summarize the SMSEs in the form of boxplots and a tabular summary, as per the simulations in the Practitioner's Corner in Chapter 1. Note that the cross-validated smoothing parameter can be obtained as follows: `npudensbw(~factor(X))$bw` (you need to first install and then load the np package).

Summarize your results in a few sentences, and make sure that you indicate both what you were expecting and what the simulations have revealed. Can you detect a Stein effect at work?

Chapter 2

Continuous Density and Cumulative Distribution Functions

> Normality is a myth; there never was, and never will be, a normal distribution. (Geary, 1947)

2.1 Overview

The first random variable that students of basic statistics typically encounter is the *discrete* random variable that we covered in Chapter 1. Once they have developed an understanding of discrete random variables, students typically proceed to *continuous* random variables, which are the focus of the present chapter.

A continuous random variable is one that can assume uncountably infinitely many values (i.e., there are infinitely many possible outcomes between any two distinct values). Some have restricted domain (e.g., $X \geq 0$ or $a \leq X \leq b$ for some finite constants a and b) and others do not (e.g., $-\infty \leq X \leq \infty$). Examples include height, weight, income, distance, and IQ. In the context of a continuous random variable, it makes no sense to talk about $\Pr(X = x)$ because $X = x$ is a *measure zero* event whose probability is zero by definition. Repeated values in a random sample cannot *theoretically*[1] occur, and as a result, one does not *count* the number of realizations of any particular value. Instead, one talks about the probability that $a < X < b$, where a and b are two constants. Such a probability is obtained from the *probability density function* (PDF), which we denote by $f(x)$. In particular,

---

[1]Of course, continuous random variables are often recorded using a fixed number of digits, and this rounding raises the possibility of encountering repeated *recorded* values of what is, in fact, a continuous random variable.

$\Pr(a \leq X \leq b) = \Pr(a < X < b) = \int_a^b f(x)\,dx$, which is simply the area under the density function of the random variable X in the interval $[a, b]$ or (a, b).[2]

Like its discrete counterpart (i.e., the probability function $p(x)$ that was studied in Chapter 1), the PDF of a continuous random variable is an object of special interest in statistics. Also, like its discrete counterpart, the PDF is generally unknown and must therefore be estimated. As in the previous chapter, there are once again three approaches that we might entertain when estimating the unknown PDF of a continuous random variable:

   i. Presume a parametric family (e.g., Gaussian) and estimate under this presumption.

   ii. Use nonsmooth nonparametric estimates (e.g., Pearson's histogram density).

   iii. Use a kernel-smoothed approach.

The first two of these are standard fare in introductory courses on data analysis, whereas the third is likely to be far less familiar to the reader. One of the drawbacks of the first approach is that if the assumed parametric family is at odds with the underlying DGP, then the resulting estimates will be *biased* and *inconsistent*. Meanwhile, one of the shortcomings of the second approach is that, since the estimates of the PDF are step functions, they are not smooth. In addition, even though they are *consistent* under certain conditions, they may not be centred on the point at which the density is being estimated. The third approach introduces some finite sample bias by smoothing the density in a particular manner, but it is *asymptotically unbiased* and *consistent*. Therefore, its finite sample performance may often be better than that of either of its peers.

2.2   Parametric Density Function Estimation

Suppose that we are interested in modeling a univariate PDF for some continuous random variable $X \in \mathbb{R}$, where $\mathbb{R}$ denotes the *real number line*. In this first example, we naïvely presume that our data were generated from the normal parametric family of distributions. The PDF is characterized by two parameters, namely the mean μ and the variance σ^2, and is given by

$$f(x; \mu, \sigma^2) = \frac{1}{\sqrt{2\pi\sigma^2}} e^{-\frac{1}{2}\left(\frac{x-\mu}{\sigma}\right)^2}.$$

The parametric density estimate $f(x; \hat{\mu}, \hat{\sigma}^2)$ is obtained by substituting the sample mean and variance for the unknown population mean and variance. This gives rise to the familiar bell-shaped density function, as can be seen in the following example (in R, the function `dnorm()` constructs the density function for a normally distributed random variable).

---

[2]Note that $\Pr(X \leq a) = \Pr(X < a)$ because $\Pr(X = x)$ is 0.

Example 2.1. Old Faithful Data.

Consider estimating the unknown PDF of the variable `eruptions`, which reports the duration (in minutes) of eruptions of the Old Faithful geyser in Yellowstone National Park, Wyoming, USA (in R, `data(faithful)` will load the dataset, `attach(faithful)` will attach). It is assumed here that the data have a normal distribution.

For the eruptions data, $\hat{\mu} = 3.488$ and $\hat{\sigma} = 1.141$. We plot the resulting density estimate $f(x; \hat{\mu}, \hat{\sigma}^2)$ along with a *rug* for the data in Figure 2.1. We test for correct parametric model specification using the Shapiro-Wilk[3] (Shapiro and Wilk, 1965) test for normality ($W = 0.8459$, P-value $9.036e - 16$) and reject the null hypothesis of a Gaussian distribution. Thus, although the normal parametric family of distributions might be appropriate when describing the density of certain statistics (e.g., the sample mean), it doesn't always provide an accurate characterization of the density of *raw* data.

As was the case when using the binomial distribution to model the boy-girl ratio in Chapter 1, we now find ourselves more or less where we began, having ruled out just one of a multitude of parametric density functions that might underlie the data. Against this backdrop, we might instead entertain both nonsmooth and smooth consistent nonparametric approaches.

2.3   Nonsmooth Density Function Estimation

2.3.1   The Histogram Density Estimator

The best-known nonsmooth nonparametric density estimator is the *histogram density* proposed by Karl Pearson (Pearson, 1895), and it is defined as follows: Let x_0 denote the *origin*, let h denote the *bin width*, and define the *bin* $[x_0 + mh, x_0 + (m + 1)h)$ for each integer $m = 0, \pm 1, \pm 2, \ldots$[4] The histogram density estimator is given by

$$f_H(x) = \frac{\text{\# of } X_i \text{ in the same bin as } x}{nh}$$

---

[3]The Shapiro–Wilk test statistic is $W = \left(\sum_{i=1}^{n} a_i X_{(i)} \right)^2 / \sum_{i=1}^{n} (X_i - \overline{X})^2$, where $X_{(i)}$ is the ith order statistic, that is, the ith-smallest number in the sample. The constants a_i are given by $(a_1, \ldots, a_n) = \frac{m'V^{-1}}{(m'V^{-1}V^{-1}m)^{1/2}}$, where $m = (m_1, \ldots, m_n)'$ is a vector of expected values of the order statistics of independent and identically-distributed standard normal random variables, and where V is the covariance matrix of those order statistics. P-values are obtained from the statistic's null distribution. We reject the null of normality at level $\alpha = \{0.01, 0.05, 0.10\}$ if $P < \alpha$.

[4]These bins are closed on the left and open on the right to avoid the possibility of an observation lying in two bins simultaneously. The R function `hist()` has the option `right=` which, if `TRUE`, uses bins that are right-closed (left-open) intervals.

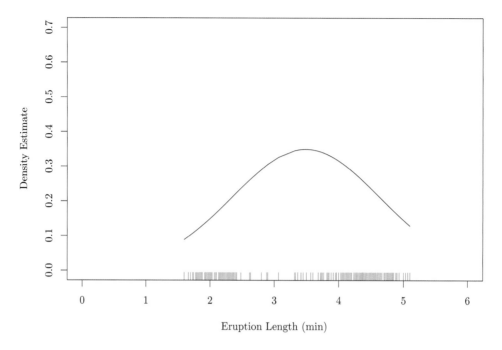

Figure 2.1: The Gaussian parametric density estimate for the eruptions data.

$$= \frac{1}{nh} \sum_{i=1}^{n} \mathbf{1}(X_i \text{ is in the same bin as } x),$$

where $\mathbf{1}(\cdot)$ is the *indicator* function that was defined in Chapter 1.

Example 2.2. Old Faithful Data.

> Figure 2.2 presents the histogram density estimate along with a rug for the `eruptions` data. The histogram estimator reveals a *bi-modal* structure in the data. The nonsmooth nature of the estimator is also readily apparent.

The histogram density estimator is known to suffer from a number of drawbacks. First, it is not particularly efficient in a statistical sense (i.e., it is more variable than need be). Second, the discontinuity of the estimator presents obstacles in the event that derivatives of density estimates are required (and they often are). Third, it is sensitive to the placement of the origin x_0 and to the bin width h. Finally, all values of x that lie in the same bin, that is, all $x \in [x_0+mh, x_0+(m+1)h)$, receive the same density estimate $f_H(x)$. It turns out that other, more efficient nonparametric estimators exist, both nonsmooth and smooth.

2.3.2   The Naïve Density Estimator

The naïve density estimator was first proposed by Fix and Hodges (1951). This estimator is, in effect, a histogram that is centred on the point x at which

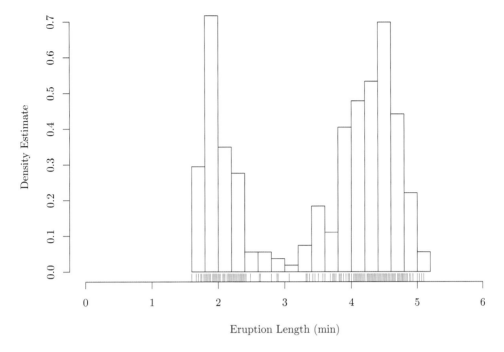

Figure 2.2: The histogram density estimate for the eruptions data.

the density is evaluated. By definition, the density function is the derivative with respect to x of the cumulative distribution function $F(x) = \Pr(X \leq x)$. For any two distinct values a and b where $a < b$, $\Pr(a < X < b) = F(b) - F(a)$. By the *fundamental theorem of calculus*[5], we obtain

$$f(x) = \lim_{h \to 0} \frac{1}{2h} \Pr(x - h < X < x + h).$$

A natural density estimator is therefore given by the empirical counterpart of the equation above, namely

$$
\begin{aligned}
f_N(x) &= \frac{1}{2h} \widehat{\Pr}(x - h < X < x + h) \\
&= \frac{1}{2h} \frac{(\# \text{ of } X_i \text{ falling in } (x - h, x + h))}{n} \\
&= \frac{1}{nh} \sum_{i=1}^{n} \frac{\mathbf{1}(X_i \text{ lies in } (x - h, x + h))}{2}.
\end{aligned}
$$

This is the *naïve density estimator*, and it can be rewritten in a particularly useful form. If X_i lies within h units of x, where x is some point at which we wish to construct our density estimate, then it is assigned a value $1/2$.

---

[5]The fundamental theorem of calculus states that differentiation and integration are essentially inverses of one another.

Otherwise, X_i is assigned a value of 0. We can thus construct a *weight function* in terms of x, X_i, and h:

$$w\left(X_i, x, h\right) = \begin{cases} \frac{1}{2} & \text{if } x - h < X_i < x + h, \\ 0 & \text{otherwise.} \end{cases}$$

Note that this is the same as expressing the weight function in terms of $z = (x - X_i)/h$, where the value $1/2$ is assigned if $-1 < z < 1$ (i.e., $|z| < 1$) and 0 is assigned if $|z| \geq 1$, i.e.,

$$w(z) = \begin{cases} \frac{1}{2} & \text{if } |z| < 1, \\ 0 & \text{otherwise.} \end{cases}$$

To see this, simply take the inequality $x - h < X_i < x + h$, subtract x, divide by h, and then multiply by -1 to obtain $1 > (x - X_i)/h > -1$, $1 > z > -1$, or $|z| < 1$. Figure 2.3 plots these weight functions.

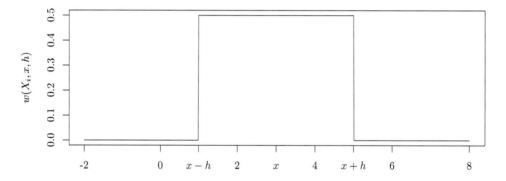

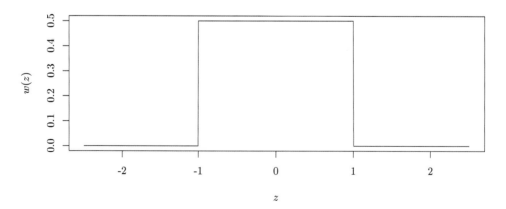

Figure 2.3: The naïve weight functions $w(X_i, x, h)$ and $w(z)$, $x = 3$, $h = 2$.

Thus, using the weight function

$$w\left(\frac{x - X_i}{h}\right) = \begin{cases} \frac{1}{2} & \text{if } \left|\frac{x-X_i}{h}\right| < 1, \\ 0 & \text{otherwise,} \end{cases}$$

where the reader will note that $w(z)$ is a uniform density function on $[-1,1]$, the naïve density estimator can be expressed as

$$f_N(x) = \frac{1}{nh} \sum_{i=1}^{n} w\left(\frac{x - X_i}{h}\right).$$

For this estimator, we place a *box* of width $2h$ and height $(2nh)^{-1}$ on each observation that lies in $(x - h, x + h)$, which corresponds to $|z| < 1$, and add these values for the entire sample to obtain $f_N(x)$. Like the histogram, however, the discontinuity of this estimator will prove to be problematic in the event that derivatives of density estimates are required.

Example 2.3. Old Faithful Data.

Figure 2.4 plots the naïve density estimate for the eruptions data. Even though this estimator is nonsmooth, one of its most appealing features is that each density estimate $f_N(x)$ is centred on the point x at which it is being evaluated. In this regard, it can be seen as an improvement on the histogram density estimator.

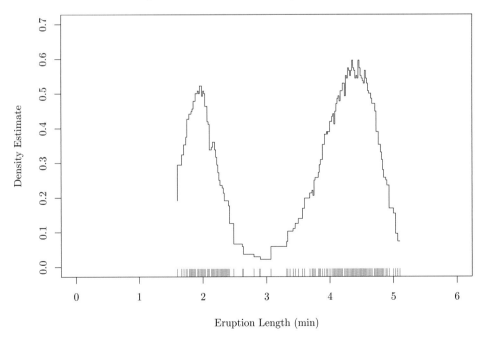

Figure 2.4: The nonsmooth naïve density estimate for the eruptions data.

2.4   Smooth Kernel Density Function Estimation

The Rosenblatt-Parzen kernel density estimator (Rosenblatt, 1956; Parzen, 1962) is the smooth (i.e., continuously differentiable) counterpart to the nonsmooth naïve density estimator of Fix and Hodges (1951). It is the most popular smooth nonparametric density estimator that is in use today.

Consider a symmetric smooth weight function (i.e., a *kernel* function) that satisfies $K(z) \geq 0$ and $\int_{-\infty}^{\infty} K(z) \, dz = 1$. The Rosenblatt-Parzen kernel density estimator is defined by

$$\hat{f}(x) = \frac{1}{nh} \sum_{i=1}^{n} K\left(\frac{x - X_i}{h}\right).$$

Observe that the only thing that distinguishes this from the nonsmooth naïve estimator of Fix and Hodges (1951) is the use of a *smooth* (i.e., continuously differentiable) weight function $K(z)$ instead of a nonsmooth uniform weight function $w(z)$.

Given that $K(z)$ is typically a symmetric density function, the Rosenblatt-Parzen estimator is an equally-weighted *mixture* of n re-scaled density functions $K\left(\frac{x-X_i}{h}\right)/h$, each having a sample realization X_i as its mean and a bandwidth h as its standard deviation. Figure 2.5 compares and contrasts the *nonsmooth* naïve weight function and the *smooth* Rosenblatt-Parzen kernel function. Note that both $w(z)$ and $K(z)$ integrate to one and are non-negative, but the similarity ends there.

The following example sheds additional light on how the Rosenblatt-Parzen density estimator is constructed.

Example 2.4. The *Mechanics* of Rosenblatt-Parzen Density Estimation.

We consider a simple illustration where our sample X_1, X_2, X_3 consists of $n = 3$ observations. We wish to construct $\hat{f}(X_1)$ for a given bandwidth h, i.e.,

$$\hat{f}(X_1) = \frac{1}{nh} \sum_{i=1}^{n} K\left(\frac{X_1 - X_i}{h}\right),$$

where we use the standard Gaussian kernel function $K(z) = \frac{1}{\sqrt{2\pi}} e^{-\frac{1}{2}z^2}$. Unlike the histogram which is the sum of boxes of height $\frac{1}{nh}$, the kernel estimator is the sum of points on curves of differing slopes and heights.

Figure 2.6 shows the density estimator evaluated on a grid of points, and includes a plot of the kernel function for each of the sample points X_1, X_2, and X_3, with vertical dashed lines at each sample point. The value of each kernel function at the point X_1 is scaled by $\frac{1}{nh}$, and their sum yields $\hat{f}(X_1)$. This is repeated for $\hat{f}(X_2)$ and $\hat{f}(X_3)$, albeit without the labels.

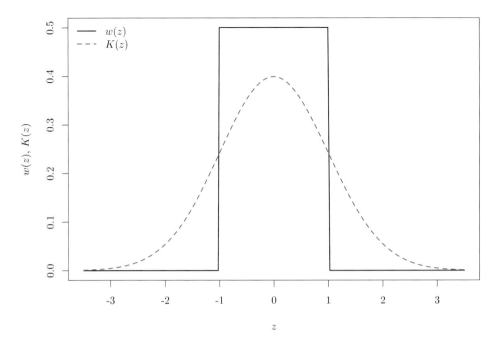

Figure 2.5: The nonsmooth naïve weight function $w(z)$ versus the smooth kernel function $K(z)$.

Example 2.5. The Rosenblatt-Parzen Density Estimator for the Old Faithful `eruptions` Data.

Figure 2.7 presents the Rosenblatt-Parzen kernel density estimate for the eruptions data using a Gaussian kernel function and an ad hoc bandwidth (we will study bandwidth selection shortly). Like the histogram and naïve density estimates, this estimate also reveals a bi-modal structure in the data. Unlike the histogram and naïve estimators, however, it is both smooth and centred on the point at which the density is estimated. The smoothness property is inherited from the Gaussian kernel function which, in this case, is (infinitely) continuously differentiable.

Figure 2.8 compares the histogram, naïve, and Rosenblatt-Parzen estimates for the eruptions data. The agreement among the three nonparametric estimators is striking. On the other hand, when these estimates are compared with the parametric estimate in Figure 2.1 that assumes a normal PDF, it is rather surprising to observe that the misspecified parametric density assigns the greatest probability to the region where, in fact, the data are most *sparse* (i.e., around 3 minutes).

The nonparametric density estimators that we have considered are not the only nonparametric methods that are available to us. For example,

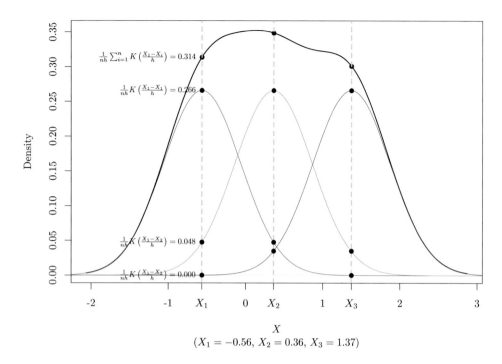

Figure 2.6: The mechanics of the Rosenblatt-Parzen kernel density estimator, $\hat{f}(X_1)$, $n = 3$, $h = 0.5$.

there also exist series-based (orthogonal series, Fourier series, etc.), logspline, nearest neighbour, and empirical likelihood density estimators. However, it is safe to say that at present, the most popular and the most widely studied nonparametric estimators are kernel-based (witness the R function `density()` that is part of the base R install). The kernel-based framework also lends itself to a range of statistical objects that are of interest to econometricians, which is why, in what follows, we restrict our attention to this particular class of nonparametric estimators.

2.4.1 Properties of the Rosenblatt-Parzen Kernel Density Estimator

We now develop the statistical underpinnings of the Rosenblatt-Parzen kernel density estimator. To begin, we demonstrate that $\hat{f}(x)$ is a *proper* density estimator *provided* that $K(z) \geq 0$, $\int K(z)\,dz = 1$, and $h > 0$ (all integrals that follow presume limits of integration $\int_{-\infty}^{\infty}$ unless specified otherwise). In order to demonstrate that $\hat{f}(x)$ is proper, we let $z = (x - X_i)/h$, which implies that $x = X_i + hz$ and $h\,dz = dx$. Therefore, we can write:

$$\int \hat{f}(x)\,dx = \frac{1}{nh} \sum_{i=1}^{n} \int K\left(\frac{x - X_i}{h}\right)\,dx$$

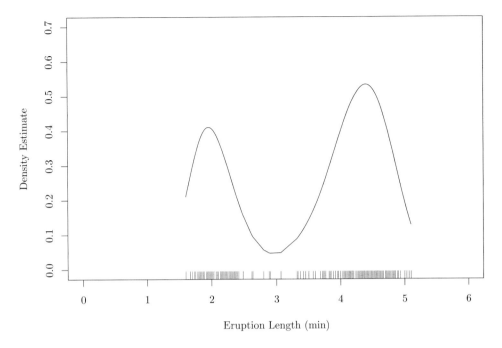

Figure 2.7: The Rosenblatt-Parzen kernel density estimate for the eruptions data.

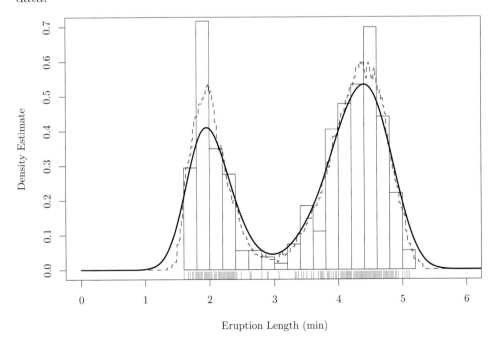

Figure 2.8: A comparison of the histogram, naïve, and Rosenblatt-Parzen density estimates for the eruptions data.

$$= \frac{1}{nh} \sum_{i=1}^{n} \int K(z) \, h \, dz$$

$$= \frac{1}{n} \sum_{i=1}^{n} \int K(z) \, dz$$

$$= 1,$$

provided that our kernel function satisfies $\int K(z) \, dz = 1$.[6] If, in addition, $K(z) \geq 0$ and $h > 0$, then $\hat{f}(x) \geq 0$ and hence $\hat{f}(x)$ is a proper density (i.e., $\hat{f}(x) \geq 0$ and $\int_{-\infty}^{\infty} \hat{f}(x) \, dx = 1$).

Having established that $\hat{f}(x)$ is proper, we now derive its pointwise bias and variance in order to obtain an expression for its pointwise MSE. Assume that $h \to 0$ as $n \to \infty$, $nh \to \infty$ as $n \to \infty$, and that the kernel function $K(z)$ is symmetric (i.e., $K(z) = K(-z)$), bounded, and non-negative. Assume also that $K(z)$ satisfies the following *second-order* regularity conditions:

$$\int K(z) \, dz = 1, \quad \int z K(z) \, dz = 0, \quad 0 < \int z^2 K(z) \, dz = \kappa_2 < \infty,$$

where the particular form of the kernel function and the value of the bandwidth are under our control. Finally, assume that the density $f(x)$ is differentiable on the real number line $\mathbb{R}$, that the first derivative $f'(x) < \infty$ is absolutely continuous on $\mathbb{R}$, that the second derivative satisfies $\int \left(f''(x) \right)^2 \, dx < \infty$, and that $\int |z^3| K(z) \, dz < \infty$. The last of these is required to satisfy a technical condition that involves the remainder term in a Taylor expansion.

Since we are using a symmetric kernel function, we can exploit this property and simplify the proofs that involve Taylor expansions of $f(t) = f(x + hz)$ around x. We use a change of variables $z = (t - x)/h$, which implies that $t = x + hz$ and $dt = h \, dz$ (x is a fixed point). The issue is simply that, when we take a Taylor expansion, integration from $-\infty$ to ∞ follows a change of variables. We also need to take a derivative based on this change of variables, and *if* this involved a change of signs (e.g., *if* we expressed $K(z)$ using the change of variables $z = (x - t)/h$, and hence $dt = -h \, dz$), then in the proofs, we would also have to deal with the fact that $\int_{-\infty}^{\infty} dt = -h \int_{\infty}^{-\infty} dz = h \int_{-\infty}^{\infty} dz$, which is an unnecessary complication *when using a symmetric kernel function*. Either way, we obtain the same result, but by exploiting kernel function symmetry, we avoid having to repeat this tedious operation over and over again. Note, however, that when we consider the kernel estimator of the cumulative distribution function (CDF) in Section 2.5, we will not be able to use this simplification because the CDF kernel is asymmetric. In any event, for symmetric kernel functions that are used to construct PDF estimates, we

---

[6]Note that this is a special case of Fubini's and Tonelli's theorems. Fubini's Theorem (Fubini, 1907) says that we can change the order of integration and summation if $\hat{f} \geq 0$ or if $\sum \int |\hat{f}| < \infty$ ($\int \sum |\hat{f}|$ - by Tonelli's theorem (Tonelli, 1909), the two are equivalent).

can always write

$$\hat{f}(x) = \frac{1}{nh} \sum_{i=1}^{n} K\left(\frac{x - X_i}{h}\right)$$

$$= \frac{1}{nh} \sum_{i=1}^{n} K\left(\frac{X_i - x}{h}\right),$$

which removes in a benign fashion many redundant lines from the proofs that follow.

By definition,

$$\text{MSE } \hat{f}(x) = \text{E}\left(\hat{f}(x) - f(x)\right)^2 = \text{Var } \hat{f}(x) + \left(\text{Bias } \hat{f}(x)\right)^2.$$

In the proofs that follow, we assume i.i.d. data. For weakly dependent processes, Robinson (1983) shows that $\hat{f}(x)$ has the same order MSE as in the i.i.d. case, and its asymptotic distribution is the same as that in the i.i.d. case. This implies that the leading bias and variance terms are the same as in the i.i.d. setting; see Wang and Phillips (2009) for the non-stationary case. See also Chapter 18 in Li and Racine (2007), who demonstrate that results pertaining to rates of convergence and asymptotic normality that are obtained under the i.i.d. assumption remain unchanged when the i.i.d. assumption is relaxed to allow for weakly dependent time series processes. This holds not only for density estimation, but also for semiparametric and nonparametric regression.

We invoke the change of variables transformation $z = (t - x)/h$. Hence $t = x + hz$ and $dt = h\, dz$ since x is a fixed point. We expand $f(x + hz)$ around x using a Taylor expansion.[7] For the pointwise expectation of the kernel density estimator, we thereby obtain

$$\text{E } \hat{f}(x) = \frac{1}{nh} \sum_{i=1}^{n} \text{E } K\left(\frac{X_i - x}{h}\right)$$

$$= \frac{1}{h} \text{E } K\left(\frac{X_1 - x}{h}\right)$$

$$= \frac{1}{h} \int K\left(\frac{t - x}{h}\right) f(t)\, dt$$

$$= \frac{1}{h} \int K(z) f(x + hz) h\, dz$$

$$= \int K(z) \left(\frac{f(x)}{0!} + \frac{hz f'(x)}{1!} + \frac{z^2 h^2 f''(x)}{2!} + \dots\right) dz$$

---

[7]A Taylor series representation of an infinitely differentiable function $f(a)$ at b is given by the infinite series $\sum_{j=0}^{\infty} \frac{(a-b)^j}{j!} f^{(j)}(b)$, where $f^{(j)}(b)$ denotes the jth derivative of f evaluated at the point b and where, by definition, $(x - a)^0 = 1$, $0! = 1$ and $f^{(0)}(b) = f(b)$. In our case, let $a = x + hz$ and $b = x$, so the Taylor expansion of $f(x + hz)$ at x is $\sum_{j=0}^{\infty} \frac{(hz)^j}{j!} f^{(j)}(x)$.

$$= f(x) \int K(z)\,dz + h f'(x) \int z K(z)\,dz + \frac{h^2}{2} f''(x) \int z^2 K(z)\,dz + \dots$$

$$= f(x) + \frac{h^2}{2} f''(x)\kappa_2 + \mathcal{R},$$

where $\mathcal{R}$ denotes a generic *remainder* term that will differ from one context to the next. This result follows from the previously stated assumptions that underlie the second-order kernel function ($\int K(z)\,dz = 1$, $\int z K(z)\,dz = 0$, etc.). For the univariate Rosenblatt-Parzen kernel density estimator that uses a second-order kernel function, the pointwise bias up to terms of $O(h^2)$ is expressed as:

$$\text{Bias } \hat{f}(x) = \text{E}\,\hat{f}(x) - f(x)$$

$$= \frac{h^2}{2} f''(x)\kappa_2$$

(this is known as the *leading* bias term). Given the assumption that $h \to 0$ as $n \to \infty$ (e.g., $h \propto 1/n^\alpha$ for some $0 < \alpha < 1$), $h^2 \propto 1/n^{2\alpha}$ goes to zero more quickly than h as $n \to \infty$. The same goes for h^3, h^4, etc. The leading term is therefore the *slowest* to converge to zero, which is why it is retained and the other terms that are of *smaller order* are ignored. Provided that $h \to 0$ as $n \to \infty$, a term of big $O(h^2)$ is also of small $o(1)$, and hence the bias vanishes in the limit (see Appendix A for details on *big and small O* notation). Observe that as the bandwidth increases, the pointwise bias increases and vice versa.

The pointwise variance is given by

$$\text{Var } \hat{f}(x) = \text{E}\left(\hat{f}(x) - \text{E}\,\hat{f}(x)\right)^2$$

$$= \text{E}\left(\frac{1}{nh}\sum_{i=1}^{n}\left(K\left(\frac{X_i - x}{h}\right) - \text{E}\,K\left(\frac{X_i - x}{h}\right)\right)\right)^2$$

$$= \frac{1}{n^2 h^2}\left(\sum_{i=1}^{n}\text{E}\,\eta_i^2 + \sum_{\substack{i=1 \\ i\neq j}}^{n}\sum_{j=1}^{n}\text{E}\,\eta_i\eta_j\right)$$

$$= \frac{1}{n^2 h^2}\left(\sum_{i=1}^{n}\text{E}\,\eta_i^2\right)$$

$$= \frac{1}{n^2 h^2}\left(\sum_{i=1}^{n}\text{E}\left(K\left(\frac{X_i - x}{h}\right) - \text{E}\,K\left(\frac{X_i - x}{h}\right)\right)^2\right)$$

$$= \frac{1}{nh^2}\,\text{E}\left(K\left(\frac{X_1 - x}{h}\right) - \text{E}\,K\left(\frac{X_1 - x}{h}\right)\right)^2$$

$$= \frac{1}{nh^2}\left(\text{E}\,K^2\left(\frac{X_1 - x}{h}\right) - \left(\text{E}\,K\left(\frac{X_1 - x}{h}\right)\right)^2\right)$$

$$= \frac{1}{nh^2} \operatorname{Var} K\left(\frac{X_1 - x}{h}\right).$$

The fourth line stems from the fact that, for independent draws, $\operatorname{E} \eta_i \eta_j = 0$ when $i \neq j$, where $\eta_i = K\left(\frac{X_i - x}{h}\right) - \operatorname{E} K\left(\frac{X_i - x}{h}\right)$. The sixth line follows from the identical distribution assumption. The second term in the second-to-last line is known from the results that were previously obtained for $\operatorname{E} \hat{f}(x)$. In order to complete the expression for the pointwise variance, we need the first term, i.e.,

$$
\begin{aligned}
\operatorname{E} K^2\left(\frac{X_1 - x}{h}\right) &= \int K^2\left(\frac{t - x}{h}\right) f(t)\, dt \\
&= \int K^2(z) f(x + hz) h\, dz \\
&= h \int K^2(z) \left(\frac{f(x)}{0!} + \frac{hz f'(x)}{1!} + \frac{z^2 h^2 f''(x)}{2!} + \dots\right) dz \\
&= h \left(f(x) \int K^2(z)\, dz + h f'(x) \int z K^2(z)\, dz + \dots\right) \\
&= h f(x) \kappa + h^2 f'(x) \int z K^2(z)\, dz + \mathcal{R},
\end{aligned}
$$

where $\kappa = \int K^2(z)\, dz$ and $\mathcal{R}$ denotes a *remainder* term. Recalling that $\operatorname{E} \hat{f}(x) = \frac{1}{h} \operatorname{E} K\left(\frac{X_1 - x}{h}\right)$, the term $\operatorname{E} K\left(\frac{X_1 - x}{h}\right)$ that appears in the expression below for the pointwise variance is given by $h \operatorname{E} \hat{f}(x)$. Using our previously derived results for $\operatorname{E} \hat{f}(x)$, we can express $\operatorname{E} K\left(\frac{X_1 - x}{h}\right)$ as $h f(x) + \frac{h^3}{2} f''(x) \kappa_2 + \mathcal{R}$. Therefore, combining this result and the above expansion of $\operatorname{E} K^2\left(\frac{X_1 - x}{h}\right)$, we can obtain an expression for the pointwise variance, which is given by

$$
\begin{aligned}
\operatorname{Var} \hat{f}(x) &= \frac{1}{nh^2} \operatorname{E} K^2\left(\frac{X_1 - x}{h}\right) - \frac{1}{nh^2}\left(\operatorname{E} K\left(\frac{X_1 - x}{h}\right)\right)^2 \\
&= \frac{1}{nh} f(x) \kappa + \frac{f'(x)}{n} \int z K^2(z)\, dz - \frac{(f(x))^2}{n} + \mathcal{R} \\
&= \frac{1}{nh} f(x) \kappa + \mathcal{R},
\end{aligned}
$$

where $\frac{1}{nh} f(x) \kappa$ is the leading term in the pointwise variance and $\mathcal{R}$ is a remainder term. Recall that, by assumption, $nh \to \infty$ as $n \to \infty$, so the *leading term* is the slowest to converge to zero as $n \to \infty$. That is, $\frac{1}{nh}$ approaches zero more slowly than $\frac{1}{n}$ or $\frac{h}{n}$, which are the terms that follow the leading term that is of $O\left(\frac{1}{nh}\right)$ in the approximation. On the first line above, the expansion of the second element $\frac{1}{nh^2}\left(\operatorname{E} K\left(\frac{X_1 - x}{h}\right)\right)^2$ has a leading term that is of the same order as the *second term* in the expansion of the first element $\frac{1}{nh^2} \operatorname{E} K^2\left(\frac{X_1 - x}{h}\right)$, which is of *smaller order* than the first term.

Consequently, after all of the work that was involved in deriving results for $\mathrm{E}\, K\left(\frac{X_1-x}{h}\right)$, once those results have been incorporated into the pointwise variance expansion, they end up being ignored because they are of *smaller order* than the leading term.

For the univariate Rosenblatt-Parzen kernel density estimator that uses a second-order kernel function, the pointwise variance up to terms of $O((nh)^{-1})$ can therefore be expressed as

$$\operatorname{Var} \hat{f}(x) = \frac{f(x)}{nh}\kappa.$$

Observe that as the bandwidth increases, the pointwise variance falls and vice versa.

Before we proceed, we will first illustrate the relationship that exists between the magnitude of h, the pointwise bias, and the pointwise variance by means of a simulated example.

Example 2.6. Pointwise Bias, Pointwise Variance, and the Bandwidth.

Consider $M = 1,000$ kernel density estimates based on samples drawn from a χ^2 distribution with $\nu = 10$ degrees of freedom. We compute the pointwise bias and variance of $\hat{f}(x)$ based on three different bandwidths – one *too large*, one *about right*, and one *too small*. Figure 2.9 summarizes the results of this exercise. As we move from left to right, the bandwidth decreases in size. Note that our focus is on pointwise behaviour, so the three figures are being simultaneously compared at a single value of x (think of placing a ruler vertically so that it intersects all three horizontal axes at the same point). The figure reveals that, as the bandwidth becomes smaller, the bias falls (i.e., the pointwise mean of the 1,000 kernel estimates approaches the true $f(x)$) and the variance increases (the pointwise 0.025th and 0.975th quantiles of the 1,000 kernel estimates get wider). We can also envision the average of the pointwise squared bias and variance across all x, that is, the *integrated* squared bias and variance. For large bandwidths, the integrated squared bias dominates the integrated variance, whereas for small bandwidths, the integrated variance dominates the integrated squared bias. For bandwidths that are *about right* (the middle figures), the integrated squared bias and the integrated variance are in balance with one other.

This Monte Carlo simulation reveals some of the subtle features that characterize the pointwise bias and variance formulae that were given in Section 2.4.1. First, observe that bias depends on the curvature $f''(x)$ which, in this example, is greatest at the mode of $f(x)$ (the figure on the left clearly reveals that the bias attains its maximum at the mode). Next, observe that as h falls (i.e., as one moves from the leftmost to the rightmost figures), the squared bias falls and the variance rises uniformly across all x. Hence the bias is *proportional* to h, while the variance is *inversely proportional to h*; this indicates that we cannot reduce one without increasing the other. This is the same trade-off that we encountered when studying smooth probability estimation in Chapter 1. It is reassuring that, regardless of whether we are studying discrete support or continuous support settings, the underlying intuition remains unchanged. In fact, as we shall see, this bias-variance trade-off is common to all kernel smoothing methods.

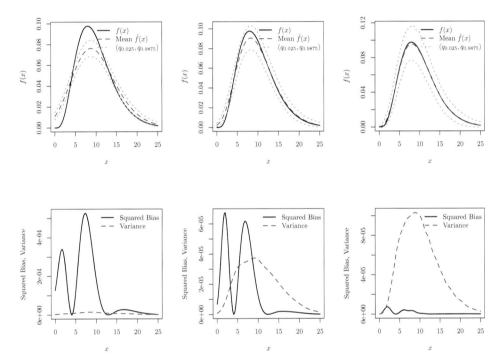

Figure 2.9: Summary of 1,000 kernel density estimates, $n = 250$, χ^2 DGP, with three bandwidths (too large [leftmost figures], about right [middle figures], too small [rightmost figures]). The upper figures plot the DGP $f(x)$ along with the pointwise mean $(1000^{-1} \sum_{m=1}^{1000} \hat{f}_m(x))$, 0.025th pointwise quantile, and 0.975th pointwise quantile. The lower figures present the pointwise squared bias $((\mathrm{E}\,\hat{f}(x) - f(x))^2)$ and pointwise variance.

The previously derived expressions for the pointwise bias and variance can be combined to obtain the pointwise MSE, which is written as

$$\mathrm{MSE}\,\hat{f}(x) = \mathrm{Var}\,\hat{f}(x) + \left(\mathrm{Bias}\,\hat{f}(x)\right)^2$$

$$= \frac{f(x)}{nh}\kappa + \left(\frac{h^2}{2}f''(x)\kappa_2\right)^2 .$$

We can construct a *global* measure of square error performance by integrating the pointwise MSE over the support of x. The IMSE is expressed as

$$\text{IMSE } \hat{f}(x) = \int \left(\frac{f(x)}{nh}\kappa + \left(\frac{h^2}{2}f''(x)\kappa_2\right)^2\right) dx$$

$$= \frac{1}{nh}\kappa \int f(x)\,dx + \left(\frac{h^2}{2}\kappa_2\right)^2 \int \left(f''(x)\right)^2 dx$$

$$= \frac{1}{nh}\kappa + \frac{h^4}{4}\kappa_2^2\Phi,$$

where $\Phi = \int \left(f''(x)\right)^2 dx$ is a constant that is specific to the unknown density $f(x)$, κ and κ_2 are constants that are specific to the kernel function $K(z)$, and $\int f(x)\,dx = 1$ holds for any density.

2.4.2 The IMSE-Optimal Bandwidth and Rate of Convergence

The IMSE expression that was derived above will prove useful for a variety of tasks. We begin by using this expression to obtain a bandwidth that globally balances squared bias and variance. Minimizing the IMSE with respect to the bandwidth h yields

$$h_{opt} = \kappa^{1/5}\kappa_2^{-2/5}\Phi^{-1/5}n^{-1/5}$$

$$= \left(\frac{\int K^2(z)\,dz}{\left(\int z^2 K(z)\,dz\right)^2 \int \left(f''(x)\right)^2 dx}\right)^{1/5} n^{-1/5}$$

$$= cn^{-1/5}.$$

Note that the constant c depends on $f''(x)$ and on properties of the kernel function $K(z)$. If $h \propto n^{-1/5}$, then the order of the leading squared bias term and of the leading variance term coincide (indeed, they ought to since h was specifically chosen to balance squared bias and variance), i.e.,

$$h^4 = O\left(\frac{1}{nh}\right) = O\left(\frac{1}{n^{4/5}}\right).$$

Plugging the optimal bandwidth into the pointwise MSE reveals that the MSE is of order $O(n^{-4/5})$ and the $\sqrt{MSE}$ is of order $O(n^{-2/5})$. This is a slower rate of convergence than what would be observed for a *correctly specified parametric model* (i.e., $O(n^{-1/2})$). We might think of this as the cost of ignorance about the underlying DGP. Nonetheless, provided that $h \to 0$ as $n \to \infty$ and $nh \to \infty$ as $n \to \infty$, the pointwise MSE of $\hat{f}(x)$ goes to zero asymptotically. We then say that $\hat{f}(x)$ is *consistent in square error*. A misspecified parametric model, on the other hand, is *inconsistent in square error* because its bias *never* vanishes, no matter how large n might be.

2.4.3 The IMSE-Optimal Kernel Function

The IMSE can be used for another task, namely determining the IMSE-optimal kernel function. If we substitute h_{opt} into the IMSE formula, then the IMSE will be

$$
\text{IMSE } \hat{f}(x) = \frac{\kappa}{nh_{opt}} + \frac{h_{opt}^4}{4}\kappa_2^2 \Phi
$$

$$
= \frac{\kappa}{n\left(\kappa^{1/5}\kappa_2^{-2/5}\Phi^{-1/5}n^{-1/5}\right)} + \frac{\left(\kappa^{1/5}\kappa_2^{-2/5}\Phi^{-1/5}n^{-1/5}\right)^4}{4}\kappa_2^2 \Phi
$$

$$
= \kappa^{4/5}\kappa_2^{2/5}\Phi^{1/5}n^{-4/5} + \frac{1}{4}\kappa^{4/5}\kappa_2^{2/5}\Phi^{1/5}n^{-4/5}
$$

$$
= \frac{5}{4}\kappa^{4/5}\kappa_2^{2/5}\Phi^{1/5}n^{-4/5}
$$

$$
= \frac{5}{4}C(K)\Phi^{1/5}n^{-4/5}.
$$

The term $C(K) = \kappa^{4/5}\kappa_2^{2/5}$ is determined solely by the kernel function, and the smaller its value, the smaller the IMSE when the optimal bandwidth is used. The unknown constant Φ is beyond our control, but it does not affect our choice of $C(K)$. All else equal, we should choose a kernel function with a small value of $C(K)$, since this will make it theoretically possible to obtain a small IMSE if the bandwidth is chosen correctly. We can engage in some *kernel carpentry* to derive an *optimal kernel function*. Without loss of generality, if $\kappa_2 \neq 1$, the kernel function can be re-scaled by $\kappa_2^{-1/2}K(\kappa_2^{-1/2}z)$, and this will not affect the value of $C(K)$.

To derive an IMSE-optimal kernel function, we must minimize $\kappa = \int K^2(z)\,dz$ subject to the constraints that $\int K(z)\,dz = 1$ and $\kappa_2 = \int z^2 K(z)\,dz = 1$ (after re-scaling). The constrained optimization problem is therefore stated as:

$$
\min_{K(z)} \int K^2(z)\,dz \quad \text{subject to} \quad \int K(z)\,dz = 1 \quad \text{and} \quad \int z^2 K(z)\,dz = 1.
$$

We can set up the Lagrangian for this problem as follows:

$$
L = \int_0^\infty K^2(z)\,dz + \lambda_1\left(\int_0^\infty K(z)\,dz - \frac{1}{2}\right) + \lambda_2\left(\int_0^\infty z^2 K(z)\,dz - \frac{1}{2}\right).
$$

Note that we are using symmetric kernel functions, so we need only integrate from 0 to ∞. The constrained minimization problem is solved using the method of *calculus of variations*. In particular, if ΔK represents a small change in the kernel function, then

$$\Delta L = \int_0^\infty 2K\left(z\right)\Delta K\left(z\right)\,dz + \lambda_1\int_0^\infty \Delta K\left(z\right)\,dz + \lambda_2\int_0^\infty z^2\Delta K\left(z\right)\,dz.$$

Collecting terms, we have

$$\Delta L = \int_0^\infty \left(2K\left(z\right) + \lambda_1 + \lambda_2 z^2\right)\Delta K\left(z\right)\,dz.$$

The necessary first order condition for a minimum is to select the function $K(z)$ that equates ΔL to zero, hence

$$2K\left(z\right) + \lambda_1 + \lambda_2 z^2 = 0 \tag{2.1}$$

and therefore

$$K(z) = -\frac{1}{2}\left(\lambda_1 + \lambda_2 z^2\right).$$

The first order conditions for the multipliers λ_1 and λ_2 are $\partial L/\partial\lambda_1 = 0$ and $\partial L/\partial\lambda_2 = 0$, or

$$\int_0^\infty K\left(z\right)\,dz = \frac{1}{2}\quad\text{and}\quad \int_0^\infty z^2 K\left(z\right)\,dz = \frac{1}{2}. \tag{2.2}$$

We now solve (2.1). Our kernel function is symmetric in z since $(-z)^2 = (+z)^2$ and it is equal to zero at $z = \pm(-\lambda_1/\lambda_2)^{1/2}$. Thus, we may take

$$K_{opt}(z) = \begin{cases} -\frac{1}{2}\left(\lambda_1 + \lambda_2 z^2\right) & \text{if } |z| < (-\lambda_1/\lambda_2)^{1/2} \\ 0 & \text{otherwise} \end{cases} \tag{2.3}$$

since $K(z) \geq 0$. The kernel function (2.3) is optimal if λ_1 and λ_2 are determined by (2.2) with $K(z)$ replaced by $K_{opt}(z)$. We can verify that $\lambda_1 = -3/(2\sqrt{5})$ and $\lambda_2 = 3/(10\sqrt{5})$ are valid solutions. Hodges and Lehmann (1956) first demonstrated that the optimal kernel function is given by

$$K_e(z) = \begin{cases} \frac{3}{4\sqrt{5}}\left(1 - \frac{1}{5}z^2\right) & \text{if } |z| < \sqrt{5} \\ 0 & \text{otherwise.} \end{cases}$$

This was first suggested in a density estimation context by Epanechnikov (1969), and hence it is often called the *Epanechnikov* kernel function.

Minimizing the IMSE has now yielded the optimal kernel function and bandwidth. For our final IMSE-related task, we define the *efficiency* of a kernel function to be

$$\text{eff}(K) = \left(\frac{C(K_e)}{C(K)}\right)^{5/4} \leq 1.$$

This compares the IMSE of a kernel function K to that of the optimal kernel function K_e ($C(K_e)$ is the lowest possible IMSE-minimizing constant $C(K) = \kappa^{4/5}\kappa_2^{2/5}$ since it is associated with the optimal kernel function). It turns out that a variety of kernel functions exhibit efficiencies that are very close to one (Silverman, 1986, page 43). In other words, the efficiency loss that arises from using a kernel function other than the optimal kernel function is negligible. Therefore, rather than choose a kernel function on the basis of IMSE, it is better to choose one that is computationally simple and that possesses the desired degree of differentiability. For this reason, the Gaussian kernel function is a very popular choice.

2.4.4 Asymptotic Normality

Let $\{X_1, X_2, \ldots, X_n\}$ be an i.i.d. sample for which we compute a Rosenblatt-Parzen kernel density estimate. Consider the ratio

$$
\begin{aligned}
Z_n &= \frac{\hat{f}(x) - \mathrm{E}\,\hat{f}(x)}{\sqrt{\mathrm{Var}\,\hat{f}(x)}} \\
&= \frac{\frac{1}{nh}\sum_{i=1}^{n} K\left(\frac{X_i-x}{h}\right) - \frac{1}{nh}\sum_{i=1}^{n} \mathrm{E}\,K\left(\frac{X_i-x}{h}\right)}{\sqrt{\mathrm{Var}\,\hat{f}(x)}} \\
&= \sum_{i=1}^{n} \left(\frac{K\left(\frac{X_i-x}{h}\right) - \mathrm{E}\,K\left(\frac{X_i-x}{h}\right)}{nh\sqrt{\mathrm{Var}\,\hat{f}(x)}} \right) \\
&= \sum_{i=1}^{n} \left(\frac{K\left(\frac{X_i-x}{h}\right) - \mathrm{E}\,K\left(\frac{X_i-x}{h}\right)}{\sqrt{n}\sqrt{\mathrm{Var}\,K\left(\frac{X_i-x}{h}\right)}} \right) \\
&= \sum_{i=1}^{n} Z_{n,i},
\end{aligned}
$$

where the denominator in the fourth line follows from the fact derived earlier that $\mathrm{Var}\,\hat{f}(x) = n^{-1}h^{-2}\,\mathrm{Var}\,K\left(\frac{X_i-x}{h}\right)$ for i.i.d. data.

Note that

(1) $Z_n = \sum_{i=1}^{n} Z_{n,i}$, where $Z_{n,i}$ is a double array, and for any *fixed* value of n $Z_{n,i}$ is i.i.d.

(2) $\mathrm{E}\,Z_{n,i} = 0$.

(3) $\mathrm{Var}\,Z_{n,i} = 1/n$.

Let

$$
\Gamma_n = \sum_{i=1}^{n} \mathrm{E}\,|Z_{n,i}|^3.
$$

The Liapounov double array central limit theorem[8] states that if conditions (1)-(3) hold and if, in addition, $\Gamma_n \to 0$ as $n \to \infty$, then $Z_n = (\hat{f}(x) - \mathrm{E}\,\hat{f}(x))/\sqrt{\mathrm{Var}\,\hat{f}(x)} \xrightarrow{d} N(0,1)$.

Since conditions (1)-(3) hold, we need to consider the behaviour of

$$
\mathrm{E}\,|Z_{n,i}|^3 = \mathrm{E}\left| \frac{K\left(\frac{X_i - x}{h}\right) - \mathrm{E}\,K\left(\frac{X_i - x}{h}\right)}{nh\sqrt{\mathrm{Var}\,\hat{f}(x)}} \right|^3
$$

$$
= \frac{\mathrm{E}\left|K\left(\frac{X_i-x}{h}\right) - \mathrm{E}\,K\left(\frac{X_i-x}{h}\right)\right|^3}{n^3 h^3 (\mathrm{Var}\,\hat{f}(x))^{3/2}}
$$

$$
\leq \frac{8\,\mathrm{E}\left|K\left(\frac{X_i-x}{h}\right)\right|^3}{n^3 h^3 (\mathrm{Var}\,\hat{f}(x))^{3/2}}.
$$

We know the limit of the denominator, but not of the numerator. Note that the second line follows from the fact that the denominator is positive, while the inequality in the last line follows from the c_r inequality[9] and Jensen's inequality[10] which, combined, tell us that $\mathrm{E}\,|A - \mathrm{E}\,A|^{2+\delta} \leq 2 \times 2^{1+\delta}\,\mathrm{E}\,|A|^{2+\delta}$.

Recall that the pointwise variance is of order $O\left(\frac{1}{nh}\right)$, and note that by a Taylor representation, we can easily obtain

$$
\mathrm{E}\left|K\left(\frac{X_i - x}{h}\right)\right|^3 = \int \left|K\left(\frac{t-x}{h}\right)\right|^3 f(t)\,dt
$$

$$
= hf(x)\int |K(z)|^3\,dz + \mathcal{R}
$$

$$
= O(h) + \mathcal{R}.
$$

Hence the leading term is of $O(h)$, which implies

$$
\mathrm{E}\,|Z_{n,i}|^3 \leq O\left(\frac{h}{n^3 h^3 (nh)^{-3/2}}\right) \text{ which is of order } O\left(h^{-1/2}n^{-3/2}\right).
$$

When we consider the i.i.d. sum $\Gamma_n = \sum_{i=1}^n \mathrm{E}\,|Z_{n,i}|^3$, we see that

$$
\Gamma_n = \sum_{i=1}^n \mathrm{E}\,|Z_{n,i}|^3
$$

---

[8] The Liapounov double array CLT is as follows. Let $\{Z_{n,i}\}_{i=1}^n$ be a double array sequence of independent random variables where $\mathrm{E}\,Z_{n,i} = 0$, $\mathrm{Var}\,Z_{n,i} = 1/n$, and $\mathrm{E}\,|Z_{n,i}|^3 < \infty$ ($\mathrm{E}\,|Z_{n,i}|^{2+\delta} < \infty$ for some $\delta > 0$). Let $\Gamma_n = \sum_{i=1}^n \mathrm{E}\,|Z_{n,i}|^3$ ($\sum_{i=1}^n \mathrm{E}\,|Z_{n,i}|^{2+\delta}$). If $\lim_{n\to\infty} \Gamma_n = 0$, then $Z_n = \sum_{i=1}^n Z_{n,i} \xrightarrow{d} N(0,1)$. See White (1984) page 112 for further details.

[9] The c_r inequality states that, for two random variables A and B, $\mathrm{E}\,|A+B|^r \leq c_r(\mathrm{E}\,|A|^r + E|B|^r)$ where $c_r = 1$ if $r \leq 1$ and $c_r = 2^{r-1}$ if $r > 1$. See White (1984) page 33 for further details.

[10] Jensen's inequality states that if $g()$ is a convex function on $\mathbb{R}$ and C is a random variable, then $g(E(C)) \leq E(g(C))$. See White (1984) page 27 for further details.

$$= n \times \text{ a term of } O\left(h^{-1/2}n^{-3/2}\right) = O\left(\frac{1}{\sqrt{nh}}\right)$$

and as a result, if $nh \to \infty$ as $n \to \infty$, then $\Gamma_n \to 0$ as $n \to \infty$. Thus, the sufficient condition for $\hat{f}(x)$ to have an asymptotic normal distribution has been satisfied.

Therefore, we write

$$\sqrt{nh}\left(\hat{f}(x) - f(x) - \text{Bias } \hat{f}(x)\right) \overset{d}{\to} N\left(0, f(x)\kappa\right).$$

In summary, we have demonstrated that the Rosenblatt-Parzen kernel density estimator $\hat{f}(x)$ is pointwise biased in finite samples, has pointwise variance $\frac{1}{nh}f(x)\kappa$, is consistent in square error provided that $h \to 0$ as $n \to \infty$ and $nh \to \infty$ as $n \to \infty$, has a limit normal distribution provided that $nh \to \infty$ as $n \to \infty$, and exhibits a rate of convergence of $O(n^{-2/5})$ in root MSE when the optimal bandwidth is used. These results are useful insofar as they pave the way for inference concerning the unknown density $f(x)$, which includes the construction of confidence bands and hypothesis testing.

2.4.5 Bandwidth Selection

A range of methods have been proposed for bandwidth selection in applied settings. It is important to be aware of the fact that, for any given sample, no method is *guaranteed* to deliver an appropriately smoothed estimator, so having a variety of approaches to choose from can be helpful. Bandwidth selection is akin to model selection in parametric settings, and therefore, its importance cannot be stressed enough. We begin with an illustration of the importance of getting the bandwidth *right* in applied settings. Optimization of the objective functions that follow is conducted using numerical algorithms that readily extend to the mixed-data multivariate setting.

Example 2.7. Old Faithful Data and Bandwidth Selection.

Figure 2.10 presents smooth kernel PDF estimates for a range of bandwidths. The figure on the upper left is said to be *undersmoothed*, while the one on the lower right is said to be *oversmoothed* (note how oversmoothing obscures the bi-modal nature of the data). This example highlights the importance of sound selection of the bandwidth in applied settings.

Ad Hoc Reference Rules

The reference rule of thumb is based on the formula for the optimal bandwidth that was derived earlier. It uses a standard family of distributions to assign a value to the term $\int f''(x)^2\,dx$ that appears in the expression for h_{opt}. For

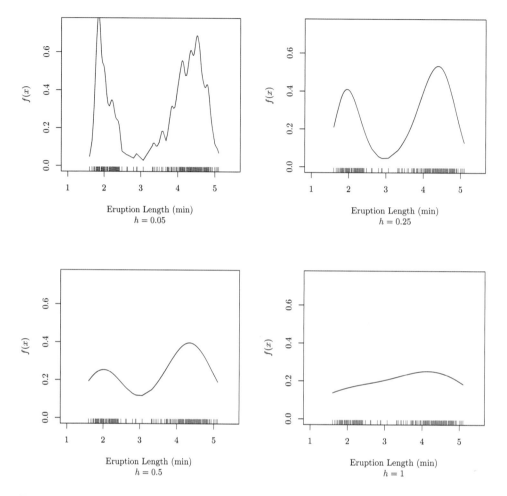

Figure 2.10: The Rosenblatt-Parzen kernel density estimate for the eruptions data, with a range of ad hoc bandwidths (upper left is undersmoothed, lower right oversmoothed).

instance, it can be shown that, for the normal family, $\int (f''(x))^2\, dx = \frac{3}{8\sqrt{\pi}\sigma^5}$. If we have adopted the standard Gaussian kernel function, then it can also be shown that

$$\kappa = \int K^2(z)\, dz = \frac{1}{2\sqrt{\pi}}, \qquad \kappa_2 = \int z^2 K(z)\, dz = 1.$$

In the end, the IMSE-optimal reference bandwidth would be

$$\hat{h} = \left(\frac{\int K^2(z)\, dz}{\left(\int z^2 K(z)\, dz\right)^2 \int \left(f''(x)\right)^2\, dx} \right)^{1/5} n^{-1/5}$$

$$= \left(\frac{4\sigma^5}{3} \right)^{1/5} n^{-1/5}$$

$$= 1.059\sigma n^{-1/5}.$$

This is the so-called 1.06-σ rule of thumb. Such rules are often used in exploratory data analysis because of their computational simplicity, but in serious work, they ought to be avoided altogether.

Plug-In Methods

Plug-in methods substitute *pilot* estimates of the unknown constant $\int f''(z)^2\,dz$ into the formula for the optimal bandwidth. These estimates might be based on, say, the rule of thumb (Sheather and Jones, 1991) that was mentioned above. Although such rules are popular, we direct the interested reader to Loader (1999) for a discussion of the relative merits of plug-in bandwidth selectors and the data-driven procedures that are discussed below.[11]

Least Squares Cross-Validation

Least squares cross-validation is a fully automatic and data-driven method of selecting the bandwidth (Rudemo, 1982; Bowman, 1984). This method is based on the principle of selecting a bandwidth that minimizes the integrated square error (ISE) of the resulting estimate. The integrated squared difference between $\hat{f}(x)$ and $f(x)$ is

$$\int \left(\hat{f}(x) - f(x)\right)^2 dx = \int \hat{f}(x)^2\,dx - 2\int \hat{f}(x)f(x)\,dx + \int f(x)^2\,dx.$$

The third term can be ignored since it does not depend on h. If we replace the first two terms with their sample counterparts and adjust for bias, then we obtain an objective function that can be numerically minimized with respect to h. The first term can be explicitly computed because it involves a convolution of the kernel function with the data. The second term is the expected value of $\hat{f}(x)$. We can replace it with its sample counterpart (the sample mean of the $\hat{f}(x)$) using the leave-one-out estimator $\hat{f}_{-i}(x)$ that uses all points except X_i to construct the density estimate, that is,

$$\hat{f}_{-i}(X_i) = \frac{1}{(n-1)h} \sum_{j=1,j\neq i}^{n} K\left(\frac{X_j - X_i}{h}\right)$$

(this removes a non-zero centring term).

---

[11]Loader writes, "We find the evidence for superior performance of plug-in approaches is far less compelling than previously claimed. In turn, we consider real data examples, simulation studies and asymptotics. Among the findings are that plug-in approaches are tuned by arbitrary specification of pilot estimators and are prone to over-smoothing when presented with difficult smoothing problems."

We then obtain the least squares cross-validated bandwidth, i.e.,

$$\hat{h} = \text{argmin}_h \left(\int \hat{f}(x)^2 \, dx - \frac{2}{n} \sum_{i=1}^{n} \hat{f}_{-i}(X_i) \right).$$

Likelihood Cross-Validation

Likelihood cross-validation yields a density estimate that has an entropy interpretation, namely that the estimate will be close to the actual density in a Kullback-Leibler sense (Kullback, 1959; Duin, 1976). Likelihood cross-validation chooses the bandwidth h that maximizes the leave-one-out log likelihood function, i.e.,

$$\hat{h} = \text{argmax}_h \sum_{i=1}^{n} \log \hat{f}_{-i}(X_i).$$

This method, which has broad applicability, was proposed by Stone (1974) and Geisser (1975). However, one of its limitations is that it tends to oversmooth thick-tailed distributions such as the Cauchy.

Bootstrap Bandwidth Selection

Faraway and Jhun (1990) have proposed a bootstrap-based method of bandwidth selection whereby the IMSE is estimated for a given bandwidth h and then minimized over all values of h. This approach uses a smoothed bootstrap method that is based on a preliminary density estimate. One of its drawbacks, however, is that the objective function is stochastic, which can give rise to numerical minimization issues. This method can also be computationally demanding.

Example 2.8. Data-Driven Bandwidth Selection for the Old Faithful Data.

> In the R package np, there exists a function `npudensbw()` that applies many of the bandwidth selection procedures that have been outlined above (see also `?bw.nrd` for some univariate bandwidth selectors). When applied to the `eruptions` data, the function yields bandwidth values of 0.3283 for the normal-reference rule of thumb option, 0.3943 for Sheather and Jones's plug-in method, 0.1026 for least squares cross-validation, and 0.1027 for likelihood cross-validation. The ad hoc reference rule that is based on an assumed unimodal density and the plug-in rule produce bandwidths that are three-to-four times greater than those delivered by likelihood and least squares cross-validation, which are both in agreement. The kernel density estimates for two of these bandwidth selectors and accompanying histograms are presented in Figure 2.11. Given that we are dealing with a bi-modal

density, the ad hoc reference and plug-in rules appear to have oversmoothed the data, thereby confirming the assertions that were made by Loader (1999).

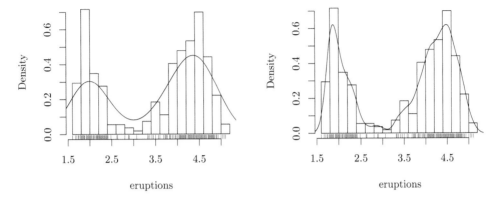

Figure 2.11: Data driven bandwidth selection for the eruptions data (Sheather and Jones's plug-in on the left, likelihood cross-validation the right).

2.4.6   Bias-Reducing Kernel Functions

Below, we engage in a bit of *kernel carpentry* in order to construct custom kernel functions that are endowed with certain properties that we desire. So-called *higher-order kernel functions* are devices that are used for bias reduction and that are also capable of reducing the resulting estimator's pointwise MSE. Many popular kernel functions such as the Gaussian that was outlined above are *second-order* kernel functions. The order of a kernel function, which we denote by ν ($\nu > 0$), is defined as the order of its first finite *nonzero* moment. For example, if $\int u K(u)\, du = 0$ and $0 < \int u^2 K(u)\, du < \infty$, then $K(\cdot)$ is said to be a second-order kernel function ($\nu = 2$). A general νth-order kernel function, where $\nu \geq 2$ is an integer, must satisfy the following conditions:

$$(1) \int K(u)\, du = 1,$$

$$(2) \int u^l K(u)\, du = 0, \quad (l = 1, \ldots, \nu - 1),$$

$$(3)\, 0 < \left| \int u^\nu K(u)\, du \right| = |\kappa_\nu| < \infty.$$

We once again adopt the notation $\kappa_\nu = \int u^\nu K(u)\, du$ for the first finite nonzero moment κ_ν (recall that for a second-order kernel function, we had $\kappa_2 = \int u^2 K(u)\, du$).

Higher-order kernel functions are surprisingly easy to construct. If $K(u)$ is symmetric around zero so that $K(u) = K(-u)$, then $\int u^{2m+1} K(u)\, du = 0$

for all positive integers m. If we wanted to construct a simple fourth-order kernel function (i.e., $\nu = 4$), then we could begin with, say, a second-order Gaussian kernel function, set up a polynomial in its argument, and solve for the roots of the polynomial subject to the desired moment constraints. For example, letting $\Phi(u) = (2\pi)^{-\frac{1}{2}} e^{-\frac{1}{2}u^2}$ be a second-order Gaussian kernel function, we could begin with the polynomial

$$K(u) = (a + bu^2)\Phi(u), \tag{2.4}$$

where a and b are two constants that must satisfy the requirements of a fourth-order kernel function. Given that $K(u)$ is an even function, $\int u^l K(u)\,du = 0$ for $l = 1, 3$. Therefore, if $K(u)$ is to satisfy Equation (2.4) with $\nu = 4$, we only need to consider the restrictions $\int K(u)\,du = 1$ and $\int u^2 K(u)\,du = 0$. The nature of $K(u)$ ensures that our constraints are *linear* in the unknown constants a and b, and can be readily obtained. These two restrictions yield the result $a = 3/2$ and $b = -1/2$, and the formula for the fourth-order univariate Gaussian kernel function is therefore given by:

$$K(u) = \left(\frac{3}{2} - \frac{1}{2}u^2\right)\frac{1}{\sqrt{2\pi}}e^{-\frac{1}{2}u^2}.$$

The full derivation of this result is left as an exercise.

If we used a fourth-order rather than a second-order kernel function to derive the pointwise bias and variance of $\hat{f}(x)$, the bias would be of order $O(h^\nu) = O(h^4)$ rather than $O(h^2)$. The variance would be unaffected and would remain of $O(1/(nh))$. With a fourth-order kernel function, the optimal bandwidth would be of order $O(n^{-1/(2\nu+1)}) = O(n^{-1/9})$ rather than $O(n^{-1/5})$ and the root MSE rate of convergence would be of order $O(n^{-\nu/(2\nu+1)}) = O(n^{-4/9})$ rather than $O(n^{-2/5}) = O(n^{-4/10})$.

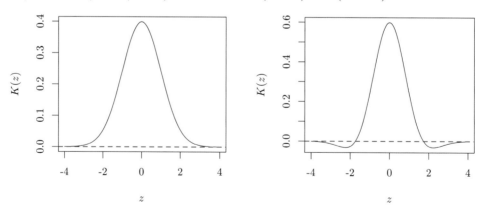

Figure 2.12: Second- and fourth-order Gaussian kernels (left and right figures, respectively).

Figure 2.12 plots the second- and fourth-order Gaussian kernel functions. It turns out that, for $\nu > 2$, no non-negative kernel function exists that satisfies conditions (1)-(3) above. This means that it becomes necessary when using higher-order kernel functions to assign negative weight to a portion of the data, which can give rise to *negative* density estimates. Clearly, this is an undesirable outcome. In any event, in finite sample applications, non-negative second-order kernel functions have often been found to yield more stable estimation results than their higher-order counterparts. Therefore, higher-order kernel functions are primarily used for theoretical purposes. Derivation of the properties of the Rosenblatt-Parzen kernel density estimator with an eighth-order kernel function is left as an exercise.

2.5 Smooth Kernel Cumulative Distribution Function Estimation

So far, we have studied kernel estimators of a PDF $f(x)$. We now turn to the study of kernel estimators of a CDF $F(x)$. Interestingly, the kernel CDF estimator has a number of useful features that are lacking in the kernel PDF estimator. Recall that the kernel estimator of a PDF is defined as

$$\hat{f}(x) = \frac{1}{nh} \sum_{i=1}^{n} K\left(\frac{x - X_i}{h}\right).$$

The kernel estimator of a CDF is defined as

$$\hat{F}(x) = \int_{-\infty}^{x} \hat{f}(t)\, dt$$

$$= \frac{1}{n} \sum_{i=1}^{n} \int_{-\infty}^{x} K\left(\frac{t - X_i}{h}\right) \frac{dt}{h}$$

$$= \frac{1}{n} \sum_{i=1}^{n} \int_{-\infty}^{\frac{x - X_i}{h}} K(u)\, du$$

$$= \frac{1}{n} \sum_{i=1}^{n} G\left(\frac{x - X_i}{h}\right)$$

where $u = (t - X_i)/h$, $du = dt/h$, and $G(a) = \int_{-\infty}^{a} K(u)\, du$.[12] Nadaraya (1964) was the first to investigate the theoretical properties of this estimator.

2.5.1 Properties of the Kernel Cumulative Distribution Function Estimator

Proceeding along the lines of our approach to smooth kernel density estimation, we now consider the pointwise MSE of $\hat{F}(x)$ in an i.i.d. setting. This will allow for IMSE-optimal bandwidth selection and for derivation of the rate of

---

[12]The kernel function K is symmetric but G is clearly not. Hence we must observe the $x - X_i$ convention.

convergence of the estimator. We apply the transformation $z = (x - t)/h$, where x is fixed, use partial integration,[13] and then take a Taylor expansion of $F(x - hz)$ around x. The pointwise expectation of $\hat{F}(x)$ is

$$\mathrm{E}\hat{F}(x) = \frac{1}{n} \sum_{i=1}^{n} \mathrm{E}\, G\left(\frac{x - X_i}{h}\right)$$

$$= \mathrm{E}\, G\left(\frac{x - X_1}{h}\right)$$

$$= \int_{-\infty}^{\infty} G\left(\frac{x - t}{h}\right) f(t)\, dt$$

$$= -\int_{\infty}^{-\infty} G(z) f(x - hz) h\, dz$$

$$= \int_{-\infty}^{\infty} G(z) f(x - hz) h\, dz$$

$$= -\int_{-\infty}^{\infty} G(z)\, dF(x - hz)$$

$$= -\{G(z) F(x - hz)\}|_{z=-\infty}^{z=+\infty} + \int_{-\infty}^{\infty} K(z) F(x - hz)\, dz$$

$$= 0 + \int_{-\infty}^{\infty} K(z) F(x - hz)\, dz$$

$$= \int K(z) \left(\frac{F(x)}{0!} - \frac{hz F'(x)}{1!} + \frac{z^2 h^2 F''(x)}{2!} - \dots\right) dz$$

$$= F(x) \int K(z)\, dz - h F'(x) \int z K(z)\, dz + \frac{h^2}{2} F''(x) \int z^2 K(z)\, dz - \dots$$

$$= F(x) \int K(z)\, dz - h f(x) \int z K(z)\, dz + \frac{h^2}{2} f'(x) \int z^2 K(z)\, dz - \dots$$

$$= F(x) + \frac{h^2}{2} f'(x) \kappa_2 + \mathcal{R},$$

which follows from the assumptions that underlie the second-order kernel function. Note that as we proceed from line three to line four, the limits of integration change because $t = \infty$ implies $hz = -\infty$ and vice versa (i.e., going from $t = -\infty$ to $t = \infty$ is the same operation as going from $hz = \infty$ to $hz = -\infty$). Note also that, as we proceed from line five to line six, $f(x - hz) d(x - hz) = d F(x - hz)$, $d(x - hz) = -h\, dz$, and hence $-f(x - hz) h\, dz = dF(x - hz)$. In line seven, we used the fact that $G(+\infty) = 1$ and $G(-\infty) = 0$, which is also true of $F(\cdot)$.

We therefore write the pointwise bias up to terms of $O(h^2)$ as

$$\mathrm{Bias}\, \hat{F}(x) = \mathrm{E}\, \hat{F}(x) - F(x)$$

---

[13]Let $A(x)$ and $B(x)$ be differentiable functions on (a, b), and assume that $A'(x)$ and $B'(x)$ are continuous on $[a, b]$. Then $\int A(x) B'(x)\, dx = A(x) B(x) - \int A'(x) B(x)\, dx$ and $\int_a^b A(x) B'(x)\, dx = A(x) B(x)|_a^b - \int_a^b A'(x) B(x)\, dx$.

$$= \frac{h^2}{2} f'(x)\kappa_2.$$

This is almost identical to the pointwise bias of $\hat{f}(x)$, where $f'(x)$ has now taken the place of $f''(x)$ in the expression that appeared previously.

We now consider the pointwise variance, which is given by

$$\operatorname{Var} \hat{F}(x) = \operatorname{E}\left(\hat{F}(x) - \operatorname{E}\hat{F}(x)\right)^2$$

$$= \frac{1}{n^2}\left(\sum_{i=1}^{n}\operatorname{E}\eta_i^2 + \sum_{\substack{i=1 \\ i \neq j}}^{n}\sum_{j=1}^{n}\operatorname{E}\eta_i\eta_j\right)$$

$$= \frac{1}{n^2}\left(\sum_{i=1}^{n}\operatorname{E}\eta_i^2\right)$$

$$= \frac{1}{n^2}\left(\sum_{i=1}^{n}\operatorname{E}\left(G\left(\frac{x - X_i}{h}\right) - \operatorname{E}G\left(\frac{x - X_i}{h}\right)\right)^2\right)$$

$$= \frac{1}{n}\left(\operatorname{E}G^2\left(\frac{x - X_1}{h}\right) - \left(\operatorname{E}G\left(\frac{x - X_1}{h}\right)\right)^2\right),$$

where $\eta_i = G\left(\frac{x-X_i}{h}\right) - \operatorname{E}G\left(\frac{x-X_i}{h}\right)$. The second term in the last line is known from our derivation of the bias of $\hat{F}(x)$. In order to complete the expression for the variance, we need

$$\operatorname{E}G^2\left(\frac{x - X_1}{h}\right) = \int_{-\infty}^{\infty}G^2\left(\frac{x - t}{h}\right)f(t)\,dt$$

$$= -\int_{\infty}^{-\infty}G^2(z)f(x - hz)h\,dz$$

$$= -\int_{-\infty}^{\infty}G^2(z)dF(x - hz)$$

$$= -(G(z)^2 F(x - hz))|_{z=-\infty}^{z=+\infty} + 2\int G(z)K(z)F(x - hz)\,dz$$

$$= 2\int G(z)K(z)\left(F(x) - hzF'(x) + \mathcal{R}\right)\,dz$$

$$= 2\int G(z)K(z)\left(F(x) - hzf(x) + \mathcal{R}\right)\,dz$$

$$= 2\left(F(x)\int G(z)K(z)\,dz - hf(x)\int zG(z)K(z)\,dz + \mathcal{R}\right)$$

where $\mathcal{R}$ is a remainder term. Note the change in the limits of integration on line two, as detailed in the derivation of $\operatorname{E}G(\cdot)$ a little earlier.

We can therefore obtain an expression for the pointwise variance,

$$\operatorname{Var}\hat{F}(x) = \frac{1}{n}\operatorname{E}G^2\left(\frac{x - X_1}{h}\right) - \frac{1}{n}\left(\operatorname{E}G\left(\frac{x - X_1}{h}\right)\right)^2$$

$$= \frac{2}{n}\left(F(x)\int G(z)K(z)\,dz - hf(x)\int zG(z)K(z)\,dz + \mathcal{R}\right)$$
$$- \frac{1}{n}\left(F(x) + \frac{h^2}{2}f'(x)\kappa_2 + \mathcal{R}\right)^2.$$

Keeping terms up to $O(h/n)$ yields

$$\text{Var}\,\hat{F}(x) = \frac{2}{n}\left(F(x)\int G(z)K(z)\,dz - hf(x)\int zG(z)K(z)\,dz\right) - \frac{1}{n}F(x)^2$$
$$= \frac{2F(x)\int G(z)K(z)\,dz - F(x)^2}{n} - \frac{2hf(x)\int zG(z)K(z)\,dz}{n}$$
$$= \frac{F(x) - F(x)^2}{n} - \frac{2hf(x)\int zG(z)K(z)\,dz}{n}$$
$$= \frac{F(x)(1 - F(x))}{n} - \frac{2hf(x)\int zG(z)K(z)\,dz}{n},$$

which follows from the fact that $\int G(z)K(z)\,dz = 1/2$ when $K(z)$ is a function that satisfies the necessary conditions for a proper density and $G(z) = \int^z K(t)\,dt$. To see this, note that

$$\int G(z)K(z)dz = \int G(z)dG(z)$$
$$= \int (1/2)d(G(z)^2)$$
$$= (1/2)G(z)^2|_{z=-\infty}^{z=+\infty}$$
$$= (1/2)(1 - 0)$$
$$= (1/2) \text{ because } G(+\infty) = 1 \text{ and } G(-\infty) = 0,$$

where $dG(z) = K(z)dz$.

This gives us the pointwise MSE for the kernel CDF estimator:

$$\text{MSE}\,\hat{F}(x) = \frac{F(x)(1 - F(x))}{n} - \frac{2hf(x)\int zG(z)K(z)\,dz}{n} + \frac{h^4}{4}\kappa_2^2\left(f'(x)\right)^2.$$

2.5.2   IMSE-Optimal Bandwidth

We can use the pointwise MSE result to obtain a global measure of square error performance, just as we did for the Rosenblatt-Parzen kernel density estimator $\hat{f}(x)$. The IMSE is given by

$$\text{IMSE}\,\hat{F}(x) = \int \frac{F(x)(1 - F(x))}{n}\,dx - \frac{2h\int zG(z)K(z)\,dz}{n}$$
$$+ \frac{h^4}{4}\kappa_2^2\int \left(f'(x)\right)^2 dx.$$

To derive the IMSE-optimal bandwidth for $\hat{F}(x)$, we take the derivative of the IMSE with respect to h, which is given by

$$\frac{d}{dh} \text{IMSE } \hat{F}(x) = -\frac{2 \int z G(z) K(z) \, dz}{n} + h^3 \kappa_2^2 \int \left(f'(x) \right)^2 \, dx.$$

Solving for the h that equates this derivative to zero, we obtain

$$h_{opt} = \left(\frac{2 \int z G(z) K(z) \, dz}{\int (f'(x))^2 \, dx \left(\int z^2 K(z) \, dz \right)^2} \right)^{1/3} n^{-1/3}.$$

If we plug this optimal bandwidth into the pointwise MSE formula that was derived above, the leading pointwise MSE term is of order $O(1/n)$, which is the *same* as that for a correctly specified parametric model. This means that the kernel estimator of a CDF has a *faster* rate of convergence than the kernel estimator of a PDF. Later on, we will see that, in multivariate settings, the kernel CDF estimator does not suffer from the *curse of dimensionality* that afflicts its kernel PDF counterpart. This has important implications for both estimation and inference. In particular, given these properties, it will at times be advantageous to transform an estimation or inference procedure into one that can be expressed in terms of $F(x)$ rather than $f(x)$.

2.5.3 Asymptotic Normality

It can also be shown via application of Liapounov's CLT that

$$\sqrt{n} \left(\hat{F}(x) - F(x) \right) \xrightarrow{d} N \left(0, F(x)(1 - F(x)) \right).$$

Note that the bias term (i.e., bias $\hat{F}(x)$) is dropped because $h = O(n^{-1/3})$ hence bias $\hat{F}(x) = O(h^2) = O(n^{-2/3}) = o(n^{-1/2})$ therefore $\sqrt{n} \text{ bias } \hat{F}(x) = o(1)$.

2.5.4 Bandwidth Selection

The reference rule of thumb is based on the formula for the optimal bandwidth that was derived above. It uses a standard family of distributions to assign a value to the term $\int \left(f'(x) \right)^2 \, dx$ that appears in the expression for h_{opt}. For instance, it can be shown that, for the normal family, $\int \left(f'(x) \right)^2 \, dx = 1/(4\sigma^3\sqrt{\pi})$. If we adopt the standard Gaussian kernel function, then it can be shown that

$$2 \int z G(z) K(z) \, dz = \frac{1}{\sqrt{\pi}}, \qquad \kappa_2 = \int z^2 K(z) \, dz = 1,$$

and hence the IMSE-optimal reference bandwidth would be

$$\hat{h} = (4\sigma^3)^{1/3} n^{-1/3}$$

$$= 1.587\sigma n^{-1/3}.$$

Because of their computational simplicity, such rules are sometimes used in exploratory data analysis, but in serious work, they ought to be avoided altogether.

Automatic bandwidth selection in the univariate context has been addressed by Bowman et al. (1998), who focus on cross-validation, and Polansky and Baker (2000), who focus on plug-in methods. More general procedures for the multivariate mixed-data case are outlined in Chapter 3.

Example 2.9. The Old Faithful Data.

> Figure 2.13 presents ECDF and smooth kernel CDF estimates for a range of bandwidths. The R function `npudistbw()` in the np package supports a number of data-driven bandwidth selection methods for kernel estimation of a CDF.

2.6   Smooth Kernel Quantile Function Estimation

Quantiles play an important role in statistics. For instance, in statistical inference, *critical values* are in fact the quantile of the distribution of a test statistic under some null hypothesis. Students are typically introduced to the concept of a quantile when they are taught in their first statistics course how to compute the *median* for some finite set of numbers. Next, they are typically taught that, if τ denotes a probability that lies in $(0, 1)$, then the τth quantile is the value such that the fraction τ of all observations in the set lie below it and $1 - \tau$ lie above it. Hence the median is the 0.50th quantile, the lower quartile is the 0.25th quantile, and so on.

The quantile function is one of many ways of describing a probability distribution, and it can serve as an alternative to the PDF $f(x)$ or the CDF $F(x)$. If we knew the distribution function of the random variable in question, we could use this to derive the quantile function, which is also called the *inverse cumulative distribution function*. It is defined as

$$q_\tau = \inf\{x : F(x) \geq \tau\} = F^{-1}(\tau),$$

where the operator inf, which is an abbreviation of *infimum*,[14] denotes the greatest lower bound of a set, that is, the largest quantity that is less than or equal to every element of a given set. Thus, the quantile function returns the minimum value of x such that the CDF $F(x)$ is no less than τ. It is characterized by the equality $F(q_\tau) = \tau$.

Example 2.10. The Gaussian (Normal) Quantile Function.

---

[14]Note that the inf function can be replaced by the min function because the CDF is right-continuous and (weakly) monotonically increasing.

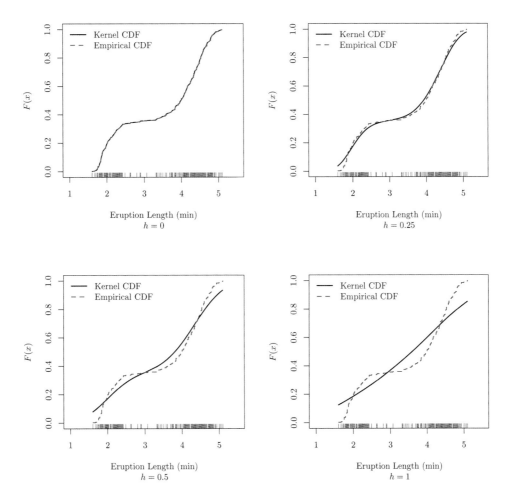

Figure 2.13: The Rosenblatt-Parzen smooth CDF and the ECDF estimates for the eruptions data for a range of bandwidths (upper left is undersmoothed, lower right oversmoothed).

Let $q_{N(\mu,\sigma^2),\tau}$ denote the τ-th quantile of a Gaussian random variable with mean μ and standard deviation σ. The Gaussian quantile function is given by

$$q_{N(\mu,\sigma^2),\tau} = \mu + \sigma\sqrt{2}\,\mathrm{erf}^{-1}(2\tau - 1),$$

where $\tau \in (0,1)$ is a probability and $\mathrm{erf}^{-1}(\cdot)$ is the inverse error function (the error function is defined as $\mathrm{erf}(x) = \frac{2}{\sqrt{\pi}} \int_0^x e^{-v^2}\,dv$). Figure 2.14 plots $F(x)$ and q_τ for the standard normal (i.e., $N(0,1)$) random variable.

In general, the quantile function is unknown. In practice, we might consider quantiles that are derived from nonparametric estimators such as the ECDF $F_n(x)$ or the smooth kernel CDF $\hat{F}(x)$ that we defined earlier. To

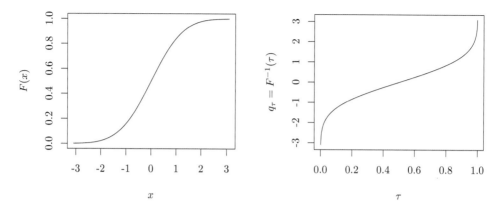

Figure 2.14: The Gaussian distribution function and quantile function.

obtain the τth quantile, we must compute the inverse of $\hat{F}(x)$. This inverse cannot be computed analytically for these estimators, and hence *numerical* approaches are used instead.

One approach is to minimize the following objective function:

$$\hat{q}_\tau = \text{argmin}_x(\tau - \hat{F}(x))^2,$$

where $(\tau - \hat{F}(x))^2 = 0$ at q_τ. Alternatively, we could compute the *quasi-inverse* (Nelsen, 2006, Definition 2.3.6, page 21). The quasi-inverse is given by

$$\hat{F}^{(-1)}(\tau) = \inf\{x : \hat{F}(x) \geq \tau\}. \tag{2.5}$$

To operationalize this inverse, we construct a very fine grid of points $x'_1, x'_2, \ldots$ that extends far beyond the support of the data. Then, for any $\tau \in (0, 1)$, the quasi-inverse is given by the value among the $x'_1, x'_2, \ldots$ that satisfies Equation (2.5).

It can be shown via application of Liapounov's CLT that

$$\sqrt{n}\,(\hat{q}_\tau - q_\tau) \xrightarrow{d} N\left(0, \frac{\tau(1 - \tau)}{f^2(q_\tau)}\right).$$

See Yang (1985) and Cheng and Sun (2006) for further details.

Example 2.11. Smooth Kernel Quantile Estimation When $X \sim \chi_5^2$, i.e., a Chi-Square Random Variable with 5 Degrees of Freedom.

> Figure 2.15 presents results for a random sample of size $n = 1,000$.
> The R function `npquantile()` in the np package uses the quasi-inverse approach.

The construction of smooth quantile functions provides a good example of nonparametric estimation in action. We went back to first principles and recalled the statistical definition of the object of interest (in this case, the quantile function), then we replaced unknowns (in this case, $F(x)$) with

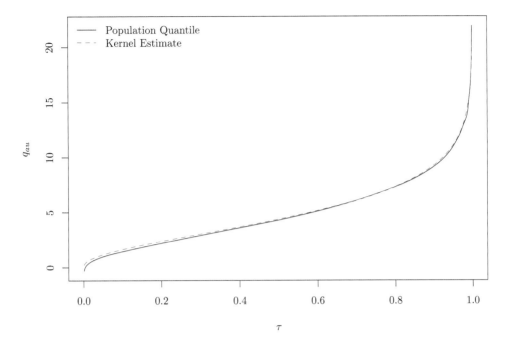

Figure 2.15: Smooth kernel quantile estimate when $X \sim \chi_5^2$, $n = 1000$.

smooth consistent nonparametric estimators. This is the essence of many of the nonparametric approaches that appear in this text. Alternatively, we could have used nonsmooth estimators such as the ECDF $F_n(x)$, but by now, we might suspect that in finite sample settings, the smooth estimator will be better behaved from an MSE perspective.

2.7 The Multivariate Extension

The treatment so far has been restricted to the univariate case. We now proceed to a multivariate setting. Let $X \in \mathbb{R}^q$ denote a random vector of dimension q, and let $f(x) = f(x_1, x_2, \ldots, x_q)$ denote a joint PDF evaluated at $x = (x_1, x_2, \ldots, x_q)'$. If $\{X_1, X_2, \ldots, X_n\}$ represents n draws of a strictly stationary continuous random vector X, where the ith draw is denoted by $X_i = (X_{i1}, X_{i2}, \ldots, X_{iq})$, then the multivariate kernel density estimator can be written as

$$\hat{f}(x) = \frac{1}{nh_1 \ldots h_q} \sum_{i=1}^n K\left(\frac{x_1 - X_{i1}}{h_1}, \ldots, \frac{x_q - X_{iq}}{h_q}\right),$$

and the multivariate kernel cumulative distribution estimator is written as

$$\hat{F}(x) = \frac{1}{n} \sum_{i=1}^n G\left(\frac{x_1 - X_{i1}}{h_1}, \ldots, \frac{x_q - X_{iq}}{h_q}\right),$$

where $K(\cdot)$ and $G(\cdot)$ are multivariate kernel functions that are suitable for estimating PDFs and CDFs, respectively (e.g., they could be multivariate density functions).

Let $z_j = (x_j - X_{ij})/h_j$, and note that

$$\int \cdots \int K(z_1, \ldots, z_q) \, dz_1 \ldots dz_q = \int_{\mathbb{R}^q} K(z) \, dz = 1 \in \mathbb{R}^1$$

$$\int_{\mathbb{R}^q} z K(z) \, dz = 0 \in \mathbb{R}^q$$

$$\int_{\mathbb{R}^q} z z' K(z) \, dz < \infty \in \mathbb{R}^q \times \mathbb{R}^q.$$

If we use the product kernel function that is outlined below, then the last two assumptions pertain to *marginal kernel functions* (i.e., $K(z_j)$, $j = 1, \ldots, q$) with means of zero, marginal variance κ_2, and zero pairwise correlation (i.e., $\int_{\mathbb{R}^q} z z' K(z) \, dz = \mathrm{diag}(\kappa_2)$, where $\mathrm{diag}(\kappa_2)$ denotes a matrix with κ_2 on its main diagonal and 0s everywhere else).

One popular choice of kernel function is the *product kernel*, which is simply a product of univariate kernel functions. For multivariate PDF estimation, it is given by

$$K\left(\frac{x_1 - X_{i1}}{h_1}, \ldots, \frac{x_q - X_{iq}}{h_q}\right) = K\left(\frac{x_1 - X_{i1}}{h_1}\right) \times \cdots \times K\left(\frac{x_q - X_{iq}}{h_q}\right)$$

$$= \prod_{j=1}^{q} K\left(\frac{x_j - X_{ij}}{h_j}\right),$$

while for multivariate CDF estimation, the product kernel function is given by

$$G\left(\frac{x_1 - X_{i1}}{h_1}, \ldots, \frac{x_q - X_{iq}}{h_q}\right) = G\left(\frac{x_1 - X_{i1}}{h_1}\right) \times \cdots \times G\left(\frac{x_q - X_{iq}}{h_q}\right)$$

$$= \prod_{j=1}^{q} G\left(\frac{x_j - X_{ij}}{h_j}\right).$$

The $K\left(\frac{x_j - X_{ij}}{h_j}\right)$ and $G\left(\frac{x_j - X_{ij}}{h_j}\right)$ are identical to the univariate kernel functions that were used previously for univariate PDF and CDF estimation, with the exception that the subscript j has been added to draw a distinction among the variables and their respective bandwidths.

We might be tempted to believe that using a product kernel function somehow imposes or assumes independence since $f(y, x) = f(y) \times f(x)$ if and only y and x are independent. However, this would be incorrect. The kernel function is simply a weighting device that imparts smoothness on the resulting estimate, with the bandwidths determining how much smoothing is applied to each component. As long as the kernel function is non-negative and it integrates to one over all of its arguments, then a proper and consistent estimator can emerge if smoothing is conducted appropriately.

Whereas $f(x)$ and $F(x)$ are always scalars regardless of the dimension of x, the same is not true of the quantile function q_τ. When $x \in \mathbb{R}^1$, the quantile function is indeed a scalar, but when $x \in \mathbb{R}^2$ it is a *contour* (set-valued). The study of multivariate quantiles remains an active area of research, with different researchers offering different answers to the seemingly simple question "what is a multivariate quantile?" For this reason, we will not be venturing beyond univariate quantiles.

2.7.1 Properties of the Multivariate Kernel Density Estimator

The proof of pointwise MSE consistency of $\hat{f}(x)$ is very similar to the one that was provided for the univariate case. In particular, we can show that

$$\text{Bias } \hat{f}(x) = \frac{\kappa_2}{2} \sum_{s=1}^{q} h_s^2 f_{ss}(x) = O\left(\sum_{s=1}^{q} h_s^2\right)$$

where again $\kappa_2 = \int z^2 K(z)\, dz$ (Li and Racine, 2007, page 25). Note that if $q = 1$, the bias expression is identical to the one that we obtained in the univariate case, i.e., $h_s^2 f_{ss}(x)\kappa_2/2 = h^2 f''(x)\kappa_2/2$, where $f_{ss}(x)$ is the second-order derivative of $f(x)$ with respect to x_s.

Letting $\eta_2 = \sum_{s=1}^{q} h_s^2$, we can also show that

$$\text{Var } \hat{f}(x) = \frac{1}{nh_1 \ldots h_q} \left(\kappa^q f(x) + O\left(\eta_2\right)\right) = O\left(\frac{1}{nh_1 \ldots h_q}\right).$$

To summarize, we obtain the pointwise MSE result

$$\text{MSE } \hat{f}(x) = O\left(\eta_2^2 + (nh_1 \ldots h_q)^{-1}\right).$$

Hence, if $\max_{1 \le s \le q} h_s \to 0$ and $nh_1 \ldots h_q \to \infty$ as $n \to \infty$, then $\hat{f}(x) \to f(x)$ in MSE (and in probability). The optimal bandwidths h_s should balance the squared bias and variance terms, i.e., $h_s^4 = O\left((nh_1 \ldots h_q)^{-1}\right)$ for all s. Minimizing the IMSE yields $h_{s,\text{opt}} = c_s\, n^{-\frac{1}{4+q}}$, where c_s is some positive constant and $s = 1, \ldots, q$. With a second-order kernel function, we obtain a pointwise RMSE that is of order $n^{-2/(4+q)}$, and hence the rate of convergence depends on the dimension q. That is, a larger q implies a slower rate of convergence. This is known as the *curse of dimensionality*.

The above results and Liapounov's CLT deliver

$$\sqrt{nh_1 \ldots h_q} \left(\hat{f}(x) - f(x) - \text{Bias } \hat{f}(x)\right) \xrightarrow{d} N\left(0, f(x)\kappa^q\right).$$

Univariate bandwidth selection methods extend naturally to the multivariate setting. The R functions `npudensbw()` and `npudens()` in the np package support the general multivariate case with differential smoothing across variables.

2.7.2 Properties of the Multivariate Kernel Cumulative Distribution Function Estimator

The proof of MSE consistency of $\hat{F}(x)$ is also very similar to the one that was provided for the univariate case. Like its univariate counterpart, the multivariate kernel estimator of $F(x)$ retains its $\sqrt{n}$ rate of convergence. However, unlike $\hat{f}(x)$, it does not suffer from the curse of dimensionality.

It can be shown by the application of Liapounov's CLT that

$$\sqrt{n}\left(\hat{F}(x) - F(x)\right) \xrightarrow{d} N\left(0, F(x)(1 - F(x))\right).$$

Bandwidth selection has been considered by Liu and Yang (2008) and Li et al. (2017), among others. Univariate bandwidth selection methods extend naturally to the multivariate setting. The R functions `npudistbw()` and `npudist()` in the np package support the general multivariate case with differential smoothing across variables.

Example 2.12. Multivariate PDF and CDF Estimation - The Old Faithful Dataset.

Figure 2.16 plots joint PDF and CDF estimates for the variables `eruptions` and `waiting` from the `faithful` dataset. There is a clear bi-modal structure in the data. These figures were generated using the R functions `npudens()`, `npudist()`, and `plot()` from the np package (`plot()` calls `npplot()` - see `?npplot()` for details).

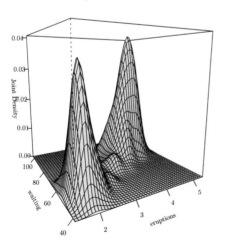 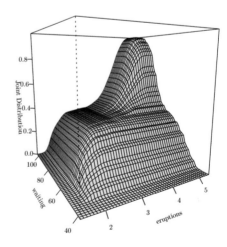

Figure 2.16: Joint PDF and CDF estimates for the Old Faithful dataset.

Having studied the theoretical underpinnings of kernel PDF and CDF estimators, we now consider the concept of *entropy*, which can be combined with these estimators to deliver a powerful and consistent approach towards statistical inference.

2.8   Entropy and Information Measures

The concept of *entropy* traces its roots to statistical mechanics and to the path-breaking work of Shannon (1948); see Golan (2017) for a thorough treatment of the subject as it pertains to econometrics. Shannon developed the notion of *information entropy*, introducing the term *bit* to describe a unit of *information*. In this framework, information is a function of probability (discrete X) or probability density (real-valued X). We first consider an illustration that involves a discrete random variable $X \in \mathcal{D}$, although with appropriate modification (e.g., by replacing $\sum_{x \in \mathcal{D}}$ with $\int_{-\infty}^{\infty} dx$), all definitions carry over to the case of a real-valued random variable.

Example 2.13. A Simple Example with a Binomial Random Variable.

> Consider a simple Bernoulli trial, $X \in \{0, 1\}$. Suppose that the *probability of success* π, with $X = 1$ being a success, is $Pr(X = 1) = p(1) = \pi = 0$. Every trial would result in $X = 0$, so what amount of information is conveyed by running this experiment? In other words, what is the *expected information* that is contained in this experiment, i.e., the *average surprise* or the *reduction in uncertainty*? Obviously, there would be zero *expected information, average surprise* or *reduction in uncertainty* in running this experiment. On the other hand, as $\pi \to 0.5$, the *expected information* in running the experiment increases. Entropy is simply a means of quantifying this *expected information*.

2.8.1   Statistical Mechanics and Information Functions

From the *statistical mechanics* perspective of Shannon (1948), entropy is a measure of uncertainty (*disorder, volatility*) associated with a random variable. For the Bernoulli trial example in which $\pi = 0$, there is no uncertainty, disorder, or volatility (the variance of X, $\pi(1 - \pi)$, is 0 when $\pi = 0$), so entropy is zero. In this experiment, entropy will increase as $\pi \to 1/2$. Entropy is not uniquely defined; there exist axiom systems that justify particular entropies. One of the more popular is given by Shannon's *information* or *surprise* function, which is defined as

$$h(x) = h(p(x)) = \log \frac{1}{p(x)}.$$

This function possesses certain *ideal* properties. It is additive, monotone decreasing, and for $h(p(x))$, $h(1) = 0$ and $h(0) \to \infty$; see Hartley (1928), among others. Shannon's information function is plotted in Figure 2.17.

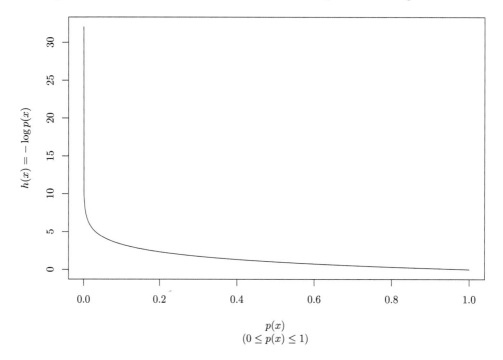

Figure 2.17: Shannon's information function $h(x)$.

If $p(x)$ is the probability of the outcome x, then $\log \frac{1}{p(x)}$ is how *surprised* we ought to be if the outcome is x. Since $p(x)$ ranges from 0 to 1, the surprise ranges from ∞ to 0. Entropy is the weighted average of the surprise across all outcomes. *Shannon's entropy* $H(X) = \mathrm{E}\, h(X)$ uses $h(p(x)) = \log \frac{1}{p(x)} = -\log p(x)$, and is the *average surprise upon discovery of the outcome of a random experiment*:

$$H(X) = \mathrm{E}\, h(X)$$
$$= -\,\mathrm{E} \log p(X)$$
$$= -\sum_{x \in \mathcal{D}} p(x) \log p(x),$$

where $p(x) \log p(x)$ is understood to be zero whenever $p(x) = 0$.

Entropy is usually measured in bits ($\log_2$), nats ($\log_e$) or bans ($\log_{10}$). There is a simple transformation of the entropy value from log base b to log base a, namely $H_b(X) = \log_b(a)(H_a(X))$.

Example 2.14. Shannon's Entropy Function $H(X)$ for a Bernoulli Trial Is Presented in Figure 2.18.

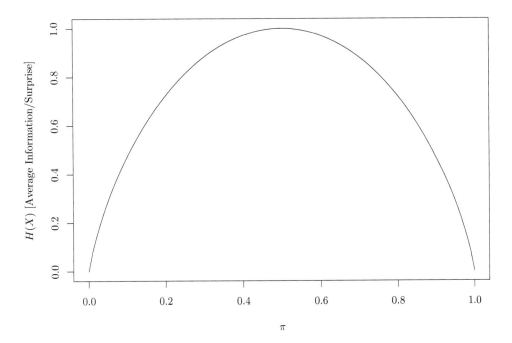

Figure 2.18: Shannon's entropy function $H(X)$, Bernoulli random variable.

Example 2.15. Shannon's Entropy Function $H(X)$ for a Binomial Random Variable.

Shannon's entropy function $H(X)$ for a binomially distributed random variable is presented in Figure 2.19.

Example 2.16. Shannon's Entropy Function for a Gaussian Random Variable Is Presented in Figure 2.20.

2.8.2 Relative Entropy

Relative entropy (Kullback-Leibler divergence, Cross entropy) can be used as a measure of how closely two probability distributions agree:

$$
\begin{aligned}
D(p||q) &= \mathrm{E}_P\left((-\log q(X)) - (-\log p(X))\right) \\
&= \sum_{x \in \mathcal{D}} p(x)((-\log q(x)) - (-\log p(x))) \\
&= \sum_{x \in \mathcal{D}} p(x)(\log p(x) - \log q(x)) \\
&= \sum_{x \in \mathcal{D}} p(x) \log \frac{p(x)}{q(x)}.
\end{aligned}
$$

Relative entropy measures divergence of q from p. It measures the inefficiency of assuming a priori that the distribution is p when the correct distribution is in fact q.

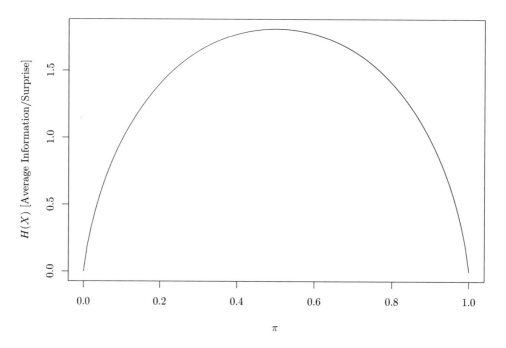

Figure 2.19: Shannon's entropy function, binomial random variable.

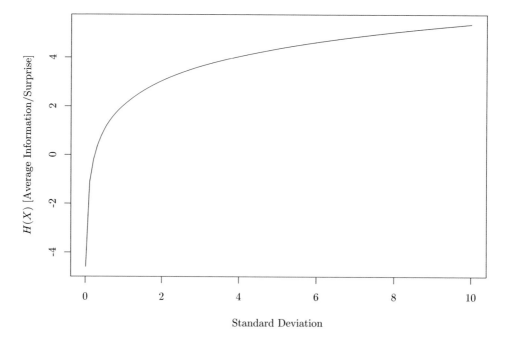

Figure 2.20: Shannon's entropy function, Gaussian random variable.

2.8.3 Joint and Conditional Entropy

We can also define the *joint* and *conditional* entropy for combinations of random variables:

$$H(X, Y) = - \sum_{x \in \mathcal{D}} \sum_{y \in \mathcal{Y}} p(x, y) \log p(x, y)$$

$$H(Y|X) = \sum_{x \in \mathcal{D}} p(x) H(Y|X = x)$$

$$= \sum_{x \in \mathcal{D}} p(x) \left(- \sum_{y \in \mathcal{Y}} p(y|x) \log p(y|x) \right)$$

$$= - \sum_{x \in \mathcal{D}} \sum_{y \in \mathcal{Y}} p(x, y) \log p(y|x).$$

Like joint and conditional probability, joint and conditional entropy are related:

$$H(X, Y) = - \sum_{x \in \mathcal{D}} \sum_{y \in \mathcal{Y}} p(x, y) \log p(y|x) p(x)$$

$$= - \sum_{x \in \mathcal{D}} \sum_{y \in \mathcal{Y}} p(x, y) \log p(y|x) - \sum_{x \in \mathcal{D}} \sum_{y \in \mathcal{Y}} p(x, y) \log p(x)$$

$$= - \sum_{x \in \mathcal{D}} \sum_{y \in \mathcal{Y}} p(x, y) \log p(y|x) - \sum_{x \in \mathcal{D}} p(x) \log p(x)$$

$$= H(Y|X) + H(X) = H(X|Y) + H(Y).$$

Conditional entropy $H(Y|X)$ measures the average amount of uncertainty in Y after we know the value of X:

$$H(Y|X) = H(X, Y) - H(X).$$

2.8.4 Mutual Information

Mutual information $I(X; Y)$ measures how much knowing the value of one random variable reduces the uncertainty about another:

$$I(X; Y) = H(X) - H(X|Y)$$

$$= H(X) + H(Y) - H(X, Y)$$

$$= \sum_{x \in \mathcal{D}} \sum_{y \in \mathcal{Y}} p(x, y) \log \frac{p(x, y)}{p(x)p(y)}$$

$$= I(Y; X) \geq 0.$$

$I(X; Y)$ is the expected value of:

$$I(x, y) = \log \frac{p(x, y)}{p(x)p(y)}.$$

It is the additional information that someone who is analyzing X gains on the margin from knowing Y.

The average mutual information of dependent variables depends on their entropy:

$$\begin{aligned} I(X;X) &= H(X) - H(X|X) \\ &= H(X) - H(X) + H(X) \\ &= H(X). \end{aligned}$$

Average mutual information is also related to relative entropy:

$$I(X;Y) = D(p(X,Y)||p(X)p(Y)).$$

If X and Y are independent, then $I(X;Y) = 0$ since in this case, $p(X,Y) = p(X)p(Y)$.

2.8.5   Entropy and Metricness

The topics that have been covered up to this point only scratch the surface. Generalized entropies that build on Shannon's can be found in the work of Rényi (1961), among others. However, one of the limitations of Shannon's relative entropy and nearly all others is that they fail to be *metric*; that is, they are not distance functions because they violate either the symmetry or the triangularity rule, or both. Hence they are measures of *divergence*, but not of *distance*. On the other hand, a metric measure allows for multiple comparisons of departures/distances.

We now turn to some of the motivating axioms that may embody what we consider to be desirable properties of any measure or index.

2.8.6   Entropy and Axiom Systems

Suppose that we require our metric for a pair of random variables X and Y to satisfy certain *ideal* properties:

- It is well-defined for both real-valued and discrete variables
- It is *normalized* to zero (say, if X and Y are independent), and it lies between 0 and 1
- It is *invariant* under continuous and strictly increasing transformations (otherwise, inadvertent transformations could produce different values)
- It is a *metric*, that is, a true measure of *distance* and not just of divergence

A relative entropy that satisfies these properties is a normalization of the Bhattacharya-Matusita-Hellinger entropy (Granger and Lin, 1994; Granger et al., 2004). It is given by

$$S_\rho = \frac{1}{2} \int_{-\infty}^{\infty} \int_{-\infty}^{\infty} \left(f_1^{1/2} - f_2^{1/2} \right)^2 \, dx \, dy$$

$$= \frac{1}{2} \int \int \left(1 - \frac{f_2^{1/2}}{f_1^{1/2}} \right)^2 dF_1(x, y).$$

The second expression, which is in moment form, is often replaced by a sample average, especially for theoretical developments. S_ρ is a generalized k-class relative entropy ($k = 1/2$) that corresponds to Hellinger distance between densities. Note that $S_\rho \in [0, 1]$, where $S_\rho = 0$ implies equality of f_1 and f_2 almost everywhere, and $S_\rho = 1$ implies that there is no overlap of the distributions (i.e., no common support). Figure 2.21 presents S_ρ under four different scenarios that involve univariate data; one where the distributions f_1 and f_2 are equal, two where the distributions are unequal but they have the same first and second moments, and one where the means differ and there is virtually no overlap.

2.8.7   Entropy, Inference, Robustness, and Consistency

Moment-based inferential procedures, which are dominant in the literature, are simple to apply and to interpret. Examples include two-sample difference in location tests (e.g., t-test) and difference in scale tests (e.g., F test). But if, for instance, we would like to know whether male and female wage distributions differ, we need to do more than simply test whether mean wages differ or whether a dummy variable in a parametric regression model is significant. Two distributions can have the same mean and variance but still be radically different. For example, suppose that female wages follow a χ^2 distribution with ν degrees of freedom and male wages follow a Gaussian distribution with mean ν and variance 2ν. Hence the two distributions have identical first and second moments (recall that a χ^2 distribution with ν degrees of freedom has mean ν and variance 2ν). If we are interested in studying wage inequality, then we might want to look beyond the mean and variance and instead take a close look at the PDF and CDF plots in Figure 2.22.

In this example, the probability of having a wage below the mean is 0.608 for females and 0.500 for males. This is in spite of the fact that the respective distributions of male and female wages have identical first and second moments. Suppose that the mean wage represents the poverty line. Then in this example, the incidence of poverty among females would be 60.8% while that among males would be 50.0%. If we are concerned about inequality, then a simple comparison of moments is not a sound strategy. Instead, we ought to carry out a comparison of the entire wage distribution for the two groups.

Moment-based tests can be problematic insofar as they sometimes lack power and they are not always consistent. Ideally, researchers would like to detect *any* difference that exists between two distributions. Parametric methods are poorly suited to this task - they may not be robust or con-

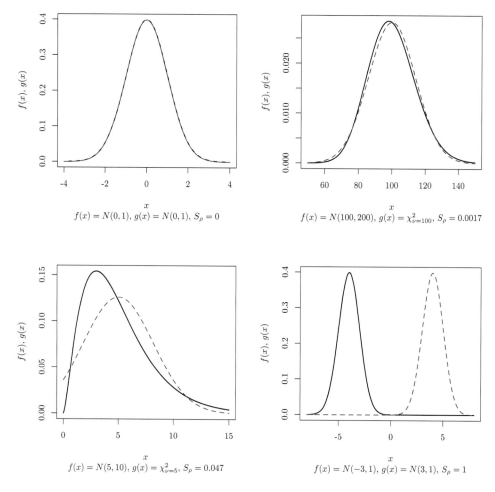

Figure 2.21: S_ρ when $f_1 = f(x)$ and $f_2 = g(x)$ represent a variety of distributions. We are comparing univariate densities, so $S_\rho = \frac{1}{2} \int \left(\sqrt{f(x)} - \sqrt{g(x)} \right)^2 dx$.

sistent, and should therefore be treated with caution. On the other hand, entropic measures of divergence can form the basis for consistent and robust alternatives to moment-based inferential procedures.

2.8.8   Kernel Estimation and Entropy

The reader has likely noticed that each of the aforementioned entropy-based measures rely on unknown probability functions or probability density functions. Replacing these unknown functions with consistent nonparametric estimates delivers a framework for sound statistical inference. The generalized mixed-data kernel density estimator (Li and Racine, 2003) that we study in

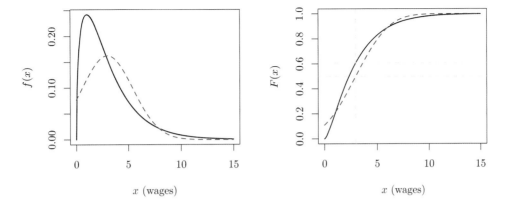

Figure 2.22: Simulated wage distributions. The dashed line is the Gaussian, while the solid line is the χ^2. The vertical dashed line in the figure on the right identifies the mean. The horizontal dashed lines in the figure on the right identify the respective probabilities of lying below the mean.

Chapter 3 is given by

$$\hat{f}(x) = \frac{1}{n} \sum_{i=1}^{n} K_\gamma(X_i, x),$$

and, going back to work by Robinson (1991), Ahmad and Li (1997), and Hong and White (2005), it can be used as a substitute for the unknown densities that appear in the entropy and information measures that have been outlined above. The generalized conditional density estimator that we study in Chapter 4 (Hall et al., 2004) is given by

$$\hat{f}(y|x) = \frac{\hat{f}(y, x)}{\hat{f}(x)},$$

and it will also prove useful in this context.

One popular method of bandwidth selection is closely tied to statistical mechanics. Likelihood cross-validation yields a density estimate that has an entropy interpretation, namely that the estimate will be close to the actual density in the Kullback-Leibler (relative entropy) sense (Kullback, 1959; Duin, 1976). The Practitioner's Corner below outlines a range of procedures for entropy-based inference that are implemented in the R package np.

2.9   Practitioner's Corner

Base R has a useful, computationally efficient function, `density()`, that can compute and plot univariate kernel density estimates $\hat{f}(x)$ using a *fast Fourier transform*. It incorporates a range of bandwidth selectors, including the normal-reference ad hoc rule and various plug-in procedures. One of its major benefits is that it can be used with extremely large sample sizes because of its use of the fast Fourier transform. The default bandwidth is `bw.nrd0()`, which implements an ad hoc rule of thumb bandwidth selector for a Gaussian kernel density estimator. See *Silverman's rule of thumb* on page 48, Equation (3.31) of Silverman (1986).

```
set.seed(42)
x <- rchisq(1000,df=5)
plot(density(x),main="")
```

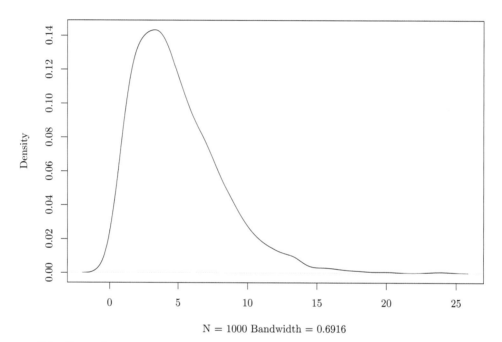

N = 1000 Bandwidth = 0.6916

The R package np contains a more general function `npudens()` that can also be used to compute the density. For the sake of illustration, we use the same bandwidth that was mentioned above. When plotting an `npdensity` object, `npplot()` is called (see `?npplot` for details). Calling the generic `plot()` function for a `npudens()` object admits a variety of options. For instance, if we wanted to construct 95% asymptotic confidence bands and add them to the plot, this could easily be accomplished, as the following code chunk demonstrates.

```
fhat <- npudens(~x,bws=bw.nrd0(x))
summary(fhat)
##
## Density Data: 1000 training points, in 1 variable(s)
##                        x
## Bandwidth(s): 0.6916
##
## Bandwidth Type: Fixed
## Log Likelihood: -2435
```

```
##
## Continuous Kernel Type: Second-Order Gaussian
## No. Continuous Vars.: 1
plot(fhat,plot.errors.style="band",plot.errors.method="asymptotic",neval=512)
```

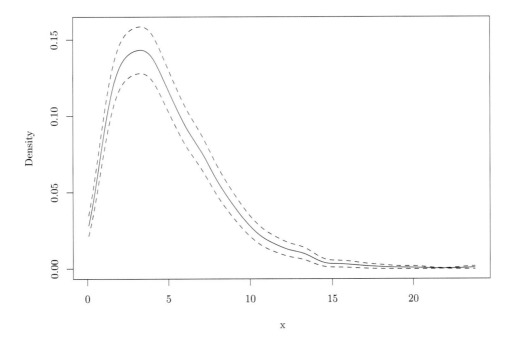

There are times when we would like to generate counterfactual density estimates or evaluate the density on a grid of user-supplied *evaluation* points (it is a convention to call the data used for estimating the density the *training* data and that used to compute the density at non-training points the *evaluation* data). To accomplish this, we use the generic R function `predict()`. We must be careful to create an evaluation dataset with the same named variable(s) as that used in the call to `npudens()`.

```
evaldata <- data.frame(x=seq(0,30,length=10))
plot(evaldata$x,predict(fhat,newdata=evaldata),xlab="$x$",ylab="Density")
rug(evaldata$x)
```

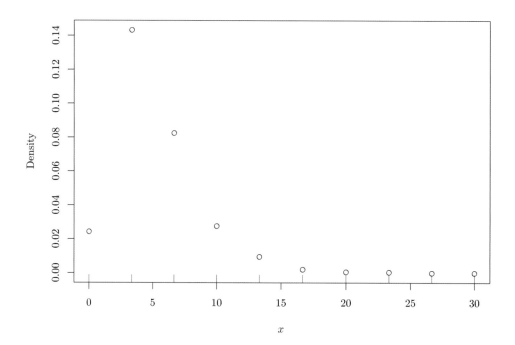

Alternatively, we could use the non-formula interface for `npudens()`. That is, instead of using `~x` and `predict(...,newdata=...)`, we could do the following (`tdat=` specifies the *training* data, `edat=` specifies the *evaluation* data, and there is no worry about `tdat` and `edat` having the same named variable):

```
x.eval <- seq(0,30,length=10)
fhat <- npudens(tdat=x,edat=x.eval,bws=bw.nrd0(x))
summary(fhat)
##
## Density Data: 1000 training points, and 10 evaluation points, in 1 variable(s)
##                      x
## Bandwidth(s): 0.6916
##
## Bandwidth Type: Fixed
## Log Likelihood: -101.1
##
## Continuous Kernel Type: Second-Order Gaussian
## No. Continuous Vars.: 1
plot(x.eval,fitted(fhat),xlab="$x$",ylab="Density")
```

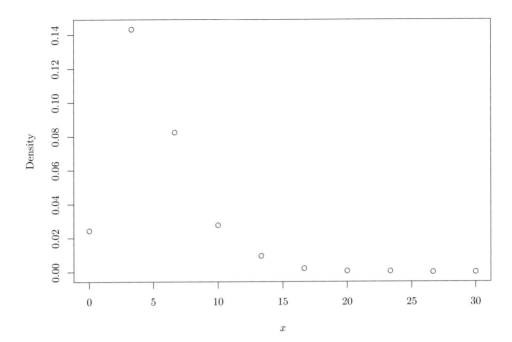

Both interfaces exist for the practitioner's convenience.

We can modify the kernel function, the order of the kernel function, and the bandwidth selection method as follows:

```
fhat <- npudens(~x,ckertype="epanechnikov",ckerorder=4,bwmethod="cv.ml")
summary(fhat)
##
## Density Data: 1000 training points, in 1 variable(s)
##                          x
## Bandwidth(s): 1.385
##
## Bandwidth Type: Fixed
## Log Likelihood: -2430
##
## Continuous Kernel Type: Fourth-Order Epanechnikov
## No. Continuous Vars.: 1
plot(fhat)
```

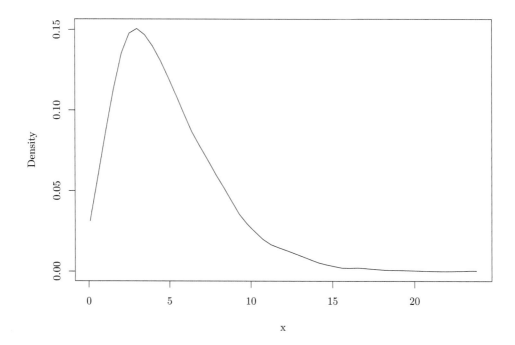

Asymptotic standard errors can be extracted from the `npdensity()` object via `se(fhat)`. See `?npudensbw` and `?npudens` for further details. See also the analogous functions `npudistbw()` and `npudist()` that are used to compute $\hat{F}(x)$.

```
Fhat <- npudist(~x)
summary(Fhat)
##
## Distribution Data: 1000 training points, in 1 variable(s)
##                       x
## Bandwidth(s): 0.4162
##
## Bandwidth Type: Fixed
##
## Continuous Kernel Type: Second-Order Gaussian
## No. Continuous Vars.: 1
plot(Fhat,plot.errors.style="band",plot.errors.method="asymptotic",neval=512)
```

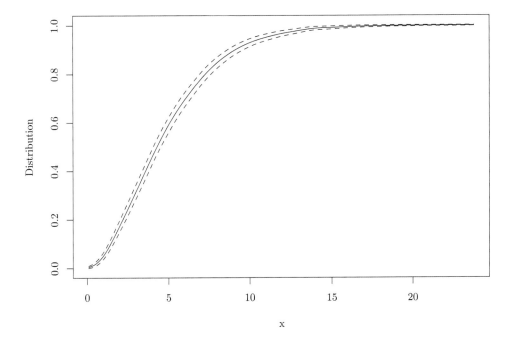

2.9.1 The Smoothed Bootstrap

Occasionally, we might wish to obtain a random sample that is drawn from our smooth kernel PDF estimate $\hat{f}(x)$ or CDF estimate $\hat{F}(x)$. For instance, if the empirical distribution is too discrete or sparse, it can be useful to take random draws from the smooth nonparametric distribution $\hat{F}(x)$ rather than its nonsmooth empirical counterpart $F_n(x)$. This procedure is known as *the smoothed bootstrap* (Efron, 1979; Silverman and Young, 1987). Because of the discrete nature of the empirical distribution $F_n(x)$, samples that are constructed from $F_n(x)$ have some rather peculiar properties. In particular, the random sample values are drawn exclusively from the original sample values, and it is common to observe repeated values in most samples. It turns out that drawing resamples from smooth kernel estimates is quite simple, since the kernel functions that are used to construct the estimators are themselves density and distribution functions. As a result, we can use a standard method for generating random numbers from a specified distribution. For example, suppose that we want to draw a random sample from a parametric distribution such as the Gaussian with mean μ and standard deviation σ. To accomplish this, we would draw random *probabilities* τ^* from the uniform $[0,1]$ distribution, and then take the quantiles $q_{\tau^*} = F^{-1}(\tau^*)$ from a Gaussian distribution with mean μ and standard deviation σ. Recall from our discussion of the mechanics of the kernel estimator $\hat{f}(x)$ that the n kernel functions $K((x - X_i)/h)$ are in fact density functions with mean X_i and standard deviation h. We take a two-step approach. First, we pick a random data point X_i from the $\{X_1, X_2, \ldots, X_n\}$ and call this X_i^*. This is equivalent to sampling from the integers $1, 2, \ldots, n$ and then selecting X_{i*}. Second, we use the standard approach to draw a random observation from a density (i.e., kernel function) that has mean X_i^* and standard deviation h. The code chunk below demonstrates the simplicity of this procedure when the Gaussian kernel function is used. Figure 2.23 plots the estimate for the original sample and for the resample (we draw $n = 1,000$ resample observations). Note that for the joint estimate below, since we are using a product kernel function, we pick a *pairwise* random data point (X_{i*1}, X_{i*2}), and then take a random draw from each element of the product kernel function independently.

```
## Credit for this example goes to Cosma Shalizi
## http://stat.cmu.edu/~cshalizi/ADAfaEPoV/
data(faithful)
n <- nrow(faithful)
x1 <- faithful$eruptions
x2 <- faithful$waiting
## First compute the data-driven bandwidths (h1,h2)
bw <- npudensbw(~x1+x2,ckertype="gaussian")
## Next, sample 1000 integers with replacement from the integers 1,2,...,n
n.boot <- 1000
i.boot <- sample(1:n,n.boot,replace=TRUE)
## Finally, generate pairwise random draws from the (x1,x2) values and
## resample from the kernels with those means and standard deviation for the
## pairwise resampled variables and bandwidths, respectively
x1.boot <- rnorm(n.boot,mean=x1[i.boot],sd=bw$bw[1])
x2.boot <- rnorm(n.boot,mean=x2[i.boot],sd=bw$bw[2])
```

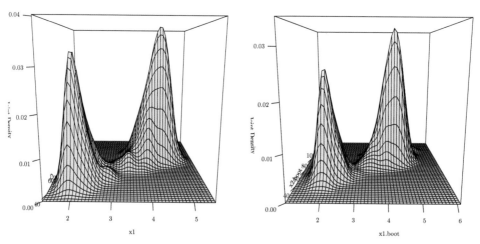

Figure 2.23: Kernel estimators of the joint density $f(x) = f(x_1, x_2)$ for the original sample (left) and for the smooth resample (right).

2.9.2   Testing Univariate Asymmetry

Testing for asymmetric behaviour dates back to the pioneering work of Crum (1923), Mitchell (1927), and Keynes (1936), who examined potential asymmetries in a number of macroeconomic series. Many macroeconomic series have been analyzed and tested for asymmetric behaviour in expansions and downturns; see the work of Timmermann and Perez-Quiros (2001), Bai and Ng (2001), Belaire-Franch and Peiro (2003), and Premaratne and Bera (2005). Existing tests are somewhat limited in application because they are designed for *continuous* processes; however, in applied settings, one often encounters discrete processes. Existing tests that examine moments and other implications of symmetry are discussed in Premaratne and Bera (2005) and Bai and Ng (2005). The latter point out that estimation of higher-order moments, such as kurtosis, have well-known difficulties. They also draw attention to the greater power of tests that are based simultaneously on several odd order moments, notwithstanding some of the issues (e.g., bias) that are associated with estimation of these moments. Methods that are based on *distributions* take into account all of the information that may be forthcoming from multiple moments, without assuming that these moments actually exist.

Consider a (strictly) stationary series $\{Y_t\}_{t=1}^T$. Let μ_y denote a measure of central tendency, say $\mu_y = \mathrm{E}\, Y_t$, let $f(y)$ denote the density function of the random variable Y_t, let $\tilde{Y}_t = -Y_t + 2\mu_y$ denote a rotation of Y_t about its mean (and let $\tilde{y} = -y + 2\mu_y$), and let $f(\tilde{y})$ denote the density function of the random variable $\tilde{Y}_t$. Note that if $\mu_y = 0$, then $\tilde{Y}_t = -Y_t$, although in general, this will not be the case. We say that a series is *symmetric about the mean* (median, mode) if $f(y) = f(\tilde{y})$ almost surely. Tests for asymmetry about the mean therefore involve the following null hypothesis:

$$H_0 : f(y) = f(\tilde{y}) \text{ almost everywhere (a.e.)}$$

against the alternative hypothesis

$$H_1 : f(y) \neq f(\tilde{y}) \text{ on a set with positive measure.}$$

The function `npsymtest()` computes the nonparametric metric entropy (normalized Hellinger of Granger et al. (2004)) outlined in Maasoumi and Racine (2009) for testing the null of symmetry using the densities/probabilities of the data and the rotated data, $f(y)$ and $f(\tilde{y})$, respectively. Y must be univariate and can be a time series, continuous, or even categorical-valued, as long as the outcomes are not character strings.

For bootstrapping the null distribution of the statistic, the option `iid` conducts simple random resampling, while `geom` conducts stationary bootstrapping using automatic block length selection via the `b.star()` function in the np package (Politis and Romano, 1994; Politis and White, 2004; Patton et al., 2009). Bootstrapping is conducted by resampling from the empirical distribution of the pooled data and the rotated data. Default bandwidths are of the plug-in variety (`bw.SJ()` for continuous variables and direct plug-in for discrete variables).

For continuous variables, we use

$$S_\rho = \frac{1}{2} \int \left(f_1^{1/2} - f_2^{1/2} \right)^2 dx$$

$$= \frac{1}{2} \int \left(1 - \frac{f_2^{1/2}}{f_1^{1/2}} \right)^2 dF_1(x),$$

where f_1 and f_2 are the marginal densities of the data and of the rotated data, respectively. The second expression, which is in moment form, is often replaced by a sample average, especially for theoretical developments. When Y is discrete/categorical, we take the sum rather than the integral over all possible outcomes. The unknown density/probability functions are replaced by nonparametric kernel estimates.

The following code chunk provides simple examples that involve both continuous and discrete data.

```
set.seed(42)
n <- 200
## Asymmetric discrete probability distribution
x <- factor(rbinom(n,2,.8))
npsymtest(x,boot.num=99)
##
## Consistent Entropy Asymmetry Test
## 99 Bootstrap Replications
##
## Test Statistic 'Srho': 0.3243     P Value: <2e-16 ***
## ---
## Signif. codes:  0 '***' 0.001 '**' 0.01 '*' 0.05 '.' 0.1 ' ' 1
## Null of symmetry is rejected at the 0.1% level
## Symmetric continuous distribution
y <- rnorm(n)
npsymtest(y,boot.num=99)
##
## Consistent Entropy Asymmetry Test
## 99 Bootstrap Replications
##
## Test Statistic 'Srho': 0.002955  P Value: 0.71
## ---
## Signif. codes:  0 '***' 0.001 '**' 0.01 '*' 0.05 '.' 0.1 ' ' 1
## Fail to reject the null of symmetry at the 10% level
```

2.9.3   Testing Equality of Univariate Densities

Maasoumi and Racine (2002) consider a metric entropy that is useful for testing whether the respective densities of two univariate random variables X and Y are equal. The function `npunitest()` computes the nonparametric metric entropy (normalized Hellinger of Granger et al. (2004)) for testing the null

$$H_0 : f(x) = g(x) \text{ almost everywhere (a.e.)}$$

against the alternative

$$H_1 : f(x) \neq g(x) \text{ on a set with positive measure.}$$

For continuous variables, we construct

$$S_\rho = \frac{1}{2} \int \left(f_1^{1/2} - f_2^{1/2} \right)^2 dx$$

$$= \frac{1}{2} \int \left(1 - \frac{f_2^{1/2}}{f_1^{1/2}} \right)^2 dF_1(x),$$

where $f_1 = f(x)$ and $f_2 = f(y)$ are the respective marginal densities of the random variables X and Y. The second expression, which is in moment form, is often replaced by a sample average, especially for theoretical developments. When X and Y are discrete/categorical, we take the sum rather than the integral over all possible outcomes. Nonparametric kernel estimates replace the unknown density/probability functions.

The null distribution is obtained via a bootstrap procedure that resamples with replacement from the pooled empirical distribution of X and Y (or of X alone for the moment version). Default bandwidths are of the plug-in variety (`bw.SJ()` for continuous variables and direct plug-in for discrete variables).

The following code chunk provides three simple examples that involve both continuous and discrete data.

```
set.seed(42)
n <- 200
## Data drawn from identical continuous distributions
x <- rnorm(n)
y <- rnorm(n)
npunitest(x,y,boot.num=99)
##
## Consistent Univariate Entropy Density Equality Test
## 99 Bootstrap Replications
##
## Test Statistic 'Srho': 0.002403  P Value: 0.88
## ---
## Signif. codes:  0 '***' 0.001 '**' 0.01 '*' 0.05 '.' 0.1 ' ' 1
## Fail to reject the null of equality at the 10% level
## Data drawn from different continuous distributions having the
## same mean and variance (would confound moment-based tests)
x <- rchisq(n,df=5)
y <- rnorm(n,mean=5,sd=sqrt(10))
npunitest(x,y,boot.num=99)
##
## Consistent Univariate Entropy Density Equality Test
## 99 Bootstrap Replications
##
## Test Statistic 'Srho': 0.04071   P Value: <2e-16 ***
## ---
## Signif. codes:  0 '***' 0.001 '**' 0.01 '*' 0.05 '.' 0.1 ' ' 1
```

```
## Null of equality is rejected at the 0.1% level
## Data drawn from different discrete distributions
x <- factor(rbinom(n,2,.5))
y <- factor(rbinom(n,2,.1))
npunitest(x,y,boot.num=99)
##
## Consistent Univariate Entropy Density Equality Test
## 99 Bootstrap Replications
##
## Test Statistic 'Srho': 0.206 P Value: <2e-16 ***
## ---
## Signif. codes:  0 '***' 0.001 '**' 0.01 '*' 0.05 '.' 0.1 ' ' 1
## Null of equality is rejected at the 0.1% level
```

2.9.4   Testing Nonlinear Pairwise Independence

Maasoumi and Racine (2002) consider a metric entropy that is useful for testing whether two random variables X and Y are pairwise independent. The function `npdeptest()` computes the nonparametric metric entropy (normalized Hellinger of Granger et al. (2004)) for testing the null hypothesis

$$H_0 : f(y, x) = f(y)f(x) \text{ almost everywhere (a.e.)}$$

against the alternative hypothesis

$$H_1 : f(y, x) \neq f(y)f(x) \text{ on a set with positive measure.}$$

For continuous variables, we construct

$$S_\rho = \frac{1}{2} \int_{-\infty}^{\infty} \int_{-\infty}^{\infty} \left(f_1^{1/2} - f_2^{1/2} \right)^2 dx\,dy$$

$$= \frac{1}{2} \int \int \left(1 - \frac{f_2^{1/2}}{f_1^{1/2}} \right)^2 dF_1(x, y),$$

where $f_1 = f(X_i, Y_i)$ is the joint density and $f_2 = g(X_i) \times h(Y_i)$ is the product of the marginal densities of the random variables X_i and Y_i. The unknown density/probability functions are replaced by nonparametric kernel estimates.

The bootstrap distribution of the $\{X_i, Y_i\}$ pairs under the null is obtained by resampling with replacement from the empirical distribution of X and generating the pairs $\{X_i^*, Y_i\}$, where X^* is the bootstrap resample. That is, we *shuffle* X and leave Y unchanged, which eliminates any pairwise dependence that might exist. By default, bandwidths for the marginal and joint densities are obtained via likelihood cross-validation.

Examples include (a) a measure/test of *fit* based on in-sample values of a variable y and fitted values $\hat{y}$, and (b) a measure of *predictability* based on a variable y and predicted values $\hat{y}$ from a user-implemented model.

The following code chunk provides a simple example that uses the actual and fitted values from a regression model. Note that in applied settings, we strongly recommend use of the default integration version of the statistic, even though we use the summation (i.e., moment) version below simply because it is computationally faster.

```
set.seed(42)
## Test/measure lack of fit between y and its fitted value from a
## regression model when x is relevant.
n <- 200
x <- rnorm(n)
y <- 1 + x + rnorm(n)
model <- lm(y~x)
y.fit <- fitted(model)
npdeptest(y,y.fit,boot.num=99,method="summation")
##
## Consistent Metric Entropy Test for Dependence
## 99 Bootstrap Replications
##
## Test Statistic 'Srho': 0.02646    P Value: <2e-16 ***
## ---
## Signif. codes:  0 '***' 0.001 '**' 0.01 '*' 0.05 '.' 0.1 ' ' 1
## Null of independence is rejected at the 0.1% level
```

2.9.5 Testing Nonlinear Serial Independence

The detection and proper measurement of *association* and *dependence* are essential tasks in economic model building and forecasting. Most commonly-used test statistics and measures of dependence are based on *correlation*, which merely reflects *linear* relations that might exist between *continuous* variables and/or Gaussian processes. These measures tend to fail when variables are discrete, and they also lack power when faced with nonlinear or non-Gaussian processes. Shannon's *mutual information* function is an alternative option that has appeared quite frequently in the literature; see Joe (1989), Robinson (1991), Skaug and Tjøstheim (1996), and Granger and Lin (1994). However, Shannon's relative entropy and nearly all others fail to be *metric* because they violate either the symmetry or the triangularity rule, or both. Hence they are measures of *divergence*, but not of *distance*; see Granger and Lin (1994) and Skaug and Tjøstheim (1996).

Granger et al. (2004) consider a metric entropy that is useful for testing for nonlinear serial independence in a univariate random variable Y. The function `npsdeptest()` computes the nonparametric metric entropy (normalized Hellinger) for testing the null

$$H_0 : f(y_t, y_{t-k}) = f(y_t)f(y_{t-k}) \text{ almost everywhere (a.e.)}$$

against the alternative

$$H_1 : f(y_t, y_{t-k}) \neq f(y_t)f(y_{t-k}) \text{ on a set with positive measure.}$$

We construct

$$S_\rho = \frac{1}{2} \int_{-\infty}^{\infty} \int_{-\infty}^{\infty} \left(f_1^{1/2} - f_2^{1/2} \right)^2 dx\, dy$$

$$= \frac{1}{2} \int \int \left(1 - \frac{f_2^{1/2}}{f_1^{1/2}} \right)^2 dF_1(x, y),$$

where $f_1 = f(y_t, y_{t-k})$ is the joint density and $f_2 = g(y_t) \times h(y_{t-k})$ is the product of the marginal densities of the random variables Y_t and Y_{t-k}. The second expression, which is in moment form, is often replaced by a sample average, especially for theoretical developments. Nonparametric kernel estimates replace the unknown density/probability functions.

The bootstrap distribution is obtained by resampling with replacement from the empirical distribution of Y_t, thereby delivering Y_t^* under the null of nonlinear serial independence. By default, bandwidths for the marginal and joint densities are obtained via likelihood cross-validation.

The following code chunk provides a simple example that involves a continuous time series. Note that in applied settings, we strongly recommend use of the default integration version of the statistic, even though we use the summation (i.e., moment) version below for the sole reason that it is computationally faster.

```
set.seed(42)
## Stationary persistent time series
Y <- arima.sim(list(ar=0.95),100)
npsdeptest(Y,lag.num=2,boot.num=99,method="summation")
##
## Consistent Metric Entropy Test for Nonlinear Dependence
## 99 Bootstrap Replications, 2 Lags
##
## Test Statistic 'Srho[1]': 0.04985    P Value: <2e-16 ***
## Test Statistic 'Srho[2]': 0.03582    P Value: <2e-16 ***
## ---
## Signif. codes:  0 '***' 0.001 '**' 0.01 '*' 0.05 '.' 0.1 ' ' 1
## Null of independence is rejected at lag 1 at the 0.1% level
## Null of independence is rejected at lag 2 at the 0.1% level
## White noise time series
set.seed(42)
Y <- rnorm(100)
npsdeptest(Y,lag.num=2,boot.num=99,method="summation")
##
## Consistent Metric Entropy Test for Nonlinear Dependence
## 99 Bootstrap Replications, 2 Lags
##
## Test Statistic 'Srho[1]': 0.003356   P Value: 0.52
## Test Statistic 'Srho[2]': 0.002402   P Value: 0.83
## ---
## Signif. codes:  0 '***' 0.001 '**' 0.01 '*' 0.05 '.' 0.1 ' ' 1
## Fail to reject the null of independence at lag 1 at the 10% level
## Fail to reject the null of independence at lag 2 at the 10% level
```

2.9.6   Bounded Domains and Boundary Corrections

Occasionally, the natural domain of a continuous random variable is not the entire real number line, but rather an interval that is known to be bounded on one or both sides. This gives rise to *boundary effects* since there are no observations to average on the other side of the bound. Boundary effects occur because the curve that is to be estimated has a discontinuity at an endpoint, and hence the usual bias expansion that depends on smoothness assumptions is no longer valid. The upshot is that the bias of $\hat{f}(x)$ is larger near the boundary. In particular, for x lying within h units of the boundary, the bias of $\hat{f}(x)$ is of $O(h)$ rather than $O(h^2)$. Furthermore, $\hat{f}(x)$ may be inconsistent for $f(x)$ near the boundary.

To overcome boundary effects, one can engage in some creative kernel carpentry whereby *boundary* or *edge* kernel functions are used; see Gasser and Müller (1979), Gasser et al. (1985), Müller (1991), Jones (1993), Chen (1999), Chen (2000), Bouezmarni and Rolin (2003), Scaillet (2004), Bouezmarni and Rombouts (2010), Igarashi (2015), and Igarashi and Kakizawa (2018). Alternatively, one can use a data-reflection approach (Boneva et al., 1971; Hall and Wehrly, 1991; Cline and Hart, 1991) or a transformation approach (Copas and Fryer, 1980; Marron and Ruppert, 1994). See Jones and Foster (1996) and Karunamunia and Zhang (2008), who propose alternative boundary bias reduction methods that combine transformation and data-reflection; see also the R package bde (Santafe et al., 2015). There also exist methods that involve creating pseudo data beyond the extremities of the density's support (Cowling and Hall, 1996). Below, we outline a few approaches that might be of interest to practitioners.

Data-Reflection

The illustration below sheds light on an extremely simple approach that involves *data-reflection*. Note, however, that this approach imposes a derivative of zero at the boundary. Suppose that X is bounded below by zero. We augment the data by adding the *reflections* of all of the points about the boundary, which produces the set $\{X_1, -X_1, X_2, -X_2, \ldots\}$. We then construct a standard kernel estimate, denoted by $\tilde{f}(x)$, for this dataset of size $2n$. An estimate based on the original data is then given by putting weight 2 on the non-negative x density and 0 on the negative x density, as follows:

$$\hat{f}(x) = \begin{cases} 2\tilde{f}(x) & \text{if } x \geq 0, \\ 0 & \text{otherwise.} \end{cases}$$

With both a lower and an upper bound, one simply reflects the data about the two bounds and then adjusts accordingly, i.e., puts weight 3 on the x density and 0 on the rest. The reflected data around a non-zero bound c

would be $\{X_i, -X_i + 2c\}_{i=1}^n$, while the reflected data around two bounds d and e would be $\{X_i, -X_i + 2d, -X_i + 2e\}_{i=1}^n$.

The estimator can also be expressed as

$$\hat{f}(x) = \frac{1}{nh} \sum_{i=1}^n \left(K\left(\frac{x - X_i}{h}\right) + K\left(\frac{x + X_i}{h}\right) \right)$$

for $x \geq 0$, and $\hat{f}(x) = 0$ for $x < 0$. There is no need to multiply $\hat{f}(x)$ by 2 since there are $2n$ terms that are summed, but in this expression, we multiply the sum by $\frac{1}{nh}$. Note that the bandwidth should be based on the original sample of n observations (Scott (1992), Page 149).

Figure 2.24 presents the uncorrected and the corrected estimates for a sample of size $n = 10000$.

```
## Use trees to speed up estimation
options(np.tree=TRUE)
## Generate data where there is an asymptote at the left boundary (worst case
## scenario)
set.seed(42)
n <- 10000
x <- sort(rexp(n))
## Compute the bandwidth for the original data
bw <- npudensbw(~x,ckertype="epanechnikov")
## Construct the standard (i.e., no boundary correction) kernel estimate
f.hat <- fitted(npudens(~x,bws=bw$bw,ckertype="epanechnikov"))
## Reflect the data, compute the reflected density, and then take the
## estimator which is 2 times the reflected density estimate for x >= 0
## (see Silverman (1986, page 30))
x.reflect <- c(x,-x)
f.reflect <- npudens(~x.reflect,bws=bw$bw,ckertype="epanechnikov")
f.boundary <- 2*predict(f.reflect,newdata=data.frame(x.reflect=x))
options(np.tree=FALSE)

## Plot the DGP, the standard estimator, and the
## boundary-corrected estimator
plot(x,dexp(x),lty=1,ylim=c(0,1),xlab="$X$",ylab="Density",type="l",
     sub=paste("Likelihood CV bandwidth:",
               formatC(f.reflect$bws$bw,format="f",digits=2),sep=""))
rug(x)
lines(x,f.boundary,col=2,lty=2,lwd=2)
lines(x,f.hat,col=3,lty=3,lwd=2)
legend("topright",
       c("DGP",
         "Reflected",
         "Standard"),
       lty=1:3,
       col=1:3,
       lwd=c(2,2,2),
       bty="n")
```

It is evident that the imposition of a zero derivative at the boundary is pulling the estimate downwards.

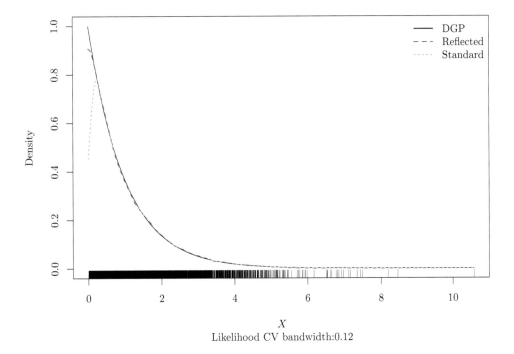

Figure 2.24: Boundary correction via data-reflection.

The function `npuniden.reflect()` in the R package np implements this univariate reflection technique for lower and upper bounds $[a, b]$.

Transformation Methods

Another way to deal with boundaries is to use an invertible function to map the limited range of X to the whole real line, find the density of the transformed variable, and then undo the transformation. Consider the following transformation for a random variable $X \in [0, 1]$,

$$Y = \log\left(\frac{X}{1-X}\right),$$

which implies

$$X = \frac{\exp(Y)}{1 + \exp(Y)}.$$

We can use the standard kernel estimator of the PDF of Y. To undo the transformation, we note that

$$\hat{g}(y) = \hat{f}(x)\left|\frac{dx}{dy}\right|,$$

and hence

$$\hat{f}(x) = \frac{\hat{g}(y)}{\left|\exp(y)/(\exp(y) + 1) - \exp(2y)/(\exp(y) + 1)^2\right|}.$$

Figure 2.25 presents the uncorrected and the corrected estimates, as well as the true density function for a $n = 500$ observation sample of data drawn from a Beta(3/4,1/4) distribution.

```
## Credit for this example goes to Cosma Shalizi
## http://stat.cmu.edu/~cshalizi/ADAfaEPoV/
set.seed(42)
n <- 500
shape1 <- 0.75
shape2 <- 0.25
x <- sort(rbeta(n,shape1,shape2))
f <- dbeta(x,shape1,shape2)
## Transform the data
y <- log(x/(1-x))
## Conduct bandwidth selection and estimation on the transformed data
f.y <- npudens(~y)
## Undo the transformation (estimate and bandwidth)
h.y <- f.y$bws$bw
f.x <- fitted(f.y)/abs(exp(y)/(exp(y)+1)-exp(2*y)/(exp(y)+1)**2)
h.x <- abs(exp(h.y)/(exp(h.y)+1)-exp(2*h.y)/(exp(h.y)+1)**2)
## Plug-in density estimate for untransformed data for comparison purposes
f.x.untrans <- density(x)
plot(x,f,type="l",ylab="Density",xlab="$X$",ylim=c(0,3),col=1,lwd=2,
    sub=paste("Likelihood CV bandwidth: ",
            formatC(h,format="f",digits=2),sep=""))
lines(x,f.x,col=2,lty=2,lwd=2)
lines(f.x.untrans,col=3,lty=3,lwd=2)
rug(x)
legend("topleft",c("DGP","Transformed","Standard"),col=1:3,lty=1:3,
        lwd=c(2,2,2),bty="n")
```

Note that likelihood cross-validation undersmoothes the density of the untransformed variable, so a direct plug-in method is used instead for the comparison. The choice of transformation must be undertaken with caution in order to avoid undesirable side-effects.

Kernel Carpentry

An alternative to transformation and reflection methods is to engage in some *kernel carpentry* whereby a custom *boundary kernel function* is generated. For $X \in [a, b]$ and a symmetric, mean zero, univariate kernel function $K(z)$ such as the Gaussian or Epanechnikov, a simple boundary kernel function is given by

$$K(z, a, b) = \begin{cases} \frac{K(z)}{G(z_b) - G(z_a)} & \text{if } z_a \leq z \leq z_b, \\ 0 & \text{otherwise,} \end{cases}$$

where $z = (x - X_i)/h$, $z_b = (b - x)/h$, and $z_a = (a - x)/h$, and where $G(z) = \int_{-\infty}^{z} K(t)\,dt$. Since $K(z)$ is a standard univariate kernel function, $G(z)$ is the CDF counterpart to the PDF $K(z)$ that we used to estimate $F(x)$. The astute reader will recognize that if $K(z)$ is, for instance, the normal density function, then this is simply the (doubly) truncated normal

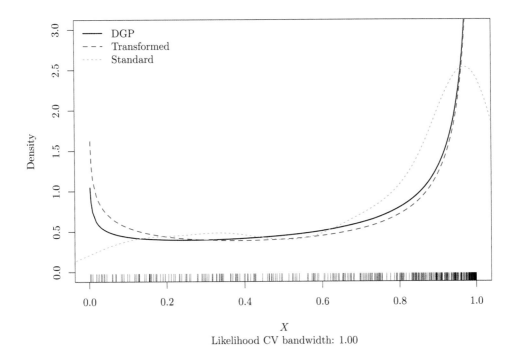

Figure 2.25: Boundary correction via transformation.

density function. To estimate a CDF, one simply uses the transformation for (doubly) truncated density functions, i.e.,

$$G(z, a, b) = \frac{G(\max(\min(z, z_b), z_a)) - G(z_a)}{G(z_b) - G(z_a)}.$$

This yields the (doubly) truncated CDF kernel function $G(z, a, b)$ that is associated with the (doubly) truncated PDF kernel function $K(z, a, b)$. The kernel function $K(z, a, b)$ will be *asymmetric* in the boundary region but it is always proper in $[a, b]$, provided that $K(z)$ is itself proper. This is very closely related to the idea of reweighting to restore missing probability mass, which was used by Diggle (1985) in the context of estimating the local intensity of a point process (he refers to this as "end-correction" [Diggle (1985); Equation (1.1)]). It is also discussed in Härdle (1990) (Page 131) and Jones (1993). The difference is that here, we perform the adjustment at the level of the kernel function rather than in an ex-post fashion after the density estimate has been constructed, although both approaches have the same effect. Figure 2.26 presents this kernel function (divided by h) for $X \in [0, 1]$ when it is constructed using 5 values of its *mode*, denoted by x.

Below, we present some simple R code that implements this kernel function, the density estimator, and a simple function for likelihood cross-validation.

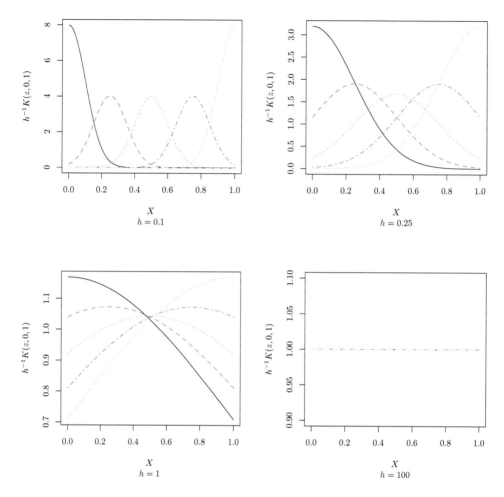

Figure 2.26: Boundary kernel function for a range of bandwidths.

```
## Create functions to compute the boundary-corrected kernel function,
## kernel estimator for X in [a,b] (X is the vector of training data,
## x the evaluation point(s)), delete-one estimate and likelihood
## cross-validation objective function - note that we divide the kernel
## function by the bandwidth hence the estimator is simply the mean of
## the kernel function evaluated at the point x
kernel <- function(X,x,h,a=0,b=1) {
    dnorm((X-x)/h)/(h*(pnorm((b-x)/h)-pnorm((a-x)/h)))
}
fhat <- function(X,h,a=0,b=1) {
    sapply(1:length(X),function(i){mean(kernel(X,X[i],h,a,b))})
}
fhat.loo <- function(X,h,a=0,b=1) {
    sapply(1:length(X),function(i){mean(kernel(X[-i],X[i],h,a,b))})
}
cv.ml.function <- function(X,h,a=0,b=1) {
    sum(log(fhat.loo(X,h,a,b)))
```

```
}
```

Figure 2.27 presents the uncorrected and the corrected estimates, as well as the true density function for a $n = 1000$ observation sample of data drawn from a Beta(5,1) distribution on $[0, 1]$.

```
## Generate data from the Beta(5,1) distribution, use likelihood
## cross-validation to select the bandwidth, create evaluation data,
## and plot the boundary-corrected and uncorrected estimates along
## with the DGP
set.seed(42)
n <- 1000
X <- sort(rbeta(n,5,1))
dgp <- dbeta(X,5,1)
## Conduct grid search for likelihood cross-validated bandwidth
h.seq<-c(seq(0.01,1.5,length=100),2^(1:20))*min(sd(X),IQR(X)/1.349)*n**(-1/5)
cv.vec <- numeric()
for(i in 1:length(h.seq)) cv.vec[i] <- cv.ml.function(X,h.seq[i])
h <- h.seq[which.max(cv.vec)]
## Construct the density estimate using the likelihood CV bandwidth
f <- fhat(X,h)
## Generate figure
plot(X,f,type="l",
     ylab="Density",
     xlab="$X$",
     ylim=c(0,max(f)),
     lty=2,
     col=2,
     lwd=2)
lines(X,fitted(npudens(~X)),col=3,lty=3,lwd=2)
lines(X,dgp,col=1,lty=1,lwd=1)
rug(X)
legend("topleft",c("DGP","Carpentry","Standard"),
       col=1:3,lty=1:3,lwd=c(2,2,2),bty="n")
```

Increasing the sample size reveals that the estimator is consistent. Its performance near the boundary regions is comparable to that in the interior region. Note, however, that certain boundary kernel functions can produce *negative* density estimates. In addition, the choice of the support interval (i.e., boundary or interior) in certain kernel functions can bring about unwanted artifacts. Simulations carried out for the uniform, Beta(5,1), and Beta(5,3) distributions, all of which lie on $[0, 1]$, indicate that the overall performance of this kernel function is quite good in all three cases ($f(0) = f(1) = 1$ for the uniform, $f(0) = 0$, $f(1) = 5$ for the Beta(5,1), and $f(0) = f(1) = 0$ for the Beta(5,3)). In particular, it outperforms the Beta kernel density estimators proposed by Chen (1999). Furthermore, it is easily extended to multivariate settings by making use of product kernel functions, and it is versatile insofar as setting either $a = -\infty$ or $b = \infty$ allows for one-sided bounds without any modification required (one would need to swap the Beta kernel for, say, the Gamma kernel when $X \in [a, \infty]$). In R, the Beta and Gamma kernel functions can be expressed as follows:

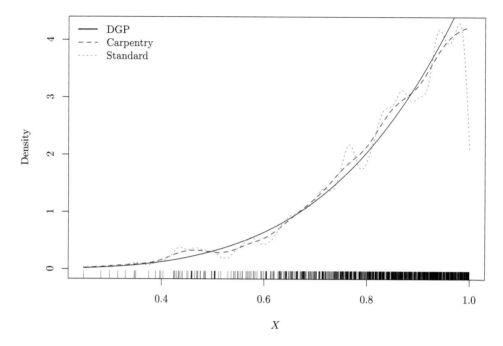

Figure 2.27: Boundary correction via kernel carpentry.

```
## Beta kernel on [a,b] (Chen (1999))
kernel <- function(x,X,h,a=0,b=1) {
    ## Rescale to lie in [0,1]
    X <- (X-a)/(b-a)
    x <- (x-a)/(b-a)
    ## No division by h, rescale to integrate to 1 on [a,b]
    dbeta(X,x/h+1,(1-x)/h+1)/(b-a)
}
## Gamma kernel on [a,infinity] (Chen (2000))
kernel <- function(x,X,h,a=0,b=Inf) {
    ## Rescale to lie in [0,Inf], b is a dummy for compatability with
    ## previous code chunk
    X <- X-a
    x <- x-a
    dgamma(X,x/h+1,1/h)
}
```

This univariate boundary kernel technique can be implemented for a range of kernel functions using `npuniden.boundary()` in the R package np.

2.9.7   Nonlinear Optimization and Multi-Starting

The objective functions for the data-driven bandwidth selection methods that were outlined earlier are *nonlinear* and may possess multiple *local* minima/maxima. That is, location of *global* minima/maxima is often complicated by the fact that the functions are not globally convex/concave. Furthermore, the optimization problems that we encountered earlier do not have *closed form* solutions, so they must be solved *numerically*. Finding a local optimum is relatively straightforward and can be achieved by means of classical local optimization methods. However, finding a global minimum or maximum of a function is far more difficult (Press et al., 1990, Page 290). *Nonlinear optimization* in the presence of local minima/maxima can be carried out via *multi-starting*. Multi-starting involves taking the most extreme result from repeated attempts at minimizing/maximizing a function that is known to have multiple local minima/maxima, where the search has been re-started each time from a different random (but sensible) initial value. When a sufficiently large number of attempts have been undertaken, we can be guardedly optimistic that a global minimum/maximum has been located. Multi-starting is a member of the *heuristic* class of search algorithms (Gilli et al., 2011) and it remains one of the most popular nonlinear optimization techniques among practitioners.

All routines in the R package np implement multi-starting and the number of multi-starts can be set via the argument `nmulti=`. In multivariate settings, where the issue of becoming trapped in local minima/maxima[15] is compounded, a large number of multi-starts may be required.

However, it is worth remembering that we work on *fixed precision* computers, and hence there isn't necessarily cause for concern if repeated attempts do not *exactly* agree with one another, as the following illustration makes clear. We simulate a sample of size $n = 100$ and conduct likelihood cross-validation based first on one and then on five restarts. We obtain the same *qualitative* bandwidths and density estimates under both scenarios; in this instance, the difference in the objective function values lies solely in the fact that the numerical optimization routine relies on a *stopping rule* that made the algorithm stop at negligibly different points on each restart. The results are nonetheless identical up to 12 digits. Thus, in this case, we were not ensnared by a local minimum/maximum. In multivariate settings, however, the optimization problem is more complex, and it wise to ensure the integrity of one's results by conducting a similar exercise to the one that is undertaken below. The objective function values over the five restarts are summarized in Table 2.1.

```
set.seed(42)
x <- rnorm(100)
bw <- npudensbw(~x,nmulti=1)
summary(bw)
```

---

[15]A co-author and I were driving from San Diego to Los Angeles for a conference on machine learning (The 33rd Symposium on the Interface of Computing Science and Statistics in June, 2001). We were discussing neural networks and nonlinear optimization, and in the middle of our conversation he remarked, "Speaking of which, I don't know if I told you, but [my wife] and I are getting divorced. I was stuck in a *local* minimum, and a bad one at that."

```
##
## Data (100 observations, 1 variable(s)):
##
## Bandwidth Selection Method: Maximum Likelihood Cross-Validation
## Formula: ~x
## Bandwidth Type: Fixed
## Objective Function Value: -147.8 (achieved on multistart 1)
##
## Var. Name: x Bandwidth: 0.4672 Scale Factor: 1.253
##
## Continuous Kernel Type: Second-Order Gaussian
## No. Continuous Vars.: 1
## Estimation Time: 0.01 seconds
bw <- npudensbw(~x,nmulti=5)
summary(bw)
##
## Data (100 observations, 1 variable(s)):
##
## Bandwidth Selection Method: Maximum Likelihood Cross-Validation
## Formula: ~x
## Bandwidth Type: Fixed
## Objective Function Value: -147.8 (achieved on multistart 2)
##
## Var. Name: x Bandwidth: 0.4672 Scale Factor: 1.253
##
## Continuous Kernel Type: Second-Order Gaussian
## No. Continuous Vars.: 1
## Estimation Time: 0.045 seconds
```

Table 2.1: Likelihood objective function value to 6 and 18 digits.

	1	2
1	-147.812	-147.811525947397968
2	-147.812	-147.811525947359115
3	-147.812	-147.811525947359144
4	-147.812	-147.811525947359939
5	-147.812	-147.811525947405215

An Illustration of Local Minima and Starting Point Selection

We consider a fairly straightforward one-dimensional minimization problem. We maximize the cross-validated likelihood function for the ordered probability estimator $\hat{p}(x)$ that was outlined in Chapter 1. We use box-constrained minimization because the smoothing parameter λ must lie in the interval $[0, 1]$. Numerical optimization routines require that the practitioner specify a *starting point*, and this can sometimes affect the location of the putative "optimal" value. For the sake of comparison, we also conduct a brute-force *grid search*, where we evaluate the likelihood function over a grid of values and select the value at which the log-likelihood function is maximized. Using the R function `optim()`, we consider numerical optimization that starts from two slightly different starting points, 0.8 and 0.9. The log-likelihood function and the values of λ that are deemed to maximize this function for the respective starting points are plotted and summarized in Figure 2.28.

```
## Functions for ordered support probability estimation
D.support <- function(X) {
  sort(unique(X))
}
Lambda <- function(X,lambda,D) {
  rowSums(sapply(1:length(D),function(i){lambda^{abs(X-D[i])}}))
}
kernel.ordered <- function(X,x,lambda,Lambda) {
  lambda^{abs(X-x)}/Lambda
}
p.ordered <- function(X,lambda,D) {
  L.X <- Lambda(X,lambda,D)
  sapply(1:length(D),function(i){mean(kernel.ordered(X,D[i],lambda,L.X))})
}
p.ordered.loo <- function(X,lambda,D) {
  L.X <- Lambda(X,lambda,D)
  sapply(1:length(X),function(i){mean(kernel.ordered(X,X[i],lambda,L.X)[-i])})
}
cv.ml.function.ordered <- function(X,lambda,D) {
    sum(log(p.ordered.loo(X,lambda,D)))
}
optim.func <- function(lambda) {cv.ml.function.ordered(X,lambda,D)}
## Create a grid for lambda and a storage vector for the likelihood
## function
lambda.seq <- seq(0,1,length=100)
cv.vec <- numeric(length(lambda.seq))
##  Simulate some data
set.seed(42)
n <- 200
p <- c(0.20, 0.20, 0.20, 0.20, 0.20)
X <- sample(c(0,1,2,9,10),n,replace=TRUE,prob=p)
D <- D.support(X)
## Conduct a grid search
for(i in 1:length(lambda.seq)) {
    cv.vec[i] <- cv.ml.function.ordered(X,lambda.seq[i],D)
}
## Conduct numerical optimization with two close starting points
## "optimal" lambda with a starting point of 0.8
foo <- optim(0.8,optim.func,method="L-BFGS-B",
             lower=0,upper=1,control=list(fnscale=-1))
lambda.0.8 <- foo$par
cv.0.8 <- foo$value
## "optimal" lambda with a starting point of 0.9
foo <- optim(0.9,optim.func,method="L-BFGS-B",
             lower=0,upper=1,control=list(fnscale=-1))
lambda.0.9 <- foo$par
cv.0.9 <- foo$value
```

```
## Grid search lambda
lambda.grid <- lambda.seq[which.max(cv.vec)]
```

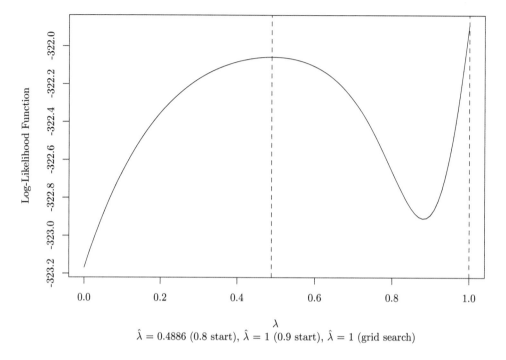

$\hat{\lambda} = 0.4886$ (0.8 start), $\hat{\lambda} = 1$ (0.9 start), $\hat{\lambda} = 1$ (grid search)

Figure 2.28: Log-likelihood function for $\lambda \in [0, 1]$.

We observe that even in the simplest of nonlinear settings, the choice of starting points matters. With a starting point of 0.8, we obtain $\hat{\lambda} = 0.4886$ and an objective function value of -322.0579. On the other hand, with a starting point of 0.9 (or with a grid search), we obtain $\hat{\lambda} = 1$ and an objective function value of -321.8876 (the value $\hat{\lambda} = 1$ is optimal here since the underlying probability function is the discrete uniform). Note that, even though a grid search on an equally-spaced grid of size 100 delivers the correct answer, this does not scale well for higher dimensions. We would need to evaluate the likelihood function over a 100×100 grid for two dimensions, a $100 \times 100 \times 100$ grid for three dimensions, and so on. This quickly becomes infeasible unless we reduce the size of the grid, in which case we suffer a loss in accuracy.

In the code chunk below, we automate the process of multi-starting for the previous example. We take `nmulti` draws from the uniform $U[0, 1]$ distribution (since $\lambda \in [0, 1]$) and re-run the optimizer `nmulti` times. We select the value of $\hat{\lambda}$ that is associated with the highest value of the objective function over all `nmulti` restarts. It is evident that local maxima are avoided and that the global maximum is indeed successfully located.

```
## Set the number of multi-starts, and then draw nmulti starting points
## in [0,1]
nmulti <- 5
lambda.init <- runif(nmulti)
## We are maximizing, so set the pre-optimization maximum for the objective
## function to -Inf
cv.opt <- -Inf
## Run the optimizer nmulti times, each time starting from different random
## initial values
for(i in 1:nmulti) {
    foo <- optim(lambda.init[i],optim.func,method="L-BFGS-B",
                 lower=0,upper=1,control=list(fnscale=-1))
    ## If we improve upon the previous maximum, save lambda and reset the
    ## maximum (cv.opt)
    if(foo$value > cv.opt) {
        cv.opt <- foo$value
        lambda.opt <- foo$par
    }
}
lambda.opt
## [1] 1
cv.opt
## [1] -321.9
```

2.9.8 Confidence Bands and Nonparametric Estimation

When constructing confidence bands for nonparametric estimators such as the Rosenblatt-Parzen kernel density estimator $\hat{f}(x)$, we encounter two challenges:

1. The estimator $\hat{f}(x)$ is biased, so our confidence bands will be centred on $\mathrm{E}\,\hat{f}(x) = f(x) + h^2 \hat{f}''(x)\kappa_2/2$ rather than $f(x)$. When the curvature $f''(x)$ is significant, our confidence bands will be quite distorted.

2. Our asymptotic results are pointwise in nature, which does not imply simultaneous coverage for all x. When using asymptotic pointwise bands, simultaneous coverage for all x can be achieved via a solution proposed by Sun and Loader (1994) that involves replacing $z_{1-\alpha/2}$ with a larger number.

The asymptotic confidence bands for the Rosenblatt-Parzen kernel density estimator are given by

$$\hat{f}(x) \pm z_{1-\alpha/2}\sqrt{\frac{\hat{f}(x)\kappa}{nh}},$$

where $1 - \alpha$ is the level of confidence.

Reliance on asymptotics has drawbacks, however, and it is often preferable to construct confidence bands via a resampling procedure such as the bootstrap. If we are concerned about our bands being centred on a biased estimate, we might want them (but not our estimate) to be bias-corrected. One approach would be to estimate $f''(x)$. However, it is more difficult to estimate derivatives of a function than the function itself, and optimal bandwidth selection for estimation of a second derivative is a non-trivial problem.

An alternative approach is to bootstrap the pointwise bias of the estimator. To accomplish this, we resample from our smooth kernel estimate $\hat{f}(x)$ rather than from the empirical distribution of the data. This is very straightforward. We compute B estimates of $\hat{f}(x)$ based on B *smooth* bootstrap replications, and the pointwise bias is then given by $B^{-1} \sum_{b=1}^{B} \hat{f}^*(x) - \hat{f}(x)$. We subtract this value from the uncorrected quantiles (or asymptotic bands) to obtain the bias-corrected confidence bands. See Calonico et al. (2018) and the accompanying R package nprobust (Calonico et al., 2017) for an alternative asymptotic procedure that is limited to the case of a single continuous variable.

A final alternative is to recognize that the kernel estimates and their uncorrected "confidence" bands are biased and to simply refer to the bands as *variability bands* since they do indeed reflect the variability of our estimate.

An Illustration of Bias-Corrected Confidence Bands

The following code chunk demonstrates the simplicity of this procedure.

```
set.seed(42)
n <- 100
neval <- 250
B <- 999
alpha <- 0.05
x <- rnorm(n)
## Compute the likelihood cross-validated bandwidth
bw <- npudensbw(~x)
## Compute the kernel estimator on a sequence of points
x.seq <- seq(-4,4,length=neval)
f <- fitted(npudens(dat=x,edat=x.seq,bws=bw$bw))
## Create matrices to hold the bootstrap replicates
f.boot.kr <- matrix(NA,B,neval)
f.boot <- matrix(NA,B,neval)
for(b in 1:B) {
  ## Resample from the raw data to get estimates of variability
  f.boot[b,]<-fitted(npudens(dat=sample(x,replace=TRUE),edat=x.seq,bws=bw$bw))
  ## Resample from the kernel estimate to bias-correct
  f.boot.kr[b,] <- fitted(npudens(dat=rnorm(n,sample(x,replace=TRUE),bw$bw)
                          ,edat=x.seq,bws=bw$bw))
}
## Compute the bootstrap pointwise bias and the true bias
bias <- colMeans(f.boot.kr) - f
true.bias <- bw$bw**2*(x.seq**2-1)*dnorm(x.seq)/2
```

We draw $n = 100$ observations from the smooth kernel estimate $\hat{f}(x)$ where $X \sim N(0,1)$. We repeat this $B = 999$ times and then compute the pointwise bootstrap bias estimate. The bootstrap bias estimate and the true bias are presented in Figure 2.29. These results are based on a Gaussian kernel function and a bandwidth ($h = 0.467$) selected via least squares cross-validation. For the Gaussian $N(0,1)$ distribution, $f''(x) = (x^2 - 1)f(x)$, and for the Gaussian kernel, $\kappa_2 = 1$. Therefore, the true bias is $h^2 f''(x)\kappa_2/2 = h^2(x^2 - 1)f(x)/2$. Figures 2.30 and 2.31 present the uncorrected and bias-corrected nonparametric confidence bands and asymptotic confidence bands.

```
dgp <- dnorm(x.seq)
ylim <- range(c(bias,true.bias))
plot(x.seq,bias,
     type="l",
     lwd=2,
     ylab="Pointwise Bias Estimate",
     xlab="$X$",
     ylim=ylim)
lines(x.seq,true.bias,col=2)
legend("bottomleft",
       c("Bootstrap Bias","True Bias ($h^2f^{''}(x)\\kappa_2/2$)"),
       col=c(1,2),
       lty=c(1,1),
       bty="n")
```

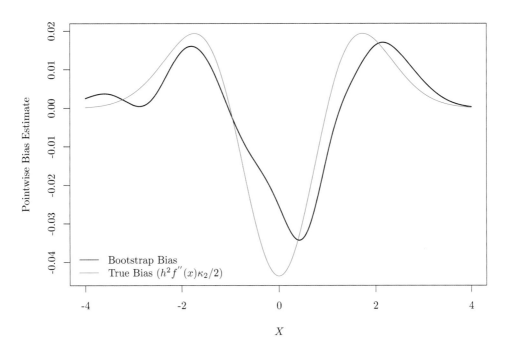

Figure 2.29: Pointwise bootstrap bias estimate.

```
par(mfrow=c(1,2),mar=c(5,4,4,2)+0.1)
bias.corr <- f - bias
q.l <- apply(f.boot,2,quantile,alpha/2)
q.u <- apply(f.boot,2,quantile,1-alpha/2)
ylim <- range(c(f,bias.corr,q.l-bias,q.u-bias,dgp))
plot(x.seq,f,
```

```
        col=1,
        type="l",
        lwd=2,
        ylim=ylim,
        xlab="$X$",
        ylab="$f(x)$")
lines(x.seq,dgp,col=2)
lines(x.seq,q.l-bias,col=3,lty=2)
lines(x.seq,q.u-bias,col=3,lty=2)
legend("topleft",
        c("$\\hat f(x)$","$f(x)$","$[q_{\\alpha/2},q_{1-\\alpha/2}]$"),
        col=c(1,2,3),
        lty=c(1,1,2),
        bty="n")
plot(x.seq,f,
        col=1,
        type="l",
        lwd=2,
        ylim=ylim,
        xlab="$X$",
        ylab="$f(x)$")
lines(x.seq,dgp,col=2)
lines(x.seq,q.l,col=3,lty=2)
lines(x.seq,q.u,col=3,lty=2)
legend("topleft",
        c("$\\hat f(x)$","$f(x)$","$[q_{\\alpha/2},q_{1-\\alpha/2}]$"),
        col=c(1,2,3),
        lty=c(1,1,2),
        bty="n")
```

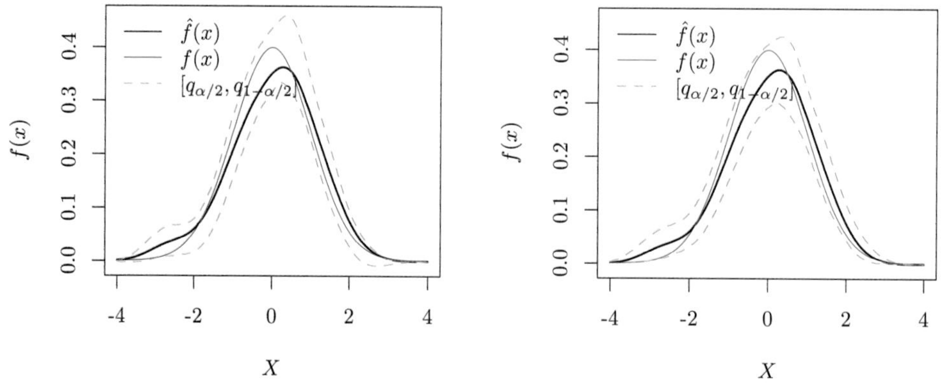

Figure 2.30: Nonparametric confidence bands; bias-corrected on the left, uncorrected on the right.

```
par(mfrow=c(1,2),mar=c(5,4,4,2)+0.1)
model <- npudens(dat=x,edat=x.seq,bws=bw$bw)
q.l <- f+qnorm(alpha/2)*model$derr
q.u <- f+qnorm(1-alpha/2)*model$derr
ylim <- range(c(f,bias.corr,q.l-bias,q.u-bias,dgp))
```

```
plot(x.seq,f,
     col=1,
     type="l",
     lwd=2,
     ylim=ylim,
     xlab="$X$",
     ylab="$f(x)$")
lines(x.seq,dgp,col=2)
lines(x.seq,q.l-bias,col=3,lty=2)
lines(x.seq,q.u-bias,col=3,lty=2)
legend("topleft",
       c("$\\hat f(x)$","$f(x)$","$[q_{\\alpha/2},q_{1-\\alpha/2}]$"),
       col=c(1,2,3),
       lty=c(1,1,2),
       bty="n")
plot(x.seq,f,
     col=1,
     type="l",
     lwd=2,
     ylim=ylim,
     xlab="$X$",
     ylab="$f(x)$")
lines(x.seq,dgp,col=2)
lines(x.seq,q.l,col=3,lty=2)
lines(x.seq,q.u,col=3,lty=2)
legend("topleft",
       c("$\\hat f(x)$","$f(x)$","$[q_{\\alpha/2},q_{1-\\alpha/2}]$"),
       col=c(1,2,3),
       lty=c(1,1,2),
       bty="n")
```

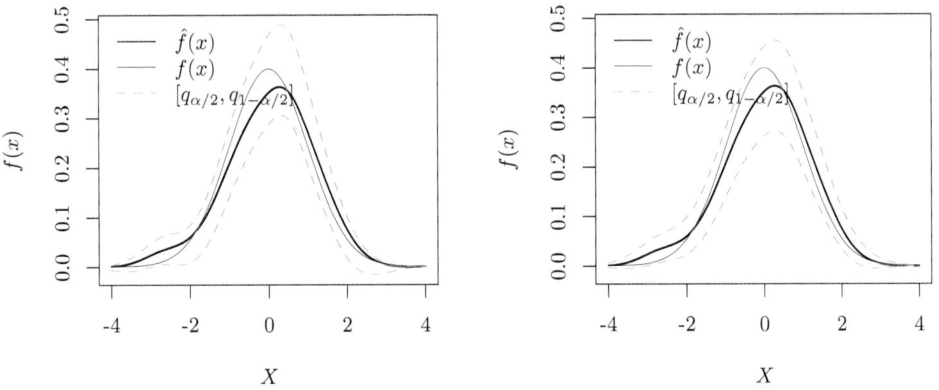

Figure 2.31: Asymptotic confidence bands; bias-corrected on the left, uncorrected on the right.

Problem Set

1. When $X \in \mathcal{D}$, we defined the sample proportion as $p_n(x) = n^{-1} \sum \mathbf{1}(X_i = x)$, and when $X \in \mathbb{R}$, we defined the histogram as $f_H(x) = (nh)^{-1} \sum \mathbf{1}(X_i$ is in the same bin as $x)$. The former is a ratio of the sum of an indicator function to the sample size n, while the latter is a ratio of the sum of an indicator function to nh, where h is the bin width. Demonstrate that each is a proper estimate of a probability mass function and a probability density function, respectively.

2. Demonstrate that the naïve density estimator $f_N(x)$ is proper.

3. Suppose that someone who is presented with an i.i.d. sample $\{X_1, X_2, \ldots, X_n\}$ would like to estimate the arithmetic mean of a continuous random variable via

$$\hat{\mu} = \int_{-\infty}^{\infty} x \hat{f}(x) \, dx,$$

   where $\hat{f}(x)$ is the Rosenblatt-Parzen kernel density estimator (you may assume that a second-order symmetric kernel function is being used).

   i. Simplify this estimator via change of variable arguments (hint - since the kernel function is symmetric, you can interchange $K((x - X_i)/h)$ and $K((X_i - x)/h)$).

   ii. Derive the bias of the simplified estimator.

   iii. Derive the variance of the simplified estimator.

   iv. What is the rate of convergence of the simplified estimator?

4. The expectation of a continuous random variable is defined as $\mu = \int_{-\infty}^{\infty} x f(x) \, dx$, while the variance of a continuous random variable is defined as $\sigma^2 = \int_{-\infty}^{\infty} (x - \mu)^2 f(x) \, dx$. For $X \in \mathbb{R}^1$, simplify the expression for σ^2 when $f(x)$ is replaced by the univariate Rosenblatt-Parzen kernel density estimator that uses a symmetric second-order kernel function. In particular, determine whether or not this estimator of σ^2 coincides with the maximum likelihood estimator of the variance, which you recall is given by

$$\hat{\sigma}^2 = n^{-1} \sum_{i=1}^{n} (X_i - \hat{\mu})^2 = n^{-1} \sum_{i=1}^{n} X_i^2 - \left(n^{-1} \sum_{i=1}^{n} X_i \right)^2,$$

   where $\hat{\mu} = n^{-1} \sum_{i=1}^{n} X_i$.

5. Consider the Rosenblatt-Parzen kernel estimator of a univariate density function, which is given by

$$\hat{f}(x) = \frac{1}{nh} \sum_{i=1}^{n} K\left(\frac{X_i - x}{h}\right),$$

where the X_i are i.i.d.

   i. Define a *higher-order kernel function* (e.g., a kernel function with the property that the order ν of its first nonzero moment is greater than 2).

   ii. What is the purpose of using a higher-order kernel function?

   iii. How does using a higher-order kernel function affect the variance?

   iv. How does using a higher-order kernel function affect the bias?

   v. Derive the IMSE and the optimal bandwidth for an eighth-order ($\nu = 8$) mean-zero symmetric kernel function.

   vi. Can you generalize your IMSE result for the eighth-order kernel function so that it applies to an arbitrary νth-order kernel function, where $\nu > 1$ is even. That is, can you express the IMSE and the resulting optimal bandwidth in terms of an even ν?

   vii. Obtain the pointwise rate of convergence of the kernel estimator $\hat{f}(x)$ that uses a νth-order kernel function (hint - use your optimal bandwidth in the formula for the root MSE and observe the power to which n is raised in your solution).

6. Consider a mean zero, symmetric, fourth-order kernel function written in polynomial form as

$$K(u) = (a + bu^2)\Phi(u),$$

where a and b are two constants that satisfy the requirements of a fourth-order kernel function (since the kernel function is symmetric, the only two restrictions that we need to consider are $\int K(u)\,du = 1$ and $\int u^2 K(u)\,du = 0$). Let $\Phi(u)$ be the standard normal kernel function given by $\Phi(u) = \frac{1}{\sqrt{2\pi}} e^{-\frac{1}{2}u^2}$. Hence $\int \Phi(u)\,du = 1$, $\int u\Phi(u)\,du = 0$, $\int u^2\Phi(u)\,du = 1$, $\int u^3\Phi(u)\,du = 0$, $\int u^4\Phi(u)\,du = 3$, $\int u^5\Phi(u)\,du = 0$, $\int u^6\Phi(u)\,du = 15$, and so on. Demonstrate that this fourth-order kernel function has a solution that is given by

$$K(u) = \left(\frac{3}{2} - \frac{1}{2}u^2\right)\Phi(u).$$

What is $\kappa_4 = \int u^4 K(u)\,du$ for this kernel function?

Chapter 3

Mixed-Data Probability Density and Cumulative Distribution Functions

> We are looking for structure in a set of numbers without imposing rigid parametric assumptions but within a statistical framework of some sort. (Chu and Marron, 1991)

3.1 Overview

As noted in Chapter 1, the first random variable that students of basic statistics typically encounter is the *discrete* random variable. Having studied discrete random variables and their associated probability functions, students then proceed to the study of *continuous* random variables and their associated probability density functions, as we did in Chapter 2. A logical next step is to study mixed discrete and continuous random variables and the joint probability density functions[1] that characterize them, but we are not aware of any introductory statistics text that considers these objects, which are known to be "parametrically awkward" (Aitchison and Aitken, 1976, page 419). On the other hand, modeling these objects in a nonparametric framework is very straightforward, and hence we fill this gap with a chapter on mixed discrete and continuous probability density functions.

In both parametric and nonparametric settings, when facing a mix of discrete and continuous data, researchers have traditionally resorted to a *frequency* approach. This involves splitting the continuous data into subsets (*cells*) according to the realizations of the discrete data. For nonparametric and correctly specified parametric models, this will of course produce consis-

---

[1]The proper name for the joint distribution of a set of mixed-data types is indeed a *density* function, and it all turns on the notion of which *measure* is used for each data type.

Table 3.1: Counts of the number of dependants present in 526 households.

numdep	0	1	2	3	4	5	6
counts	252	105	99	45	16	7	2

tent estimates. However, for a given sample size, as the number of subsets increases, the amount of data in each cell falls, which leads to a *sparse data* problem. In such cases, there may be insufficient data in each subset to deliver sensible density estimates, since the estimates will be highly variable.

Example 3.1. Wooldridge's wage1 Data.

By way of illustration, consider the wage1 dataset (Wooldridge, 2002), which is a cross-section of wage data based on a random sample of $n = 526$ observations from the U.S. Current Population Survey for the year 1976. Consider two variables, one of which is continuous (`lwage`) and the other of which is discrete (`numdep`). `lwage` is the logarithm of an individual's average hourly earnings, and `numdep` is the individual's number of dependants $\{0, 1, \ldots, 6\}$. The number of observations in each cell is tabulated in Table 3.1. We can now appreciate the dilemma that is faced by the practitioner. We could split our data into cells and model a separate density of the continuous variable `lwage` based on the data in each cell. However, we see from Table 3.1 that there are only 2 households with 6 dependants, so we would be attempting to model a PDF based on only 2 observations. This would not be reliable, *even if we have correctly specified the parametric model*. It might in fact be beneficial to *borrow* information from other cells, that is, to *shrink* the cell estimates towards a *pooled* estimate. This is in fact what the kernel methods that are described below are designed to accomplish.

3.2 Smooth Mixed-Data Kernel Density and Cumulative Distribution Function Estimation

Suppose that we are faced with a dataset consisting of two random variables, one of which is continuous ($X^c \in \mathbb{R}$) and the other of which is discrete ($X^d \in \mathcal{D}$ with cardinality c). We would like to model their joint density function $f(x) = f(x^c, x^d)$, where the superscripts ^{c} and ^{d} denote continuous and discrete data types, respectively, and where $x = (x^c, x^d) \in \mathbb{R} \times \mathcal{D}$.

Using a product kernel function as we did in Chapters 1 and 2 for the multivariate extensions of $\hat{p}(x)$ and $\hat{f}(x)$, the kernel estimator of $f(x^c, d^d)$ is defined as

$$\hat{f}(x^c, x^d) = \frac{1}{nh} \sum_{i=1}^{n} K\left(\frac{X_i^c - x^c}{h}\right) L(X_i^d, x^d, \lambda),$$

where $K(\cdot)$ and $L(\cdot)$ are univariate continuous and categorical kernel functions, respectively. We assume without loss of generality that the discrete variable X^d is a nominal categorical variable (i.e., it is unordered). Hence we can use Aitchison and Aitken's unordered kernel function, which you recall is defined as

$$L(X_i^d, x^d, \lambda) = \begin{cases} 1 - \lambda & \text{if } X_i^d = x^d \\ \lambda/(c-1) & \text{otherwise,} \end{cases}$$

where $\lambda \in [0, (c-1)/c]$ and $\sum_{t^d \in \mathcal{D}} L(t^d, x^d, \lambda) = 1$. We assume that $K(z)$ is a standard second-order kernel, i.e., it is real-valued, non-negative, bounded, and symmetric, and it satisfies $K(z) \geq 0$, $\int_{-\infty}^{\infty} K(z)\, dz = 1$, $\int_{-\infty}^{\infty} z K(z)\, dz = 0$, and $0 < \int_{-\infty}^{\infty} z^2 K(z)\, dz = \kappa_2 < \infty$.

3.2.1   Properties of the Mixed-Data Smooth Kernel Density Estimator

Under standard regularity conditions, it can be shown that the bias of $\hat{f}(x^c, x^d)$ up to $O(h^2 + \lambda)$ is

$$\text{Bias } \hat{f}(x^c, x^d) = -\frac{\lambda(cf(x^c, x^d) - f(x^c))}{c-1} + \frac{h^2}{2} f''(x^c, x^d)\kappa_2,$$

where $f(x^c) = \sum_{x^d \in \mathcal{D}} f(x^c, x^d)$. The variance of $\hat{f}(x^c, x^d)$ up to $O(1/(nh))$ can be shown to be

$$\text{Var } \hat{f}(x^c, x^d) = \frac{f(x^c, x^d)}{nh} \kappa.$$

Note that the variance does not depend on λ and it is of the same order as the univariate Rosenblatt-Parzen estimator. The IMSE-optimal smoothing parameters can be shown to be

$$h_{opt} = \left(\frac{\kappa}{\sum_{x^d} \int \phi_3^2\, dx^c - \frac{\left(\sum_{x^d} \int \phi_2 \phi_3\, dx^c\right)^2}{\sum_{x^d} \int \phi_2^2\, dx^c}}\right)^{1/5} n^{-1/5},$$

$$\lambda_{opt} = \frac{h_{opt}^2 \sum_{x^d} \int \phi_2 \phi_3\, dx^c}{2 \sum_{x^d} \int \phi_2^2\, dx^c}$$

$$= \frac{\sum_{x^d} \int \phi_2 \phi_3\, dx^c}{2 \sum_{x^d} \int \phi_2^2\, dx^c} \left(\frac{\kappa}{\sum_{x^d} \int \phi_3^2\, dx^c - \frac{\left(\sum_{x^d} \int \phi_2 \phi_3\, dx^c\right)^2}{\sum_{x^d} \int \phi_2^2\, dx^c}}\right)^{2/5} n^{-2/5},$$

where $\phi_2 = (cf(x^c, x^d) - f(x^c))/(c - 1)$ and $\phi_3 = f''(x^c, x^d)\kappa_2$. Plugging these IMSE-optimal bandwidths back into the formula for the MSE or IMSE reveals that this *bivariate* kernel estimator has the same rate of convergence as the *univariate* Rosenblatt-Parzen kernel density estimator (i.e., the root MSE is of order $O(n^{-2/5})$). Note that the discrete variable contributes to the bias but not the variance of the estimator, which is a feature of all mixed-data kernel estimators.

Application of Liapounov's CLT delivers

$$\sqrt{nh}\left(\hat{f}(x) - f(x) - \text{Bias}\,\hat{f}(x)\right) \xrightarrow{d} N\left(0, f(x)\kappa\right).$$

Similar results hold when the discrete variable is ordered, and their derivation is left as an exercise.

Bandwidth selection proceeds in exactly the same manner as in Chapter 2; least squares and likelihood cross-validation extend easily to this setting. See Li and Racine (2003) for the theoretical underpinnings of least squares cross-validation in a mixed-data context.

Example 3.2. Log-Wages and Number of Dependants.

Figure 3.1 presents the joint PDF estimate for `lwage` (continuous) and `numdep` (ordered).

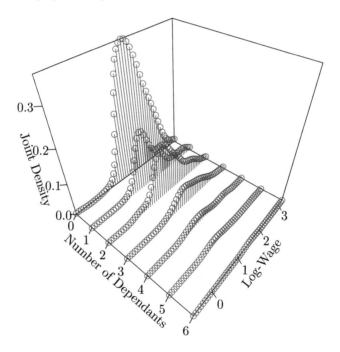

Figure 3.1: Mixed-data bivariate kernel density estimate for the joint PDF of lwage (continuous) and numdeps (ordered).

3.2.2 Properties of the Mixed-Data Smooth Kernel Cumulative Distribution Estimator

Consider the kernel estimator of a joint cumulative distribution function for one continuous and one ordered discrete variable, $\hat{F}(x^c, x^d)$, which we define as

$$\hat{F}(x^c, x^d) = \int_{-\infty}^{x^c} \sum_{t^d \leq x^d} \hat{f}(t^c, t^d) \, dt^c$$

$$= \frac{1}{n} \sum_{i=1}^{n} \int_{-\infty}^{x^c} K\left(\frac{t^c - X_i^c}{h}\right) \frac{dt^c}{h} \sum_{t^d \leq x^d} l(X_i^d, t^d, \lambda)$$

$$= \frac{1}{n} \sum_{i=1}^{n} G\left(\frac{x^c - X_i^c}{h}\right) \mathcal{L}(X_i^d, x^d, \lambda)$$

where $G(\cdot)$ and $\mathcal{L}(\cdot)$ are the cumulative counterparts to $K(\cdot)$ and $l(\cdot)$ that were outlined in Chapters 1 and 2. Under standard regularity conditions, it can be shown that the bias is of order $O(h^2 + \lambda)$ and that the variance is of order $O(1/n)$. Application of Liapounov's CLT delivers

$$\sqrt{n}\left(\hat{F}(x) - F(x)\right) \xrightarrow{d} N\left(0, F(x)(1 - F(x))\right).$$

Note that this estimator's root IMSE is of order $O(1/\sqrt{n})$, just like its univariate counterparts.

A least squares cross-validation procedure for selecting h and λ has been proposed by Li et al. (2017), who also provide theoretical support for this estimator. The functions `npudistbw()` and `npudist()` in the R package np implement this approach.

Example 3.3. Log-Wages and Number of Dependants.

> Figure 3.2 presents the joint CDF estimate for `lwage` (continuous) and `numdep` (ordered).

3.3 The Multivariate Extension

Extension of the preceding results to the multivariate setting is fairly straightforward. With minor modification, each of the estimators that we have outlined thus far has a natural multivariate counterpart. In a multivariate setting, the probability density function $f(x)$ might encompass a combination of continuous, unordered, and ordered variables (here, x is a vector but $f(x)$ is clearly a scalar). Suppose that we have q continuous, r unordered, and s ordered variables. The product kernel for estimating the joint density function is given by

$$\prod_{j=1}^{q} h_j^{-1} K\left(\frac{x_j^c - X_{ij}^c}{h_j}\right) \prod_{j=1}^{r} L(X_{ij}^u, x_j^u, \lambda_j^u) \prod_{j=1}^{s} l(X_{ij}^o, x_j^o, \lambda_j^o)$$

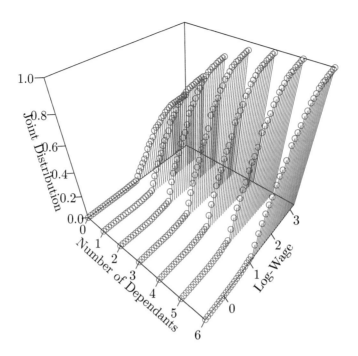

Figure 3.2: Mixed-data bivariate kernel density estimate for the joint CDF of lwage (continuous) and numdeps (ordered).

and the resulting estimator is

$$\hat{f}(x) = \frac{1}{n} \sum_{i=1}^{n} \prod_{j=1}^{q} h_j^{-1} K\left(\frac{x_j^c - X_{ij}^c}{h_j}\right) \prod_{j=1}^{r} L(X_{ij}^u, x_j^u, \lambda_j^u) \prod_{j=1}^{s} l(X_{ij}^o, x_j^o, \lambda_j^o),$$

where the superscripts ^{c}, ^{u} and ^{o} serve to distinguish the continuous, unordered and ordered variables, respectively. Note that x is a $(q + r + s)$-dimensional vector that consists of q continuous, r unordered, and s ordered variables, and that each variable in the product kernel has its own smoothing parameter. When using the R package np, the operators `factor()` and `ordered()` allow you to cast your variables according to their type, and the appropriate kernels are subsequently automatically applied without any additional input from the user (the default data type is `numeric()`, which is taken to be continuous).

To simplify notation and provide for a parsimonious object that can handle any combination of data types, define the *generalized* product kernel function

$$K_\gamma(X_i, x) = \prod_{j=1}^{q} h_j^{-1} K\left(\frac{x_j^c - X_{ij}^c}{h_j}\right) \prod_{j=1}^{r} L(X_{ij}^u, x_j^u, \lambda_j^u) \prod_{j=1}^{s} l(X_{ij}^o, x_j^o, \lambda_j^o)$$

so that the estimator of the multivariate mixed-data joint PDF is expressed more concisely as

$$\hat{f}(x) = \frac{1}{n} \sum_{i=1}^{n} K_\gamma(X_i, x),$$

where $\gamma = (h_1, h_2, \ldots, h_q, \lambda_1^u, \lambda_2^u, \ldots, \lambda_r^u, \lambda_1^o, \lambda_2^o, \ldots, \lambda_s^o)$.

If instead we are modeling the multivariate mixed-data joint CDF $F(x)$, which is defined only for ordered data types, then the resulting estimator is given by

$$\hat{F}(x) = \frac{1}{n} \sum_{i=1}^{n} \prod_{j=1}^{q} G\left(\frac{x_j^c - X_{ij}^c}{h_j}\right) \prod_{j=1}^{s} \mathcal{L}(X_{ij}^o, x_j^o, \lambda_j^o)$$

$$= \frac{1}{n} \sum_{i=1}^{n} G_\gamma(X_i, x),$$

where $\gamma = (h_1, h_2, \ldots, h_q, \lambda_1^o, \lambda_2^o, \ldots, \lambda_s^o)$.

Both of these estimators are biased in finite samples but they are less variable than their empirical nonsmooth counterparts. The leading bias of $\hat{f}(x)$ is of order $O(\sum_{j=1}^{q} h_j^2 + \sum_{j=1}^{r} \lambda_j^u + \sum_{j=1}^{s} \lambda_j^o)$, while that of $\hat{F}(x)$ is of order $O(\sum_{j=1}^{q} h_j^2 + \sum_{j=1}^{s} \lambda_j^o)$. The leading variance terms are identical to those noted for the estimators' multivariate continuous-only counterparts, so we can once again obtain the results

$$\sqrt{n \prod_{j=1}^{q} h_j} \left(\hat{f}(x) - f(x) - \text{Bias } \hat{f}(x)\right) \xrightarrow{d} N\left(0, f(x)\kappa^q\right)$$

and

$$\sqrt{n} \left(\hat{F}(x) - F(x)\right) \xrightarrow{d} N\left(0, F(x)(1 - F(x))\right).$$

Observe that there is no curse of dimensionality associated with the multivariate kernel CDF estimator. Smoothing parameter selection proceeds in the same manner as in the univariate case, with the modification that a vector of smoothing parameters must now be selected; see Li and Racine (2003) and Li et al. (2017) for further details.

3.4 Smooth Kernel Copula Function Estimation with Mixed-Data

Copulae are functions that "couple" multivariate distribution functions to their one-dimensional marginal distribution functions (Nelsen, 2006, page 1). Copulae are popular because they provide scale-free measures of dependence among components of random vectors. They are useful when the objective is to characterize co-monotonicity among variables or to analyze the behaviour of variables that simultaneously assume large (or small) values. Given that the study of copulae entails the study of (unknown) marginal and joint distributions, nonparametric approaches have obvious appeal. They are a solid alternative to parametric copulae, which can rarely be generalized beyond two variables. A number of nonparametric approaches that have been proposed do, however, suffer from certain limitations that restrict their general utility. There is now a growing interest in estimation of copulae with discrete marginals and/or a mix of discrete and continuous marginals (see e.g., Smith and Khaled (2012) for a Bayesian approach), and the recent development of nonparametric approaches with mixed-data types is ideally-suited to this task. Below we describe a data-driven approach that supports mixed-data types and that does not suffer from some of the complications that are associated with many existing kernel-based methods.

Copula-based methods have attracted the attention of practitioners in a range of disciplines. For instance, in a comprehensive survey of multivariate GARCH models, Bauwens et al. (2006) provide an overview of the parametric copula-MGARCH (Multivariate GARCH) framework. These models are specified by GARCH equations for the conditional variances, marginal distributions for each series, and a conditional copula function. The copula's parameters are time-varying and may even be functions of past data. The benefit of such approaches, at least in the bivariate case, is the flexible nature of their joint distributions. Trivedi and Zimmer (2007) have written an accessible monograph that outlines uses of parametric copulae in applied econometrics, with particular emphasis on estimation and misspecification. An appealing aspect of parametrically specified copulae is that estimation and inference are based on standard maximum likelihood procedures. We direct the interested reader to these encyclopedic references that capture the salient features of parametric copulae in an econometric context. Semiparametric copula models, which are more flexible than fully parametric models but not as flexible as nonparametric models, have been considered by Tsukahara (2005), Chen et al. (2006) and Chen et al. (2009b), among others. The approach that we propose allows practitioners to overcome the potential limitations of parametric copulae by embracing nonparametric methods that are computationally efficient and that handle the range of ordered categorical and continuous data types that are often encountered in applied settings.

We take an inversion approach to estimation of the copula and, in a similar fashion to Fermanian and Scaillet (2003), we exploit Sklar's theorem (Nelsen, 2006, Corollary 2.3.7) to produce copulae directly from the joint distribution function. Given a bivariate distribution function H with continuous marginals F and G, we can *invert* (Nelsen, 2006, page 51) to obtain the copula using

$$C(u_x, u_y) = H(F^{-1}(u_x), G^{-1}(u_y)).$$

Here, we produce copulae directly from the joint distribution function using $C(u_x, u_y) = H(F^{-1}(u_x), G^{-1}(u_y))$, as opposed to the typical approach that instead uses $H(x, y) = C(F(x), G(y))$. Of course, the object $C(\cdot)$ is well-defined regardless of which representation is used, and it must coincide with $H(\cdot)$. Taking this approach, we directly obtain $\hat{H}(x, y) = \hat{H}(\hat{F}^{-1}(\hat{u}_x), \hat{G}^{-1}(\hat{u}_y)) = \hat{C}(\hat{u}_x, \hat{u}_y)$. The approach that is proposed by Fermanian and Scaillet (2003) is for continuous data types only, and it makes use of ad-hoc bandwidths ($h_i = \hat{\sigma}_i n^{-1/5}$, $j = 1, 2$) that are not optimal for either copula or copula density estimation. For each marginal, we use the associated bandwidth that was used to compute $\hat{H}(x, y)$, and we compute $\hat{u}_x$ and $\hat{u}_y$ directly, thereby delivering $\hat{C}(\hat{u}_x, \hat{u}_y)$. Therefore, each marginal sample realization (i.e., X_i) has direct $\hat{u}_{X_i} = \hat{F}(X_i)$, where

$$\hat{F}(x) = \int_{-\infty}^{x} \hat{f}(v) \, dv = \frac{1}{n} \sum_{i=1}^{n} \mathcal{G}\left(\frac{x - X_i}{h}\right),$$

and where $\mathcal{G}(x) = \int_{-\infty}^{x} K(v) \, dv$ and $K(v)$ is a standard kernel used for density estimation such as the Gaussian or Epanechnikov. This directly delivers $\hat{H}(x, \infty) = \hat{C}(\hat{u}_x, 1)$, guaranteeing that the quantiles $\hat{F}^{-1}(\hat{u}_x)$, the $\hat{u}_x$, and the $\hat{C}(\hat{u}_x, 1)$ estimates are internally consistent, which is axiomatically desirable. Furthermore, if we need to evaluate the copula at a (u_x, u_y) pair other than the sample $(\hat{u}_{X_i}, \hat{u}_{Y_i})$, we can compute the *quasi-inverse* (see Nelsen (2006), Definition 2.3.6, page 21). We adopt this approach in our implementation which we now briefly describe. The quasi inverse is given by

$$F^{(-1)}(u) = \inf\{x : F(x) \geq u\}. \tag{3.1}$$

To operationalize this inverse, we construct a very fine grid of points $x_1', x_2', \dots$ that extends far beyond the support of the data. Then, for any $u \in [0, 1]$, the quasi-inverse is the value among the $x_1', x_2', \dots$ that satisfies Equation (3.1).

This approach avoids the use of boundary corrections and ensures that there is no divergence between the marginals derived from the copula and those used to construct the copula. In addition, standard distributional theory holds since this approach is based on direct application of conventional kernel estimators (see, e.g., Liu and Yang (2008)).

For copula density estimation, we can use the same approach, again avoiding the complications that arise from the use of boundary kernels and so forth. The copula density is

$$c(u) = \frac{\partial^d C(u_1, \dots, u_d)}{\partial u_1 \cdots \partial u_d} \tag{3.2}$$

$$= \frac{f(F_1^{-1}(u_1), \dots, F_d^{-1}(u_d))}{f_1(F_1^{-1}(u_1)) \cdots f_d(F_d^{-1}(u_d))}. \tag{3.3}$$

It is *scale free* by design and, for independent random variates, it is clearly equal to one. The copula density is the ratio of the joint PDF to what it would have been under independence. For mixed-data types, we suggest the least squares cross-validation bandwidth selector of Li and Racine (2003).

3.4.1   Copulae and Dependence

As pointed out by Fermanian and Scaillet (2003) and a number of other authors, there are two reasons why copulae are popular. First, they serve to characterize independence and co-monotonicity among variables. Second, they facilitate analysis of the behaviour of variables when they simultaneously assume large (or small) values. We briefly discuss these applications below.

Independence and Co-monotonicity

Copulae characterize independence and co-monotonicity between random variables. It is well known that a set of random variables are independent if and only if their joint PDFs (CDFs) are equal to the product of their marginal PDFs (CDFs). In terms of the copula function, this means that independence is characterized by $C(u) = \prod_{j=1}^{d} u_j$ for all u. Furthermore, each random variable is almost surely a strictly increasing function of any of the others (co-monotonicity) if and only if $C(u) = \min\{u_1, \ldots, u_d\}$ for all u.

Copulae are also intimately related to standard measures of dependence between two real-valued random variables X and Y. Indeed, the population versions of Kendall's tau (Kendall, 1938), Spearman's rho (Spearman, 1904), Gini's gamma (Gini, 1914), and Blomqvist's beta (Blomqvist, 1950) can be expressed as:

$$\tau_{x,y} = 1 - 4 \int_0^1 \int_0^1 \frac{\partial C(u_x, u_y)}{\partial u_x} \frac{\partial C(u_x, u_y)}{\partial u_y} \, du_x \, du_y,$$

$$\rho_{x,y} = 12 \int_0^1 \int_0^1 C(u_x, u_y) \, du_x \, du_y - 3,$$

$$\gamma_{x,y} = 4 \int_0^1 \int_0^1 [C(u_x, 1 - u_x) + C(u_x, u_x)] \, du_x - 2,$$

$$\beta_{x,y} = 4C(1/2, 1/2) - 1.$$

Note that the derivations used to obtain Equation (3.3) are the same as those that deliver objects such as, e.g., $\partial C(u_x, u_y)/\partial u_x$ in the equation above.

Tail Dependence

Copulae can be used to analyze how two random variables behave together when they simultaneously assume large (or small) values. For example, in finance, they are useful for examining the joint behaviour of large negative returns (large losses). This type of behaviour can be described by *positive quadrant dependence* (Lehmann, 1966).

Two random variables X and Y are *positively quadrant dependent* (PQD) if, for all (x, y) in $\mathbb{R}^2$,

$$\Pr(X \le x, Y \le y) \ge \Pr(X \le x) \Pr(Y \le y). \tag{3.4}$$

That is, two random variables are PQD if the probability that they are simultaneously small is at least as great as it would be if they were independent. When dealing with more than two variables, we say that they are *positively orthant dependent* (POD). Inequality (3.4) can be rewritten in terms of the copula C of the two random variables, since it is equivalent to the condition $C(u_x, u_y) \geq u_x u_y$ for all (u_x, u_y) in $[0,1]^2$. By applying Bayes's rule, one can also rewrite inequality (3.4) as $\Pr(X \leq x | Y \leq y) \geq \Pr(X \leq x)$. The PQD condition may be strengthened by requiring the conditional probability to be a non-increasing function of y. This implies that the probability of a small value of the return X does not increase as the value of the other return increases. It corresponds to particular monotonicities in the tails. We say that a random variable X is left tail decreasing in Y, denoted $\text{LTD}(X|Y)$, if $\Pr(X \leq x | Y \leq y)$ is a non-increasing function of y for all x. This, in turn, is equivalent to the condition that, for all u_x in $[0, 1]$, $C(u_x, u_y)/u_y$ is non-increasing in u_y, or $\partial C(u_x, u_y)/\partial u_y \leq C(u_x, u_y)/u_y$ for almost all u_y.

The notions of independence, PQD, and LTD are characterized in terms of copulae, and hence they may be verified once copulae have been estimated. Generalization of these concepts to a setting that involves mixed-data kernel copula estimators is straightforward. Inference has been considered by Denuit and Scaillet (2004) and Scaillet (2005), among others.

We can make use of the R function `npcopula()` in the np package for estimation of multivariate copulae defined over mixed-data types.

Example 3.4. Simulated Data Illustration.

Figure 3.3 presents a simulated example of a mixed-data copula and copula density.

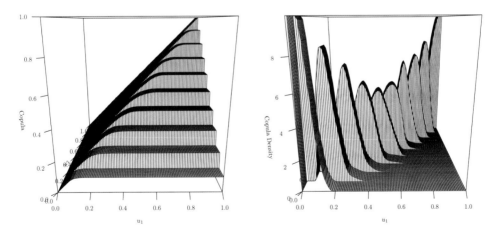

Figure 3.3: Simulated illustration of a mixed-data copula and copula density.

3.5 Practitioner's Corner

3.5.1 Testing Equality of Mixed-Data Multivariate Densities

There exist a number of kernel-based tests of equality of distribution functions, although most of them presume that the underlying variable is *continuous* in nature; see Ahmad and van Belle (1974), Mammen (1992), Fan and Gencay (1993), Li (1996), Fan and Ullah (1999), and the references therein. Li et al. (2009a) propose a nonparametric test for equality of multivariate densities encompassing both continuous and categorical data. This test can be implemented via the `npdeneqtest()` function in the R package np. Let X and Y be multivariate vectors of dimension $q + r$, where q denotes the number of continuous variables and r denotes the number of discrete/categorical variables. Suppose that we wish to test the null

$$H_0 : f(x) = g(x) \text{ almost everywhere (a.e.)}$$

against the alternative

$$H_1 : f(x) \neq g(x) \text{ on a set with positive measure.}$$

A test statistic based on the integrated squared density difference is given by

$$I = \int (f(x) - g(x))^2 \, dx$$
$$= \int (f(x)dF(x) + g(x)dG(x) - f(x)dG(x) - g(x)dF(x)),$$

where $F(\cdot)$ and $G(\cdot)$ are the CDFs of X and Y, respectively, and where $\int dx = \sum_{x^d \in \mathcal{D}} \int dx^c$. We replace the first occurrences of $f(\cdot)$ and $g(\cdot)$ by their leave-one-out kernel estimates, and replace $F(\cdot)$ and $G(\cdot)$ by their ECDFs. The resulting statistic is denoted by I_n. Li et al. (2009a) demonstrate that, under the null of equality,

$$T_n = \sqrt{n_1 n_2 \prod_{j=1}^{q} h_j} \, \frac{I_n}{\sigma_n} \rightarrow N(0,1) \text{ in distribution,}$$

where σ_n^2 is the variance of I_n. Under the alternative, the statistic diverges to $+\infty$, so the test is one-sided and results in rejection when the statistic is sufficiently large.

The test that uses critical values taken from the asymptotic distribution displays finite sample size distortions. Hence the `npdeneqtest()` function employs bootstrap resampling to obtain the finite sample distribution of the statistic. This provides a test that has correct size. The bootstrap resamples are obtained by resampling from the empirical distribution of the pooled data; that is, they are drawn from a common multivariate distribution under the null. Bandwidths are obtained by default via likelihood cross-validation.

The following code chunk provides two simple examples that involve a mix of continuous and discrete data. Note that the two samples must be data frames with identically named variables (e.g., the variables `wages` and `experience` must be common to both data frames, with females represented in sample A and males represented in sample B).

```
set.seed(42)
n <- 250
## Distributions are equal
sample.A <- data.frame(a=rnorm(n),b=factor(rbinom(n,2,.5)))
sample.B <- data.frame(a=rnorm(n),b=factor(rbinom(n,2,.5)))
npdeneqtest(sample.A,sample.B,boot.num=99)
##
## Consistent Density Equality Test
## 99 Bootstrap Replications
##
## Test Statistic 'Tn': -0.6911 P Value: 0.83
## ---
## Signif. codes:  0 '***' 0.001 '**' 0.01 '*' 0.05 '.' 0.1 ' ' 1
## Fail to reject the null of equality at the 10% level
## Distributions are unequal
sample.A <- data.frame(a=rnorm(n),b=factor(rbinom(n,2,.5)))
sample.B <- data.frame(a=rnorm(n,sd=10),b=factor(rbinom(n,2,.25)))
npdeneqtest(sample.A,sample.B,boot.num=99)
##
## Consistent Density Equality Test
## 99 Bootstrap Replications
##
## Test Statistic 'Tn': 55.74   P Value: <2e-16 ***
## ---
## Signif. codes:  0 '***' 0.001 '**' 0.01 '*' 0.05 '.' 0.1 ' ' 1
## Null of equality is rejected at the 0.1% level
```

3.5.2 Generating Copula Function Contours

The copula and copula density estimates that have been presented in this chapter are not always of direct interest. Instead, *contours* (iso-probability/iso-density lines) are often a preferred means of summarizing the copula estimates. The following code chunk demonstrates how one can plot bivariate copula function contours.

```
require(MASS)
set.seed(42)
## Simulate correlated Gaussian data (rho(x,y)=0.99)
n <- 1000
n.eval <- 100
rho <- 0.99
mu <- c(0,0)
Sigma <- matrix(c(1,rho,rho,1),2,2)
mydat <- mvrnorm(n=n, mu, Sigma)
mydat <- data.frame(x=mydat[,1],
                    y=ordered(as.integer(cut(mydat[,2],
```

```
                         quantile(mydat[,2],seq(0,1,by=.1)),
                         include.lowest=TRUE))-1))
q.min <- 0.0
q.max <- 1.0
grid.seq <- seq(q.min,q.max,length=n.eval)
grid.dat <- cbind(grid.seq,grid.seq)
## Estimate the copula (bw object obtained from npudistbw())
bw.cdf <- npudistbw(~x+y,data=mydat)
copula <- npcopula(bws=bw.cdf,data=mydat,u=grid.dat)
## Plot the copula
contour(grid.seq,grid.seq,matrix(copula$copula,n.eval,n.eval),
        xlab="$u_1$",
        ylab="$u_2$",
        sub="Copula Contour")
```

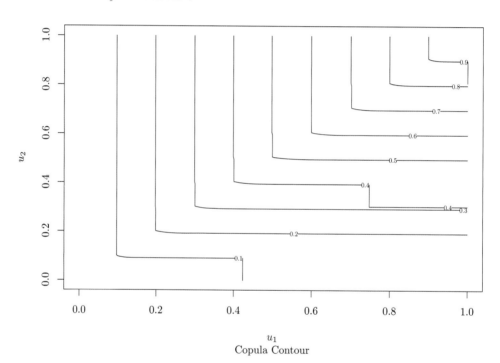

Copula Contour

Problem Set

1. Consider the kernel estimator of a joint density function for one continuous and one discrete variable, $\hat{f}(x^c, x^d)$, given by

$$\hat{f}(x^c, x^d) = \frac{1}{nh} \sum_{i=1}^{n} K\left(\frac{X_i^c - x^c}{h}\right) L(X_i^d, x^d, \lambda),$$

where $K(\cdot)$ and $L(\cdot)$ are continuous and categorical kernel functions, respectively, $X^c \in \mathbb{R}$, $X^d \in \mathcal{D} = \{0, 1, \ldots, c-1\}$, and c is the number of outcomes for the discrete variable. Assume that the discrete variable X^d is a nominal categorical variable (i.e., it is unordered). Hence we might use Aitchison and Aitken's unordered kernel function, which is given by

$$L(X_i^d, x^d, \lambda) = \begin{cases} 1 - \lambda & \text{if } X_i^d = x^d \\ \lambda/(c-1) & \text{otherwise,} \end{cases}$$

where $\lambda \in [0, (c-1)/c]$ and $\sum_{t^d \in \mathcal{D}} L(t^d, x^d, \lambda) = (1-\lambda) + (c-1)\lambda/(c-1) = 1$. Assume that $K(z)$ is a standard *second-order* kernel, i.e., it is real-valued, non-negative, bounded, and symmetric, and it satisfies $K(z) \geq 0$, $\int_{-\infty}^{\infty} K(z)\,dz = 1$, $\int_{-\infty}^{\infty} zK(z)\,dz = 0$, and $\int_{-\infty}^{\infty} z^2 K(z)\,dz = \kappa_2 < \infty$. Suppose that you are presented with i.i.d. draws from $f(x^c, x^d)$. It might be helpful to note that when taking expectations with respect to a discrete and a continuous random variable, you need to do the following

$$\mathrm{E}\,K\left(\frac{X_1^c - x^c}{h}\right) L(X_1^d, x^d, \lambda) = \sum_{t^d \in \mathcal{D}} \int_{-\infty}^{\infty} K\left(\frac{t^c - x^c}{h}\right) L(t^d, x^d, \lambda) \times$$
$$f(t^c, t^d)\,dt^c.$$

You can exploit the *product kernel* setup, so

$$\sum_{t^d \in \mathcal{D}} \int_{-\infty}^{\infty} K\left(\frac{t^c - x^c}{h}\right) L(t^d, x^d, \lambda) f(t^c, t^d)\,dt^c$$

is equal to

$$\sum_{t^d \in \mathcal{D}} L(t^d, x^d, \lambda) \int_{-\infty}^{\infty} K\left(\frac{t^c - x^c}{h}\right) f(t^c, t^d)\, dt^c.$$

You will likely want to take a (univariate) Taylor expansion of the density around the continuous variable. No such thing is needed when considering the discrete variable, so you will take an expansion of $f(x^c + zh, t^d)$ around x^c, letting $f'(x^c, t^d) = df(x^c, t^d)/dx^c$ and so forth. It may also be of interest to note that $f(x^c, x^d) + \sum_{t^d \in \mathcal{D}, t^d \neq x^d} f(x^c, t^d) = \sum_{t^d \in \mathcal{D}} f(x^c, t^d)$ and that $\sum_{t^d \in \mathcal{D}} f(x^c, t^d) = f(x^c)$. When considering certain expansions, it will also be useful to note that λ turns out to be of the same order as h^2, which implies that terms of $O(h^2\lambda)$ will be of the same order as terms of $O(h^4)$, etc.

   i. What is the bias of this estimator up to terms of $O(h^2)$ and $O(\lambda)$?

   ii. What is the variance of this estimator up to terms of $O(1/(nh))$?

   iii. Obtain the optimal bandwidths and rate of convergence for this estimator.

Chapter 4

Conditional Probability Density and Cumulative Distribution Functions

> Essentially, all models are wrong, but some are useful. (Box, 1976)

4.1 Overview

Conditional density and distribution functions underpin many statistical objects that are of interest to practitioners, such as the conditional moments appearing in Chapter 5. They are, however, rarely modelled directly in parametric settings and they have received limited attention in a kernel context. Nevertheless, they are extremely useful for a range of tasks. While direct estimation of the conditional density function is often interesting in its own right, it can be useful for modeling binary, multinomial, or count outcome data (see Cameron and Trivedi (1998) for a thorough treatment of count data models). Modeling conditional quantiles can be achieved via estimation and inversion of a conditional CDF and regression analysis, which entails modeling conditional means, depends directly on the conditional density function. Hence the conditional PDF and CDF constitute the backbone of many popular statistical methods.

The conditional PDF is defined as

$$f(y|x) = \frac{f(y,x)}{f(x)}.$$

The conditional PDF will be used in subsequent chapters to define and construct the local constant estimator of a conditional mean (regression) function. It will also be used to construct nonparametric binary choice and count outcome models.

The conditional CDF for continuous y is defined as

$$F(y|x) = \int_{-\infty}^{y} \frac{f(t,x)}{f(x)} \, dt.$$

The conditional CDF is useful for a variety of purposes, including the construction of fully nonparametric quantile estimators and the estimation of conditional value at risk.

4.2   Smooth Kernel Conditional Density Function Estimation

Let $f(y,x)$ and $f(x)$ denote the joint and marginal densities of (X,Y) and X, respectively, where we allow Y and X to consist of continuous, unordered, and ordered variables. In what follows, we refer to Y as a dependent variable and to X as a covariate. We use $\hat{f}(y,x)$ and $\hat{f}(x)$ to denote kernel[1] estimators of $f(y,x)$ and $f(x)$, and we estimate the conditional density $f(y|x) = f(y,x)/f(x)$ by

$$\hat{f}(y|x) = \frac{\hat{f}(y,x)}{\hat{f}(x)}. \qquad (4.1)$$

The estimator of $f(z) = f(y,x)$ is given by

$$\hat{f}(z) = \frac{1}{n} \sum_{i=1}^{n} K_{\gamma_z}(Z_i, z),$$

while the estimator of $f(x)$ is given by

$$\hat{f}(x) = \frac{1}{n} \sum_{i=1}^{n} K_{\gamma_x}(X_i, x).$$

It is important to note that the bandwidths for the conditioning data are the same in $\hat{f}(z)$ and $\hat{f}(x)$; that is, we *do not* use separate data-driven estimators of $f(z)$ and $f(x)$. Hall et al. (2004) demonstrate that

$$\sqrt{n \prod_{j=1}^{q^y} h_j^y \prod_{j=1}^{q^x} h_j^x} \left(\hat{f}(y|x) - f(y|x) - \text{Bias } \hat{f}(y|x) \right) \xrightarrow{d} N\left(0, \text{AVar } \hat{f}(y|x)\right),$$

where $\prod_{j=1}^{q^y} h_j^y \prod_{j=1}^{q^x} h_j^x$ is the product of bandwidths for the $q^y + q^x$ continuous variables in $Z = (X,Y)$ (Hall et al. (2004) consider the case

---

[1] We use the multivariate mixed-data product kernel notation for our estimators, i.e., $\hat{f}(x) = n^{-1} \sum_{i=1}^{n} K_{\gamma}(X_i, x)$ where $K_{\gamma}(X_i, x) = \prod_{j=1}^{q} h_j^{-1} K\left(\frac{x_j^c - X_{ij}^c}{h_j}\right) \prod_{j=1}^{r} L(X_{ij}^u, x_j^u, \lambda_j^u) \prod_{j=1}^{s} l(X_{ij}^o, x_j^o, \lambda_j^o)$, as outlined in Chapter 3.

where $q^y = 1$). Note that $\text{AVar}\,\hat{f}(y|x)$ denotes the pointwise variance modulo the $n\prod_{j=1}^{q^y} h_j^y \prod_{j=1}^{q^x} h_j^x$ terms that appear in the denominator of $\text{Var}\,\hat{f}(y|x)$. For example, in the univariate x case, $\text{Var}\,\hat{f}(x) = f(x)\kappa/nh$, so $\text{AVar}\,\hat{f}(x) = nh\,\text{Var}\,\hat{f}(x) = f(x)\kappa$. The interested reader may find detailed formulas for the bias and variance in Hall et al. (2004) and Li and Racine (2007).

4.2.1   Bandwidth Selection

Least Squares Cross-Validation

We can choose the bandwidth vector γ_z by cross-validated minimization of a weighted integrated square error. Using the notation $\int dz = \sum_{z^d} \int dz^c$, the weighted integrated square difference between $\hat{f}(\cdot)$ and $f(\cdot)$ is

$$
\begin{aligned}
I_n &= \int \left(\hat{f}(y|x) - f(y|x) \right)^2 f(x)\,dz \\
&= \int \left(\hat{f}(y|x) \right)^2 f(x)\,dz - 2\int \hat{f}(y|x) f(y|x) f(x)\,dz + \int \left(f(y|x) \right)^2 f(x)\,dz \\
&\equiv I_{1n} - 2I_{2n} + I_{3n}.
\end{aligned}
$$

This is similar to the least squares cross-validation procedure for unconditional density estimation that was discussed in Chapter 2. Note that I_{3n} is independent of γ_z, so minimizing I_n over γ_z is equivalent to minimizing $I_{1n} - 2I_{2n}$. For details on the theoretical underpinnings of data-driven bandwidth selection for this method, see Hall et al. (2004) and Bashtannyk and Hyndman (2001).

Likelihood Cross-Validation

We might also choose bandwidths via likelihood cross-validation. Likelihood cross-validation yields a conditional density estimate that has an entropy interpretation, namely that the estimate will be close to the actual conditional density in a Kullback-Leibler sense (Duin, 1976). The optimal γ_z is obtained via maximization of the log likelihood function given by

$$
\mathcal{L} = \sum_{i=1}^{n} \log \hat{f}_{-i}(Y_i|X_i),
$$

where $\hat{f}_{-i}(Y_i|X_i)$ is the leave-one-out estimator defined in Chapter 2.

Example 4.1. Modeling an Italian GDP Panel.
  We consider an Italian GDP growth panel that covers 21 regions over the period 1951-1998 (millions of Lire, 1990=base). There are two variables, `gdp` and `year`, and 1,008 observations in total. We treat `gdp` as continuous and `year` $(1951, 1952, \ldots)$ as an ordered

discrete variable. We then estimate the density of `gdp` conditional on `year`. Figure 4.1 plots the estimated conditional density, $\hat{f}(\text{gdp}|\text{year})$, based on bandwidths $\hat{h}_{\text{gdp}} = 0.715$ and $\hat{\lambda}_{\text{year}} = 0.671$ that have been selected via likelihood cross-validation.

Figure 4.1 reveals that the distribution of income has evolved from being unimodal in the early 1950s to being markedly bimodal in the 1990s. This result is robust insofar as it is observed regardless of whether bandwidths are chosen using simple rules-of-thumb or data-driven methods such as least squares or likelihood cross-validation. This evolution might not be captured by parametric models of the income distribution. For instance, the (unimodal) log-normal distribution, which is a popular parametric framework for modeling income distributions, is incapable of revealing the multi-modal structure of this dataset. However, this multi-modal structure is readily revealed by the kernel method.

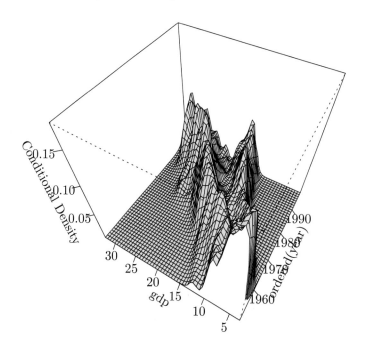

Figure 4.1: Nonparametric conditional PDF estimate for the Italian GDP panel.

4.2.2   The Presence of Irrelevant Covariates

Choosing appropriate bandwidths for the estimator defined in (4.1) in a general multivariate mixed-data setting can be tricky. In the mixed-data case, plug-in rules tend to be prohibitively complex, and a major difficulty is that there does not exist a general formula for optimal bandwidths. A more significant issue is that it can be difficult to determine which components of X are relevant to the problem of conditional inference. For example, if the jth component of X is independent of Y, then that component is irrelevant to the estimation of the density of Y given X. Thus, it should ideally be dropped before conducting inference. Hall et al. (2004) show that the least squares cross-validation method that has been outlined above overcomes these difficulties. It automatically determines the irrelevant components by assigning them large bandwidths and consequently shrinking them towards the uniform distribution on the respective marginals. This effectively removes irrelevant components by suppressing their contribution to the variance of the estimator; their bias is already small as a result of their independence of Y. Cross-validation also provides important information about which components are relevant. The relevant components are precisely those that have been assigned bandwidths of conventional size by the cross-validation procedure. Cross-validation gives rise to asymptotically optimal smoothing for relevant components and elimination of irrelevant components by means of oversmoothing.

Hall et al. (2004) demonstrate that the behaviour of the bandwidths for irrelevant conditioning variables in X ought to be the opposite of that of the optimal bandwidths for the relevant components of X. In particular, optimal smoothing of the irrelevant components entails $h \to \infty$ as $n \to \infty$. This result has also been established in a regression context; see Hall et al. (2007) for further details. We will examine this subject in the Practitioner's Corner of this chapter.

Figure 4.2 illustrates the behaviour of $K(z)/h = K((x - X_i)/h)/h$ as h increases for a Gaussian kernel function. We plot $K(z)/h$ for $x = 0$ when the $X_i \sim N(0, 1)$; hence, the X_i lie mostly in the range $(-3.5, \ldots, 3.5)$ even though their support is in fact the real number line. We observe that, as h increases, the kernel function shrinks towards a constant function $K(0)$. Obviously, $\int \hat{f}(x)\,dx = 1$ for any h, so as h increases, the probability mass gets spread over increasingly large intervals. This implies that $\hat{f}(x) \to 0$, with $\hat{f}(x) > 0$ for finite h. Eventually, as h increases, we hit a point at which $K(z)/h$ is a constant function in the range $(-3.5, \ldots, 3.5)$. Once this occurs, *equal* weight is placed on each X_i in our sample, which we call *uniform smoothing*. For the Gaussian kernel function, $K(0) = 0.3989$, so as h increases, $K(z) \to 0.3989$ and $K(z)/h \to 0$, with $K(z)/h > 0$ for finite h. Thus, for the estimator $\hat{f}(y|x)$, we can see that $\hat{f}(y|x) \to \hat{f}(y)$ as $h_x \to \infty$. We say that the large bandwidth has shrunk the distribution of X towards its uniform marginal (this result is left as an exercise).

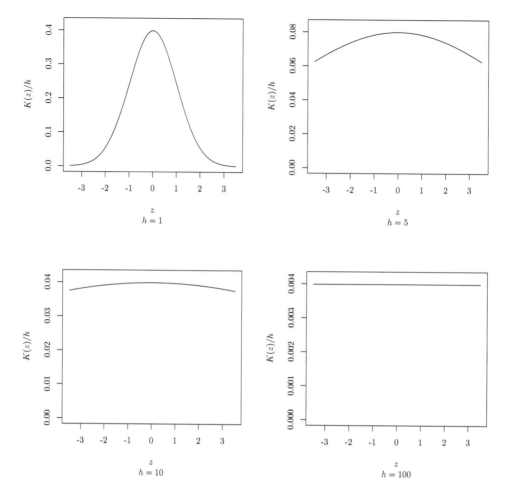

Figure 4.2: Effect of oversmoothing on $K(z)/h$.

4.3 Smooth Kernel Conditional Cumulative Distribution Function Estimation

Li and Racine (2008) propose a kernel-based nonparametric conditional CDF estimator and an associated nonparametric conditional quantile estimator that admit a mix of discrete and continuous data. While bandwidth selection for kernel quantile regression remains an open research topic, they employ a modification of the bandwidth selector for a conditional PDF that was proposed by Hall et al. (2004). We use $F(y|x)$ to denote the conditional CDF of Y given $X = x$ and $f(x)$ to denote the marginal density of X. We can estimate $F(y|x)$ by

$$\hat{F}(y|x) = \frac{\int_{-\infty}^{y} \hat{f}(t, x)\, dt}{\hat{f}(x)}$$

$$= \frac{n^{-1} \sum_{i=1}^{n} G\left(\frac{y - Y_i}{h_y}\right) K_{\gamma_x}(X_i, x)}{\hat{f}(x)},$$

where $G(\cdot)$ is a kernel CDF that is chosen by the researcher (e.g., the standard normal CDF), h_y is the bandwidth associated with Y, and $K_{\gamma_x}(X_i, x)$ is a generalized mixed-data product kernel function. For discrete Y, $\int_{-\infty}^{y}$ is replaced by $\sum_{t \in \mathcal{D}, t \leq y}$ and $G\left(\frac{y - Y_i}{h_y}\right)$ is replaced by $\mathcal{L}(Y_i, y, \lambda_y)$.

It can be shown that

$$\sqrt{n \prod_{j=1}^{q} h_j} \left(\hat{F}(y|x) - F(y|x) - \text{Bias } \hat{F}(y|x)\right) \xrightarrow{d} N(0, \text{AVar } \hat{F}(y|x)).$$

See Li and Racine (2008) for further details. Note that here, we have considered the case of a univariate Y; however, the extension to multivariate and mixed-data Y is straightforward. The R function `npcdist()` in the np package supports multivariate Y objects via, e.g., `F <- npcdist(y1+y2~x)`.

4.3.1 Bandwidth Selection

Li et al. (2013) suggest choosing bandwidths $\gamma = (h_y, \gamma_x)$ by minimizing

$$CV(\gamma) = n^{-1} \sum_{i=1}^{n} \int \left(\mathbf{1}(Y_i \leq y) - \hat{F}_{-i}(y|X_i)\right)^2 \mathcal{M}(X_i) M(y) dy, \qquad (4.2)$$

where $\mathcal{M}(\cdot)$ and $M(\cdot)$ are trimming functions. One problem with (4.2) is that it involves numerical integration which is computationally costly. An alternative that is proposed by Li et al. (2013) replaces integration over y by a sample average over the Y_js,

$$CV_\Sigma(\gamma) = \frac{1}{n(n-1)} \sum_{i=1}^{n} \sum_{j \neq i}^{n} \left(\mathbf{1}(Y_i \leq Y_j) - \hat{F}_{-i}(Y_j|X_i)\right)^2 \mathcal{M}(X_i).$$

These approaches are asymptotically equivalent and their behaviour is similar in finite sample settings.

Example 4.2. Modeling an Italian GDP Panel.

We consider an Italian GDP growth panel that covers 21 regions over the period 1951-1998 (millions of Lire, 1990=base). There are two variables, `gdp` and `year`, and 1,008 observations in total. We treat `gdp` as continuous and `year` $(1951, 1952, \dots)$ as an ordered discrete variable. We then estimate the distribution of `gdp` conditional on `year`, $\hat{F}(\text{gdp}|\text{year})$, which is plotted in Figure 4.3.

While Figures 4.1 and 4.3 are intended to convey similar information, the conditional CDF in Figure 4.3 does so in a manner that is better suited to the estimation of, say, a conditional quantile, which is the topic to which we now turn.

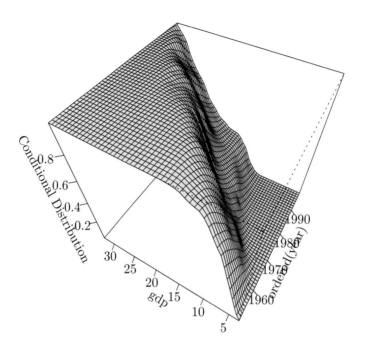

Figure 4.3: Nonparametric conditional CDF estimates for the Italian GDP panel.

4.4   Conditional Quantile Function Estimation

4.4.1   Parametric Conditional Quantile Function Estimation

The estimation of regression functions is one of the most common tasks that are regularly undertaken by practitioners of statistics and econometrics. However, the regression function is not always representative of the covariates' impact on the dependent variable. For example, when the dependent variable is left (or right) censored, the relationship that is captured by the regression function tends to be distorted. In such cases, conditional quantiles above (or below) the censoring point are a robust alternative. Furthermore, the conditional quantile function summarizes the conditional distribution of a dependent variable more comprehensively than the conditional mean function. A conditional τth quantile ($\tau \in (0,1)$) of a conditional distribution function $F(\cdot|x)$ is defined by

$$q_\tau(x) = \inf\{y : F(y|x) \geq \tau\} = F^{-1}(\tau|x),$$

or equivalently, $F(q_\tau(x)|x) = \tau$.

It is interesting to note that parametric quantile regression (Koenker and Bassett, 1978) is based on the familiar model

$$Y_i = \beta_0 + \beta_1 X_i + \epsilon_i,$$

which also forms the basis for simple linear regression. The least squares estimator of $\beta = (\beta_0, \beta_1)'$ is obtained by minimizing the sum of squared residuals, i.e.,

$$\text{argmin}_{\beta \in \mathbb{R}^2} \sum_{i=1}^{n} \rho(Y_i - \beta_0 - \beta_1 X_i),$$

where $\rho(a) = a^2$ delivers the *conditional mean*. Meanwhile, for the τth conditional quantile function $q_\tau(x)$, Koenker and Bassett (1978) propose obtaining $\beta_\tau = c(\beta_{0,\tau}, \beta_{1,\tau})'$ by solving

$$\text{argmin}_{\beta \in \mathbb{R}^2} \sum_{i=1}^{n} \rho_\tau(Y_i - \beta_0 - \beta_1 X_i),$$

where $\rho_\tau(a) = a(\tau - \mathbf{1}(a < 0))$ is the so-called *check function*. This delivers a linear parametric *regression quantile*. Given that such models can obviously be misspecified, it is advisable to perform a test for correct specification (Otsu, 2009). While the parametric approach starts from a linear regression model, the nonparametric approach that is outlined below starts with the *definition* of a conditional quantile, i.e., the inverse of a conditional CDF. It then plugs in the kernel estimator of the unknown conditional CDF and inverts this object via the *quasi-inverse* procedure that was defined in Section 2.6. Note also that an important rationale for using quantile regression is that it provides more information about the conditional distribution of a dependent variable than the conditional mean function. To the extent that the nonparametric approach is based *directly* on the conditional distribution, the information that it encompasses is comprehensive; the various quantiles τ then allow us to divide this information into manageable *slices*.

Example 4.3. Modeling an Italian GDP Panel.

We consider an Italian GDP growth panel that covers 21 regions over the period 1951-1998 (millions of Lire, 1990=base). There are two variables, gdp and year, and 1,008 observations in total. We estimate a set of parametric regression quantiles for gdp conditional on year. Figure 4.4 presents the 0.25, 0.50 (median), and 0.75 conditional quantiles for the Italian GDP panel, along with box plots[2] of the raw data. The nonsmooth quantile estimates that are generated by the box plot can be directly compared to those obtained via parametric quantile regression. Although the

---

[2] A box-and-whisker plot (sometimes called a *box plot*) is a histogram-like method of displaying data that was invented by J. Tukey. To create a box-and-whisker plot, one draws a box with ends at the quartiles Q_1 and Q_3. The statistical median M is represented by a horizontal line in the box, and the *whiskers* are extended to the farthest points that are not outliers (i.e., that are within $3/2$ times the interquartile range of Q_1 and Q_3). Every point that is more than $3/2$ times the interquartile range from the end of the box is represented by a dot.

estimates are somewhat close, they are not in complete agreement, which suggests that there might be some nonlinearity that is neglected by the parametric model. This could be confirmed by a specification test.

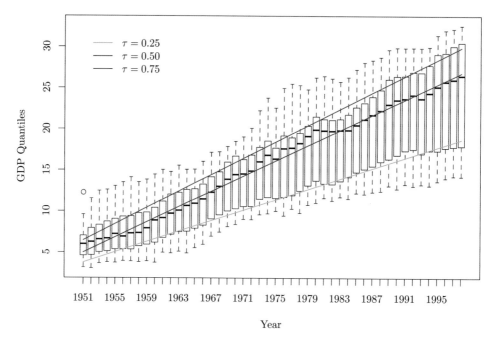

Figure 4.4: Parametric conditional quantile estimates for the Italian GDP panel, $\tau = (0.25, 0.50, 0.75)$.

If we perform a test for correct parametric specification (Otsu, 2009) of the $\tau = 0.50$th conditional quantile, we obtain a Wald statistic $W = 14.9203$ and a P-value of 0.0049. This results in rejection at all conventional levels of the null hypothesis that the parametric model is correctly specified. Hence we might instead consider a consistent nonparametric approach.

One problem that practitioners sometimes encounter when using parametric quantile methods is the *quantile crossing* phenomenon. Given that the CDF is nondecreasing and the quantile function is the inverse of the CDF, it must be the case that $q_{\tau_1}(x) \geq q_{\tau_2}(x)$ for any τ_1, $\tau_2 \in [0, 1]$ that satisfy $\tau_1 \geq \tau_2$ (e.g., the 90th percentile cannot be less than the 80th percentile). However, it is not uncommon for parametric regression quantiles to violate this axiom, and hence a variety of methods have been developed to *rearrange* the quantile estimates when this occurs. See, for instance, the re-arrangement method proposed by Chernozhukov et al. (2010). See also Qu and Yoon (2015), who propose solving a constrained optimization problem to avoid such occurrences.

4.4.2 Smooth Kernel Conditional Quantile Function Estimation

Estimation of conditional quantiles is straightforward once we have obtained an estimate of the conditional CDF, such as the one that is plotted in Figure 4.3. We can directly estimate the conditional quantile function $q_\tau(x)$ by taking the quasi-inverse (Nelsen, 2006, Definition 2.3.6, page 21) of the estimated conditional CDF function, i.e.,

$$\hat{q}_\tau(x) = \inf\{y : \hat{F}(y|x) \geq \tau\} \equiv \hat{F}^{-1}(\tau|x).$$

Li and Racine (2008) demonstrate that $\hat{q}_\tau(x) \to q_\tau(x)$ in probability and that

$$\sqrt{n \prod_{j=1}^{q} h_j} \left(\hat{q}_\tau(x) - q_\tau(x) - \text{Bias}\, \hat{q}_\tau(x)\right) \overset{d}{\to} N(0, \text{AVar}\, \hat{q}_\tau(x)),$$

where the above results are for the multivariate mixed-data case that we studied in Chapter 3. The theoretical underpinnings of this method can be found in Li and Racine (2008). The function `npqreg()` in the R package np implements this method. Note that it is impossible for quantiles derived from the inverse CDF to cross, provided that the CDF estimator is proper (i.e., $\hat{F}(-\infty|x) = 0$, $\hat{F}(\infty|x) = 1$, and $\hat{F}(y|x)$ is nondecreasing in y). Since $\hat{F}(y|x)$ is a sum of CDF kernels that are themselves monotone nondecreasing, $\hat{F}(y|x)$ is *guaranteed* to be monotone nondecreasing in y. Therefore, the quantile crossing phenomenon cannot occur in this context.

Example 4.4. Modeling an Italian GDP Panel.

> We consider an Italian GDP growth panel that covers 21 regions over the period 1951-1998 (millions of Lire, 1990=base). There are two variables, `gdp` and `year`, and 1,008 observations in total. We treat `gdp` as continuous and `year` $(1951, 1952, \dots)$ as an ordered discrete variable. We then estimate a set of quantiles for `gdp` conditional on `year`. Figure 4.5 presents the 0.25, 0.50 (median), and 0.75 conditional quantiles for the Italian GDP panel, along with box plots of the raw data. The nonsmooth quantile estimates generated by the box plot can therefore be easily compared to those obtained via direct estimation of the smooth CDF. It is clear that the two sets of quantile estimates are in agreement.

An alternative method that uses kernel-smoothed quantile functions is outlined in Racine and Li (2017).

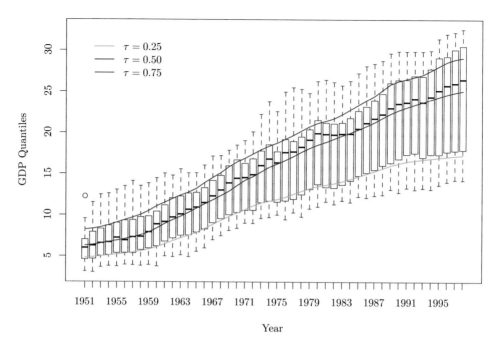

Figure 4.5: Nonparametric conditional quantile estimates for the Italian GDP panel, $\tau = (0.25, 0.50, 0.75)$.

4.5   Binary Choice and Multinomial Choice Models

4.5.1   Parametric Binary Choice and Multinomial Choice Models

Aldrich and Nelson (1995) outline the classical parametric treatment of binary and multinomial choice models, which we now briefly describe. The classical treatment begins with a linear regression model of the form

$$Y_i^* = \beta_0 + \beta_1 X_i + \epsilon_i,$$

where Y_i^* is treated as continuous. It is assumed that $Y_i \in \{0, 1\}$ and that we observe $Y_i = 1$ if $Y_i^* \geq 0$, i.e., if $\beta_0 + \beta_1 X_i + \epsilon_i > 0$. Otherwise, we observe $Y_i = 0$. It is easy to see that if we regress Y_i on X_i, then the conditional mean $\beta_0 + \beta_1 X_i$ coincides with $\Pr(Y = 1 | X = x)$, *provided that* the parametric model is correctly specified. Next, it is often pointed out that if one conducts a least squares regression of the binary Y_i on X_i, then the estimate $\hat{Y}_i = \hat{\beta}_0 + \hat{\beta}_1 X_i$ could be either negative or greater than one; in this case, it would be *improper*. To correct this, the index $\beta_0 + \beta_1 X_i$ is *squashed* by a function that lies in $[0, 1]$. Since a CDF must lie in $[0, 1]$, one might use the Logistic CDF, which delivers the *binary choice Logit model* $\left(F(x) = 1 / \left(1 + e^{-(\beta_0 + \beta_1 x)}\right)\right)$. Alternatively, the Gaussian CDF delivers the *binary choice Probit model.* Both of these models are estimated via the method of maximum likelihood.

We are modeling a conditional probability $\Pr(Y = 1|X = x) = f(Y = 1|x)$, which is a conditional PDF for a binary $Y \in \{0, 1\}$. A nonparametric approach would recognize this fact and model $f(y|x)$ using a mixed-data kernel estimator of a conditional PDF. In contrast, the classical parametric approach begins with a linear regression model and then applies some band-aids to patch up its shortcomings. This was also the case when we considered parametric quantile regression in Section 4.4.1. A natural worry is that such models are misspecified and hence inconsistent. Tests for correct specification of binary and multinomial choice models have been proposed to assist in the diagnosis of this problem. See Hausman and McFadden (1984) and Mora and Moro-Egido (2008) for tests that apply to multinomial Logit and ordered discrete outcome models, respectively. See also Li and Racine (2013) for a consistent nonparametric test that applies to binary and multinomial choice models.

4.5.2 Smooth Kernel Binary Choice and Multinomial Choice Models

Kernel PDF estimators for mixed-data can also be applied to the estimation of *conditional mode* models. Consider a discrete outcome $Y \in \mathcal{D} = \{0, 1, \ldots, c - 1\}$, which might denote, by way of example, the number of successful patent applications by firms. We define the *mode* of Y conditional on $X = x$ by

$$M(x) = \text{argmax}_{y \in \mathcal{D}} f(y|x).$$

To understand this approach, suppose that $y \in \{0, 1, 2\}$ and that $f(Y = 0|x) = 0.1$, $f(Y = 1|x) = 0.7$, and $f(Y = 2|x) = 0.2$, where $f(y|x) = f(Y = y|X = x) = \Pr(Y = y|X = x)$. To make a conditional prediction about Y given $X = x$, you would naturally choose the most likely outcome which in this case, given $X = x$, is $Y = 1$. This is the *conditional mode* of a discrete random variable Y.

In order to estimate a conditional mode $M(x)$, we need to model the conditional density. Let us call $\hat{M}(x)$ the estimated conditional mode, which is given by

$$\hat{M}(x) = \text{argmax}_{y \in \mathcal{D}} \hat{f}(y|x),$$

where $\hat{f}(y|x)$ is the mixed-data kernel estimator of $f(y|x)$ defined in (4.1), and where Y is discrete. The function `npconmode()` in the R package np implements this method.[3] By way of example, suppose that we would like to use this method to model a binary indicator of low birth weights.

---

[3]This procedure can be used without modification for binary, multinomial, and count outcome models.

Example 4.5. Modeling Low Birth Weight (binary outcome, 0/1).

Using data on birth weights that are taken from the R MASS library (Venables and Ripley, 2002), we estimate a parametric Logit model and a nonparametric conditional mode model. The conditional density that is required for the latter is estimated using Equation (4.1), which is based on the method of Hall et al. (2004). We use likelihood cross-validation for bandwidth selection. We assess the estimators' classification ability via a comparison of their confusion matrices.[4] The outcome y is a binary indicator of low infant birth weight (low), although this method could also handle unordered and ordered multinomial outcomes without any modification. In this example, $n = 189$ and there are 7 explanatory variables in x, smoke, race, ht, ui, ftv, age, and lwt, all of which are defined below.

- low indicator of birth weight less than 2.5kg ($1 = < 2.5$kg)
- smoke smoking status during pregnancy ($1 =$ smoker)
- race mother's race ($1 =$ white, $2 =$ black, $3 =$ other)
- ht history of hypertension ($1 =$ hypertensive)
- ui presence of uterine irritability ($1 =$ present)
- ftv number of physician visits during the first trimester
- age mother's age in years
- lwt mother's weight in pounds at last menstrual period

Note that all variables in this example other than age and lwt are categorical. We compute the *confusion* matrices for each model, and summarize the results in Tables 4.1 and 4.2.

Table 4.1: Parametric Logit confusion matrix.

	0	1
0	119	11
1	34	25

Table 4.2: Smooth kernel nonparametric confusion matrix.

	0	1
0	127	3
1	27	32

---

[4]A *confusion matrix* is a tabulation of the actual outcomes versus those predicted by a model. The diagonal elements are the correctly predicted outcomes and the off-diagonal elements are the incorrectly predicted (confused) outcomes.

The nonparametric model correctly classifies $(127 + 32)/189 = 84.1\%$ of low/high (i.e., 0/1) birth weights, while the Logit model correctly classifies only $(119 + 25)/189 = 76.2\%$. Applying the Hosmer and Lemeshow (2013) test for correct parametric specification of the Logit model, we obtain a χ^2 goodness-of-fit test statistic of 16.007 and a P-value of 0.042. Hence, we reject the null of correct specification at the 5% level.

Example 4.6. Modeling Choice of Healthcare Provider (multinomial outcome, i.e., $Y \in \{\text{notreat, private, public}\}$).

In this example, we estimate a parametric multinomial Logit model and a nonparametric conditional mode model using data on choice of healthcare provider. We then assess their classification ability by comparing their confusion matrices. The outcome is an indicator of choice of healthcare provider (`notreat/private/public`), although the nonparametric method could also handle binary outcomes without any modification. In this application, there are $n = 2716$ observations and 4 predictors. The data are taken from the 1995 South African October Household Survey (Statistics South Africa, 1995, Koch (2017)), and is limited to children under the age of 12 who have been ill within the 30 days prior to the survey. The outcome variable is `hlthsk` (factor), which takes on values

- `notreat1` ill child was not treated for illness
- `private` ill child was treated in private facility
- `public1` ill child was treated in public facility

The covariates include

- `inc` 1995 household reported earnings (numeric)
- `insure` ill child has health insurance (factor)
- `time.med` distance to health facility in minutes (ordered factor)
- `rd.age` measures policy; those under 6 are eligible to receive free health care (factor)

We compute the confusion matrices for the multinomial Logit and the nonparametric conditional mode models, and summarize the results in Tables 4.3 and 4.4.

Table 4.3: Parametric multinomial Logit confusion matrix.

	notreat	private	public
notreat	0	111	485
private	0	358	418
public	0	180	1164

Table 4.4: Smooth kernel nonparametric confusion matrix.

	notreat	private	public
notreat	71	74	451
private	6	355	415
public	6	108	1230

Note that the multinomial Logit has difficulty predicting the notreat outcomes (such *corner solutions* are not uncommon for parametric binary/multinomial choice models). The in-sample correct classification ratios (CCRs) are 56% and 61% for the multinomial Logit and nonparametric models, respectively.

4.6   Practitioner's Corner

We model the joint density of two random variables that have been drawn from a bivariate normal distribution with correlation $\rho_{xy} = 0.5$ in the first instance and $\rho_{xy} = 0.0$ in the second instance. We are interested in the ability of likelihood cross-validation to automatically smooth out an *irrelevant* predictor without resorting to pre-testing. Figure 4.6 presents the conditional density estimate $\hat{f}(y|x)$ for each case.[5]

```
par(mfrow=c(1,2),cex=.6,mar=c(4,2,2,2))
require(MASS)
n <- 1000
rho <- 0.5
mu <- c(0,0)
Sigma <- matrix(c(1,rho,rho,1),2,2)
set.seed(42)
foo <- mvrnorm(n=n, mu, Sigma)
x <- foo[,1]
y <- foo[,2]
f <- npcdens(y~x)
plot(f,view="fixed",main="",theta=55,phi=10,
    sub=paste("$\\rho_{xy}=0.5$, $h_x = ",
    format(f$bw$xbw,digits=3),
    "$, $h_y = ",format(f$bw$ybw,digits=3),"$",sep=""))
## X and Y independent
n <- 1000
rho <- 0.0
mu <- c(0,0)
Sigma <- matrix(c(1,rho,rho,1),2,2)
set.seed(42)
foo <- mvrnorm(n=n, mu, Sigma)
x <- foo[,1]
```

---

[5]In order to use the function `mvrnorm()`, you must first load the R package MASS (Venables and Ripley, 2002).

```
y <- foo[,2]
f.irr <- npcdens(y~x)
plot(f.irr,view="fixed",main="",theta=55,phi=10,
     sub=paste("$\\rho_{xy}=0.0$, $h_x = ",
     format(f.irr$bw$xbw,digits=3),
     "$, $h_y = ",format(f.irr$bw$ybw,digits=3),"$",sep=""))
```

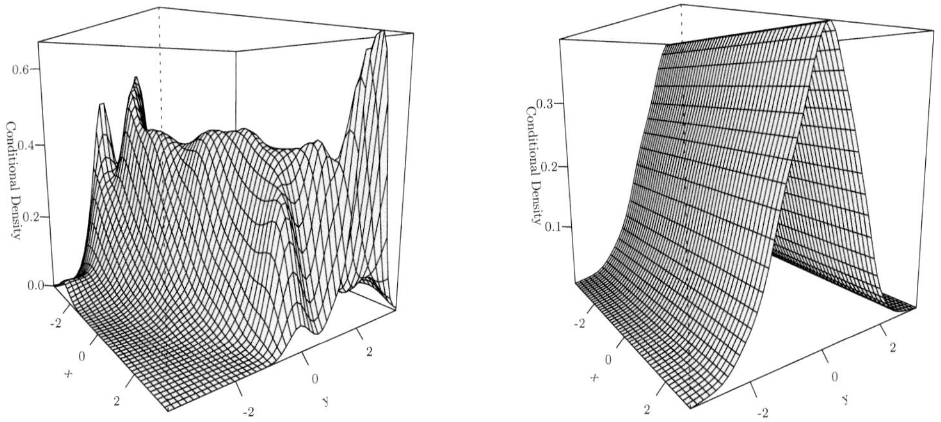

Figure 4.6: Conditional density estimates, X and Y joint normal random variates.

As detailed in Hall et al. (2004), when X and Y are independent, the least squares cross-validation procedure shrinks X towards its uniform marginal. In effect, X is *smoothed out* of the resulting estimate; further examination of this result is left as an exercise. Figure 4.7 presents the unconditional density estimate $\hat{f}(y)$.

```
f.uni <- npudens(~y)
plot(f.uni,sub=paste("$h_y = ",format(f.uni$bw,digits=3),"$",sep=""))
```

Note that the unconditional likelihood cross-validated bandwidth h_y is indistinguishable from the one that is obtained when $\hat{f}(y|x)$ is estimated and X and Y are independent. For independent random variables, we know that $f(y,x) = f(y)f(x)$ and that $f(y|x) = f(y,x)/f(x) = f(y)$; however we did not know ex ante that this was the case at hand. Nonetheless, the data-driven bandwidth selection procedure delivered an estimate such that $\hat{f}(y|x) = \hat{f}(y)$. Thus, the rate of convergence of $\hat{f}(y|x)$ *must* be the same as in the one-dimensional case. In retrospect, this is rather remarkable, since we have established that the procedure delivers automatic dimensionality reduction when appropriate by oversmoothing irrelevant predictors.

We observe the same phenomenon when dealing with the conditional CDF estimator.

```
par(mfrow=c(1,2),cex=.6,mar=c(4,2,2,2))
n <- 1000
rho <- 0.5
```

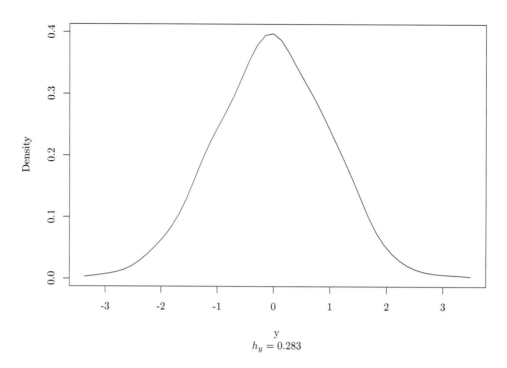

Figure 4.7: Univariate (unconditional) density estimate for Y.

```
mu <- c(0,0)
Sigma <- matrix(c(1,rho,rho,1),2,2)
set.seed(42)
foo <- mvrnorm(n=n, mu, Sigma)
x <- foo[,1]
y <- foo[,2]
F <- npcdist(y~x)
plot(F,view="fixed",main="",theta=55,phi=10,
    sub=paste("$\\rho_{xy}=0.5$, $h_x = ",
    format(F$bw$xbw,digits=3),
    "$, $h_y = ",format(F$bw$ybw,digits=3),"$",sep=""))
## X and Y independent
n <- 1000
rho <- 0.0
mu <- c(0,0)
Sigma <- matrix(c(1,rho,rho,1),2,2)
set.seed(42)
foo <- mvrnorm(n=n, mu, Sigma)
x <- foo[,1]
y <- foo[,2]
F.irr <- npcdist(y~x)
plot(F.irr,view="fixed",main="",theta=55,phi=10,
    sub=paste("$\\rho_{xy}=0.0$, $h_x = ",
    format(F.irr$bw$xbw,digits=3),
    "$, $h_y = ",format(F.irr$bw$ybw,digits=3),"$",sep=""))
```

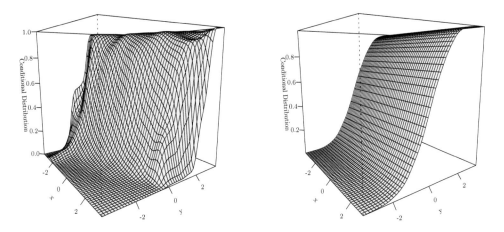

Figure 4.8: Conditional distribution estimates, X and Y joint normal random variates.

```
F.uni <- npudist(~y)
plot(F.uni,sub=paste("$h_y = ",format(F.uni$bw,digits=3),"$",sep=""))
```

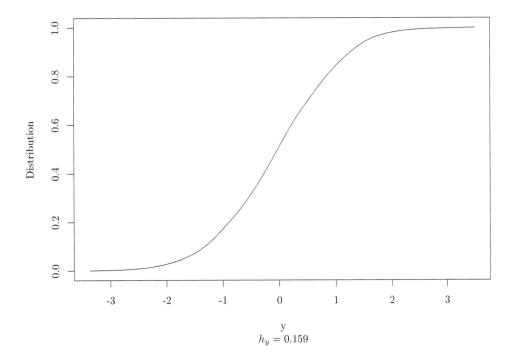

Figure 4.9: Univariate (unconditional) distribution estimate for Y.

4.6.1 Generating Counterfactual Predictions

We consider the conditional probability of having a low birth weight newborn as a function of the mother's age and whether she was a smoker. Although these are simple point estimates, we could of course enrich our analysis by, for instance, adding variability bounds to the estimates or conducting a test of equality of conditional probabilities.

```
par(mfrow=c(2,1),mar=c(5,4,4,2)+0.1)
require(MASS)
data(birthwt)
birthwt$low <- factor(birthwt$low)
birthwt$smoke <- factor(birthwt$smoke)
## Estimate the conditional probability of low birth weight as a function of
## age and smoking status
f <- npcdens(low~age+smoke,data=birthwt)
## Generate two data frames to predict the probability of low birth weight
## (low=1) as a function of age and smoking status (smoke=1 indicates a
## smoker)
foo.smoke <- with(birthwt,data.frame(low=factor("1",levels=levels(low)),
                                     smoke=factor("1",levels=levels(smoke)),
                                     age=min(age):max(age)))
foo.nosmoke <- with(birthwt,data.frame(low=factor("1",levels=levels(low)),
                                       smoke=factor("0",levels=levels(smoke)),
                                       age=min(age):max(age)))
## Generate the conditional probability that low=1 for smokers and nonsmokers
f.low.smoke <- predict(f,newdata=foo.smoke)
f.low.nosmoke <- predict(f,newdata=foo.nosmoke)
## Plot the conditional probability estimates versus age
plot(foo.smoke$age,f.low.smoke,
     type="l",
     ylab="$\\hat f(1\\vert x)=Pr(low=1\\vert age,smoke)$",
     xlab="Age",
     lwd=2)
lines(foo.nosmoke$age,f.low.nosmoke,col=2,lty=2,lwd=2)
legend("topright",c("Smoker","Nonsmoker"),col=1:2,lty=1:2,lwd=c(2,2),bty="n")
## Plot the increased risk of having a low birth weight newborn for smokers
## as a function of age
plot(foo.smoke$age,f.low.smoke-f.low.nosmoke,type="l",lwd=2,
     ylab="Increased Probability of Low Birth Weight",
     xlab="Age")
```

4.6.2 Bootstrapping Counterfactual Predictions

Suppose that we would like to bootstrap nonparametric confidence bands for the increased probability of a low birth weight for smokers relative to nonsmokers. We may do this either under the null that there is no effect of smoking or under the alternative. The two code chunks that follow show how to implement the bootstrap for both the parametric and the nonparametric conditional probability estimators. Uncommenting one line will impose the null on the bootstrap procedure. One can present results in either tabular

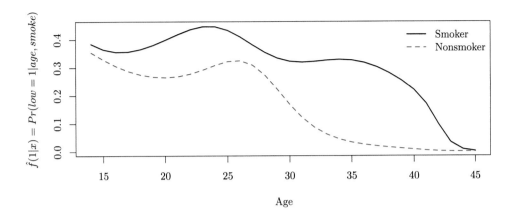

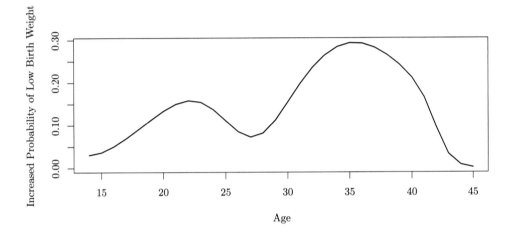

Figure 4.10: Probability of delivering a low birth weight infant as a function of mother's age and smoking status (top), and increased risk from smoking (bottom).

or graphical form and assess whether the increased risk is indeed significant. Under the alternative, one should verify whether the lower bound of the nonparametric pointwise confidence band is greater than zero for some or all of its support. Under the null, one should verify whether the estimate exceeds its upper bound for some or all of its support.

```
require(MASS)
data(birthwt)
birthwt$low <- factor(birthwt$low)
birthwt$smoke <- factor(birthwt$smoke)
## Generate counterfactual data matrices
age.seq <- with(birthwt,min(age):max(age))
foo.smoke <- with(birthwt,data.frame(low=factor("1",levels=levels(low)),
                                     smoke=factor("1",levels=levels(smoke)),
                                     age=age.seq))
```

```
foo.nosmoke <- with(birthwt,data.frame(low=factor("1",levels=levels(low)),
                                smoke=factor("0",levels=levels(smoke)),
                                age=age.seq))
## Fit the parametric model
model <- glm(low~(smoke+
            poly(age,degree=3))^2,
            family=binomial(link=logit),
            data=birthwt)
## Obtain the difference in probabilities
p.increased <- predict(model,newdata=foo.smoke,type="response") -
    predict(model,newdata=foo.nosmoke,type="response")
## Set the number of bootstrap replications
B <- 999
## Create a matrix to store the bootstrapped counterfactuals
p.increased.matrix <- matrix(NA,B,length(age.seq))
for(b in 1:B) {
    ## Draw a pairwise bootstrap resample
    birthwt.boot <- birthwt[sample(NROW(birthwt),replace=TRUE),]
    ## Impose null of no relationship between smoke and low
    ## birthwt. If the next line of code is commented out the
    ## bootstrap is under the alternative, uncommented under the null
    ## birthwt.boot$smoke <- birthwt.boot$smoke[sample(NROW(birthwt)),]
    model <- glm(low~(smoke+
                    poly(age,degree=3))^2,
                family=binomial(link=logit),
                data=birthwt.boot)
    p.increased.matrix[b,]<-predict(model,newdata=foo.smoke,type="response") -
        predict(model,newdata=foo.nosmoke,type="response")

}
## Construct pointwise 5th and 95th quantiles
q.05 <- apply(p.increased.matrix,2,quantile,0.05,type=1)
q.95 <- apply(p.increased.matrix,2,quantile,0.95,type=1)
## Plot results
ylim <- range(c(q.05,q.95,p.increased))
plot(age.seq-0.5,p.increased,type="l",
    ylim=ylim,
    xlab="Age",
    ylab="Increased Probability of Low Birth Weight")
lines(age.seq-0.5,q.05,col=2,lty=2)
lines(age.seq-0.5,q.95,col=2,lty=2)
abline(h=0,lty=2,col="grey")

require(np)
require(MASS)
data(birthwt)
birthwt$low <- factor(birthwt$low)
birthwt$smoke <- factor(birthwt$smoke)
## Generate counterfactual data matrices
age.seq <- with(birthwt,min(age):max(age))
foo.smoke <- with(birthwt,data.frame(low=factor("1",levels=levels(low)),
                                smoke=factor("1",levels=levels(smoke)),
                                age=age.seq))
```

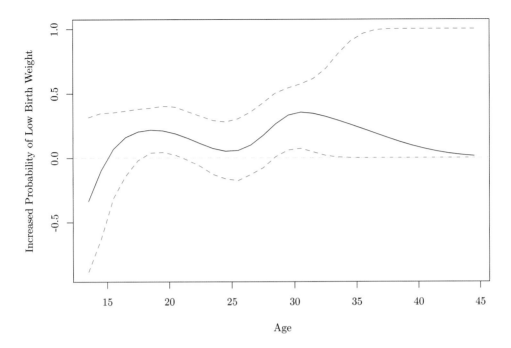

Figure 4.11: Bootstrap confidence bands for the parametric estimate of the increased probability of delivering a low birth weight infant for smokers.

```
foo.nosmoke <- with(birthwt,data.frame(low=factor("1",levels=levels(low)),
                                       smoke=factor("0",levels=levels(smoke)),
                                       age=age.seq))
## Fit the nonparametric model and retrieve bandwidths
model <- npcdens(low~smoke+age,data=birthwt)
bws <- c(model$bws$ybw,model$bws$xbw)
## Obtain the difference in probabilities
p.increased <- predict(model,newdata=foo.smoke,type="response") -
    predict(model,newdata=foo.nosmoke,type="response")
## Set the number of bootstrap replications
B <- 999
## Create a matrix to store the bootstrapped counterfactuals
p.increased.matrix <- matrix(NA,B,length(age.seq))
for(b in 1:B) {
    ## Draw a pairwise bootstrap resample
    birthwt.boot <- birthwt[sample(NROW(birthwt),replace=TRUE),]
    ## Impose null of no relationship between smoke and low
    ## birthwt. If the next line of code is commented out the
    ## bootstrap is under the alternative, uncommented under the null
    ## birthwt.boot$smoke <- birthwt.boot$smoke[sample(NROW(birthwt)),]
    model <- npcdens(low~smoke+age,data=birthwt.boot,bws=bws)
    p.increased.matrix[b,]<-predict(model,newdata=foo.smoke,type="response")-
        predict(model,newdata=foo.nosmoke,type="response")
}
## Construct pointwise 5th and 95th quantiles
q.05 <- apply(p.increased.matrix,2,quantile,0.05,type=1)
```

```
q.95 <- apply(p.increased.matrix,2,quantile,0.95,type=1)
## Plot results
ylim <- range(c(q.05,q.95,p.increased))
plot(age.seq-0.5,p.increased,type="l",
     ylim=ylim,
     xlab="Age",
     ylab="Increased Probability of Low Birth Weight")
lines(age.seq-0.5,q.05,col=2,lty=2)
lines(age.seq-0.5,q.95,col=2,lty=2)
abline(h=0,lty=2,col="grey")
```

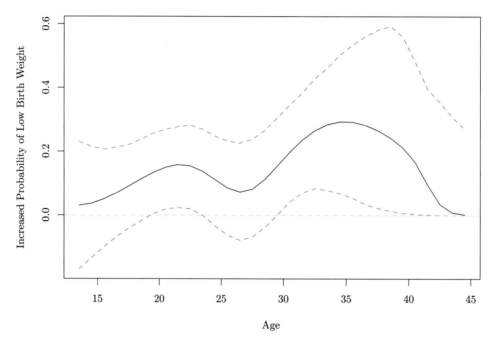

Figure 4.12: Bootstrap confidence bands for the nonparametric estimate of the increased probability of delivering a low birth weight infant for smokers.

Note that `plot()` calls `npplot()` for objects that are produced by the np package. The following line of code automates the construction of nonparametric confidence bands; see `?npplot` for details.

```
plot(model,
     plot.errors.method="bootstrap",
     plot.errors.quantiles=c(0.05,0.95),
     plot.errors.style="band",
     plot.errors.type="quantiles")
```

4.6.3 The Smoothed Bootstrap

Occasionally, we might wish to obtain a random sample that is drawn from our smooth kernel conditional PDF estimate $\hat{f}(y|x)$ or conditional CDF estimate $\hat{F}(y|x)$. The code that appears in this subsection demonstrates how this can be accomplished. In contrast to the unconditional PDF case that was discussed in the Practitioner's Corner in Chapter 2, the wrinkle here is that we select a point with probability that is proportional to the kernel function for x at the point at which the conditional object is to be evaluated. That is, we resample the integers 1 through n with probability $K((X_j - X_i)/h)/\sum_{i=1}^{n} K((X_j - X_i)/h)$ when resampling the jth sample realization. This procedure could be used to construct bias-corrected bootstrap and asymptotic confidence bands in exactly the same manner as was done for the unconditional PDF in Chapter 2. The following code chunk implements this procedure using the Old Faithful data.

```
## Credit for this example goes to Cosma Shalizi
## http://stat.cmu.edu/~cshalizi/ADAfaEPoV/
par(mfrow=c(1,2),cex=.6,mar=c(4,2,2,2))
set.seed(42)
data(faithful)
y <- faithful$eruptions
x <- faithful$waiting
n <- nrow(faithful)
## First compute the bandwidth vector for the conditional density
## estimate using a Gaussian kernel
bw <- npcdensbw(y~x,ckertype="gaussian")
## Next generate draws from the conditional kernel density estimate
## when using a Gaussian kernel with weights proportional to K((X_j-X_i)/h)
y.boot <- numeric()
x.boot <- numeric()
for(j in 1:n) {
    p <- dnorm((x[j]-x)/bw$xbw[1])/sum(dnorm((x[j]-x)/bw$xbw[1]))
    j.boot <- sample(1:n,replace=TRUE,prob=p)[1]
    y.boot[j] <- rnorm(1,y[j.boot],bw$ybw[1])
    x.boot[j] <- rnorm(1,x[j.boot],bw$xbw[1])
}
## Plot the conditional density for the actual sample
plot(npcdens(y~x,bws=c(bw$ybw[1],bw$xbw[1])),
     view="fixed",
     theta=300,
     phi=50,
     main="")
## Plot the conditional density for the bootstrap sample
plot(npcdens(y~x,
             data=data.frame(y=y.boot,x=x.boot),
             bws=c(bw$ybw[1],bw$xbw[1])),
     view="fixed",
     theta=300,
     phi=50,
     main="")
```

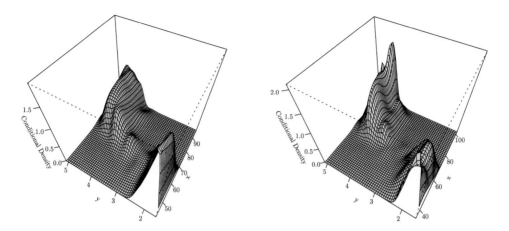

Figure 4.13: Conditional PDF estimate and smooth bootstrap resample and the associated conditional PDF estimate.

4.6.4 Assessing Model Performance

When parametric models are used in applied data analysis, testing for model adequacy is highly recommended. When the parametric model is *rejected* by the data, practitioners often adopt nonparametric methods. However, even if the nonparametric alternative exhibits an *apparent* improvement in fit, there is no guarantee that it will perform better than the parametric model that has been deemed inadequate.

This is widely appreciated in the time series literature, where out-of-sample predictive performance is of paramount importance. Corradi and Swanson (2002) ponder whether it might be the case that simple linear time series models provide forecasts that are at least as accurate as more sophisticated nonlinear models. They write, "If this were shown to be the case, there would be no point in using nonlinear models for out-of-sample prediction, even if the linear models could be shown to be incorrectly specified, say based on the application of in-sample nonlinearity tests." By way of example, Medeiros et al. (2006) use autoregressive neural network models (AR-NN) of financial time series. However, having rejected linearity, they fit an AR-NN model and conduct a rigorous postmortem analysis of each model's ability to predict stock returns, and conclude that the "NN modeling strategy ... is not any better than a linear model with a constant composition of variables. A nonlinear model cannot therefore be expected to do better than a linear one." See also Racine (2001) for an alternative example that involves a comparison of neural networks and linear predictors.

The flip side to the preceding argument is that there is no guarantee that a parametric model that *passes* a model adequacy test will perform any better than a nonparametric model. Overspecified parametric models can pass model adequacy tests, even though they entail a loss of efficiency and may be outperformed by alternative specifications. In addition, some model adequacy tests are *inconsistent* and lack power. Hence a failure to reject the null parametric model may simply be a reflection of the *inadequacy* of certain model adequacy tests. And as White (2000) cautions us, extensive parametric specification searches make it more likely that the observed favourable performance of a model is the result of luck rather than superior fit; he labels such practices *data snooping.*

If we focus instead on out-of-sample predictive performance, this provides a sound statistical basis for discriminating between competing models. Out-of-sample predictive performance is the metric of choice for time series researchers; see Diebold and Mariano (1995), West and McCracken (1998), and McCracken (2000). Although there are some in the time series literature who advocate in-sample predictive evaluation (Inoue and Kilian, 2004), there is nonetheless a large body of research that makes a convincing case for sample-splitting mechanisms whereby the full sample is split into two sub-samples - one for estimation and the other for predictive evaluation; see Corradi and Swanson (2007) and the references therein.

Racine and Parmeter (2014) provide an alternative time series test for predictive accuracy that uses a resampling-based repeated splitting mechanism. This approach, which is also applicable to cross sectional settings, overcomes some of the limitations that are associated with existing tests, namely their reliance on a single split of the data and constraints on the minimum size of the hold-out sample that are driven by power considerations.

The approach that Racine and Parmeter (2014) propose is rooted in the notion of *apparent* versus *true* error estimation; for a detailed overview of apparent, true, and excess error, see Efron (1982), Chapter 7. In-sample measures of fit assess *apparent error*, which is more optimistic than *true error* since a model is selected to *fit* the data best. For a given loss function, an in-sample measure of performance such as expected loss might be computed, thereby providing an estimate of the apparent error that arises from the modeling process. However, all such in-sample measures are fallible and are therefore unreliable guides for model selection. For example, unadjusted R^2 fails to take model complexity into account, while adjusted R^2 measures are not defined for many semi- and nonparametric methods. Information-based measures such as AIC can be biased if the sequence of competing parametric models is nonnested. See Ye (1998) and Shen and Ye (2002) for details.

The approach of Racine and Parmeter (2014) makes use of the empirical distribution function of a model's true error, which allows one to test whether a given model's expected true error is statistically smaller than that of a competing model. This is achieved by leveraging repeated splits of the data rather than just one, and by computing the estimated loss based on the hold-out data for each split. We will then reach a conclusion that one model's expected true error is statistically smaller than that of another, and hence we can expect it to be closer to the true DGP. Even though both models are, at best, approximations, one is therefore to be preferred over the other.

The basic idea is that the data are split into two independent samples of size n_1 and n_2. The first n_1 observations are used for model fitting and the remaining $n_2 = n - n_1$ observations are used for model evaluation. The latter might entail, by way of example, construction of a correct classification ratio (CCR) based on the remaining independent n_2 observations. That is, given that we know the outcomes in the evaluation data, this approach delivers an estimate of true performance; readers who are familiar with the Diebold and Mariano (1995) test for predictive accuracy will immediately recognize this strategy. However, this estimate of true performance is sensitive to the particular division of the data into two independent subsets, which might not be representative of the DGP. Thus, one might mistakenly favour an inferior model, depending on which data points end up in each of the two samples. To overcome this limitation, the process is repeated a large number of times. Each time, the original sample is shuffled and the models are refitted on the *training* data (the n_1 observations) and evaluated on the independent *evaluation* data (the $n_2 = n - n_1$ hold-out observations). This repeated sample-splitting experiment will produce two vectors of length S that represent draws from the distribution of, e.g., actual CCRs for each model. For (strictly) stationary dependent processes, we cannot use sample splitting directly; however, we can use resampling methods that are appropriate for such processes. When each resample is the outcome of an appropriate resampling methodology, it mimics dependence that is present in the original series and can itself be split; see Patton et al. (2009) and the function `b.star()` in the np package. These two vectors of draws can then be used to discriminate between the two models.

Specifically, presume that $Z_i = (X_i, Y_i)$ represent random draws from a (strictly) stationary ergodic process with unknown distribution function F,

$$Z_1, Z_2, \ldots, Z_{n_1} \sim F.$$

We observe $Z_1 = z_1, Z_2 = z_2, \cdots, Z_{n_1} = z_{n_1}$, and in what follows, we let $Z^{n_1} = (Z_1, Z_2, \ldots, Z_{n_1})$ and $z^{n_1} = (z_1, z_2, \ldots, z_{n_1})$. Having observed $Z^{n_1} = z^{n_1}$, we fit a model $\hat{g}(\cdot)$ that will be used to predict some *future* (unseen) values of the response variable, which we denote

$$\hat{g}_{z^{n_1}}(x^{n_2}).$$

The superscript n_2 indicates a new set of observations, $z^{n_2} = (z_{n_1+1}, z_{n_1+2}, \ldots, z_n)$, which are distinct from $z^{n_1} = (z_1, z_2, \ldots, z_{n_1})$. Note that $n_2 = n - n_1$. We are interested in estimating a quantity known as *expected true error* (Efron, 1982, page 51). If we were estimating a regression function, the *true error* would be the loss function evaluated over the model's residuals, i.e.,

$$E_{n_2, F}\left[\ell\left(Y^{n_2} - \hat{g}_{Z^{n_1}}(X^{n_2})\right)\right].$$

The loss function, which is specified by the researcher and satisfies certain regularity conditions, is denoted by $\ell(\cdot)$ and the regression model is denoted by $\hat{g}_{Z^{n_1}}(X^{n_2})$. The notation $E_{n_2,F}$ indicates an expectation over the new point(s)

$$Z_{n_1+1}, Z_{n_1+2}, \ldots, Z_n \sim F,$$

which are independent of $Z_1, Z_2, \cdots, Z_{n_1}$, the variables that determine $\hat{g}_{Z^{n_1}}(\cdot)$. Note that $Z = (Y, X)$. We refer to Z^{n_1} as the *training set*. Next, define *expected true error* as

$$E\left(E_{n_2,F}\left[\ell(\cdot)\right]\right),$$

which is the expectation over all potential models $\hat{g}_{Z^{n_1}}(\cdot)$ for a given loss function $\ell(\cdot)$. Formally, for two models that are indexed by A and B, we state the null and the alternative as

$$H_0 : E\left(E_{n_2,F^A}\left[\ell(\cdot)\right]\right) - E\left(E_{n_2,F^B}\left[\ell(\cdot)\right]\right) = 0$$

and

$$H_A : E\left(E_{n_2,F^A}\left[\ell(\cdot)\right]\right) - E\left(E_{n_2,F^B}\left[\ell(\cdot)\right]\right) > 0.$$

When comparing two approximate models, for a given loss function $\ell(\cdot)$, the one with the lower *expected true error* is to be preferred in applied settings since it is expected to lie closest to the true DGP. Rejection of the null leads to the selection of model B over model A.

A realization of *true error* is based on the observed $z^{n_2} = (z_{n_1+1}, z_{n_1+2}, \ldots, z_n)$. We may therefore construct the ECDF of realized true error based on S such splits of the data. Given two competing models, we can use their respective ECDFs of realized true error to determine whether one model has statistically significantly lower expected true error than another. Note that here, we are dealing with a paired two-sample problem where we are testing for equivalence of expected true error based on two vectors of realizations of true error that have been constructed from the competing models. The pairing arises from potential correlation of predictions obtained from competing models. Thus, the procedure that we consider is strictly data-driven and nonparametric in nature.

When the data represent independent draws, we proceed as follows:

- Resample without replacement pairwise from $z = \{x_i, y_i\}_{i=1}^n$ and call these resamples $z_* = \{x_i^*, y_i^*\}_{i=1}^n$. This applies a random *shuffle* to the data.
- Let the first n_1 of the shuffled observations $z_*^{n_1} = \{x_i^*, y_i^*\}_{i=1}^{n_1}$ form a training sample and the remaining $n_2 = n - n_1$ observations $z_*^{n_2} = \{x_i^*, y_i^*\}_{i=n_1+1}^n$ form an evaluation sample.
- Holding the degree of smoothing of the kernel model and the functional form of the parametric model fixed at those used for the full sample, fit each model on the training observations $(z_*^{n_1})$ and obtain predicted values from the remaining evaluation observations $(z_*^{n_2})$.

- If using the average square prediction error (ASPE) as the measure of loss, compute the ASPE of each model, which we denote by $\text{ASPE}^A = n_2^{-1} \sum_{i=n_1+1}^{n}(y_i^* - \hat{g}_{z^{n_1}}^A(x_i^*))^2$ and $\text{ASPE}^B = n_2^{-1} \sum_{i=n_1+1}^{n}(y_i^* - \hat{g}_{z^{n_1}}^B(x_i^*))^2$.

- Repeating this a large number of times yields S draws, $\{\text{ASPE}_s^A, \text{ASPE}_s^B\}_{s=1}^{S}$. We refer to the respective ECDFs as $\hat{F}_S^A$ and $\hat{F}_S^B$, where each places mass $1/S$ at ASPE_s^A and ASPE_s^B. We can now use $\hat{F}_S^A$ and $\hat{F}_S^B$ to discriminate between models; for instance, we can perform a paired t-test of the hypothesis based on each model's mean ASPE.

The focus until now has been on minimizing *loss*, e.g., expected true square error loss. However, the problem could have equivalently been expressed in terms of maximizing *gain* insofar as gain is the mirror image of loss. In this case, we would naturally prefer the model with the largest expected true gain.

Below, we consider a simple paired test of differences in means for two distributions of expected true CCRs. The CCRs are taken from three parametric Logit models and from the nonparametric binary outcome model that has been outlined in this chapter. In this example, a higher expected true CCR is equivalent to a lower expected true error.

We use the MASS package's `birthwt` data that appeared previously in this chapter. The null hypothesis is that a parametric and a nonparametric model have equal expected true CCR. The alternative hypothesis is that the nonparametric model has higher expected true CCR. Rejection of the null indicates that the nonparametric model performs significantly better than the parametric model on independent data drawn from the same DGP.

```
## This code chunk illustrates the RP test (Revealed Performance)
## detailed in Racine and Parmeter (2014)
require(np)
options(np.messages=FALSE)
set.seed(42)
## This function takes a confusion matrix and formats it correctly if
## it is unbalanced and returns the CCR as well.
CM <- function(cm) {
  factor.values.eval <- colnames(cm)
  CM <- matrix(0,nrow(cm),nrow(cm))
  rownames(CM) <- rownames(cm)
  colnames(CM) <- rownames(cm)
  for(i in 1:ncol(cm)) {
    CM[,(1:nrow(cm))[rownames(cm)==factor.values.eval[i]]] <- cm[,i]
  }
  return(list(CM=CM,CCR=sum(diag(CM))/sum(CM)))
}
## Load the birthwt data
library(MASS)
data(birthwt)
## Create a data frame that has up to 4th order polynomials. We will
```

```
## use the BIC-optimal parametric model that will allow for
## interactions and some nonlinearity.
bwt <- with(birthwt,data.frame(low=factor(low),
                               race=factor(race),
                               smoke=factor(smoke),
                               ht=factor(ht),
                               ui=factor(ui),
                               ftv=ordered(ftv),
                               age=age,
                               agesq=age**2,
                               agecu=age**3,
                               agequ=age**4,
                               lwt=lwt,
                               lwtsq=lwt**2,
                               lwtcu=lwt**3,
                               lwtqu=lwt**4))
## Set the size of the evaluation data (n.eval) and the training data
## (n.train), number of multistarts for bandwidth selection (nmulti)
## and number of train/eval splits (M)
nmulti <- 1
n.eval <- 10
n <- nrow(bwt)
n.train <- n-n.eval
M <- 100
## Create storage vectors
ccr.linear <- numeric(M)
ccr.linint <- numeric(M)
ccr.BIC <- numeric(M)
ccr.kernel <- numeric(M)
## Copy the full sample into the object train
train <- bwt
## Fit the parametric Logit model for the full sample.
##
## Linear
logit.linear <- glm(low~
                    smoke+
                    race+
                    ht+
                    ui+
                    age+
                    lwt+
                    ftv,
                    family=binomial(link=logit),
                    data=train)
## Linear Logit model with interactions
logit.linint <- glm(low~
                    (smoke+
                     race+
                     ht+
                     ui+
                     age+
                     lwt+
                     ftv)^2,
```

```
                         family=binomial(link=logit),
                         data=train)
## BIC-optimal Logit model
logit.BIC <- glm(low ~ .,
                    family = binomial(link=logit),
                    data = train)
logit.BIC <- stepAIC(logit.BIC, ~ .^3,
                        trace=FALSE,
                        k=log(nrow(birthwt)))
## Get the bandwidths for the nonparametric model for the full sample.
bw <- npcdensbw(low~
                    smoke+
                    race+
                    ht+
                    ui+
                    age+
                    lwt+
                    ftv,
                    data=train,
                    nmulti=nmulti)
## Apparent (in-sample) performance
ccr.app.linear <- with(train,CM(table(low,ifelse(predict(update(logit.linear),
                        type="response",newdata=train)>0.5,1,0))))$CCR
ccr.app.linint <- with(train,CM(table(low,ifelse(predict(update(logit.linint),
                        type="response",newdata=train)>0.5,1,0))))$CCR
ccr.app.BIC <- with(train,CM(table(low,ifelse(predict(update(logit.BIC),
                        type="response",newdata=train)>0.5,1,0))))$CCR
ccr.app.kernel <- npconmode(bws=bw,newdata=train)$CCR.overall
## Conduct the M train/eval splits
for(m in 1:M) {
    ## Shuffle the data into independent training and evaluation samples.
    ii <- sample(1:n,replace=FALSE)
    train <- bwt[ii[1:n.train],]
    ## glm() can't deal with < all ftv cases
    while(length(unique(train$ftv))<length(unique(bwt$ftv))) {
        ii <- sample(1:n,replace=FALSE)
        train <- bwt[ii[1:n.train],]
    }
    eval <- bwt[ii[(n.train+1):n],]
    ## Extract the correct classification ratios for the independent
    ## evaluation data where we know the outcomes (update() refits the
    ## Logit model on train, the nonparametric model will
    ## automatically update taking train from the environment when it
    ## is called by predict()).
    ccr.linear[m]<-with(eval,CM(table(low,ifelse(predict(update(logit.linear),
                        type="response",newdata=eval)>0.5,1,0))))$CCR
    ccr.linint[m]<-with(eval,CM(table(low,ifelse(predict(update(logit.linint),
                        type="response",newdata=eval)>0.5,1,0))))$CCR
    ccr.BIC[m] <- with(eval,CM(table(low,ifelse(predict(update(logit.BIC),
                        type="response",newdata=eval)>0.5,1,0))))$CCR
    ccr.kernel[m] <- npconmode(bws=bw,newdata=eval)$CCR.overall
}
## Conduct a paired t-test that the mean expected true CCR for each model
```

Table 4.5: Apparent versus expected true model performance (higher values are preferred) and P-values from a test for equality of expected true performance. The cases considered are the kernel versus linear index Logit models, kernel versus linear index with interaction Logit models, and kernel versus BIC-optimal index Logit models. Rejection of the null implies that the kernel-based model has significantly higher mean CCR on independent data.

	Apparent	Expected	Rank	P-value
Linear	0.762	0.690	3	0.030
Lin-Int	0.825	0.624	4	0.000
BIC	0.698	0.695	2	0.042
Kernel	0.841	0.716	1	NA

```
## is equal versus the alternative that the kernel-based model has a
## significantly larger expected true CCR than the BIC-optimal Logit model.
p.linear <- t.test(ccr.kernel,ccr.linear,alternative="greater",
                paired=TRUE)$p.value
p.linint <- t.test(ccr.kernel,ccr.linint,alternative="greater",
                paired=TRUE)$p.value
p.BIC <- t.test(ccr.kernel,ccr.BIC,alternative="greater",paired=TRUE)$p.value
p <- c(p.linear,p.linint,p.BIC,NA)
## Apparent performance
apparent <- c(ccr.app.linear,ccr.app.linint,ccr.app.BIC,ccr.app.kernel)
## Expected true performance
true <- c(mean(ccr.linear),mean(ccr.linint),mean(ccr.BIC),mean(ccr.kernel))
```

Table 4.5 summarizes the results from this exercise. The kernel model exhibits statistically significantly better expected true performance (as measured by CCR) than any of the parametric models that are considered, including the BIC-optimal approach. As expected, the in-sample (apparent) measures are always more optimistic than the realized (expected) measures. Interestingly, this is an illustration that uses a small sample ($n = 189$) and a large number of covariates (8) which, according to some, ought to disqualify the use of nonparametric kernel smoothing methods. In this case, the so-called curse of dimensionality does not prevent the kernel method from outperforming a number of parsimonious parametric models.

4.6.5 Average Treatment Effects and Propensity Score Matching

The measurement of average treatment effects (ATE), initially confined to the assessment of dose-response relationships in medical settings, is a popular approach that has been adopted in a broad range of disciplines. Examples include assessing human-capital losses arising from war (Ichino and Winter-Ebmer, 1998), the effectiveness of job training programs (Lechner, 1999), and the effectiveness of right heart catheterization (RHC) for critically ill patients admitted to an intensive care unit (Li et al., 2008, 2009b), among others.

One of the most popular approaches towards the measurement of treatment effects involves the estimation of a *propensity score* which is defined as the *conditional probability* of receiving treatment. Estimation of the propensity score was originally undertaken with parametric index models such as the Logit or Probit. There is an extensive literature on semiparametric and nonparametric estimation of treatment effects; see Hahn (1998) and Hirano et al. (2003) by way of illustration. The advantage of pursuing a nonparametric approach in this setting is rather obvious, as misspecification of the propensity score may impact significantly upon the magnitude and even the sign of the estimated treatment effect. In many settings mismeasurement induced by misspecification can be extremely costly – envision for a moment the societal cost of incorrectly concluding that a novel and beneficial cancer treatment in fact causes harm.

In what follows, we use a dummy variable, $T_i \in \{0, 1\}$, to indicate whether an individual has received treatment or not. We let $T_i = 1$ for the treated, 0 for the untreated. Letting $Y_i(T_i)$ denote the outcome, then, for $i = 1, \ldots, n$, we write

$$Y_i = T_i Y_i(1) + (1 - T_i) Y_i(0).$$

Interest lies in the average treatment effect defined as follows,

$$\tau = \mathrm{E}[Y_i(1) - Y_i(0)].$$

Let X_i denote a vector of pre-treatment variables. One issue that immediately surfaces in this setting is that, for each individual i, we either observe $Y_i(0)$ or $Y_i(1)$, but not both. Therefore, in the absence of additional assumptions, the treatment effect cannot be consistently estimated. One popular assumption is the *unconfoundedness condition* (Rosenbaum and Rubin, 1983), which presumes that, conditional on X_i, the treatment indicator T_i is independent of the potential outcome.

Define the conditional treatment effect by $\tau(x) = \mathrm{E}[Y_i(1) - Y_i(0)|X_i = x]$. Assuming that the unconfoundedness condition holds, one can easily show that (e.g., Theorem 4 of Rosenbaum and Rubin (1983))

$$\tau(x) = \mathrm{E}[Y_i|T_i = 1, X_i = x] - \mathrm{E}[Y_i|T_i = 0, X_i = x]. \qquad (4.3)$$

The two terms on the right-hand side of (4.3) can be estimated consistently by any nonparametric estimation technique. Presuming the unconfoundedness condition holds, the average treatment effect can be obtained via simple averaging over $\tau(x)$ and is given by

$$\tau = \mathrm{E}[\tau(X_i)]. \qquad (4.4)$$

Letting $E(Y_i|X_i, T_i)$ be denoted by $g(X_i, T_i)$, we then have

$$Y_i = g(X_i, T_i) + \epsilon_i, \tag{4.5}$$

with $E(\epsilon_i|X_i, T_i) = 0$.

Defining $g_0(X_i) = g(X_i, T_i = 0)$ and $g_1(X_i) = g(X_i, T_i = 1)$, we can re-write (4.5) as

$$
\begin{aligned}
Y_i &= g_0(X_i) + [g_1(X_i) - g_0(X_i)]T_i + \epsilon_i \\
&= g_0(X_i) + \tau(X_i)T_i + \epsilon_i,
\end{aligned} \tag{4.6}
$$

where $\tau(X_i) = g_1(X_i) - g_0(X_i)$.

From (4.6) it is easy to show that $\tau(X_i) = \mathrm{Cov}(Y_i, T_i|X_i)/\mathrm{Var}(T_i|X_i)$. Letting $\mu(X_i) = \Pr(T_i = 1|X_i) \equiv E(T_i|X_i)$ (because T_i equals 0 or 1), we may write

$$\tau = E[\tau(X_i)] = E\left\{\frac{(T_i - \mu_i(X_i))Y_i}{\mathrm{Var}(T_i|X_i)}\right\}.$$

By noting that $\mathrm{Var}(T_i|X_i) = \mu(X_i)(1 - \mu(X_i))$, this can be written as

$$
\begin{aligned}
\tau &= E\left\{\frac{(T_i - \mu_i(X_i))Y_i}{\mu(X_i)(1 - \mu(X_i))}\right\} \\
&= E\left\{\frac{T_iY_i}{\mu(X_i)} - \frac{1 - Y_i}{1 - \mu(X_i)}\right\}.
\end{aligned}
$$

Since $\mu(X_i) = \Pr(T_i = 1|X_i) = E(T_i|X_i)$, we can use either a conditional probability estimator or a conditional mean estimator to estimate $\mu(X_i)$. To avoid division by zero one needs to ensure that $\hat{\mu}(X_i) \in (0, 1)$, and it is worth noting that the local constant conditional mean estimator outlined in Chapter 6 and the conditional probability estimator outlined in this chapter are both *guaranteed* to deliver *proper* probabilities, i.e., will deliver $\hat{\mu}(X_i) \in [0, 1]$ though this *is not guaranteed* to be the case when using local polynomial estimators with order ≥ 1. See Li et al. (2009b) for further details.

We consider the performance of parametric and nonparametric propensity score models based upon data taken from the Study to Understand Prognoses and Preferences for Outcomes and Risks of Treatments (SUPPORT). These data were used in a study by Connors et al. (1996) who considered 30-day, 60-day, and 180-day survival (they also considered categories of admission diagnosis and categories of comorbidities illness as covariates). We restrict attention to 180-day survival by way of example, while we ignore admission diagnosis and comorbidities illness due to the prevalence of missing observations among these covariates. Nevertheless, even though we omit admission diagnosis and comorbidities illness as covariates, we indeed observe results that are qualitatively and quantitatively similar to those reported in Connors et al. (1996) and Lin et al. (1998). The variables we consider are as follows:

- Y: Outcome - 1 if death occurred within 180 days, zero otherwise

- T: Treatment - 1 if a Swan-Ganz catheter was received by the patient when they were hospitalized, zero otherwise.
- X_1: Sex - 0 for female, 1 for male
- X_2: Race - 0 if black, 1 if white, 2 if other
- X_3: Income - 0 if under 11K, 1 if 11–25K, 2 if 25–50K, 3 if over 50K
- X_4: Primary disease category - 1 if Acute Respiratory Failure, 2 if Congestive Heart Failure, 3 if Chronic Obstructive Pulmonary Disease, 4 if Cirrhosis, 5 if Colon Cancer, 6 if Coma, 7 if Lung Cancer, 8 if Multiple Organ System Failure with Malignancy, 9 if Multiple Organ System Failure with Sepsis
- X_5: Secondary disease category - 1 if Cirrhosis, 2 if Colon Cancer, 3 if Coma, 4 if Lung Cancer, 5 if Multiple Organ System Failure with Malignancy, 6 if Multiple Organ System Failure with Sepsis, 7 if NA
- X_6: Medical insurance - 1 if Medicaid, 2 if Medicare, 3 if Medicare & Medicaid, 4 if No insurance, 5 if Private, 6 if Private & Medicare
- X_7: Age - age (converted to years from Y/M/D data stored with 2 decimal accuracy)

Based upon a parametric Logit model, Connors et al. (1996) report that those receiving right-heart catheterization are more likely to die within 180 days than those who did not which was a controversial finding. Lin et al. (1998) report that, when further adjustments were made, the risk of death is lower than that reported by Connors et al. (1996) and they conclude that "results of our sensitivity analysis provide additional insights into this important study and imply perhaps greater uncertainty about the role of RHC than those stated in the original report."

Lin et al. (1998) note that cardiologists' and intensive care physicians' belief in the efficacy of RHC for guiding therapy for certain patients is so strong that "it has prevented the conduct of a randomized clinical trial" (RCT) while Connors et al. (1996) note that "the most recent attempt at an RCT was stopped because most physicians refused to allow their patients to be randomized."

Below we estimate the propensity score using a parametric Logit model and nonparametric conditional probability model, compute the ATE for both estimates, and then construct nonparametric confidence intervals for the estimates. We also report the confusion matrices and correct classification ratios.

```
set.seed(42)
library(np)
options(np.tree=TRUE,np.messages=FALSE)
rhc <- read.table("data/rhc.dat",header=TRUE)
## Parametric
ps.logit <- glm(swang1~
                factor(sex)+
                factor(race)+
                factor(income)+
```

```
                    factor(cat1)+
                    factor(cat2)+
                    factor(ninsclas)+
                    age,
                    family = binomial(link = logit),
                    data=rhc)
## Compute the propensity score, i.e., P(Y=1|x)
ps.par <- ps.logit$fit
## Compute the parametric confusion matrix and ATE
cm.par <- table(rhc$swang1,ifelse(ps.par>0.5,1,0))
ate.par <- mean(rhc$swang1*rhc$death/ps.par -
                (1-rhc$swang1)*rhc$death/(1-ps.par))
## Nonparametric
bw <- npcdensbw(factor(swang1)~
                factor(sex)+
                factor(race)+
                factor(income)+
                factor(cat1)+
                factor(cat2)+
                factor(ninsclas)+
                age,
                cxkertype="epanechnikov",
                nmulti=1,
                data=rhc)
model.np <- npcdens(bw,data=rhc)
phat <- fitted(model.np)
## The conditional probability corresponds to Pr(Y=y|x). We want
## Pr(Y=1|x) to be consistent with the Logit model.
ps.np <- ifelse(rhc$swang1==1,phat,1-phat)
## Compute the confusion matrix and nonparametric ATE
cm.np <- table(rhc$swang1,ifelse(ps.np>0.5,1,0))
ate.np <- mean(rhc$swang1*rhc$death/ps.np -
               (1-rhc$swang1)*rhc$death/(1-ps.np))
```

The confusion matrices for the parametric and nonparametric propensity score estimators are as follows:

Table 4.6: Parametric confusion matrix.

	0	1
0	2841	710
1	1197	987

Table 4.7: Nonparametric confusion matrix.

	0	1
0	2893	658
1	1113	1071

An examination of these confusion matrices indicates that the nonparametric model is better able to predict who receives treatment and who does not than the parametric model; the correct classification ratios for the parametric and nonparametric approaches are *0.6675* and *0.6912*, respectively.

```
## Bootstrap the ATEs
B <- 1000
ate.par.res <- numeric(length=B)
ate.np.res <- numeric(length=B)
rhc.orig <- rhc
for(i in 1:B) {
  rhc <- rhc.orig[sample(seq(1,nrow(rhc)),replace=TRUE),]
  ## Parametric
  ps.logit <- glm(swang1~
                  factor(sex)+
                  factor(race)+
                  factor(income)+
                  factor(cat1)+
                  factor(cat2)+
                  factor(ninsclas)+
                  age,
                  family = binomial(link = logit),
                  data=rhc)
  ps.par.res <- ps.logit$fit
  ate.par.res[i] <- mean(rhc$swang1*rhc$death/ps.par.res -
                  (1-rhc$swang1)*rhc$death/(1-ps.par.res))
  ## Nonparametric (this call will use the resampled rhc and the
  ## pre-computed bandwidths)
  phat.res <- predict(model.np,data=rhc)
  ps.np.res <- ifelse(rhc$swang1==1,phat.res,1-phat.res)
  ate.np.res[i] <- mean(rhc$swang1*rhc$death/ps.np.res -
                  (1-rhc$swang1)*rhc$death/(1-ps.np.res))
}
```

The parametric and nonparametric ATEs are *0.07176* and *0.007923*, respectively, and their 95% bootstrapped nonparametric confidence intervals are *[0.04585,0.09969]* and *[-0.0285,0.02281]*, respectively. These confidence intervals indicate that the parametric model suggests a statistically significant increased risk of death for those receiving RHC, while the nonparametric model yields no significant difference. The nonparametric results overturn the controversial parametric results leading us to conclude that patients receiving RHC treatment *do not* in fact appear to suffer an increased risk of death, and indicate that the controversial findings reported by Connors et al. (1996) may well be an artifact of parametric misspecification.

For related literature that uses matching instead of the estimation of a propensity score see Heckman et al. (1997), Heckman et al. (1998), and Dehejia and Wahba (1999).

Problem Set

1. Define the conditional density estimator $\hat{f}(y|x)$ for the bivariate case as

$$\hat{f}(y|x) = \frac{\hat{f}(y, x)}{\hat{f}(x)}$$

where

$$\hat{f}(y, x) = \frac{1}{nh_y h_x} \sum_{i=1}^{n} K\left(\frac{y - Y_i}{h_y}\right) K\left(\frac{x - X_i}{h_x}\right)$$

and where

$$\hat{f}(x) = \frac{1}{nh_x} \sum_{i=1}^{n} K\left(\frac{x - X_i}{h_x}\right).$$

Demonstrate that $\hat{f}(y|x) \to \hat{f}(y)$ as $h_x \to \infty$. That is, show that the conditional density estimator $\hat{f}(y|x)$ approaches the unconditional density estimator $\hat{f}(y)$ as the bandwidth $h_x \to \infty$.

2. Consider the `birthwt` data from the R package MASS. Fit a Logit model where the outcome is `low` (=1 if low birth weight, 0 otherwise) and the covariates are `age` (mother's age in years) and `smoke` (=1 if the mother smoked during pregnancy, 0 otherwise). The model should allow for interaction between `age` and `smoke`. Generate a counterfactual that plots the probability of low birth weight as a function of age for smokers and non-smokers. For instance, a model that is linear in `age` with an `age/smoke` interaction could be estimated as follows:

```
require(MASS)
data(birthwt)
birthwt$low <- factor(birthwt$low)
birthwt$smoke <- factor(birthwt$smoke)
model <- glm(low~(smoke+
            poly(age,degree=1))^2,
            family=binomial(link=logit),
            data=birthwt)
summary(model)
## Generate two data frames to predict the probability of low birth
## weight (low=1) as a function of age and smoking status (smoke=1
## indicates a smoker)
low.smoke<-with(birthwt,data.frame(low=factor("1",levels=levels(low)),
```

```
                        smoke=factor("1",levels=levels(smoke)),
                        age=min(age):max(age)))
low.nosmoke<-with(birthwt,data.frame(low=factor("1",levels=levels(low)),
                        smoke=factor("0",levels=levels(smoke)),
                        age=min(age):max(age)))
p.lin.low.smoke <- predict(model,newdata=low.smoke,type="response")
p.lin.low.nosmoke <- predict(model,newdata=low.nosmoke,type="response")
## Plot the counterfactual probabilities for smokers and nonsmokers
plot(low.smoke$age,p.lin.low.smoke,
     ylim=range(c(p.lin.low.smoke,p.lin.low.nosmoke)),
     ylab="$Pr(low=1\\vert age,smoke)$",
     xlab="Age",
     type="l",lwd=2)
lines(low.smoke$age,p.lin.low.nosmoke,col=2,lty=2,lwd=2)
legend("topright",c("Smoker","Nonsmoker"),col=1:2,lty=1:2,
       lwd=c(2,2),bty="n")
## Plot the increased risk of low birth weight associated with smoking
plot(low.smoke$age,p.lin.low.smoke-p.lin.low.nosmoke,type="l",lwd=2,
     ylab="Increased Probability of Low Birth Weight",
     xlab="Age")
abline(h=0,lty=2,col="grey")
```

   i. Repeat this for a model that is quadratic in age (**degree=2**), cubic
      in age (**degree=3**), and quartic in age (**degree=4**). Based on the
      AIC criterion, which parametric model would you prefer?
  ii. Compare the preferred parametric and the nonparametric proba-
      bility and increased risk estimates. Comment on any differences.

Part II

Conditional Moment Functions and Related Statistical Objects

Chapter 5

Conditional Moment Functions

Statistics may be boring, but it does have its moments. (anonymous)

5.1 Overview

A *moment* is a specific quantitative measure of the shape of a set of points. If the points represent probability density, then the zeroth moment is the total probability (i.e., one), the first moment is the mean, the second central moment (with shift) is the variance, the third central moment (with normalization and shift) is the skewness, and the fourth central moment (with normalization and shift) is the kurtosis. The rth moment about the origin of the random variable Y is denoted by μ'_r and is defined as

$$\mu'_r = \mathrm{E}\, Y^r.$$

The rth moment about the mean of the random variable Y (i.e., the rth *central* moment) is defined as

$$\mu_r = \mathrm{E}((Y - \mu'_1)^r).$$

Skewness is defined as $\mu_3/(\mu_2)^{3/2}$ and kurtosis is defined as $\mu_4/(\mu_2)^2$. These unconditional *descriptive statistics* (i.e., the mean, variance, skewness, and kurtosis) are useful for summarizing location, scale, symmetry, and how heavy-tailed a distribution is. When we condition a moment on a set of covariates that may explain its variation, we are then dealing with a *conditional moment*. The rth *conditional* moment about the origin of the random variable Y given $X = x$ is defined as

$$\mu'_r(x) = \mathrm{E}(Y^r | X = x).$$

The rth *conditional* moment about the conditional mean of the random variable Y given $X = x$ is defined as

$$\mu_r(x) = \mathrm{E}((Y - \mu_1'(x))^r | X = x).$$

The most commonly encountered conditional moment is the *conditional mean* $\mu_1'(x) = \mathrm{E}(Y|X = x)$ since it is the object of predominant interest in *regression analysis*. The *conditional variance* $\mu_2(x) = \mathrm{E}((Y - \mu_1'(x))^2 | X = x)$ is a widely studied moment in finance, where it is referred to as the *conditional volatility*. Also popular in finance is the study of *conditional skewness*, which goes by the moniker *conditional asymmetry*.

Unconditional and conditional moments are respectively defined in terms of the unconditional and conditional PDF and CDF of a random variable Y. For instance, the rth moment about the origin for a continuous random variable $Y \in \mathbb{R}$ is given by

$$\mu_r' = \mathrm{E}\,Y^r$$
$$= \int_{-\infty}^{\infty} y^r f(y)\, dy$$
$$= \int_{-\infty}^{\infty} y^r\, dF(y),$$

where $f(y)$ and $F(y)$ respectively denote the unconditional PDF and CDF of Y. The rth moment about the origin for a discrete random variable $Y \in \mathcal{D}$ is given by

$$\mu_r' = \mathrm{E}\,Y^r$$
$$= \sum_{y \in \mathcal{D}} y^r p(y).$$

The rth conditional moment about the origin for a continuous random variable $Y \in \mathbb{R}$ is given by

$$\mu_r'(x) = \mathrm{E}(Y^r | X = x)$$
$$= \int_{-\infty}^{\infty} y^r f(y|x)\, dy$$
$$= \int_{-\infty}^{\infty} y^r\, dF(y|x),$$

where $f(y|x)$ and $F(y|x)$ respectively denote the conditional PDF and CDF of Y given X. The point being made is that regardless of whether one is interested in unconditional or conditional moments, they are functions of *unknown* unconditional or conditional PDFs and CDFs. We studied nonparametric estimation of density and distribution functions in Chapter 1, Chapter 2, and Chapter 3 and conditional density and distribution functions in Chapter 4. It doesn't take too much imagination to appreciate the essence of nonparametric estimation of conditional moments; one simply plugs in a smooth consistent nonparametric estimator of the unknown unconditional or conditional PDF or CDF and simplifies where possible. One can then determine the statistical properties of the resulting method, construct a suitable scheme for smoothing parameter and bandwidth selection, and describe the limiting distribution.

We will now study a conditional moment that is very popular in applied statistics, namely the conditional mean or *regression* function.

Chapter 6

Conditional Mean Function Estimation

If all you have is a hammer, everything looks like a nail. (Maslow, 1966)

6.1 Overview

Regression analysis, which involves the estimation of *conditional mean* functions, is one of the most popular statistical methods in existence. Its objective is to measure the *expected value* of a variable Y, given a vector of predictors X. This statistical tool is designed to get at questions such as "what is the expected hourly wage of a married Asian female who holds an undergraduate degree in chemical engineering and who has five years of work experience in her sector?" Regression analysis also involves the estimation of *marginal effects*, i.e., how Y responds to *changes* in the predictors, and the determination of whether such responses are *statistically significant*.

The conditional mean function (i.e., the *regression* function) for a continuously distributed $Y \in \mathbb{R}$ is defined as

$$
\begin{aligned}
g(x) &= \mathrm{E}(Y|X = x) \\
&= \int y \frac{f(y, x)}{f(x)}\, dy \\
&= \frac{\int y f(y, x)\, dy}{f(x)} \\
&= \frac{m(x)}{f(x)},
\end{aligned} \tag{6.1}
$$

where the conditioning and the dependent variables are both treated as random variables.[1] Note that the limits of integration, which are omitted

---

[1]The assumption that the design X is non-random or *fixed in repeated samples* is

to avoid unnecessary notational clutter, are $\pm\infty$ unless stated otherwise. Using the shorthand notation $\mathrm{E}(Y|X = x) = \mathrm{E}(Y|x)$, the conditional mean relationship under the assumption of additive errors[2] is given by

$$y = \mathrm{E}(Y|x) + \epsilon$$
$$= g(x) + \epsilon.$$

The unknown functions in this relationship are the joint and marginal PDFs, $f(y, x)$ and $f(x)$, respectively.

The *marginal effects function* for continuously distributed $x \in \mathbb{R}$ is simply the first partial derivative function, and it is defined as

$$\begin{aligned}
\beta(x) &= \frac{dg(x)}{dx} \\
&= \frac{f(x)m'(x) - m(x)f'(x)}{f^2(x)} \\
&= \frac{m'(x)}{f(x)} - \frac{m(x)}{f(x)}\frac{f'(x)}{f(x)} \\
&= \frac{m'(x)}{f(x)} - g(x)\frac{f'(x)}{f(x)}.
\end{aligned} \tag{6.2}$$

Reflect momentarily on the definition of the conditional mean function $g(x)$ and the marginal effects function $\beta(x)$ in Equations (6.1) and (6.2). They involve unknown joint and marginal densities (and derivatives thereof in the case of $\beta(x)$), which are nonlinear functions of y and x. If you were given the task of estimating, say, the unknown object $\beta(x) = \frac{m'(x)}{f(x)} - g(x)\frac{f'(x)}{f(x)}$, it might be difficult to justify the assumption that the derivative $\beta(x)$ is *not* a function of x and is instead a constant. We will return to this issue in due course.

There are two approaches that one might entertain when estimating unknown conditional mean and marginal effects functions:

   i. Presume a parametric relationship (e.g., additive and linear in the predictors) and estimate under this presumption.

   ii. Use a kernel-smoothed approach.

Note that these were also the options that we considered when we wanted to estimate an unknown density function. Of course, the kernel-based approach isn't the only nonparametric estimation method that is available to practitioners, but given its considerable popularity in applied settings, it is the only one that we will be entertaining here. Alternative approaches that are based on Fourier series, regression splines, smoothing splines, polynomial

---

sometimes invoked in parametric settings to simplify the theoretical analysis. We take no such shortcuts in what follows.

   [2]Nonseparable error models are sometimes necessary, which somewhat complicates the analysis; see Altonji and Matzkin (2005).

series, nearest neighbours, and wavelets can also be found in the literature (Gallant, 1987; Wahba, 1990; de Boor, 2001; Gençay et al., 2002; Wang, 2011).

6.2   Parametric Conditional Mean Models

The parametric approach requires that a number of assumptions be made about the underlying DGP. For instance, the classical *linear regression* specification presumes that Y (or some transformation of Y) can be expressed as a linear function of X (or some transformation of X). The complete mathematical specification of such a model involves a set of guesses about the underlying DGP, i.e.,

- $Y_i = \beta_0 + \beta_1 X_{i1} + \beta_2 X_{i2} + \cdots + \beta_q X_{iq} + \varepsilon_i$ is the *true* model (i.e., it is *correctly specified*)
- $\mathrm{E}(\varepsilon_i | X_{i1}, \ldots X_{iq}) = 0$ (errors are *exogenous*)
- $\mathrm{E}(\varepsilon_i^2 | X_{i1}, \ldots X_{iq}) = \sigma^2$ (errors are *homoskedastic*)
- $\mathrm{E}(\varepsilon_i \varepsilon_j | X_{i1}, \ldots X_{iq}, X_{j1}, \ldots X_{jq}) = \sigma_{ij} = 0$, $i \neq j$ (errors are *serially uncorrelated*)
- $f(\varepsilon) = \frac{1}{\sqrt{2\pi\sigma^2}} e^{-\frac{1}{2}\left(\frac{\varepsilon-\mu}{\sigma}\right)^2}$ (the errors are *normally distributed*; this assumption is required when conducting maximum likelihood estimation, for example)

This is the *classical parametric Fisherian* approach that casts statistical estimation as a problem involving a *finite* number of parameters (here $\beta_0, \beta_1, \ldots, \beta_q$, μ and σ^2). This imposes a rigid parametric structure on the underlying DGP which, if incorrect, leads to biased and inconsistent estimation of the conditional mean. Note that it isn't just the conditional mean whose functional form must be specified in advance; if the conditional variance/covariance function or the density function of the population disturbances are incorrectly specified, this can invalidate inference.

Example 6.1. Correctly and Incorrectly Specified Parametric Regression Models.

> We first consider the case where the practitioner has correctly assumed that a linear-in-predictor regression model is appropriate. The following table presents a summary of the model $Y_i = \beta_0 + \beta_1 X_i + \varepsilon_i$ fitted by the method of maximum likelihood when the DGP is $\mathrm{E}(Y|x) = 1 + x$, the errors are normal, and none of the remaining pertinent assumptions are violated. We draw $n = 100$ observations from the underlying DGP.

> In this instance, the estimates are sound since the practitioner has correctly guessed the true model. That is, the practitioner has drawn from the (infinite-dimensional) space of candidate

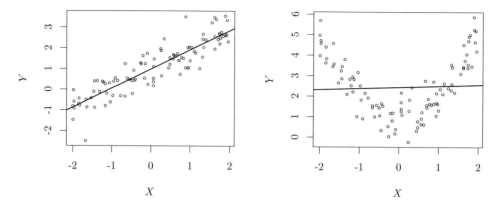

Figure 6.1: Linear regression estimates for two DGPs. The parametric model on the left is correctly specified and consistent, while the model on the right is incorrectly specified and inconsistent.

Table 6.1: Correctly specified parametric model summary.

	Estimate	Std. Error	t value	Pr(>|t|)
(Intercept)	0.9918	0.0560	17.72	0.0000
x	0.9275	0.0464	19.98	0.0000

functions the one function that happens to coincide with the underlying DGP. A scatterplot of the data reveals a clear relationship between X and Y. The coefficient of determination for the correctly specified linear model is 0.803, while the t and F statistics indicate that the intercept and slope parameter estimates are highly significant ($F = 399.3934, 1, 98$). A test for correct specification of the conditional mean function delivers a P-value of 0.629; hence we would fail to reject the null at all conventional levels that the linear model is correctly specified (Ramsey, 1969).

Next, we consider the case where the practitioner has incorrectly assumed that a linear-in-predictor regression model is appropriate. The following table presents a summary of the model $Y_i = \beta_0 + \beta_1 X_i + \varepsilon_i$ fitted by the method of maximum likelihood when the DGP is $E(Y|x) = 1 + x^2$, the errors are normal, and all underlying assumptions other than a correctly specified conditional mean function hold true.

Table 6.2: Incorrectly specified parametric model summary.

	Estimate	Std. Error	t value	Pr(>|t|)
(Intercept)	2.4430	0.1449	16.86	0.0000
x	0.0577	0.1201	0.48	0.6319

In this instance, the practitioner has failed to correctly guess the true model and the outcome is consequently disappointing. A scatterplot of the data reveals that there is an unmistakable relationship between X and Y; however, the incorrectly specified linear model's coefficient of determination is only 0.0024, while the t and F statistics for this model indicate that X and Y are unrelated ($F = 0.231, 1, 98$). A test for correct specification of the conditional mean function delivers a P-value of 1.4098×10^{-37} and hence we would reject the null at all conventional levels that the linear model is correctly specified (Ramsey, 1969). Of course, in multivariate settings, we cannot use visual aids to gain insight into what the underlying relationship might be, and as we consider alternative parametric specifications, we open a Pandora's pre-test box that gives rise to complications regarding statistical inference. The data and model fits for both the correctly and the incorrectly specified models are plotted in Figure 6.1.

As a preview of things to come, we also estimate the unknown conditional mean using a data-driven nonparametric method (the *local linear* estimator). The estimates are presented in Figure 6.2. It is evident that the smooth nonparametric approach is able to adapt to the underlying DGP without requiring any functional form assumptions from the practitioner.

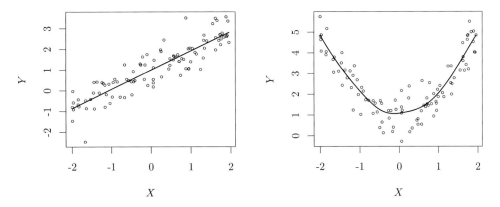

Figure 6.2: Consistent nonparametric regression (local linear) estimates for two DGPs.

6.2.1   (Re)-interpretation of Conditional Mean Models

Parametric regression results are typically reported as in Table 6.1 and the scalar coefficient estimates are given an interpretation along the lines of "$\hat{\beta}_1$ is the effect on the dependent variable y of a marginal increase in the predictor x". When a model is linear in predictors, these are referred to as *slope coefficients*. The t-statistics and P-values that are reported in Table 6.1 pertain to null hypotheses of the form $H_0\colon \beta_1 = 0$, and hence they are in fact being used to infer whether $dg(x)/dx = 0$ for all x. These are called *tests of significance* and their interpretation under H_0 is that the predictor is irrelevant, that is, it has no explanatory power in the model. When dealing with continuous data types, each of the coefficient estimates is the first partial derivative of the dependent variable y with respect to a predictor x. As soon as we depart from a model that is linear in predictors and that does not contain any interaction terms, the coefficient estimates and the aforementioned test statistics no longer have a straightforward interpretation. For instance, consider a model that is quadratic in a predictor, $Y_i = \beta_0 + \beta_1 X_i + \beta_2 X_i^2 + \epsilon_i$. The coefficients β_1 and β_2 are components of the *derivative function* $dg(x)/dx = \beta_1 + 2\beta_2 x$ but they are not independently meaningful. If the model was instead $Y_i = \beta_0 + \beta_1 \cos(\beta_2 X_i) + \epsilon_i$, then $dg(x)/dx = -\beta_1\beta_2 \sin(\beta_2 X_i)$ and it would therefore make little sense to reduce a nonlinear relationship such as this to a simple scalar.

In a nonlinear setting, we tend to use derivative functions rather than scalars to model marginal effects.[3] These derivative functions can be reported in tabular form, where there is a column of x values and another column of associated marginal effects estimates $\hat\beta(x)$. Alternatively, the relationship can be depicted in graphical form where the marginal effect $\hat\beta(x)$ is plotted as a function of x. In any event, reducing the derivative estimate $\hat\beta(x)$ to a scalar is often just as ill-advised as reducing the fitted values $\hat g(x)$ from a regression model to a scalar, since these both tend to be functions of the predictors x. While such a reduction might be comparatively easy to interpret, it is important to remember that "easy to interpret" is not a very defensible statistical criterion; *consistency*, *minimum variance*, and *unbiasedness* are far more important.

The absence of any sound statistical reason for defaulting to a simple linear model calls to mind the tale of the drunk who, after leaving a bar one night, is looking for his lost keys under a street lamp. The story goes something like this.

> A man is on his hands and knees crawling around a street lamp. A stranger walks by and asks "What are you doing? Can I help?" "Looking for my lost keys..." is the reply. The stranger asks "Where did you lose them?" "In the alley behind that building..." is the reply. The stranger asks "Why are you looking here?" "Because the light is better here!" is the reply.

The relevance of this metaphor to model specification should by this point

---

[3]Recall that the space of models is dense but there is only one model that gives rise to a constant scalar-valued derivative function. This is the *additive* model that is *linear in predictors* and that *lacks any interaction terms*.

be obvious. Modeling a derivative as a constant β_1 rather than a function $\beta(x)$ simply because it is easier to interpret is just as erroneous as looking for one's keys in a particular location solely because the light is better.

6.2.2 Counterfactual Experiments and Conditional Mean Models

Interesting relationships are often complex. If you seek to truly understand them, it may require some effort, but you will be rewarded with insights that might otherwise escape your notice. When faced with an unknown statistical relationship, practitioners often make simplifying assumptions that are intended to facilitate their understanding of the matter at hand. This typically involves reducing some object of interest to a *scalar* quantity. While this reductionist approach may appear simple, there is a risk that oversimplification, in a statistical approximation context, will lead to biased, inconsistent estimation and unsound inference.

Consider the following example that involves an earnings equation in which hourly wages are modelled as a function of an employee's potential experience. Let $y = g(x) + \epsilon$, where y is the wage rate, x is potential experience, ϵ is a stochastic disturbance term that satisfies $E(\epsilon|X = x) = 0$, and $g(x) = E(Y|X = x)$ is the unknown conditional mean function. Suppose that you would like to determine the impact of an additional year of potential experience on expected wage. In this context, the object of interest is the *marginal effect function* $\beta(x)$, which is simply the first derivative of $g(x)$ with respect to x.

If you were content with the assumption of a linear relationship $g(x) = \beta_0 + \beta_1 x$, then the marginal effect function given your guess about the underlying DGP would be $\beta(x) = \beta_1$, that is, a scalar whose value can be estimated via the classical approach. Thus, your simplifying assumption, which may or may not be warranted, has reduced the relevant result from an element of a *function space* to an element of a *parameter space*. That is, a vector has been reduced to a scalar.

The theory of human capital (Becker, 1993) predicts that wages will first rise, then plateau, and then eventually fall as one gains experience. Using data from the 1976 U.S. Current Population Survey, we fit two models - one that is linear and another that is quadratic in potential experience.

Figure 6.3 presents the fitted values and marginal effects estimates for the linear and quadratic specifications. Note that the former reduces the marginal effect to a scalar. The coefficients of variation for the linear and quadratic models are $R^2 = 0.0124$ and $R^2 = 0.104$, respectively. A summary of the regression results for each model appears in Table 6.3 and Table 6.4.

For the sake of argument, suppose that the quadratic specification is a faithful description of the underlying DGP. Then the practitioner who has mistakenly reduced the marginal effect to a scalar would tell you that its value

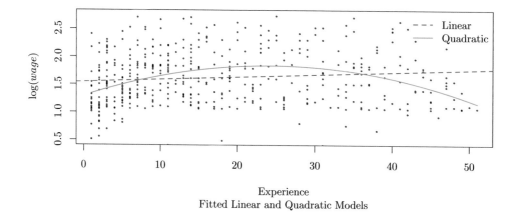

Experience
Fitted Linear and Quadratic Models

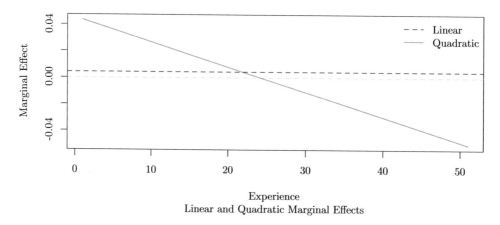

Experience
Linear and Quadratic Marginal Effects

Figure 6.3: Parametric earnings functions and marginal effects functions (U.S. Current Population Survey, 1976).

is 0.0044. The marginal effect is, however, *positive* and large in magnitude at low levels of experience and *negative* and large in magnitude at high levels of experience. This result is consistent with the theory of human capital. The linear and quadratic models' marginal effects are plotted in Figure 6.3.

Things become more interesting when we move beyond the single predictor case. Here, it is common to assume *additivity*, i.e., that $g(x_1, x_2) = g_1(x_1) + g_2(x_2)$, and this is often further reduced to the standard additive linear formulation $g(x_1, x_2) = \beta_0 + \beta_1 x_1 + \beta_2 x_2$. This is not an innocuous assumption since it implies that the value of one predictor cannot influence another predictor's marginal effects. For instance, it would indeed be difficult to justify the point of view that the marginal effect of an additional year of potential experience ought to be the same for university-educated professionals and for those with only a high school diploma.

There are some who advocate the use of *average derivatives*, which also

Table 6.3: Linear model summary.

	Estimate	Std. Error	t value	Pr(>|t|)
(Intercept)	1.5490	0.0370	41.87	0.0000
exper	0.0044	0.0017	2.57	0.0106

Table 6.4: Nonlinear (quadratic) model summary.

	Estimate	Std. Error	t value	Pr(>|t|)
(Intercept)	1.2953	0.0495	26.18	0.0000
exper	0.0455	0.0059	7.77	0.0000
expersq	-0.0009	0.0001	-7.31	0.0000

involves a scalar representation of the marginal effect function. This is again difficult to justify, particularly when a test is performed to determine whether the average is equal to zero and failure to reject the null results in a false conclusion that there is no relationship between the predictor and the outcome.[4] We will resist this reductionist urge and proceed according to the recognition that interesting relationships are complex.

A promising approach towards the interpretation of nonlinear relationships involves the construction of simple counterfactuals whereby an *interesting individual* is identified and then a specific question is answered on this basis. For instance, one might ask how an additional year of potential experience affects the wages of a married female with one year of experience under her belt. This involves a comparison of $g(female, married, exper = 1)$ with $g(female, married, exper = 2)$. Regardless of whether the model is linear or nonlinear, parametric or nonparametric, it is always possible to compute $\hat{g}(female, married, exper = 2)$ - $\hat{g}(female, married, exper = 1)$, construct confidence bands, and test the null hypothesis that there is no difference. In the code chunk below, a comparison is undertaken of 1 versus 2 years of potential experience and then of 50 versus 51 years of potential experience. We consider a simple linear additive model and a nonlinear model that allows for interaction among all predictors and that adopts a polynomial of degree 2 for potential experience.

For the simple linear additive model, the marginal effect is obviously the same regardless of whether the individual is starting from a low or a high level of experience. The less restrictive nonlinear model makes no such assumption, but it is just as capable of answering the question that is posed in this counterfactual exercise. In R, we invoke the **predict()** function for the estimated model. Thus, instead of talking about parameters, we seek to

---

[4]This is a necessary but not a sufficient condition for concluding that there is no relationship. A necessary and sufficient condition is that the derivative function $\beta(x)$ is zero for all x (almost everywhere). Reporting the derivative at the *average value of the predictor* is also difficult to justify.

provide answers to interesting questions, and we are able to do so in a robust
fashion when our analysis is based on a consistent nonparametric estimation
framework.

```
model.lm.nonlin <- lm(lwage~(female+married+exper+expersq)^2-exper:expersq,
                      data=wage1)
model.lm <- lm(lwage~female+married+exper,data=wage1)
## Generate data frames with the same named variables as those in the
## regression equation
newdata.1<-with(wage1,data.frame(female=factor("Female",levels=levels(female)),
                      married=factor("Married",levels=levels(married)),
                      exper=1,
                      expersq=1))
newdata.2<-with(wage1,data.frame(female=factor("Female",levels=levels(female)),
                      married=factor("Married",levels=levels(married)),
                      exper=2,
                      expersq=2**2))
newdata.50<-with(wage1,data.frame(female=factor("Female",levels=levels(female)),
                      married=factor("Married",levels=levels(married)),
                      exper=50,
                      expersq=50**2))
newdata.51<-with(wage1,data.frame(female=factor("Female",levels=levels(female)),
                      married=factor("Married",levels=levels(married)),
                      exper=51,
                      expersq=51**2))
## Construct the counterfactual for the nonlinear then linear model moving
## from 1 to 2 year's worth of potential experience
nonlin.12 <- predict(model.lm.nonlin,newdata=newdata.2)-
          predict(model.lm.nonlin,newdata=newdata.1)
lin.12 <- predict(model.lm,newdata=newdata.2)-
          predict(model.lm,newdata=newdata.1)
nonlin.12
##          1
## 0.006676
lin.12
##          1
## 0.001276
## Construct the counterfactual for the nonlinear then linear model moving
## from 50 to 51 year's worth of potential experience
nonlin.5051 <- predict(model.lm.nonlin,newdata=newdata.51)-
          predict(model.lm.nonlin,newdata=newdata.50)
lin.5051 <- predict(model.lm,newdata=newdata.51)-
          predict(model.lm,newdata=newdata.50)
nonlin.5051
##          1
## -0.01692
lin.5051
##          1
## 0.001276
```

The coefficients of variation for the linear and nonlinear models are
$R^2 = 0.1853$ and $R^2 = 0.2815$, respectively. Summaries of the results for
each model appear in Table 6.6 and Table 6.7.

Table 6.5: Counterfactual wage differences for married females due to a one-year increase in potential experience (Δ PE) under nonlinear ($\beta_n(x)$) and linear ($\beta_l(x)$) parametric specifications.

Δ PE	$\hat{\beta}_n(x)$	$\hat{\beta}_l(x)$
1-2	0.006676	0.001276
50-51	-0.016918	0.001276

Table 6.6: Linear parametric model summary.

	Estimate	Std. Error	t value	Pr($>|$t$|$)
(Intercept)	1.5011	0.0498	30.12	0.0000
femaleMale	0.3597	0.0426	8.45	0.0000
marriedNotmarried	-0.2221	0.0459	-4.84	0.0000
exper	0.0013	0.0016	0.78	0.4345

One might ask "why not compute the counterfactual for the entire range of potential experience?" The following code chunk does just this, controlling as above for sex and marital status.

```
exper.seq <- 1:51
beta.lm <- numeric()
beta.lm.nonlin <- numeric()
for(i in 1:(length(exper.seq)-1)) {
 ## Generate data frames with the same named variables as those in the
 ## regression equation
 newdata.a<-with(wage1,data.frame(female=factor("Female",levels=levels(female)),
                  married=factor("Married",levels=levels(married)),
                  exper=exper.seq[i],
                  expersq=exper.seq[i]**2))
 newdata.b<-with(wage1,data.frame(female=factor("Female",levels=levels(female)),
                  married=factor("Married",levels=levels(married)),
                  exper=exper.seq[i+1],
                  expersq=exper.seq[i+1]**2))
   ## Construct the counterfactual for the nonlinear then linear model
   ## for a sequence of years of potential experience (1-51)
   beta.lm.nonlin[i] <- predict(model.lm.nonlin,newdata=newdata.b)-
      predict(model.lm.nonlin,newdata=newdata.a)
   beta.lm[i] <- predict(model.lm,newdata=newdata.a)-
      predict(model.lm,newdata=newdata.b)
}
## Compute the analytic derivative with the same controls
beta.analytic <- with(wage1,coef(model.lm.nonlin)[4]
                  +2*coef(model.lm.nonlin)[5]*exper)
```

These types of counterfactual experiments involve the construction of *numerical derivatives* while *controlling* for the remaining predictors in the model. One could alternatively take the analytic derivative of the nonlinear function while controlling for sex and marital status, and this would accom-

Table 6.7: Nonlinear parametric (quadratic with interactions) model summary.

	Estimate	Std. Error	t value	Pr($>$|t|)
(Intercept)	1.4289	0.1084	13.18	0.0000
femaleMale	0.2572	0.1195	2.15	0.0318
marriedNotmarried	-0.2256	0.1129	-2.00	0.0461
exper	0.0074	0.0111	0.67	0.5035
expersq	-0.0002	0.0002	-1.04	0.2968
femaleMale:marriedNotmarried	-0.2588	0.0928	-2.79	0.0055
femaleMale:exper	0.0272	0.0119	2.29	0.0222
femaleMale:expersq	-0.0005	0.0003	-2.09	0.0368
marriedNotmarried:exper	0.0268	0.0121	2.23	0.0264
marriedNotmarried:expersq	-0.0005	0.0003	-1.80	0.0722

plish the exact same goal. Figure 6.4 presents such a comparison for the example above, although a summary could have also been provided in tabular form. Pointwise confidence bands could be added to the table or figure using either the asymptotic distribution or an appropriate bootstrap procedure (the latter is preferred in applied settings, while the former is required to prove the validity of the bootstrap procedure). See the Practitioner's Corner in Chapter 4 for an illustration of the bootstrap in a nonparametric context. As an aside, note that in Table 6.6, the linear model's partial derivative with respect to years of potential experience does not differ significantly from zero. Some practitioners might incorrectly interpret this result as lending support to the conclusion that the predictor X and the outcome Y are unrelated. We will discuss model-free consistent tests for predictor relevance in due course.

Figure 6.4 reveals what, in hindsight, is obvious. Scalar parameters corresponding to the continuous predictors in linear additive models without any interaction terms are partial derivatives and they can be interpreted directly. In nonlinear models, however, these parameters are components of a partial derivative function and they are not independently of much interest. The additivity assumption and the lack of interaction terms have the effect of *controlling* for off-axis predictors because this restriction has been imposed ex ante. In general, conducting a counterfactual exercise for a particular individual is equivalent to computing a partial derivative in the nonlinear model while controlling for the off-axis predictors (i.e., holding them constant at some interesting values). The parametric mindset might then need a reset. Given that the interest lies in partial derivatives, which tend to be functions of the various predictors and parameters in one's model, it is straightforward to evaluate an estimated partial derivative function while controlling for off-axis predictors, if desired. The above exercise, which was undertaken with parametric models, is a clear illustration of this fact. When we move on to

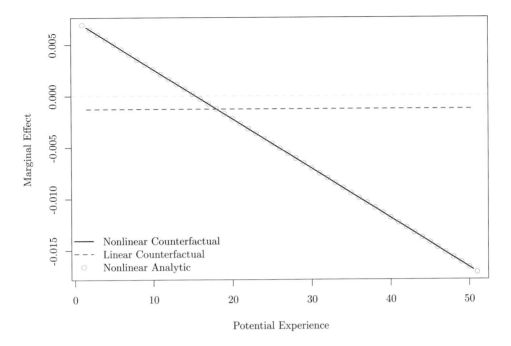

Figure 6.4: Comparison of counterfactual and analytic derivatives controlling for off-axis predictors.

nonparametric models, we will take the same approach when summarizing and reporting our results (we refer to such estimates as *partial* to reflect the fact that off-axis predictors are held fixed). In contrast, the preference for interpreting a scalar parameter in a linear additive model often results in a gross oversimplification. Examining a more general analytic partial derivative function directly while controlling for the levels of the remaining predictors is a robust alternative. The same goes for summarizing the conditional mean function itself. An empirical illustration in the Practitioner's Corner includes a plot of the mean and derivative functions with multivariate and mixed predictors.

Before we proceed, it is worth pointing out that we are not suggesting that parametric regression methods are incorrect and we are certainly not calling for their outright dismissal (their theoretical pedigree is unassailable). It is not the theory of linear regression that is incorrect, rather, it is the application that is at times problematic. Linear regression should not be approached as if it is a simple recipe to be followed, i.e., "pour equal amounts of data and linear model into blender, push button, report scalar". If the parametric model that one writes down does not reflect the underlying DGP, one ends up with inconsistent estimates and unsound inference. On the other hand, consistent nonparametric regression methods can shed light on relationships that might otherwise remain hidden from one's view.

6.3   Local Constant Kernel Regression

The *Nadaraya-Watson* estimator, which was originally proposed by Nadaraya (1965) and Watson (1964), is a very popular nonparametric regression method. It is the limiting case of the *local polynomial* estimator when the degree of the polynomial is zero (Fan, 1992), and hence it is also known as the *local constant* estimator. Local polynomial estimators, which we will be studying later in this chapter, were developed to correct for *boundary bias* in the local constant estimator.

We begin our foray into nonparametric regression by considering the local constant estimator when there is only one predictor in the model. This estimator is elegant in its simplicity; it is obtained by replacing the unknown conditional density $f(y|x) = f(y, x)/f(x)$ that appears in the definition of the conditional mean with its consistent nonparametric counterpart, $\hat{f}(y|x)$.

For continuously distributed $Y \in \mathbb{R}$, the local constant kernel regression estimator of the conditional mean is defined as

$$\hat{g}(x) = \int y \frac{\hat{f}(y, x)}{\hat{f}(x)} \, dy$$
$$= \frac{\hat{m}(x)}{\hat{f}(x)}.$$

The estimated nonparametric regression function is written as

$$y = \hat{g}(x) + \hat{\epsilon}.$$

Exploiting the symmetry of the kernel function for Y, i.e., $K\left(\frac{y-Y_i}{h_y}\right) = K\left(\frac{Y_i-y}{h_y}\right)$, we write the kernel estimators $\hat{f}(y, x)$ and $\hat{f}(x)$ as follows:

$$\hat{f}(y, x) = \frac{1}{nh_x h_y} \sum_{i=1}^{n} K\left(\frac{X_i - x}{h_x}\right) K\left(\frac{y - Y_i}{h_y}\right),$$
$$\hat{f}(x) = \frac{1}{nh_x} \sum_{i=1}^{n} K\left(\frac{X_i - x}{h_x}\right).$$

It turns out that the numerator of $\hat{g}(x)$, $\int y\hat{f}(y, x) \, dy$, can be simplified. Let $z_x = (X_i - x)/h_x$ and $z_y = (y - Y_i)/h_y$. Using Tonelli and Fubini's theorems to interchange the order of summation and integration, we can write

$$\int y\hat{f}(y, x) \, dy = \int y \frac{1}{nh_x h_y} \sum_{i=1}^{n} K(z_x)K(z_y) \, dy$$
$$= \frac{1}{nh_x h_y} \sum_{i=1}^{n} K(z_x) \int yK(z_y) \, dy$$

$$= \frac{1}{nh_x h_y} \sum_{i=1}^{n} K(z_x) \int (Y_i + h_y z_y) K(z_y) \, h_y dz_y$$

$$= \frac{1}{nh_x h_y} \sum_{i=1}^{n} K(z_x) \left(Y_i h_y \int K(z_y) \, dz_y + h_y^2 \int z_y K(z_y) \, dz_y \right)$$

$$= \frac{1}{nh_x} \sum_{i=1}^{n} Y_i K(z_x),$$

provided that our kernel satisfies $\int K(z) \, dz = 1$ and $\int z K(z) \, dz = 0$. Therefore, the simplified version of the local constant kernel estimator of a conditional mean is given by

$$\hat{g}(x) = \frac{\frac{1}{nh} \sum_{i=1}^{n} Y_i K\left(\frac{X_i - x}{h}\right)}{\frac{1}{nh} \sum_{i=1}^{n} K\left(\frac{X_i - x}{h}\right)},$$

where we have dropped the redundant $_x$ subscript on h since the bandwidths for the Y_i and the X_i no longer need to be distinguished. This form of the estimator with the simplified $\hat{m}(x)$ is what is used in the proofs that follow. The simplified expression for the discrete $Y \in \mathcal{D}$ case differs from what appears above and is left as an exercise. Note that this estimator does not smooth the Y_i and that a common bandwidth h *must* be used in $\hat{m}(x)$ and $\hat{f}(x)$ (this bandwidth will be optimized for the estimation of conditional mean functions).

As an aside, we could also express $\hat{g}(x)$ as

$$\hat{g}(x) = \sum_{i=1}^{n} Y_i W\left(\frac{X_i - x}{h}\right),$$

where $W\left(\frac{X_i - x}{h}\right) = K\left(\frac{X_i - x}{h}\right) / \sum_{j=1}^{n} K\left(\frac{X_j - x}{h}\right)$. Written this way, it is evident that $\hat{g}(x)$ is a locally weighted average of the Y_i. Observe that as $h \to \infty$, $W\left(\frac{X_i - x}{h}\right) \to K(0) / \sum_{j=1}^{n} K(0) = 1/n$. That is, as h increases, the *conditional* mean estimator shrinks towards the *unconditional* mean of Y. This property is illustrated in Figure 6.5 where the DGP is $y = 1 + \sin(4\pi x) + \epsilon$ with $x \sim U[0, 1]$.

There is yet another interpretation of $\hat{g}(x)$. Instead of using the plug-in principle (i.e., replacing $f(y|x)$ with $\hat{f}(y|x)$), the local constant estimator can alternatively be obtained by solving a *weighted least squares* (WLS) problem, i.e.,

$$\hat{g}(x) = \operatorname{argmin}_\alpha \sum_{i=1}^{n} (Y_i - \alpha)^2 K\left(\frac{X_i - x}{h}\right).$$

The proof that this yields the estimator $\hat{g}(x)$ that was obtained previously is left as an exercise. In this instance, we are carrying out a locally weighted regression of Y_i on a *constant* α (later, we will consider the more general

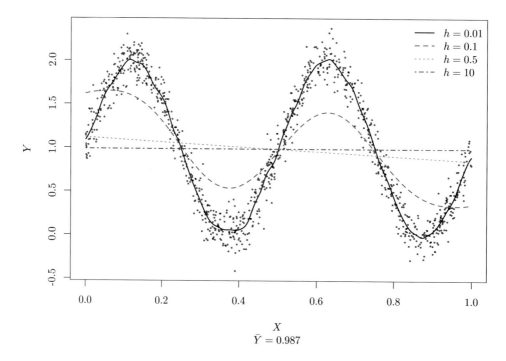

Figure 6.5: The behaviour of the local constant estimator as h increases (as $h \to \infty$, $\hat{g}(x) \to \bar{Y}$).

case). It is rather remarkable that, under very general conditions, we can obtain a consistent nonparametric estimator of an unknown conditional mean using only a linear regression of Y on an intercept term and the Gaussian density or some other kernel as a weight function. One might never have suspected that a simple parametric linear regression function and a simple parametric density function could be combined to this effect.

6.3.1   Estimator Properties

In this section, we derive expressions for the pointwise bias and variance of the local constant estimator $\hat{g}(x)$. We proceed in three stages. First, we adopt an expansion of $\hat{g}(x) = \hat{m}(x)/\hat{f}(x)$ that generates an expression with a non-stochastic denominator ($\hat{f}(x)$ is stochastic). Next, we use this expansion to derive the pointwise bias of $\hat{g}(x)$. This involves Taylor representations and application of the *law of iterated expectations* (also known as the *law of total expectation*). Finally, we use a similar approach to derive the pointwise variance of $\hat{g}(x)$. We begin with detailed proofs and establish each new proof construct. Some minor details of the last few results that are needed to complete the proofs are left as an exercise for the interested reader. This exercise ought to be a simple matter once the main results and proof concepts have been digested. When needed, we will call on some of the properties of

$\hat{f}(x)$ that we established in Chapter 2.

An Expansion to Deal with a Random Denominator

In what follows, we only retain the terms that are required to obtain the desired result. The remaining terms in the expansion are relegated to a generic remainder term, $\mathcal{R}$. The skeptical reader may verify that any additional terms that might be included are of smaller order than the leading terms retained below. The number and order of the terms retained will depend on whether we are deriving an expression for the pointwise bias or the pointwise variance.

Observe that $\hat{g}(x) = \hat{m}(x)/\hat{f}(x)$ is a ratio of two correlated random variables. Given the linearity of the expectations operator (i.e., $\mathrm{E}\,A/B \neq \mathrm{E}\,A/\mathrm{E}\,B$), in order to properly deal with the random denominator $\hat{f}(x)$, we use a series expansion and express $\hat{g}(x)$ as follows:

$$
\begin{aligned}
\hat{g}(x) &= \frac{\hat{m}(x)}{\hat{f}(x)} \\
&= \frac{\mathrm{E}\,\hat{m}(x) + \hat{m}(x) - \mathrm{E}\,\hat{m}(x)}{\mathrm{E}\,\hat{f}(x) + \hat{f}(x) - \mathrm{E}\,\hat{f}(x)} \\
&= \frac{\mathrm{E}\,\hat{m}(x) + (\hat{m}(x) - \mathrm{E}\,\hat{m}(x))}{\mathrm{E}\,\hat{f}(x)\left(1 + \frac{\hat{f}(x) - \mathrm{E}\,\hat{f}(x)}{\mathrm{E}\,\hat{f}(x)}\right)} \\
&= \frac{\mathrm{E}\,\hat{m}(x) + (\hat{m}(x) - \mathrm{E}\,\hat{m}(x))}{\mathrm{E}\,\hat{f}(x)}\left(1 + \frac{\hat{f}(x) - \mathrm{E}\,\hat{f}(x)}{\mathrm{E}\,\hat{f}(x)}\right)^{-1} \\
&= \frac{\mathrm{E}\,\hat{m}(x) + (\hat{m}(x) - \mathrm{E}\,\hat{m}(x))}{\mathrm{E}\,\hat{f}(x)} \times \\
&\qquad \left(1 - \frac{\hat{f}(x) - \mathrm{E}\,\hat{f}(x)}{\mathrm{E}\,\hat{f}(x)} + \left(\frac{\hat{f}(x) - \mathrm{E}\,\hat{f}(x)}{\mathrm{E}\,\hat{f}(x)}\right)^2 + \mathcal{R}\right) \\
&= \frac{\mathrm{E}\,\hat{m}(x)}{\mathrm{E}\,\hat{f}(x)} + \frac{(\hat{m}(x) - \mathrm{E}\,\hat{m}(x))}{\mathrm{E}\,\hat{f}(x)} - (\mathrm{E}\,\hat{m}(x))\left(\frac{\hat{f}(x) - \mathrm{E}\,\hat{f}(x)}{(\mathrm{E}\,\hat{f}(x))^2}\right) \\
&\quad - \frac{(\hat{m}(x) - \mathrm{E}\,\hat{m}(x))(\hat{f}(x) - \mathrm{E}\,\hat{f}(x))}{(\mathrm{E}\,\hat{f}(x))^2} + \mathcal{R}, \qquad (6.3)
\end{aligned}
$$

provided that $|(\hat{f}(x) - \mathrm{E}\,\hat{f}(x))/\mathrm{E}\,\hat{f}(x)| < 1$ and that $\mathrm{E}\,\hat{f}(x) \neq 0$. Note that this expansion has resulted in an expression of $\hat{g}(x)$ that no longer contains the random variable $\hat{f}(x)$ in the denominator. Instead, it contains $\mathrm{E}\,\hat{f}(x)$, which is non-stochastic. Furthermore, the terms involving $(\hat{f}(x) - \mathrm{E}\,\hat{f}(x))/\mathrm{E}\,\hat{f}(x)$ are of $O(h^2)$ and vanish as $n \to \infty$, provided that $h \to 0$ as $n \to \infty$. This expression will form the basis of the expressions for the pointwise bias and variance of $\hat{g}(x)$.

To obtain the pointwise bias, we will express $\mathrm{E}\,\hat{g}(x)$ using the representation in Equation (6.3). We observe that the expectation of the second and third terms in the last line of Equation (6.3) is zero, and hence we may write

$$
\begin{aligned}
\mathrm{E}\,\hat{g}(x) &= \frac{\mathrm{E}\,\hat{m}(x)}{\mathrm{E}\,\hat{f}(x)} + 0 - 0 - \frac{\mathrm{E}\left((\hat{m}(x) - \mathrm{E}\,\hat{m}(x))(\hat{f}(x) - \mathrm{E}\,\hat{f}(x))\right)}{(\mathrm{E}\,\hat{f}(x))^2} + \mathcal{R} \\
&= \frac{\mathrm{E}\,\hat{m}(x)}{\mathrm{E}\,\hat{f}(x)} - \frac{\mathrm{Cov}(\hat{m}(x), \hat{f}(x))}{(\mathrm{E}\,\hat{f}(x))^2} + \mathcal{R}.
\end{aligned}
\tag{6.4}
$$

We can use this result to obtain an expression for the pointwise bias, which is given by $\mathrm{Bias}\,\hat{g}(x) = \mathrm{E}\,\hat{g}(x) - g(x)$.

To obtain an expression for the pointwise variance, we first observe that

$$
\hat{g}(x) = \frac{\mathrm{E}\,\hat{m}(x)}{\mathrm{E}\,\hat{f}(x)} + \frac{\hat{m}(x) - \mathrm{E}\,\hat{m}(x)}{\mathrm{E}\,\hat{f}(x)} - (\mathrm{E}\,\hat{m}(x))\left(\frac{\hat{f}(x) - \mathrm{E}\,\hat{f}(x)}{(\mathrm{E}\,\hat{f}(x))^2}\right) + \mathcal{R},
$$

and that

$$
\mathrm{E}\,\hat{g}(x) = \frac{\mathrm{E}\,\hat{m}(x)}{\mathrm{E}\,\hat{f}(x)} + \mathcal{R}.
$$

This yields

$$
\hat{g}(x) - \mathrm{E}\,\hat{g}(x) = \frac{\hat{m}(x) - \mathrm{E}\,\hat{m}(x)}{\mathrm{E}\,\hat{f}(x)} - (\mathrm{E}\,\hat{m}(x))\left(\frac{\hat{f}(x) - \mathrm{E}\,\hat{f}(x)}{(\mathrm{E}\,\hat{f}(x))^2}\right) + \mathcal{R}.
\tag{6.5}
$$

Therefore, taking the expectation of the square of Equation (6.5), the pointwise variance $\mathrm{E}\left((\hat{g}(x) - \mathrm{E}\,\hat{g}(x))^2\right)$ can be expressed as

$$
\begin{aligned}
\mathrm{Var}\,\hat{g}(x) &= \mathrm{E}\left(\frac{\hat{m}(x) - \mathrm{E}\,\hat{m}(x)}{\mathrm{E}\,\hat{f}(x)}\right)^2 + (\mathrm{E}\,\hat{m}(x))^2\,\mathrm{E}\left(\frac{\hat{f}(x) - \mathrm{E}\,\hat{f}(x)}{(\mathrm{E}\,\hat{f}(x))^2}\right)^2 \\
&\quad - 2\,(\mathrm{E}\,\hat{m}(x))\,\mathrm{E}\left(\frac{\hat{m}(x) - \mathrm{E}\,\hat{m}(x)}{\mathrm{E}\,\hat{f}(x)}\right)\left(\frac{\hat{f}(x) - \mathrm{E}\,\hat{f}(x)}{(\mathrm{E}\,\hat{f}(x))^2}\right) + \mathcal{R} \\
&= \frac{\mathrm{Var}\,\hat{m}(x)}{(\mathrm{E}\,\hat{f}(x))^2} + (\mathrm{E}\,\hat{m}(x))^2 \frac{\mathrm{Var}\,\hat{f}(x)}{(\mathrm{E}\,\hat{f}(x))^4}
\end{aligned}
\tag{6.6}
$$

$$
- 2\,\mathrm{E}\,\hat{m}(x)\frac{\mathrm{Cov}(\hat{m}(x), \hat{f}(x))}{(\mathrm{E}\,\hat{f}(x))^3} + \mathcal{R}.
\tag{6.7}
$$

Once we have obtained expressions for the respective right hand side terms in Equations (6.4) and (6.7), our derivation of the pointwise mean and variance of $\hat{g}(x)$ is complete. Note that the covariance term is present in both equations, although it will turn out to be ignorable when obtaining an expression for the pointwise bias. That is, we will establish that the second term on the right hand side of Equation (6.4) is of smaller order than the leading term. On the other hand, derivation of the covariance expression will indeed be required for our determination of the pointwise variance of $\hat{g}(x)$. We proceed by obtaining (or recalling) the expressions that appear in Equations (6.4) and (6.7) and then using these to derive formulas for the pointwise mean and variance of $\hat{g}(x)$. Once we have obtained these results, we can then derive IMSE-optimal bandwidths and limit distributions of the estimator. More practical issues such as data-driven bandwidth selection will also be discussed. While these derivations are somewhat lengthy, they give rise to simple and intuitive expressions that will inform the reader's understanding of the finite-sample behaviour of the local constant regression estimator $\hat{g}(x)$.

Assumptions

In everything that follows, we assume that $g(x)$ and $f(x)$ are twice continuously differentiable in a neighbourhood of x. Let $\int K(z)\,dz = 1$, $\int zK(z)\,dz = 0$, and $\int z^2 K(z)\,dz = \kappa_2 < \infty$. Let $h \to 0$ as $n \to \infty$ and $nh \to \infty$ as $n \to \infty$. We assume that $\{Y_i, X_i\}$ are i.i.d. and that X_i is orthogonal to ϵ. We also assume that $f''(x)$ is bounded and continuous in a neighbourhood of x. We now focus our attention on obtaining an expression for the pointwise bias of $\hat{g}(x)$.

Pointwise Bias

Equation (6.4) reveals that we require two new expressions in addition to those that have previously been obtained for $\hat{f}(x)$. These are the expectation of $\hat{m}(x)$, $\mathrm{E}\,\hat{m}(x)$, and the covariance of the numerator and the denominator of $\hat{g}(x)$, $\mathrm{Cov}(\hat{m}(x), \hat{f}(x))$. The expression $\mathrm{E}\,\hat{f}(x) = f(x) + h^2 f''(x)\kappa_2/2$ was already derived in Chapter 2, and we will make use of it shortly.

First, we consider the numerator $\mathrm{E}\,\hat{m}(x)$ in the first term on the right hand side of Equation (6.4). Assuming i.i.d. draws and a second-order kernel function, if we use the law of iterated expectations and keep terms up to $O(h^2)$, we observe that

$$
\begin{aligned}
\mathrm{E}\hat{m}(x) &= \mathrm{E}\left(\mathrm{E}_{X_i}\,\hat{m}(x)\right) \\
&= \mathrm{E}\left(\frac{1}{nh}\sum_{i=1}^{n}\mathrm{E}(Y_i|X_i)K\left(\frac{X_i - x}{h}\right)\right) \\
&= \mathrm{E}\left(\frac{1}{nh}\sum_{i=1}^{n}g(X_i)K\left(\frac{X_i - x}{h}\right)\right) \\
&= \frac{1}{nh}\sum_{i=1}^{n}\mathrm{E}\,g(X_i)K\left(\frac{X_i - x}{h}\right) \\
&= \frac{1}{h}\,\mathrm{E}\,g(X_1)K\left(\frac{X_1 - x}{h}\right)
\end{aligned}
$$

$$= \frac{1}{h} \int g(t) K\left(\frac{t-x}{h}\right) f(t)\, dt$$

$$= \int g(x+hz) f(x+hz) K(z)\, dz$$

$$= \int \left(g(x) + hzg'(x) + \frac{h^2 z^2}{2} g''(x) + \mathcal{R}\right) \times$$

$$\left(f(x) + hzf'(x) + \frac{h^2 z^2}{2} f''(x) + \mathcal{R}\right) K(z)\, dz$$

$$= g(x)f(x) \int K(z)\, dz + hg(x)f'(x) \int zK(z)\, dz + hg'(x)f(x) \int zK(z)\, dz$$

$$+ h^2 g'(x)f'(x) \int z^2 K(z)\, dz + \frac{h^2}{2} g''(x)f(x) \int z^2 K(z)\, dz \qquad (6.8)$$

$$+ \frac{h^2}{2} g(x)f''(x) \int z^2 K(z)\, dz + \mathcal{R}$$

$$= g(x)f(x) + \frac{h^2}{2} \left(2g'(x)f'(x) + g''(x)f(x) + g(x)f''(x)\right)\kappa_2 + \mathcal{R}, \qquad (6.9)$$

where E_{X_i} is the expectation conditional on X_i, that is, $\mathrm{E}(\cdot|X_i)$.

Next, we consider the numerator $\mathrm{Cov}(\hat{m}(x), \hat{f}(x))$ in the second term on the right hand side of Equation (6.4). Assuming i.i.d. draws and a second-order kernel function, if we use the law of iterated expectations and keep terms up to $O(1/(nh))$, we observe that

$$\mathrm{Cov}\left(\hat{m}(x), \hat{f}(x)\right) = \mathrm{E}\left((\hat{m}(x) - \mathrm{E}\,\hat{m}(x))(\hat{f}(x) - \mathrm{E}\,\hat{f}(x))\right)$$

$$= \mathrm{E}\left(\mathrm{E}_{X_i}\left((\hat{m}(x) - \mathrm{E}(\mathrm{E}_{X_i}\,\hat{m}(x)))(\hat{f}(x) - \mathrm{E}\,\hat{f}(x))\right)\right)$$

$$= \mathrm{E}\left(\frac{1}{nh}\sum_{i=1}^{n}\left(g(X_i)K\left(\frac{X_i - x}{h}\right) - \mathrm{E}\,g(X_i)K\left(\frac{X_i - x}{h}\right)\right)\right.$$

$$\left.\times \frac{1}{nh}\sum_{i=1}^{n}\left(K\left(\frac{X_i - x}{h}\right) - \mathrm{E}\,K\left(\frac{X_i - x}{h}\right)\right)\right)$$

$$= \mathrm{E}\left(\frac{1}{nh}\sum_{i=1}^{n}\phi_i \frac{1}{nh}\sum_{i=1}^{n}\eta_i\right)$$

$$= \mathrm{E}\,\frac{1}{(nh)^2}\left(\sum_{i=1}^{n}\phi_i\eta_i + \sum_{i=1}^{n}\sum_{j=1,i\neq j}^{n}\phi_i\eta_j\right)$$

$$= \frac{1}{nh^2}\,\mathrm{E}\,\phi_1\eta_1$$

$$= \frac{1}{nh^2}\,\mathrm{E}\left(\left(g(X_1)K\left(\frac{X_1 - x}{h}\right) - \mathrm{E}\,g(X_1)K\left(\frac{X_1 - x}{h}\right)\right)\right.$$

$$\left.\times \left(K\left(\frac{X_1 - x}{h}\right) - \mathrm{E}\,K\left(\frac{X_1 - x}{h}\right)\right)\right)$$

$$= \frac{1}{nh^2} \, \mathrm{E} \left(\left(g(X_1)K\left(\frac{X_1-x}{h}\right) - \mathrm{E}\, g(X_1)K\left(\frac{X_1-x}{h}\right) \right) K\left(\frac{X_1-x}{h}\right) \right)$$

$$- \frac{1}{nh^2} \, \mathrm{E} \left(\left(g(X_1)K\left(\frac{X_1-x}{h}\right) - \mathrm{E}\, g(X_1)K\left(\frac{X_1-x}{h}\right) \right) \mathrm{E}\, K\left(\frac{X_1-x}{h}\right) \right)$$

$$= \frac{1}{nh^2} \left(\mathrm{E}\, g(X_1)K^2\left(\frac{X_1-x}{h}\right) - \mathrm{E}\, g(X_1)K\left(\frac{X_1-x}{h}\right) \mathrm{E}\, K\left(\frac{X_1-x}{h}\right) \right)$$

$$= \frac{1}{nh^2} \left(hg(x)f(x) \int K^2(z)\, dz + \mathcal{R} - (hg(x)f(x) + \mathcal{R})(hf(x) + \mathcal{R}) \right)$$

$$= \frac{g(x)f(x)}{nh} \kappa + \mathcal{R}, \tag{6.10}$$

where $\phi_i = g(X_i)K\left(\frac{X_i-x}{h}\right) - \mathrm{E}\, g(X_i)K\left(\frac{X_i-x}{h}\right)$, $\eta_i = K\left(\frac{X_i-x}{h}\right) - \mathrm{E}\, K\left(\frac{X_i-x}{h}\right)$, and the second term in the fifth equality has expectation zero under the i.i.d. assumption. Note that the second term in the eighth equality equals zero and the expressions in the ninth equality should be apparent since their derivation is similar to what has been done previously. In particular, the derivation of $\mathrm{E}\, g(X_1)K^2\left(\frac{X_1-x}{h}\right)$ is very similar to that of $\mathrm{E}\, g(X_1)K\left(\frac{X_1-x}{h}\right)$, which was provided earlier; rather than repeat it here, we instead leave it as an exercise. See line 5 in Equation (6.9) and multiply all subsequent lines by h to adjust for the presence of the $1/h$ term.

This allows us to obtain the pointwise bias of $\hat{g}(x)$ using Equation (6.4). Equation (6.9) is of $O(h^2)$, while Equation (6.10) is of $O(1/(nh))$. The latter term is of smaller order than the former (recall results for $\hat{f}(x)$ where the bias was of $O(h^2)$ and the variance was of $O(1/(nh))$). Using previous results that were established for $\hat{f}(x)$ in Chapter 2 and the result in Equation (6.9), if we retain terms up to $O(h^2)$ for $\mathrm{E}\, \hat{f}(x)$ in the denominator, then the leading term in the expression for $\mathrm{E}\, \hat{g}(x)$ in Equation (6.4) is given by

$$\frac{\mathrm{E}\, \hat{m}(x)}{\mathrm{E}\, \hat{f}(x)} = \frac{\mathrm{E}\, \hat{m}(x)}{f(x) + \frac{h^2 f''(x)}{2}\kappa_2}$$

$$= \frac{\mathrm{E}\, \hat{m}(x)}{f(x)} \left(1 + \frac{h^2 f''(x)}{2f(x)}\kappa_2 \right)^{-1}$$

$$= \frac{\mathrm{E}\, \hat{m}(x)}{f(x)} \left(1 - \frac{h^2 f''(x)}{2f(x)}\kappa_2 + \left(\frac{h^2 f''(x)}{2f(x)}\kappa_2 \right)^2 + \mathcal{R} \right)$$

$$= \frac{\left(g(x)f(x) + \frac{h^2}{2}\left(2g'(x)f'(x) + g''(x)f(x) + g(x)f''(x) \right)\kappa_2 + \mathcal{R} \right)}{f(x)}$$

$$\times \left(1 - \frac{h^2 f''(x)}{2f(x)}\kappa_2 + \mathcal{R} \right)$$

$$= \frac{g(x)f(x)}{f(x)} + \frac{h^2}{2f(x)}\left(2g'(x)f'(x) + g''(x)f(x) + g(x)f''(x) \right)\kappa_2$$

$$
- \frac{g(x)f(x)}{f(x)} \frac{h^2 f''(x)}{2f(x)} \kappa_2 + \mathcal{R}
$$

$$
= g(x) + \frac{h^2}{2f(x)} \left(2g'(x)f'(x) + g''(x)f(x) \right) \kappa_2 + \mathcal{R}.
$$

Using this result and keeping terms of $O(h^2)$, the pointwise bias of $\hat{g}(x)$, $\mathrm{E}\,\hat{g}(x) - g(x)$, is therefore given by

$$
\text{Bias}\,\hat{g}(x) = \frac{h^2}{2f(x)} \left(2g'(x)f'(x) + g''(x)f(x) \right) \kappa_2.
$$

Note that this bias is of the same order as the bias of $\hat{f}(x)$, which the reader might recall is given by $h^2 f''(x)\kappa_2/2$. Moreover, as in the case of $\hat{f}(x)$, the bias of $\hat{g}(x)$ increases as h increases. We now turn our attention to the pointwise variance of $\hat{g}(x)$.

Pointwise Variance

Equation (6.7) reveals that to obtain the pointwise variance of $\hat{g}(x)$, we require an expression for $\text{Var}\,\hat{m}(x)$ in addition to the results that were established above. Using the law of iterated expectations, we observe that $\text{Var}\,\hat{m}(x)$ can be written as

$$
\text{Var}\,\hat{m}(x) = \mathrm{E}\left(\text{Var}_{X_i}\,\hat{m}(x) \right) + \text{Var}\left(\mathrm{E}_{X_i}\,\hat{m}(x) \right),
$$

where Var_{X_i} is the variance conditional on X_i, that is, $\text{Var}(\cdot|X_i)$. We consider each component in turn. Assuming i.i.d. draws, we can express $\mathrm{E}\left(\text{Var}_{X_i}\,\hat{m}(x) \right)$ as

$$
\mathrm{E}\left(\text{Var}_{X_i}\,\hat{m}(x) \right) = \mathrm{E}\left(\text{Var}_{X_i}\left(\frac{1}{nh} \sum_{i=1}^{n} Y_i K\left(\frac{X_i - x}{h} \right) \right) \right)
$$

$$
= \mathrm{E}\left(\frac{1}{n^2 h^2} \sum_{i=1}^{n} \text{Var}(Y_i|X_i) K^2\left(\frac{X_i - x}{h} \right) \right.
$$

$$
\left. + \frac{1}{n^2 h^2} \sum_{i=1}^{n} \sum_{j=1,i\neq j}^{n} \text{Cov}(Y_i, Y_j|X_i, X_j) K\left(\frac{X_i - x}{h} \right) K\left(\frac{X_j - x}{h} \right) \right)
$$

$$
= \frac{1}{nh^2} \mathrm{E}\,\sigma^2(X_1) K^2\left(\frac{X_1 - x}{h} \right)
$$

$$
= \frac{1}{nh^2} \int \sigma^2(t) K^2\left(\frac{t - x}{h} \right) f(t)\,dt
$$

$$
= \frac{1}{nh} \int \sigma^2(x + hz) f(x + hz) K^2(z)\,dz
$$

$$
= \frac{1}{nh} \sigma^2(x) f(x) \kappa + \mathcal{R}, \tag{6.11}
$$

where $\sigma^2(x) = E((Y - E(Y|X = x))^2|X = x) = E(\epsilon^2|X = x)$ is the second conditional moment about the conditional mean, as outlined in Chapter 5, and where the second term in the second equality is zero under the i.i.d. assumption.

We can express $\mathrm{Var}\,(\mathrm{E}_{X_i}\,\hat{m}(x))$ as

$$
\mathrm{Var}\,(\mathrm{E}_{X_i}\,\hat{m}(x)) = \mathrm{Var}\,\left(\frac{1}{nh}\sum_{i=1}^{n} g(X_i)K\left(\frac{X_i - x}{h}\right)\right)
$$

$$
= \frac{1}{n^2h^2}\left(\sum_{i=1}^{n}\mathrm{Var}\,\left(g(X_i)K\left(\frac{X_i - x}{h}\right)\right)\right. \tag{6.12}
$$

$$
\left. + \sum_{i=1}^{n}\sum_{j=1,i\neq j}^{n}\mathrm{Cov}\,\left(g(X_i)K\left(\frac{X_i - x}{h}\right), g(X_j)K\left(\frac{X_j - x}{h}\right)\right)\right)
$$

$$
= \frac{1}{nh^2}\left(\mathrm{E}\,g(X_1)^2 K^2\left(\frac{X_1 - x}{h}\right) - \left(\mathrm{E}\,g(X_1)K\left(\frac{X_1 - x}{h}\right)\right)^2\right), \tag{6.13}
$$

where the second term in the second equality is zero under the i.i.d. assumption. With a bit of algebra, the first term on the right hand side of Equation (6.13) can be expressed as

$$
\frac{1}{nh^2}\,\mathrm{E}\,g^2(X_1)K^2\left(\frac{X_1 - x}{h}\right) = \frac{1}{nh^2}\int g^2(t)K^2\left(\frac{t - x}{h}\right)f(t)\,dt
$$

$$
= \frac{1}{nh}\int g^2(x + hz)f(x + hz)K^2(z)\,dz
$$

$$
= \frac{1}{nh}g^2(x)f(x)\kappa + \mathcal{R},
$$

while the second term on the right hand side of Equation (6.13) can be expressed as

$$
\frac{1}{nh^2}\left(\mathrm{E}\,g(X_1)K\left(\frac{X_1 - x}{h}\right)\right)^2 = \frac{1}{nh^2}\left(\int g(t)K\left(\frac{t - x}{h}\right)f(t)\,dt\right)^2
$$

$$
= \frac{1}{n}g^2(x)f^2(x) + \mathcal{R},
$$

which is of smaller order $O(1/n)$ than the leading term in Equation (6.11). We leave the details as an exercise for the interested reader. Retaining terms up to $O(1/(nh))$, we can combine these results to obtain the pointwise variance of $\hat{m}(x)$, which is given by

$$
\mathrm{Var}\,\hat{m}(x) = \mathrm{E}\,(\mathrm{Var}_{X_i}\,\hat{m}(x)) + \mathrm{Var}\,(\mathrm{E}_{X_i}\,\hat{m}(x))
$$

$$
= \frac{\sigma^2(x)f(x) + g^2(x)f(x)}{nh}\kappa + \mathcal{R}.
$$

We now have all of the results that are needed to evaluate the expansion of the pointwise variance of $\hat{g}(x)$ in Equation (6.7). With a bit of algebra and care, if we retain terms up to $O(1/nh)$, the first term on the right hand side of Equation (6.7) is given by

$$\frac{\text{Var}\,\hat{m}(x)}{(\text{E}\,\hat{f}(x))^2} = \frac{\frac{\sigma^2(x)f(x)+g^2(x)f(x)}{nh}\kappa}{\left(f(x)+\frac{h^2 f''(x)}{2}\kappa_2\right)^2}$$

$$= \frac{\sigma^2(x)+g^2(x)}{nhf(x)}\kappa + \mathcal{R}.$$

Retaining terms up to $O(1/nh)$, the second term on the right hand side of Equation (6.7) is given by

$$(\text{E}\,\hat{m}(x))^2\frac{\text{Var}\,\hat{f}(x)}{(\text{E}\,\hat{f}(x))^4} = (g(x)f(x)+\mathcal{R})^2\frac{\frac{f(x)}{nh}\kappa + \mathcal{R}}{\left(f(x)+\frac{h^2 f''(x)}{2}\kappa_2\right)^4}$$

$$= \frac{g^2(x)}{nhf(x)}\kappa + \mathcal{R},$$

while the third term on the right hand side of Equation (6.7) is given by

$$-2\,\text{E}\,\hat{m}(x)\frac{\text{Cov}(\hat{m}(x),\hat{f}(x))}{(\text{E}\,\hat{f}(x))^3} = -2(g(x)f(x)+\mathcal{R})\frac{\frac{g(x)f(x)}{nh}\kappa + \mathcal{R}}{\left(f(x)+\frac{h^2 f''(x)}{2}\kappa_2\right)^3}$$

$$= -2\frac{g^2(x)}{nhf(x)}\kappa + \mathcal{R}.$$

Hence, from Equation (6.7), we can express the pointwise variance of $\hat{g}(x)$ up to terms of $O(1/nh)$ as

$$\text{Var}\,\hat{g}(x) = \frac{\sigma^2(x)+g^2(x)}{nhf(x)}\kappa + \frac{g^2(x)}{nhf(x)}\kappa - 2\frac{g^2(x)}{nhf(x)}\kappa$$

$$= \frac{\sigma^2(x)}{nhf(x)}\kappa.$$

Observe that as the bandwidth increases (decreases), the pointwise variance falls (rises). This was also the case for the univariate PDF estimator that was outlined in Chapter 2.

The derivations that have been outlined above, which were made necessary by the presence of the random denominator in $\hat{g}(x)$, result in expressions that have a surprisingly simple form. They are the direct counterparts, albeit with an extra layer of approximation, to the formulas for the pointwise bias and variance of $\hat{f}(x)$ that we derived in Chapter 2. Furthermore, the same intuition that we established previously about the behaviour of the bandwidth, the pointwise bias, and the pointwise variance applies here. We once again observe that the pointwise bias is of $O(h^2)$ and the pointwise variance is of $O(1/(nh))$ when a second-order kernel function is used. Before we proceed any further, we first provide a simulated example that elucidates the relationship between the magnitude of the bandwidth h, the pointwise bias, and the pointwise variance of the local constant estimator.

Example 6.2. Local Constant Regression, Pointwise Bias, Pointwise Variance, and the Bandwidth.

Consider $Y_i = \sin(2\pi X_i) + \epsilon_i$ with $X \sim U[0, 1]$ and $\epsilon \sim N(0, \sigma^2)$. We obtain $M = 1,000$ local constant kernel regression estimates based on three different bandwidths (one *too large*, one *about right*, one *too small*) and use these to compute the pointwise bias and variance of $\hat{g}(x)$. Figure 6.6 summarizes the results of this exercise. As we move from left to right, the bandwidth falls. If you consider the pointwise behaviour at any given value of x in all three figures, you can see that as the bandwidth shrinks in size, the bias falls and the variance increases. That is, the pointwise mean of the 1,000 kernel estimates approaches the true $g(x)$ and the pointwise 0.025th and 0.975th quantiles of the 1,000 kernel estimates get wider. Furthermore, if you can envision the average of the pointwise squared bias and variance across all x (i.e., the *integrated* squared bias and variance), you can see that for large bandwidths, the former dominates the latter, whereas for small bandwidths, the latter dominates the former. For bandwidths that are *about right* (the middle figures), the integrated squared bias and the integrated variance are in balance with one another.

This simulation reveals a number of features of the pointwise bias and variance formulae for the local constant estimator. First, observe that bias depends on the curvature $g''(x)$ and the density $f(x)$. Next, observe that as h falls (i.e., as one moves from the leftmost to the rightmost figures), the squared bias falls and the variance rises uniformly across x. Thus, the bias is *proportional* to h and the variance is *inversely proportional to h*, which reveals that we cannot reduce one without increasing the other. Finally, note that the pointwise bias formula contains the term $g'(x)f'(x)/f(x)$. As we approach the tails of the design X, $f(x) \to 0$, and hence the bias increases provided that $g'(x)f'(x)$ does not approach zero at the same rate. Boundary bias can clearly be seen in the three lowermost plots in Figure 6.6. For a given bandwidth, the bias is higher than it is in the interior as $x \to 0$ or $x \to 1$.

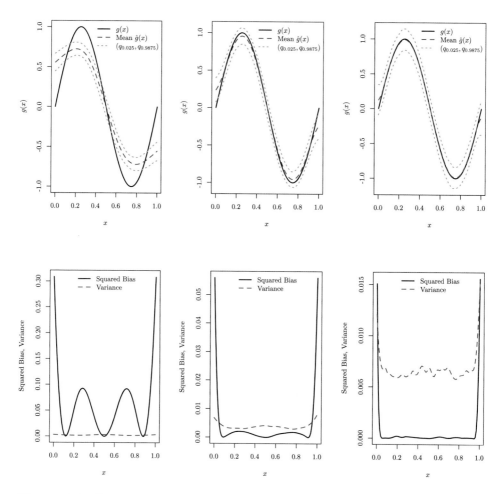

Figure 6.6: Summary of 1,000 local constant kernel regression estimates, $n = 250$, $Y_i = \sin(2\pi X_i) + \epsilon_i$ DGP, with three bandwidths (too large [leftmost figures], about right [middle figures], too small [rightmost figures]). The upper figures plot the DGP $g(x)$ along with the pointwise mean $(1000^{-1} \sum_{m=1}^{1000} \hat{g}_m(x))$, 0.025th pointwise quantile, and 0.975th pointwise quantile. The lower figures present the pointwise squared bias $((\mathrm{E}(\hat{g}(x)) - g(x))^2)$ and pointwise variance.

6.3.2 The IMSE-Optimal Bandwidth and Kernel Function

The MSE of the local constant estimator $\hat{g}(x)$ is the sum of its pointwise variance and the square of its pointwise bias. It is given by

$$\mathrm{MSE}\,\hat{g}(x) = \frac{\sigma^2(x)}{nhf(x)}\kappa + \frac{h^4\kappa_2^2}{4}\left(2\frac{g'(x)f'(x)}{f(x)} + g''(x)\right)^2.$$

The IMSE is given by

$$\mathrm{IMSE}\,\hat{g}(x) = \frac{\kappa}{nh}\int \sigma^2(x)f^{-1}(x)\,dx$$

$$+ \frac{h^4 \kappa_2^2}{4} \int \left(2g'(x)f'(x)f^{-1}(x) + g''(x) \right)^2 dx.$$

We can minimize the IMSE with respect to h to obtain the IMSE-optimal bandwidth, which is given by

$$h_{opt} = \left(\frac{\kappa \int \sigma^2(x)f^{-1}(x)\, dx}{\kappa_2^2 \int \left(2g'(x)f'(x)f^{-1}(x) + g''(x) \right)^2 dx} \right)^{1/5} n^{-1/5}.$$

The optimal bandwidth delivers an estimator $\hat{g}(x)$ whose IMSE and pointwise MSE are of $O(n^{-4/5})$ and whose root-IMSE and root-MSE are of $O(n^{-2/5})$. This is the same rate that was obtained in Chapter 2 for the univariate PDF estimator $\hat{f}(x)$.

The IMSE-optimal kernel function is identical to the one that was obtained in Chapter 2 in the context of density estimation, and its derivation is not repeated here. This is unsurprising, given that the variance and the bias are of the same order as in the density case; in addition, the variance is again proportional to κ and the squared bias is again proportional to κ_2^2. Thus, the IMSE can once again be expressed as $\frac{5}{4}\kappa^{4/5}\kappa_2^{2/5}\Phi^{1/5}n^{-4/5}$, where the constant Φ is not the same as in the density case but this does not affect the derivation of the optimal kernel since it is independent of Φ.

6.3.3   Asymptotic Normality

Application of Liapounov's CLT yields

$$\sqrt{nh}\left(\hat{g}(x) - g(x) - \text{Bias}\,\hat{g}(x) \right) \overset{d}{\to} N\left(0, \frac{\sigma^2(x)\kappa}{f(x)} \right).$$

These results pave the way for inference concerning the unknown conditional mean $g(x)$, which includes the construction of confidence bands and hypothesis testing.

6.3.4   Outlier-Resistant Local Constant Kernel Regression

Nonparametric kernel methods are occasionally criticized for their lack of robustness to the presence of contaminated data that might arise due to measurement error, data entry errors, and the like. Methods that are robust in this traditional statistical sense are often referred to as *resistant* since they *resist* the presence of a small number of bad data values. However, this carries a cost insofar as in the absence of outliers, robust estimators are less efficient than their non-robust counterparts. Below, we describe a method proposed by Leung (2005) for resistant robust kernel regression in the presence of outliers in the Y-direction.

Recall that the local constant estimator of $g(x)$ is given by

$$\hat{g}(x) = \operatorname{argmin}_\alpha \sum_{i=1}^{n} \rho(Y_i - \alpha) K\left(\frac{X_i - x}{h}\right),$$

where $\rho(a) = a^2$. A resistant local constant estimator can be obtained by replacing $\rho(\cdot)$ with $\rho_c(\cdot)$ (Leung, 2005)

$$\tilde{g}(x) = \operatorname{argmin}_\alpha \sum_{i=1}^{n} \rho_c(Y_i - \alpha) K\left(\frac{X_i - x}{h}\right),$$

where ρ_c is a function (Huber, 1964) that underlies the class of so-called M *estimators*. It is defined as (Maronna et al., 2006, page 26)

$$\rho_c(u) = \begin{cases} u^2 & \text{if } |u| \le c, \\ 2c|u| - c^2 & \text{if } |u| > c. \end{cases}$$

In order to compute $\tilde{g}(x)$, the resistance parameter c must be specified by the user. A popular rule of thumb is $c = 1.345 \times s$, where s is a robust measure of scale such as the median absolute deviation about the median. It ensures 95% efficiency relative to the homoskedastic Gaussian error benchmark. Although this approach is more computationally demanding than the non-robust alternative, simulations and applications provided by Leung (2005) indicate that in the presence of outlying Y values, it can be quite useful.

Related work includes Stone (1977) and Cleveland (1979), who consider resistant local polynomial fitting using weighted least squares. This method is referred to as *lowess*, which stands for *locally weighted regression*. The robustness stems from iterative fitting whereby assigned weights are inversely proportional to the residuals from the previous fit; hence, outliers tend to be downweighted. Cantoni and Ronchetti (2001) consider smoothing splines with robust smoothing parameter selection, along similar lines as Leung (2005). Fan and Jiang (2000) look at robust one-step local polynomial estimators but do not address the issue of bandwidth selection. Wang and Scott (1994) focus on locally weighted polynomials, with fitting being undertaken via linear programming. See also Čížek and Härdle (2006), who consider robust estimation of dimension-reduction regression models.

6.3.5   Bandwidth Selection

In Chapters 1 through 4, when we studied kernel-based estimation of probability mass/density functions and distribution functions, we were mindful of the need to tailor smoothing parameter selection methods to the particular object that was being estimated. By now, we appreciate the smoothing parameter's leading role in this framework, and this remains the case when the focus shifts to estimation of regression functions. Unfortunately, in a regression setting, practitioners often adopt ad hoc reference rules that are designed for, say, density estimation; this virtually guarantees that the regression estimate will be suboptimal. We will study a set of fully automatic, data-driven methods that tend to perform well in a wide range of settings. They all admit mixed-data types and scale well in a multivariate environment. Although these methods are numerically intensive, they have many desirable features. The R package np includes a function `npregbw()` that implements these approaches. Minimization of the objective functions that follow is carried out using numerical algorithms that are suitable for the mixed-data multivariate predictor setting.

A Direct Plug-In Method

Ruppert et al. (1995) propose a direct plug-in method whereby the unknown objects that appear in the expression for the IMSE-optimal bandwidth are replaced by kernel estimates. The function `dpill()` in the R package KernSmooth (Wand, 2015) implements this procedure using a standard normal kernel. An initial estimate of $g(x)$ is obtained via least squares quartic fits over blocks of data, with the number of blocks selected according to Mallows' C_p criterion. Strictly speaking, `dpill()` is a plug-in estimator for the local linear method that is discussed below; the local linear estimator's optimal bandwidth is h_{opt} given above, without the $g'(x)f'(x)f^{-1}(x)$ term. It is worth noting, however, that this approach does not scale to the multivariate mixed-data case and that the function `dpill()` is limited to a single continuous predictor.

Least Squares Cross-validation

Least squares cross-validation chooses the h that minimizes the following objective function:

$$CV(h) = n^{-1} \sum_{i=1}^{n} (Y_i - \hat{g}_{-i}(X_i))^2 M(X_i),$$

where $\hat{g}_{-i}(X_i) = \sum_{l \neq i}^{n} Y_l K_\gamma(X_l, X_i) / \sum_{l \neq i}^{n} K_\gamma(X_l, X_i)$ is the leave-one-out kernel estimator of $g(X_i)$, and $0 \leq M(\cdot) \leq 1$ is a weight function that compensates for difficulties arising from division by zero or slow convergence due to boundary effects. The cross-validated bandwidth is given by $\hat{h} = \operatorname{argmin}_h CV(h)$. Theoretical underpinnings for the multivariate mixed-data local constant, local linear, and generalized local polynomial approaches have been provided by Racine and Li (2004), Li and Racine (2004), and Hall and Racine (2015), respectively.

Generalized Cross-Validation

Generalized cross-validation (GCV) is an approach that was proposed by Craven and Wahba (1979). Note that the kernel estimator can be expressed as

$$(\hat{g}(X_1), \ldots, \hat{g}(X_n))^{\mathrm{T}} = H(h)Y,$$

where $Y = (Y_1, \ldots, Y_n)^{\mathrm{T}}$ and $H(h)$ is an $n \times n$ hat matrix that depends on the Xs, h, and $K(\cdot)$. The GCV method selects the h that minimizes

$$GCV(h) = \left(n^{-1} \operatorname{tr}(I - H(h)) \right)^{-2} n^{-1} \sum_{i=1}^{n} (Y_i - \hat{g}(X_i))^2.$$

The generalized cross-validated bandwidth is given by $\hat{h} = \operatorname{argmin}_h GCV(h)$.

An Information-Theoretic Bandwidth Selector

Hurvich et al. (1998) propose an information criterion for smoothing parameter selection in nonparametric models. It is based on the minimization of

$$\mathrm{AIC}_c(h) = \log \left(n^{-1} \sum_{i=1}^{n} (Y_i - \hat{g}(X_i))^2 \right) + 1 + \left(\frac{2 \left(\operatorname{tr} H(h) + 1 \right)}{n - \operatorname{tr} H(h) - 2} \right).$$

The AIC_c-optimal bandwidth, which is given by $\hat{h} = \operatorname{argmin}_h \mathrm{AIC}_c(h)$, penalizes undersmoothing more severely than least squares and generalized cross-validation. It can therefore be useful when undersmoothing is a potential issue.

Example 6.3. Data-Driven Bandwidth Selection for the Old Faithful Data.

> In Figure 6.7, we revisit the Old Faithful data and plot the result of a local constant regression of `eruptions` (eruption time in minutes) on `waiting` (waiting time to the next eruption in minutes). The cross-validated bandwidth is obtained using the method of Hurvich et al. (1998) and is given by $\hat{h} = \operatorname{argmin}_h AIC_c(h)$. The reader can confirm that least squares cross-validation results in a similar fit for this example.

6.3.6   A Coefficient of Determination for Nonparametric Regression

The *coefficient of determination* is frequently reported as a summary measure of in-sample fit. For linear parametric models, this is based on a decomposition of sums of squares, which is not applicable to nonlinear models. However, there exists a unit-free measure of goodness-of-fit for nonparametric regression models that is the counterpart to the linear coefficient of determination

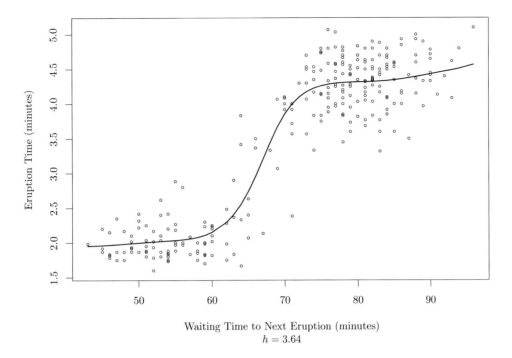

Figure 6.7: Local constant regression, Old Faithful data.

(Doksum and Samarov, 1995). Letting Y_i denote the ith realization of Y and $\hat{Y}_i = \hat{g}(X_i)$ the fitted value for observation i, we may define R^2 as

$$R^2 = \frac{\left(\sum_{i=1}^n (Y_i - \bar{Y})(\hat{Y}_i - \bar{Y})\right)^2}{\sum_{i=1}^n (Y_i - \bar{Y})^2 \sum_{i=1}^n (\hat{Y}_i - \bar{Y})^2}.$$

This measure *always* lies in the range $[0, 1]$, with $R^2 = 1$ corresponding to a perfect fit to the sample data and $R^2 = 0$ corresponding to a total absence of predictive power beyond that of the unconditional mean of Y. In the special case where $\hat{Y}_i$ is a least squares estimate of a linear model with an intercept term, it can be shown that this R^2 is identical to the standard measure computed as $\sum_{i=1}^n (\hat{Y}_i - \bar{Y})^2 / \sum_{i=1}^n (Y_i - \bar{Y})^2$. This result is left as an exercise. See also Su and Ullah (2013) who consider a alternate measure of nonparametric goodness-of-fit.

6.3.7 Local Constant Marginal Effects

Nonparametric estimation of the marginal effects function is a central task in many applied settings. Recalling the definition of $\beta(x)$ that is given in Equation (6.2), if we replace the unknown objects with their kernel estimators, we obtain the local constant estimator of $\beta(x)$. This turns out to be the *analytic* derivative of the local constant kernel estimator of $g(x)$ when common bandwidths are used for all components. This estimator of the marginal effects function is given by

$$
\begin{aligned}
\hat{\beta}(x) &= \frac{d\hat{g}(x)}{dx} \\
&= \frac{\hat{f}(x)\hat{m}'(x) - \hat{m}(x)\hat{f}'(x)}{\hat{f}^2(x)} \\
&= \frac{\hat{m}'(x)}{\hat{f}(x)} - \frac{\hat{m}(x)}{\hat{f}(x)}\frac{\hat{f}'(x)}{\hat{f}(x)} \\
&= \frac{\hat{m}'(x)}{\hat{f}(x)} - \hat{g}(x)\frac{\hat{f}'(x)}{\hat{f}(x)},
\end{aligned}
$$

where

$$
\hat{m}'(x) = -\frac{1}{nh^2}\sum_{i=1}^{n} Y_i K'\left(\frac{X_i - x}{h}\right),
$$

$$
\hat{f}'(x) = -\frac{1}{nh^2}\sum_{i=1}^{n} K'\left(\frac{X_i - x}{h}\right).
$$

The definitions of $\hat{m}(x)$, $\hat{f}(x)$, and $\hat{g}(x)$ have already been provided and are not repeated here.

In order to address the presence of a random denominator, we mirror the approach that was taken when we studied the properties of $\hat{g}(x)$ and we express $\hat{\beta}(x)$ as follows:

$$
\hat{\beta}(x) = \frac{(\hat{m}'(x) - \hat{g}(x)\hat{f}'(x))}{\hat{f}(x)}
$$

$$
= \frac{\mathrm{E}(\hat{m}'(x) - \hat{g}(x)\hat{f}'(x)) + (\hat{m}'(x) - \hat{g}(x)\hat{f}'(x)) - \mathrm{E}(\hat{m}'(x) - \hat{g}(x)\hat{f}'(x))}{\mathrm{E}\,\hat{f}(x) + \hat{f}(x) - \mathrm{E}\,\hat{f}(x)}
$$

$$
= \frac{\mathrm{E}\,\hat{m}'(x) - \mathrm{E}\,\hat{g}(x)\hat{f}'(x) + (\hat{m}'(x) - \mathrm{E}\,\hat{m}'(x)) - (\hat{g}(x)\hat{f}'(x) - \mathrm{E}\,\hat{g}(x)\hat{f}'(x))}{\mathrm{E}\,\hat{f}(x) + \hat{f}(x) - \mathrm{E}\,\hat{f}(x)}
$$

$$
= \frac{\left(\mathrm{E}\,\hat{m}'(x) - \mathrm{E}\,\hat{g}(x)\hat{f}'(x) + (\hat{m}'(x) - \mathrm{E}\,\hat{m}'(x)) - (\hat{g}(x)\hat{f}'(x) - \mathrm{E}\,\hat{g}(x)\hat{f}'(x))\right)}{\mathrm{E}\,\hat{f}(x)\left(1 + \frac{\hat{f}(x) - \mathrm{E}\,\hat{f}(x)}{\mathrm{E}\,\hat{f}(x)}\right)}
$$

$$
= \frac{\left(\mathrm{E}\,\hat{m}'(x) - \mathrm{E}\,\hat{g}(x)\hat{f}'(x) + (\hat{m}'(x) - \mathrm{E}\,\hat{m}'(x)) - (\hat{g}(x)\hat{f}'(x) - \mathrm{E}\,\hat{g}(x)\hat{f}'(x))\right)}{\mathrm{E}\,\hat{f}(x)}
$$

$$
\times \left(1 + \frac{\hat{f}(x) - \mathrm{E}\,\hat{f}(x)}{\mathrm{E}\,\hat{f}(x)}\right)^{-1}
$$

$$
= \frac{\left(\mathrm{E}\,\hat{m}'(x) - \mathrm{E}\,\hat{g}(x)\hat{f}'(x) + (\hat{m}'(x) - \mathrm{E}\,\hat{m}'(x)) - (\hat{g}(x)\hat{f}'(x) - \mathrm{E}\,\hat{g}(x)\hat{f}'(x))\right)}{\mathrm{E}\,\hat{f}(x)}
$$

$$\times \left(1 - \frac{\hat{f}(x) - \mathrm{E}\,\hat{f}(x)}{\mathrm{E}\,\hat{f}(x)} + \mathcal{R} \right)$$

$$= \frac{\mathrm{E}\,\hat{m}'(x)}{\mathrm{E}\,\hat{f}(x)} - \frac{\mathrm{E}\,\hat{g}(x)\hat{f}'(x)}{\mathrm{E}\,\hat{f}(x)} + \frac{(\hat{m}'(x) - \mathrm{E}\,\hat{m}'(x))}{\mathrm{E}\,\hat{f}(x)} - \frac{(\hat{g}(x)\hat{f}'(x) - \mathrm{E}\,\hat{g}(x)\hat{f}'(x))}{\mathrm{E}\,\hat{f}(x)}$$

$$- \mathrm{E}\,\hat{m}'(x) \left(\frac{\hat{f}(x) - \mathrm{E}\,\hat{f}(x)}{(\mathrm{E}\,\hat{f}(x))^2} \right) + \mathrm{E}\,\hat{g}(x)\hat{f}'(x) \left(\frac{\hat{f}(x) - \mathrm{E}\,\hat{f}(x)}{(\mathrm{E}\,\hat{f}(x))^2} \right)$$

$$- (\hat{m}'(x) - \mathrm{E}\,\hat{m}'(x)) \left(\frac{\hat{f}(x) - \mathrm{E}\,\hat{f}(x)}{(\mathrm{E}\,\hat{f}(x))^2} \right)$$

$$+ (\hat{g}(x)\hat{f}'(x) - \mathrm{E}\,\hat{g}(x)\hat{f}'(x)) \left(\frac{\hat{f}(x) - \mathrm{E}\,\hat{f}(x)}{(\mathrm{E}\,\hat{f}(x))^2} \right) + \mathcal{R}.$$

To obtain expressions for the pointwise bias and variance of $\hat{\beta}(x)$, we only need to consider the properties of $\hat{m}'(x)$ and $\hat{f}'(x)$ since we have already derived the pointwise expectation and variance of $\hat{f}(x)$, $\hat{m}(x)$, and $\hat{g}(x)$, and the covariance of $\hat{m}(x)$ and $\hat{f}(x)$. Vinod and Ullah (1988) outline the following results that the reader may verify:

$$\mathrm{E}\,\hat{f}'(x) = f'(x) + \frac{h^2}{2}f'''(x)\kappa_2 + \mathcal{R},$$

$$\mathrm{Var}\,\hat{f}'(x) = \frac{f(x)}{nh^3} \int K'^2(z)\,dz + \mathcal{R},$$

$$\mathrm{E}\,\hat{m}'(x) = (g(x)f(x))'$$
$$+ \frac{h^2}{2}\left(g(x)f'''(x) + g'''(x)f(x) + 3g'(x)f''(x) + 3g''(x)f'(x) \right)\kappa_2$$
$$+ \mathcal{R},$$

$$\mathrm{Var}\,\hat{m}'(x) = \frac{(\sigma^2(x) + g^2(x))f(x)}{nh^3} \int K'^2(z)\,dz + \mathcal{R}.$$

Following a similar approach to our previous derivation of the pointwise mean and variance of $\hat{g}(x)$, we can show that, with a second-order kernel function, the pointwise bias of $\hat{\beta}(x)$ up to terms of $O(h^2)$ is given by

$$\mathrm{Bias}\,\hat{\beta}(x) = \frac{h^2}{2}\left(g'''(x) + 2\left(\frac{g'(x)f''(x)}{f(x)} + \frac{g''(x)f'(x)}{f(x)} - g'(x)\left(\frac{f'(x)}{f(x)} \right)^2 \right) \right)\kappa_2$$

and retaining terms up to $O(1/(nh^3))$, the pointwise variance is given by

$$\mathrm{Var}\,\hat{\beta}(x) = \frac{\sigma^2(x)}{nh^3 f(x)} \int K'^2(z)\,dz.$$

These results rely on the same proof constructs that were established earlier, and we leave their derivation as an exercise for the interested reader.

As the bandwidth increases, the pointwise variance falls and the pointwise bias increases. Note that consistent estimation requires $nh^3 \to \infty$ as $n \to \infty$ in addition to $h \to 0$ as $n \to \infty$.

Application of Liapounov's CLT delivers the asymptotic property

$$\sqrt{nh^3}\left(\hat{\beta}(x) - \beta(x) - \text{Bias}\,\hat{\beta}(x)\right) \xrightarrow{d} N\left(0, \frac{\sigma^2(x)}{f(x)}\int K'^2(z)\,dz\right),$$

provided that h is of $O(n^{-1/7})$. These results are useful insofar as they pave the way for inference concerning the unknown marginal effects function $\beta(x)$, including the construction of confidence bands and hypothesis testing.

See Rilstone and Ullah (1989) for an alternative method of obtaining local constant marginal effects. Smoothing parameter selection that is tailored to $\beta(x)$ has been addressed by Henderson et al. (2015).

Example 6.4. The Marginal Effects Function for the Old Faithful Data.

In Figure 6.8, we revisit the Old Faithful data and plot the local constant estimates of both $g(x)$ and $\beta(x)$ when `eruptions` (eruption time in minutes) is regressed on `waiting` (waiting time to the next eruption in minutes). Clearly, $\hat{g}(x)$ is a monotone increasing function, which implies that $\hat{\beta}(x) \geq 0$. The largest value of $\hat{\beta}(x)$ occurs around the 65 minute mark.

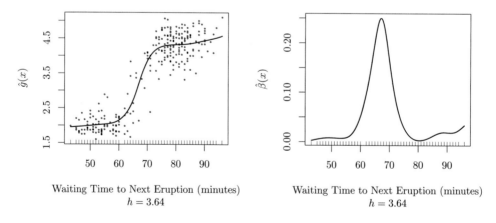

Figure 6.8: Local constant estimator $\hat{g}(x)$ (left) and marginal effects function $\hat{\beta}(x)$ (right), Old Faithful data.

6.4 Local Polynomial Kernel Regression

The local constant estimator was proposed six decades ago by Nadaraya (1965) and Watson (1964). Though popular, it suffers from *boundary bias*, which we explain in more detail below. The *local polynomial* estimator is a more recent development that overcomes this issue. The authoritative text on local polynomial kernel estimation is Fan and Gijbels (1996). Suppose that we wish to approximate the unknown conditional mean function $g(x)$ at some point x_0 in a neighbourhood of x. Assume that the derivative of order $p+1$ at x_0, $g^{(p+1)}(x_0)$, exists and is finite. A Taylor representation of $g(x)$ at x_0 is given by

$$g(x) = \sum_{j=0}^{\infty} \frac{(x-x_0)^j}{j!} g^{(j)}(x_0)$$

$$= g(x_0) + (x-x_0)g'(x_0) + \cdots + \frac{(x-x_0)^p}{p!} g^{(p)}(x_0).$$

We could fit this polynomial locally by solving a weighted least squares problem, i.e.,

$$\hat{\alpha} = \mathrm{argmin}_{\alpha_0,\dots,\alpha_p} \sum_{i=1}^{n} \left(Y_i - \sum_{j=0}^{p} \alpha_j (x - X_i)^j \right)^2 K\left(\frac{x-X_i}{h} \right).$$

The local polynomial estimator of $g(x)$ is the locally weighted intercept term $\hat{g}(x) = \hat{\alpha}_0$, while the jth-order order derivative estimates, $j = 1, 2, \dots, p$, are given by the remaining locally weighted coefficients $\hat{\alpha}_1, \hat{\alpha}_2, \dots, \hat{\alpha}_p$. That is, the first derivative is $\hat{\beta}(x) = \hat{\alpha}_1$, and so forth. When $p > 0$, $\hat{\beta}(x)$ is no longer the *analytic* derivative of the estimated conditional mean $\hat{g}(x)$, as it was in the local constant case. This can have unintended consequences for constrained estimation; see Racine (2016) for details. Note that it is not necessary to use deviations about x for the local polynomial fit. That is, we could get rid of the $(x - X_i)^j$ terms and instead minimize

$$\sum_{i=1}^{n} \left(Y_i - \sum_{j=0}^{p} \alpha_j X_i^j \right)^2 K\left(\frac{x-X_i}{h} \right), \tag{6.14}$$

where $\hat{g}(x) = \sum_{j=0}^{p} \hat{\alpha}_j x^j$ and where $\hat{\alpha}_1, \hat{\alpha}_2, \dots, \hat{\alpha}_p$ are once again the locally weighted derivative estimates, that is, the marginal effects functions (see the R example in the Practitioner's Corner). In matrix form, we denote the design matrix by $\mathbf{X}$,

$$\mathbf{X} = \begin{pmatrix} 1 & X_1 & \cdots & X_1^p \\ \vdots & \vdots & \cdots & \vdots \\ 1 & X_n & \cdots & X_n^p \end{pmatrix}$$

and we let

$$\mathbf{Y} = \begin{pmatrix} Y_1 \\ \vdots \\ Y_n \end{pmatrix} \quad \text{and} \quad \alpha = \begin{pmatrix} \alpha_0 \\ \vdots \\ \alpha_p \end{pmatrix}.$$

Let $\mathbf{K}$ denote the diagonal weight matrix

$$\mathbf{K} = \begin{pmatrix} K(z_1) & \cdots & 0 \\ \vdots & \ddots & \vdots \\ 0 & \cdots & K(z_n) \end{pmatrix}$$

where $z_i = (x - X_i)/h$. Using matrix algebra, the weighted least squares problem in Equation (6.14) can be written as

$$\min_{\alpha} (\mathbf{Y} - \mathbf{X}\alpha)^{\mathrm{T}} \mathbf{K} (\mathbf{Y} - \mathbf{X}\alpha)$$

and its solution is given by

$$\hat{\alpha} = \left(\mathbf{X}^{\mathrm{T}} \mathbf{K} \mathbf{X} \right)^{-1} \mathbf{X}^{\mathrm{T}} \mathbf{K} \mathbf{Y}.$$

Thus, $\hat{g}(X_i) = \mathbf{X}_i^{\mathrm{T}} \hat{\alpha}$, where $\mathbf{X}_i^{\mathrm{T}}$ is a $1 \times (p+1)$ vector that denotes the ith row of the $n \times (p+1)$ matrix $\mathbf{X}$. Ruppert and Wand (1994) provide first order asymptotic expansions for the bias and variance of $\hat{g}(x)$.

This estimator has the property that, as $h \to \infty$, $\hat{g}(x)$ approaches a global polynomial of degree p. So if $p = 1$, then as $h \to \infty$, $\hat{g}(X_i) \to \mathbf{X}_i^{\mathrm{T}} \hat{\beta}$, where $\hat{\beta} = \left(\mathbf{X}^{\mathrm{T}} \mathbf{X} \right)^{-1} \mathbf{X}^{\mathrm{T}} \mathbf{Y}$ is the global (unweighted) OLS coefficient vector for the simple linear regression model $Y_i = \beta_0 + \beta_1 X_i + \epsilon_i$.

By way of illustration, consider the local linear estimator. The local linear $(p = 1)$ and local constant $(p = 0)$ estimators of $g(x)$ have identical pointwise variance. However, retaining terms of $O(h^2)$, the pointwise bias of the single-predictor local linear estimator is given by

$$h^2 \left(\frac{1}{2} g''(x) \right) \kappa_2$$

while the pointwise bias of the local constant estimator is given by

$$h^2 \left(\frac{1}{2} g''(x) + \frac{g'(x) f'(x)}{f(x)} \right) \kappa_2.$$

We observe that the $1/f(x)$ term in the expression for the pointwise bias of the local constant estimator gives rise to the boundary bias phenomenon that we mentioned earlier. On the other hand, the $1/f(x)$ term does not appear in the expression for the pointwise bias of the local linear estimator, which indicates that it does not suffer from boundary bias. Unlike its local constant counterpart, however, in some settings, the local linear estimator is known to suffer from singularity issues. A solution to this problem that involves shrinkage is outlined in Seifert and Gasser (2000); see also Cheng et al. (1997). These methods are baked into the functions `npregbw()` and `npreg()` in the R package np.

Example 6.5. Local Linear Regression, Pointwise Bias, Pointwise Variance, and the Bandwidth.

Consider $M = 1,000$ local linear kernel regression estimates where $X \sim U[0,1]$, $\epsilon \sim N(0, \sigma^2)$ and $Y_i = \sin(2\pi X_i) + \epsilon_i$. We compute the pointwise bias and variance of $\hat{g}(x)$ based on three different choices of bandwidths (one *too large*, one *about right*, one *too small*). Figure 6.9 summarizes the results of this exercise.

This Monte Carlo simulation reveals a feature of the formula for the pointwise bias of the local linear estimator, namely that bias depends on the curvature $g''(x)$ but *not* on the density $f(x)$. We should therefore not expect to observe any boundary bias. It is clear from Figure 6.9 that the bias is the same at the boundaries and in the interior. A comparison of Figure 6.9 and Figure 6.6 reveals that the local linear method is indeed very effective at removing boundary bias. It turns out that this is a feature that is shared by all *odd* degree local polynomial estimators. Thus, moving from the local constant to the local linear estimator has the advantage of removing boundary bias, but it comes at the cost of *losing* the ability to smooth out an irrelevant (continuous) predictor. Below, we will consider an approach that overcomes this limitation via joint selection of the polynomial degree and the bandwidth.

Example 6.6. Local Linear Estimation in Practice - The `Prestige` Data.

Figure 6.10 illustrates how, as $h \to \infty$ (the oversmoothed case in Figure 6.10), $\hat{g}(x) \to \hat{\beta}_0 + \hat{\beta}_1 x$, that is, the local linear estimator converges to the global linear least squares estimator. This example uses the `Prestige` data from the `car` package (Fox and Weisberg, 2011). The dataset consists of $n = 102$ observations. The dependent variable is the prestige of Canadian occupations (the *Pineo-Porter score*) and the explanatory variable is average income for each occupation measured in 1971 Canadian dollars.

6.5 The Multivariate Local Polynomial Extension

A general pth degree local polynomial estimator for the multivariate predictor case is more notationally cumbersome. The general multivariate case is considered by Masry (1996a; see also Masry, 1996b), who establishes the uniform almost sure convergence rate and a pointwise asymptotic normality result for the local polynomial estimator of $g(x)$ and its derivatives up to degree p. Following the carefully considered notation in Masry (1996a), we define

$$r = (r_1, \ldots, r_q), \quad r! = r_1! \times \cdots \times r_q!,$$

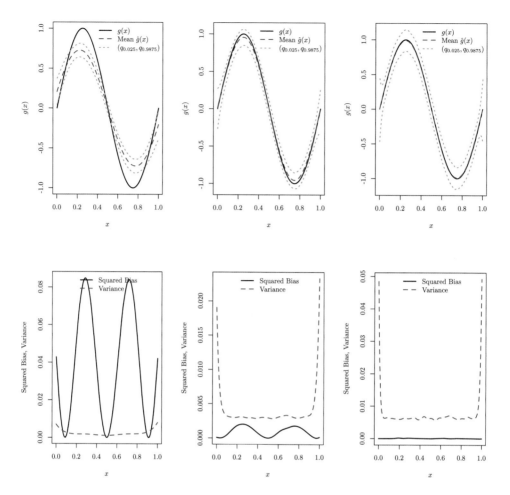

Figure 6.9: Summary of 1,000 local linear kernel regression estimates, $n = 250$, $Y_i = \sin(2\pi X_i) + \epsilon_i$ DGP, with three bandwidths (too large [leftmost figures], about right [middle figures], too small [rightmost figures]). The upper figures plot the DGP $g(x)$ along with the pointwise mean ($1000^{-1} \sum_{m=1}^{1000} \hat{g}_m(x)$), 0.025th pointwise quantile, and 0.975th pointwise quantile. The lower figures present the pointwise squared bias ($[\mathrm{E}(\hat{g}(x)) - g(x)]^2$) and pointwise variance.

$$\bar{r} = \sum_{j=1}^{q} r_j,$$

$$x^r = x_1^{r_1} \times \cdots \times x_q^{r_q},$$

$$\sum_{0 \le \bar{r} \le p} = \sum_{j=0}^{p} \sum_{r_1=0}^{j} \cdots \sum_{r_q=0}^{j}, \quad (\text{with } \bar{r} \equiv r_1 + \cdots + r_q = j), \quad \text{and}$$

$$(D^r g)(x) = \frac{\partial^r g(x)}{\partial x_1^{r_1} \ldots \partial x_q^{r_q}}.$$

Assuming that $g(x)$ has derivatives of total degree $p + 1$ at a point x, we

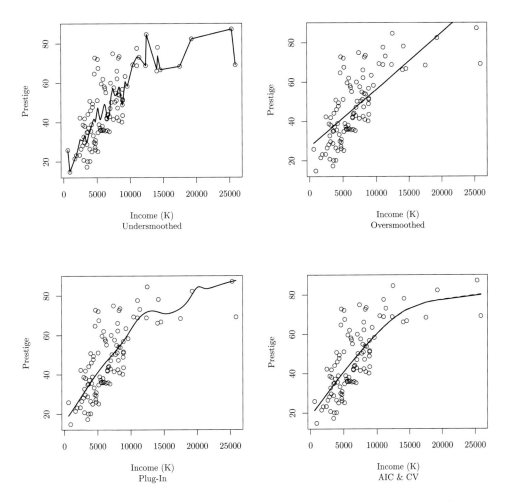

Figure 6.10: Nonparametric local linear regression with a variety of bandwidths for the Prestige data.

can approximate $g(z)$ locally using a multivariate polynomial of total degree p,

$$g(z) \stackrel{\sim}{=} \sum_{0 \leq \bar{r} \leq p} \frac{1}{r!} (D^r g)(v)|_{v=x} (z - x)^r. \tag{6.15}$$

Define a multivariate weighted least squares function by

$$\sum_{i=1}^{n} \left(Y_i - \sum_{0 \leq \bar{r} \leq p} b_r(x)(X_i - x)^r \right)^2 K_\gamma(X_i, x), \tag{6.16}$$

where $K_\gamma(X_i, x)$ is the generalized product kernel that was outlined in Chapter 3. Note that only the q continuous predictors appear in the polynomial, whereas the $q + r + s$ continuous, unordered, and ordered predictors appear in $K_\gamma(X_i, x)$.

Minimizing Equation (6.16) with respect to each $b_r(x)$ gives an estimate $\hat{b}_r(x)$. By (6.15), we know that $r!\hat{b}_r(x)$ estimates $(D^r g)(x)$, and hence $(D^r \hat{g})(x) = r!\hat{b}_r(x)$. For a general treatment of multivariate bandwidth selection for the local linear kernel estimator when all predictors are continuous, see Yang and Tschernig (1999). The mixed-data local constant and local linear cases with data-driven selection of γ have been considered by Racine and Li (2004) and Li and Racine (2004), respectively, while the infinite-order case has been considered by Hall and Racine (2015).

It can be shown via application of Liapounov's CLT that

$$\sqrt{n \prod_{j=1}^{q} h_j} \left(\hat{g}(x) - g(x) - \text{Bias } \hat{g}(x)\right) \xrightarrow{d} N\left(0, \frac{\sigma^2(x)\kappa^q}{f(x)}\right).$$

These results are useful insofar as they pave the way for inference concerning the unknown conditional mean $g(x)$, which includes the construction of confidence bands and hypothesis testing.

6.6   Local Polynomial Kernel Regression and Shrinkage

In applied settings, the degree of the local polynomial is often set to be one greater than the largest derivative that the practitioner needs to estimate. Alternatively, one might simply opt for the local linear or local constant estimators with the understanding that they are both consistent, even though they possess different properties. A particularly interesting property of the local polynomial estimator is that as the bandwidth $h \to \infty$, it shrinks towards a global least squares polynomial fit of degree p. See Kiefer and Racine (2009) and Kiefer and Racine (2017) for theory that links kernel smoothing to Bayesian shrinkage and related Stein effects. In particular,

- If $p = 0$, then as $h \to \infty$, the local constant estimator $\hat{g}(x)$ shrinks towards $\bar{Y}$, which is the unconditional mean of Y.
- If $p = 1$, then as $h \to \infty$, the local linear estimator $\hat{g}(x)$ shrinks towards $\hat{\beta}_0 + \hat{\beta}_1 X_i$, which is the least squares linear regression of Y_i on X_i.
- If $p = 2$, then as $h \to \infty$, the local quadratic estimator $\hat{g}(x)$ shrinks towards $\hat{\beta}_0 + \hat{\beta}_1 X_i + \hat{\beta}_2 X_i^2$, which is the least squares regression of Y_i on X_i and X_i^2 (a similar property holds for $p = 3, 4, \ldots$).

If you knew *ex ante* that X and Y are unrelated, then you would model Y by its unconditional mean or equivalently, by a local constant estimator with a large bandwidth value h. *If* you knew *ex ante* that there is, say, a quadratic relationship between X and Y, then you would use a parametric regression that is quadratic in X to model Y or equivalently, a local quadratic estimator with a large bandwidth value h. Unfortunately, we cannot know ex ante that these are the properties of the underlying DGP. We will come back to this issue after we consider the notion of *analytic* functions.

In mathematics, an *analytic* function is one that is locally given by a convergent power series (Wikipedia, 2017). A function is analytic if and only if it is equal to its Taylor series in some neighbourhood of every point in its support.

- Any polynomial is an analytic function. If a polynomial has degree p, then any terms in its Taylor series expansion that are of degree larger than p must immediately vanish to 0; hence the series will be trivially convergent.

- The exponential function is analytic. Any Taylor series for this function converges not only for x close enough to x_0, as in the definition, but for all values of x in its support.

- Trigonometric, logarithm, and power functions are analytic on any open subset of their support.

- The absolute value function is not everywhere analytic because it is not differentiable at 0. Piecewise functions are typically not analytic where the pieces meet.

The class of analytic functions is dense and encompasses virtually any transformation that practitioners might use when modeling nonlinear relationships. This includes polynomial expansions, logarithmic transformations, trigonometric and exponential transformations, exponentiated polynomials, etc.

As noted earlier, in applied settings, practitioners tend to either adopt the local constant or local linear variants, or choose a local polynomial whose degree is slightly greater than the order of the maximum derivative that needs to be estimated. Although such ad hoc determination of the polynomial degree is not necessarily optimal, it is both theoretically and practically challenging to jointly determine the polynomial degree and the value of the bandwidth. Hall and Racine (2015) propose a data-driven cross-validation procedure for the joint determination of the multivariate polynomial degree vector and bandwidth vector. After providing the underlying theory, they demonstrate that this approach can lead to improvements in both finite-sample efficiency and rates of convergence. If the true DGP is in fact an analytic function (e.g., a polynomial whose degree does not depend on the sample size), the method of Hall and Racine (2015) is capable of attaining the $\sqrt{n}$ rate that is typically associated with correctly specified parametric models. Moreover, the estimator is shown to be uniformly consistent for a much larger class of DGPs. This result is achieved via joint optimization of the bandwidth vector and the polynomial degree vector. Bernstein polynomials are used rather than the *raw* polynomials that appeared earlier in the Taylor approximation, and the degree of the polynomial is allowed to differ for each predictor; otherwise, the standard local polynomial approach is followed. The joint optimization of the cross-validation function with respect to the polynomial degree vector, whose entries are integers, and the bandwidth vector, whose entries are real-valued non-negative bounded scalars, is a *mixed-integer* problem that can be handled by the NOMAD solver (Le Digabel, 2011; Abramson et al., 2011) in the R package crs (Racine and Nie, 2017; Nie and Racine, 2012). The R function npglpreg() in the crs package implements this approach to generalized local polynomial regression.

In the following code chunk, the functions npreg() and npglpreg() in the np and crs packages, respectively, are used to carry out multivariate local polynomial estimation. Illustrations of the broader behaviour of the approach of Hall and Racine (2015) can be found in the Practitioner's Corner at the end of this chapter.

```
require(np)
require(crs)
options(np.messages=FALSE,crs.messages=FALSE)
set.seed(42)
n <- 250
x1 <- runif(n,-2,2)
x2 <- runif(n,-2,2)
dgp <- x1**3+x2
y <- dgp + rnorm(n,sd=0.5*sd(dgp))
## Local constant estimation (local polynomial with degree=0)
ghat.lc <- npreg(y~x1+x2,nmulti=5)
ghat.glp.lc <- npglpreg(y~x1+x2,cv="bandwidth",degree=c(0,0),nmulti=5)
summary(ghat.lc$bws)
summary(ghat.glp.lc)
## Local linear estimation (local polynomial with degree=1)
ghat.ll <- npreg(y~x1+x2,regtype="ll",nmulti=5)
ghat.glp.ll <- npglpreg(y~x1+x2,cv="bandwidth",degree=c(1,1),nmulti=5)
summary(ghat.ll$bws)
summary(ghat.glp.ll)
## Local quadratic estimation (local polynomial with degree=2)
ghat.glp.lq <- npglpreg(y~x1+x2,cv="bandwidth",degree=c(2,2),nmulti=5)
summary(ghat.glp.lq)
## Generalized local polynomial estimation (joint selection of
## polynomial degree and bandwidth vectors)
ghat.glp <- npglpreg(y~x1+x2,nmulti=5)
summary(ghat.glp)
```

Example 6.7. A Comparison of the Local Constant, Local Linear, and Generalized Local Polynomial Estimators.

Figure 6.11 compares the finite-sample behaviour of the local constant, local linear, and generalized local polynomial estimators. All bandwidths have been selected by means of least squares cross-validation. The DGP is given by $g(x) = sin(2\pi x)$, where $x \sim U[0, 1]$. It is evident that all three approaches yield quality representations of the underlying DGP, with estimates growing smoother as the order of the polynomial increases. The respective cross-validated bandwidths are 0.0236, 0.03, and 1.7734×10^5, and the cross-validated degree for the generalized local polynomial

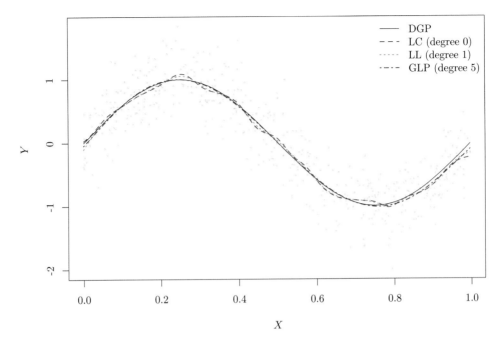

Figure 6.11: Cross-validated local constant, local linear, and generalized local polynomial estimators.

estimator is 5. In this instance, a polynomial of degree 5 combined with a large bandwidth (1.7734×10^5) gives rise to a very good fit, and it would likely outperform its local constant and local linear peers if evaluated on independent data drawn from this particular DGP.

6.7 Multivariate Mixed-Data Marginal Effects

Consider a multivariate conditional mean function $g(x) = E(Y|X = x)$ where x is a vector composed of q continuous, r unordered, and s ordered predictors, i.e., $x = (x_1^c, \ldots, x_q^c, x_1^u, \ldots, x_r^u, x_1^o, \ldots, x_s^o)^{\mathrm{T}}$. Let $\beta_j(x)$ denote the *marginal effects* function that is associated with the jth predictor. If the jth predictor $x_j \in \mathbb{R}$ is continuous, then $\beta_j(x)$ is the first partial derivative function of $g(x)$ with respect to x_j. If the jth predictor x_j^u is unordered and an element of, say, the discrete set $\mathcal{D} = \{a, b, c\}$, we first require a base category, which we will take to be $x_j^u = a$. The marginal effects function $\beta_j(x)$ is the finite difference between the conditional mean $g(x)$ evaluated at either $x_j^u = b$ or $x_j^u = c$ and $g(x)$ evaluated at $x_j^u = a$. If the jth predictor is ordered, then we have two options. The first option is to take finite differences as in the unordered case. The second option is to take finite differences between *successive* elements of the ordered set. Hence $\beta_j(x)$ would be defined as the finite difference between the conditional mean function $g(x)$ evaluated at $x_j^u = b$ and at $x_j^u = a$, and the finite difference between $g(x)$ evaluated at $x_j^u = c$ and at $x_j^u = b$. Thus, to recap, if we partition the vector of predictors x into x_j and $x_{(-j)}$, where $x_{(-j)}$ contains all predictors other than x_j, then we may write $x = (x_{(-j)}, x_j)$ and define the marginal effects function as

$$\beta_j(x) = \begin{cases} \partial g(x)/\partial x_j & \text{if } x_j \in \mathbb{R}, \\ \Delta_j g(x) = g(x_{(-j)}, x_j = l) - g(x_{(-j)}, x_j = \mathcal{D}_0) & \text{if } x_j \in \mathcal{D}, \end{cases}$$

where $l \in \{\mathcal{D}_0, \ldots, \mathcal{D}_{c-1}\}$, $\mathcal{D}_0$ denotes the base category, and $\mathcal{D} = \{\mathcal{D}_0, \ldots, \mathcal{D}_{c-1}\}$. Given that we are dealing with general nonlinear surfaces, $\beta_j(x)$ may naturally change as the elements of x change. Thus, we treat $\beta_j(x)$ as a *function* of x rather than restricting it to be a scalar.

Realize that this is *exactly* what practitioners do when they estimate a regression function that is linear and additive in predictors and that contains intercept-shifting dummy variables. For instance, suppose that you specify the model $\alpha_0 + \delta_b \mathbf{1}(x_1 = b) + \delta_c \mathbf{1}(x_1 = c) + \alpha_1 x_2 + \epsilon$, where $x_1 \in \mathcal{D} = \{a, b, c\}$, $\mathbf{1}(x_1 = b) = 1$ if $x_1 = b$, $\mathbf{1}(x_1 = c) = 1$ if $x_1 = c$, and $x_2 \in \mathbb{R}$. The marginal effects function $\beta(x)$ for the discrete predictor $x_1 \in \mathcal{D}$ is given by δ_b or δ_c, which respectively correspond to the finite difference between $g(x; \alpha, \delta)$ evaluated at $x_1 = a$ and at $x_1 = b$, and the finite difference between $g(x; \alpha, \delta)$ evaluated at $x_1 = a$ and at $x_1 = c$. Furthermore, for the continuous predictor $x_2 \in \mathbb{R}$, $\partial g(x; \alpha, \delta)/\partial x_2 = \alpha_1$, which is the first derivative function. It is presumed to be a constant that depends on neither the value of x_2 nor the level of x_1 (in our terminology, we refer to the *levels* of a *factor* or categorical predictor).

When constructing the marginal effects function $\beta_j(x)$, one must always take into account the values that are assumed by the predictors other than x_j, which we denote by $x_{(-j)}$. It would be perfectly reasonable to leave them at their sample realizations, i.e., the vector X_i^T. Alternatively, one might hold the values of the remaining predictors constant at their respective medians or modes for all $i = 1, \ldots, n$. The former might be appropriate when conducting inference where the null relating to $\beta_j(x)$ holds *almost everywhere*. The latter might be the preferred option when plotting $\beta_j(x)$ since the off-axis predictors will then be held constant, which is axiomatically desirable. In the Practitioner's Corner at the end of this chapter, we construct and interpret marginal effects surfaces in a multivariate mixed-data context. We illustrate how smooth results for the continuous predictors can be produced when the off-axis predictors are held constant.

6.7.1   A Consistent Test for Predictor Relevance

As we discussed in Chapter 2, parametric tests are sometimes *inconsistent*, i.e., they lack power in the direction of certain alternatives. This arises because the user must specify the set of alternatives under which the null will be rejected, and hence there may exist some alternatives that a particular test cannot detect. Furthermore, depending on the hypothesis that is being tested, a test's validity might hinge on *correct* parametric specification of the model. That is, it might rely on an assumption that the model is a faithful representation of the underlying DGP.

There exist a range of nonparametric procedures that have been proposed for the *consistent* testing of certain hypotheses. The power of consistent tests lies in the fact that as $n \to \infty$, the probability of rejecting H_0 when H_0 is false approaches 1. This is not necessarily true in a parametric context. We begin with an illustration that involves a simple test for predictor relevance in a parametric regression framework.

Example 6.8. Testing for Predictor Relevance.

Consider the linear regression model,

$$Y_i = g(X_i; \alpha) + \epsilon_i$$
$$= \alpha_0 + \alpha_1 X_i + \epsilon_i,$$

and a sample of simulated data that is drawn from a DGP to be revealed shortly. We perform a common *test of significance*, which involves the null hypothesis $H_0 \colon dg(x; \alpha)/dx = \beta(x; \alpha) = \alpha_1 = 0$. Failure to reject the null implies that the predictor x has no explanatory power *in the model* $g(x; \alpha) = \alpha_0 + \alpha_1 x$. Based on this simple t-test, a practitioner might conclude that there is no relationship between X and Y in the underlying DGP. But this conclusion holds only if the model is correctly specified. Practitioners generally intend to test the hypothesis $H_0 \colon dg(x)/dx = \beta(x) = 0$ almost everywhere (a.e.), and the assumed model specification reduces this to a problem of testing whether the scalar α_1 differs significantly from 0. Table 6.7.1 summarizes the estimated model.

We fail to reject H_0 simply because the true model is $Y_i = \alpha_0 + \alpha_1 X_i^2 + \epsilon_i$, with $X_i \sim U[-1, 1]$. That is, even though there is indeed a strong relationship between X and Y that happens to be nonlinear, the linear fit yields a coefficient $\hat{\alpha}_1$ that is on average equal to 0.

	Estimate	Std. Error	t value	Pr($>$|t|)
(Intercept)	1.1169	0.0353	31.66	0.0000
x	-0.0054	0.0605	-0.09	0.9287

We now consider a consistent nonparametric test of a predictor's significance in a nonparametric regression setting (Racine, 1997; Racine et al., 2006). One first partitions the vector of predictors x into two parts - the predictor x_j whose significance is being tested and the remaining explanatory variables $x_{(-j)}$. Recall that we defined the partial derivative function with respect to the jth predictor as

$$\beta_j(x) = \begin{cases} \partial g(x)/\partial x_j & \text{if } x_j \in \mathbb{R}, \\ \Delta_j g(x) = g(x_{(-j)}, x_j = l) - g(x_{(-j)}, x_j = \mathcal{D}_0) & \text{if } x_j \in \mathcal{D}, \end{cases}$$

where $l \in \{\mathcal{D}_0, \ldots, \mathcal{D}_{c-1}\}$.

This approach is the counterpart to the simple t-test that is commonly performed in parametric regression settings. In our framework, we are interested in a consistent test of the hypothesis $\beta_j(x) = 0$ a.e., as opposed to the hypothesis that a coefficient in a potentially misspecified model is equal to 0.

If the unknown conditional mean function $g(x)$ is independent of the predictor x_j, then the unknown marginal effects function $\beta_j(x)$ is zero almost everywhere. We write this as

$$g(x) \perp x_j | x_{(-j)} \Leftrightarrow \beta_j(x) = 0,$$

where $\perp x_j | x_{(-j)}$ denotes conditional orthogonality.

The null and alternative hypotheses can be stated as

$$H_0: \quad \beta_j(x) = 0 \text{ for all } x \text{ (a.e.),}$$
$$H_A: \quad \beta_j(x) \neq 0 \text{ for some } x \text{ on a set with a positive measure.}$$

Aggregating over the support of the random variable X, we have

$$H_0: \quad \lambda = \mathrm{E}\left(\beta_j(X)^2\right) = 0,$$
$$H_A: \quad \lambda = \mathrm{E}\left(\beta_j(X)^2\right) > 0.$$

A feasible pivotal test statistic is given by

$$\hat{\lambda} = \begin{cases} \frac{1}{n}\sum_{i=1}^{n}\left(\frac{\hat{\beta}_j(X_i)}{\hat{\sigma}_{\hat{\beta}_j(X_i)}}\right)^2 & \text{if } x_j \in \mathbb{R}, \\ \frac{1}{n}\sum_{i=1}^{n}\sum_{l=1}^{c-1}\left(\frac{\hat{\beta}_j(X_i)}{\hat{\sigma}_{\hat{\beta}_j(X_i)}}\right)^2 & \text{if } x_j \in \mathcal{D}. \end{cases}$$

If the null hypothesis is true, then λ will be identically equal to zero. To obtain a feasible test statistic, one replaces the unknown marginal effects function $\beta(x)$, which is either a derivative or a set of finite differences, with a consistent kernel estimator, and substitutes the sample moment for the unknown population moment. It is widely known that asymptotic approximations result in tests that have poor size properties. This is because they give rise to critical values that are not functions of the smoothing parameters, which vanish asymptotically, whereas the test statistic's value depends on the degree of smoothing. In practice, resampling methods tend to be preferable (Robinson, 1991). The bootstrap yields null distributions that adapt to the degree of smoothing and delivers more robust tests than those based on asymptotic approximations. The function `npsigtest()` in the R package np performs tests of predictor relevance and can be used on objects obtained from `npreg()`. A joint test procedure is also available (see `?npsigtest()` for options).

Example 6.9. Testing for Predictor Relevance in an Earnings Equation Setting.

We conduct a test of significance for each predictor in the earnings equation model that is considered in the Practitioner's Corner in this chapter. The variables `female` and `married` are unordered categorical predictors, while `educ`, `exper`, and `tenure` are treated as continuous. Results based on a local linear regression with AIC_c bandwidths are presented in the following code chunk.

```
data(wage1)
ghat <- npreg(lwage ~ female + married + educ + exper + tenure,
              regtype="ll",
              bwmethod="cv.aic",
              data=wage1)
npsigtest(ghat)
##
## Kernel Regression Significance Test
## Type I Test with IID Bootstrap (399 replications, Pivot = TRUE, joint = FALSE)
## Explanatory variables tested for significance:
## female (1), married (2), educ (3), exper (4), tenure (5)
##
##                female married  educ exper tenure
## Bandwidth(s): 0.01979  0.1523 7.848 8.432  41.61
##
## Individual Significance Tests
## P Value:
## female  <2e-16 ***
## married 0.0050 **
## educ    <2e-16 ***
## exper   <2e-16 ***
## tenure  0.0025 **
## ---
## Signif. codes:  0 '***' 0.001 '**' 0.01 '*' 0.05 '.' 0.1 ' ' 1
```

Fan and Li (1996), Chen and Fan (1999), Lavergne and Vuong (2000), and Delgado and Manteiga (2001) propose alternative nonparametric tests of significance of continuous predictors in nonparametric regression models. See also Lavergne (2001) and the references therein for a non-smoothing nonparametric test of regression constancy over subsamples.

6.8   Time Series Kernel Regression

All of the results that were derived above pertained to an i.i.d. setting. Nonetheless, similar results have been obtained for weakly dependent processes. In particular, it can be demonstrated that the leading terms of the pointwise bias and pointwise variance expressions for density, conditional density, and conditional moment estimation are *identical* to those obtained in the i.i.d. case; see Li and Racine (2007) for additional details. For instance, Masry (1996a) and Masry (1996b) have shown that $\hat{g}(x)$ for weakly dependent processes has the same order MSE and the same asymptotic distribution as in the i.i.d. case. For the mixed-data weakly dependent case, see Ouyang et al. (2009). Recent work by Sun and Li (2011), among others, has addressed the non-stationary case. The general conclusion is that bandwidth selection, estimation, and inference can proceed *without modification*; only the non-stationary case requires a separate treatment, which is to be expected.

Example 6.10. Kernel Regression for an AR(1) Process.

> As the following code chunk illustrates, the function `npreg()` in the R package np supports time series objects. Desired lags for a series can be generated with the `lag()` function. Figure 6.12 presents a simulated time series and a local constant kernel estimate. The DGP is given by $Y_t = 0.9Y_{t-1} + \epsilon_t$, which is a linear stationary AR(1) process. Given the uncertainty regarding the appropriate lag order, we include four lags of Y_t in the nonparametric model.
>
> Note how the bandwidths in the code chunk are large for lags that exceed 1. This is because the local constant estimator that uses a product kernel and cross-validated bandwidth selection has the ability to automatically remove irrelevant predictors without any pre-testing (Hall et al., 2007). To see this, note that if $h_2 = h_3 = h_4 \to \infty$, then $K((Y_{t-k} - y_{t-k})/h_k) \to K(0)$ for $k = 2, 3, 4$. Therefore, $\prod_{k=1}^{4} K((Y_{t-k}-y_{t-k})/h_k) = K((Y_{t-1}-y_{t-1})/h_1)K(0)^3$ and $\hat{g}(x) = \sum_{t=5}^{t} Y_t K((Y_{t-1} - y_{t-1})/h_1)K(0)^3 / \sum_{t=5}^{t} K((Y_{t-1} - y_{t-1})/h_1)K(0)^3 = \sum_{t=5}^{t} Y_t K((Y_{t-1} - y_{t-1})/h_1) / \sum_{t=5}^{t} K((Y_{t-1} - y_{t-1})/h_1)$, which is the one-predictor local constant kernel estimator. If lags 2, 3, and 4 are irrelevant and the cross-validated $\hat{h}_2$, $\hat{h}_3$, and $\hat{h}_4$ are large, then cross-validation has effectively shrunk a four-dimensional nonparametric estimator towards a one-dimensional nonparametric estimator that, appropriately, converges at the one-dimensional rate. The intuition that underlies this property is straightforward. If an irrelevant predictor is unknowingly included in a local constant regression, then its presence does not give rise to any bias. Hence, the estimator bias with respect to this predictor is the same, regardless of the asso-

ciated bandwidth. On the other hand, the additional noise that arises from this predictor increases the estimator's overall variability. The variance falls as the bandwidth that is associated with this predictor increases in size. Since cross-validation essentially seeks to optimize the square-error properties of the estimator, it assigns a large bandwidth value to this predictor since overall variability is reduced without any effect on bias. As described above, this essentially removes the irrelevant predictor from the resulting estimate. It is rather impressive that cross-validation has differentiated the relevant and the irrelevant predictors by oversmoothing the latter and optimally smoothing the former. This is one reason why we might not want to write-off the local constant estimator simply because it exhibits boundary bias. In effect, in the presence of irrelevant predictors, cross-validation delivers a dimensionality reduction procedure, which is not what occurs in a parametric setting.

To recapitulate, even though we included four lags of Y in the model due to uncertainty about how many lags we ought to incorporate, the cross-validated local constant estimator in effect *smoothed out* lags 2, 3, and 4. This resulted in an estimator that included the only relevant predictor, namely the first lag of Y. Application of the consistent test for parameter relevance that was detailed earlier indicates (correctly) that lags 2, 3, and 4 are irrelevant predictors. Moreover, refitting the model with just a single lag produces the same fit, which confirms that each of the estimates uses only one predictor.

```
## Simulate data from a stationary univariate AR(1) process
set.seed(42)
n <- 100
y <- arima.sim(n = n, list(ar = c(0.9)))
## Conduct local constant estimation of y on four lags
ghat.4 <- npreg(y~lag(y,-1)+lag(y,-2)+lag(y,-3)+lag(y,-4))
## Examine the model summary
summary(ghat.4)
##
## Regression Data: 96 training points, in 4 variable(s)
##              lag(y, -1) lag(y, -2) lag(y, -3) lag(y, -4)
## Bandwidth(s):    0.6519      1.952     2.5e+08   58583015
##
## Kernel Regression Estimator: Local-Constant
## Bandwidth Type: Fixed
## Residual standard error: 0.8801
## R-squared: 0.8245
##
## Continuous Kernel Type: Second-Order Gaussian
## No. Continuous Explanatory Vars.: 4
## Conduct a nonparametric significance test
```

```
npsigtest(ghat.4)
##
## Kernel Regression Significance Test
## Type I Test with IID Bootstrap (399 replications, Pivot = TRUE, joint = FALSE)
## Explanatory variables tested for significance:
## lag(y, -1) (1), lag(y, -2) (2), lag(y, -3) (3), lag(y, -4) (4)
##
##                 lag(y, -1) lag(y, -2) lag(y, -3) lag(y, -4)
## Bandwidth(s):     0.6519      1.952     2.5e+08    58583015
##
## Individual Significance Tests
## P Value:
## lag(y, -1) <2e-16 ***
## lag(y, -2) 0.44
## lag(y, -3) 0.94
## lag(y, -4) 0.90
## ---
## Signif. codes:  0 '***' 0.001 '**' 0.01 '*' 0.05 '.' 0.1 ' ' 1
## Re-fit the model using only 1 lag
ghat.1 <- npreg(y~lag(y,-1))
## Plot the data and nonparametric fit
plot(y,lwd=2)
lines(ts(fitted(ghat.4),start=5),col=2,lty=2,lwd=2)
points(ts(fitted(ghat.1),start=2),col=3)
legend("topright",c("$Y_t$",
    "$\\hat Y_t=\\hat g(Y_{t-1},Y_{t-2},Y_{t-3},Y_{t-4})$",
    "$\\hat Y_t=\\hat g(Y_{t-1})$"),
    lty=c(1,2,NA),col=1:3,lwd=c(2,2,NA),
    pch=c(NA,NA,1),bty="n")
```

The generalized local polynomial estimator of Hall and Racine (2015) offers the promise, through the cross-validated joint selection of the polynomial degree and bandwidth vectors, of both removing irrelevant predictors by shrinking them towards a constant function (degree zero, large bandwidth) *and* shrinking the estimator towards a global polynomial of the appropriate order. We examine how it performs in the case of the above linear time series AR(1) DGP where there is lag and polynomial degree uncertainty.

```
## npglpreg() does not support time series objects, so we
## manually create the lagged series
y.lag.1 <- c(rep(NA,1),y[1:(n-1)])
y.lag.2 <- c(rep(NA,2),y[1:(n-2)])
y.lag.3 <- c(rep(NA,3),y[1:(n-3)])
y.lag.4 <- c(rep(NA,4),y[1:(n-4)])
model <- npglpreg(y~y.lag.1+y.lag.2+y.lag.3+y.lag.4,
                nmulti=5,degree.max=5)
summary(model)
## Call:
## npglpreg.formula(formula = y ~ y.lag.1 + y.lag.2 + y.lag.3 +
##     y.lag.4, nmulti = 5, degree.max = 5)
```

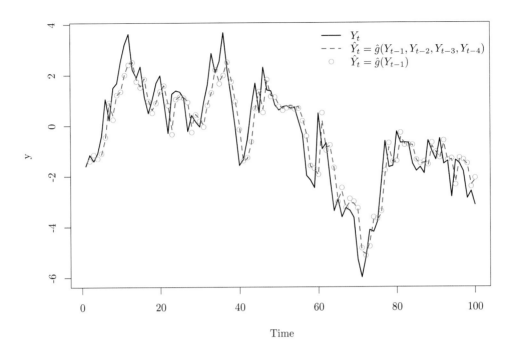

Figure 6.12: Local constant estimation of a stationary univariate AR(1) time series, $Y_t = 0.9Y_{t-1} + \epsilon_t$.

```
##
## Generalized Local Polynomial Kernel Regression
##
## Polynomial type: Bernstein
## Using (local) Seifert & Gasser shrinkage for cross-validation
## There are 4 continuous predictors
## Bandwidth type: fixed
## Continuous kernel type: gaussian
## Continuous kernel order: 2
## Bandwidth for y.lag.1: 2488961 (scale factor = 2143265)
## Bandwidth for y.lag.2: 15108900 (scale factor = 13166144)
## Bandwidth for y.lag.3: 86182070 (scale factor = 76031125)
## Bandwidth for y.lag.4: 5602996 (scale factor = 4981916)
## Degree for y.lag.1: 1
## Degree for y.lag.2: 0
## Degree for y.lag.3: 0
## Degree for y.lag.4: 0
## Training observations: 96
## Multiple R-squared: 0.812
## Cross-validation score: 0.84938168
## Number of multistarts: 5
## Estimation time: 45.6 seconds
## Fit a model that is linear, uses only the relevant predictor,
## and uses the same data as the nonparametric model
model.lm <- lm(y~y.lag.1,subset=5:n)
summary(model.lm)
```

```
##
## Call:
## lm(formula = y ~ y.lag.1, subset = 5:n)
##
## Residuals:
##     Min      1Q  Median     3Q     Max
## -1.936  -0.643  -0.035  0.670   2.780
##
## Coefficients:
##                 Estimate Std. Error t value Pr(>|t|)
## (Intercept)     -0.0564     0.0947     -0.6     0.55
## y.lag.1          0.9089     0.0451     20.1   <2e-16 ***
## ---
## Signif. codes:  0 '***' 0.001 '**' 0.01 '*' 0.05 '.' 0.1 ' ' 1
##
## Residual standard error: 0.912 on 94 degrees of freedom
## Multiple R-squared:  0.812, Adjusted R-squared:  0.81
## F-statistic:  406 on 1 and 94 DF,  p-value: <2e-16
## Examine the first five fitted values from the nonparametric
## and linear AR(1) models
cbind(fitted(model),fitted(model.lm))[1:5,]
##        [,1]     [,2]
## 5 -1.0356  -1.0356
## 6 -0.4089  -0.4089
## 7  0.8985   0.8985
## 8  0.1420   0.1420
## 9  1.3060   1.3060
```

We observe that, in this setting, the estimator lives up to its potential. It correctly selects the degree for the first lag; the AR(1) process is a linear process, so the degree 1 with a large bandwidth is appropriate. It also correctly selects a large bandwidth and a constant function (degree 0) for the remaining lags. This results in a globally linear model that is a function of the first lag of Y only, and delivers a $\sqrt{n}$-consistent estimator that is identical to what would be obtained if the true functional form and the relevance of the predictors were known a priori. In this case, the generalized local polynomial approach gives rise to what is known as the *oracle* estimator.

Example 6.11. Predicting Percentage Changes in U.S. Weekly Gas Prices.

We consider a series obtained from the U.S. Energy Information Administration on the weekly percentage change in U.S. gas prices from 08/20/1990 to 11/13/2017. Adopting a 20-year rolling window, we fit a local constant model and compare it to an ARIMA(p, d, q) model that is fit with the `auto.arima()` function in the R package forecast (Hyndman and Khandakar, 2008). The forecasts from each of the models and the series are plotted in Figure 6.13. The models' relative efficiency, based on their average predicted square error, is also noted, with a value less than 1 indicating superior performance of the kernel approach.

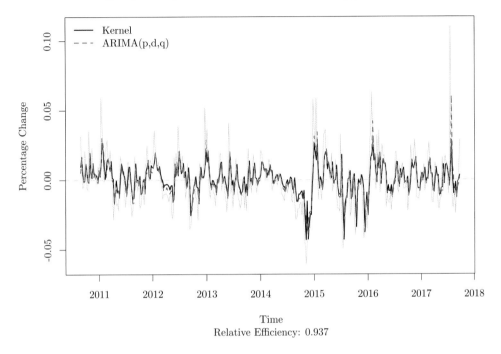

Figure 6.13: Percentage change in US weekly gas prices.

6.9 Shape Constrained Kernel Regression

Background and Overview

Economic theory often imposes constraints on underlying relationships (i.e., monotonicity, concavity, homogeneity, etc.). If the constraints that are imposed are in agreement with the underlying DGP, they can potentially produce a nonparametric estimator that is both *statistically and theoretically consistent*. This endeavour has a rich history. The Fourier Flexible Form (FFF) estimator of Gallant (1981) is a series-based estimator that is capable of handling restrictions, although a monotonicity constraint can be difficult to impose. Matzkin (1991) has considered identification and estimation of general nonparametric problems with economic constraints. Yatchew and Bos (1997) have developed a series-based estimator that can handle general constraints, while Beresteanu (2005) has introduced a spline-based procedure that can handle multiple, general, and derivative-based constraints.

Powerful methods of imposing monotonicity in nonparametric regression settings have been proposed by Hall et al. (2001) and Hall and Huang (2001). Du et al. (2013) generalize these approaches and propose a shape constrained nonparametric regression method that allows equality or inequality constraints to be imposed on derivatives of any order. This encompasses many of the approaches that have been mentioned above and provides a flexible framework for shape constrained nonparametric regression. We describe this approach below and refer the interested reader to the literature that we have cited for additional details.

A Quadratic Program Approach

The goal of shape constrained nonparametric estimation is to estimate an unknown conditional mean function $g(x)$ subject to constraints on $g^{(\mathbf{s})}(x)$, where $\mathbf{s}$ is a q-vector that is of the same dimension as x. We restrict our attention to the q continuous predictor setting since we are talking about shape constrained derivatives, although this framework is also able to handle other types of constraints. The elements of $\mathbf{s}$ represent the order of the partial derivative that is taken with respect to each element of x. Thus, $\mathbf{s} = (0, 0, \ldots, 0)$ represents the function itself, while $\mathbf{s} = (1, 0, \ldots, 0)$ represents $\partial g(x)/\partial x_1$. In general, for $\mathbf{s} = (s_1, s_2, \ldots, s_q)$, we have

$$g^{(\mathbf{s})}(x) = \frac{\partial^{s_1} g(x) \cdots \partial^{s_q} g(x)}{\partial x_1^{s_1} \cdots \partial x_q^{s_q}}.$$

Consider the class of kernel regression smoothers that can be written as a linear combination of the response Y_i, i.e.,

$$\hat{g}(x) = \sum_{i=1}^{n} H_i(x) Y_i,$$

where $H_i(x)$ is an element of the *nonparametric hat matrix* that was outlined in our earlier discussion of generalized cross-validation (Craven and Wahba, 1979). All of the kernel regression methods that we have studied thus far belong to this class, as do a range of additional kernel smoothers such as, for instance, the Priestley-Chao estimator (Priestley and Chao, 1972) and the Gasser-Müller estimator (Gasser and Müller, 1979).

Du et al. (2013) consider constraints on the estimate $\hat{g}(x)$ that are of the form $l(x) \leq \hat{g}^{(\mathbf{s})}(x) \leq u(x)$ for arbitrary $u(\cdot)$, $l(\cdot)$, and $\mathbf{s}$. Their generalization of $\hat{g}(x)$ follows that of Hall and Huang (2001), and is given by

$$\hat{g}(x|p) = \sum_{i=1}^{n} H_i(x) p_i Y_i.$$

In what follows, $\hat{g}^{(\mathbf{s})}(x|p) = \sum_{i=1}^{n} H_i^{(\mathbf{s})}(x) p_i Y_i$, where $H_i^{(\mathbf{s})}(x) = \frac{\partial^{s_1} H_i(x) \cdots \partial^{s_q} H_i(x)}{\partial x_1^{s_1} \cdots \partial x_q^{s_q}}$. Under this notation, $\mathbf{s}$ represents a $q \times 1$ vector of non-negative integers that indicate the order of the partial derivative of the kernel smoother's weighting function. By way of example, using $\hat{g}(x|p)$ to generate an unrestricted local constant estimator would entail setting $p_i = 1$, $i = 1, \ldots, n$, and

$$H_i(x) = \frac{K_\gamma(X_i, x)}{\sum_{j=1}^n K_\gamma(X_j, x)},$$

where $K_\gamma(\cdot)$ is a generalized product kernel that admits both continuous and categorical data and γ is a vector of bandwidths. We have a constrained local constant estimator when $p_i \neq 1$ for some i. In this framework, the same bandwidths are used for both the constrained and the unconstrained estimator, and hence standard bandwidth selection methods are appropriate.

Let p_u be an n-vector of 1's and let p be the vector of weights that must be selected. To impose the constraints, we choose $p = \hat{p}$ to minimize the distance from p to the uniform weights $p_i = 1 \ \forall i$. This is intuitively appealing since, as noted above, $p_i = 1 \ \forall i$ for the unconstrained estimator. Whereas Hall and Huang (2001) consider probability weights (i.e., $0 \leq p_i \leq 1$, $\sum_i p_i = 1$) and distance measures that are suitable for probability weights (i.e., Hellinger), Du et al. (2013) adopt a different approach. They allow for both positive and negative weights, drop the requirement that $\sum_i p_i = 1$, and use an alternative distance measure. In particular, they forgo the power divergence metric of Cressie and Read (1984), which was used by Hall and Huang (2001), since it is only valid for probability weights. Instead, they adopt the L_2 distance metric $D(p) = (p_u - p)^{\mathrm{T}}(p_u - p)$, which is ideally suited to the task at hand. The problem is to simply select the weights p that minimize $D(p)$ subject to $l(x) \leq \hat{g}^{(\mathbf{s})}(x) \leq u(x)$ and possibly additional constraints that are of a similar form. One may use standard quadratic programming methods to obtain a solution.

Example 6.12. Estimating a Deterministic Production Frontier.

> We simulate data from $X \sim U[0, 1]$ and generate a frontier that is given by $\sqrt{x}$. One-sided errors are drawn from a half-normal distribution. We impose monotonicity ($g'(x) \geq 0$), concavity ($g''(x) \leq 0$), and the constraint that the frontier function is deterministic ($y \leq g(x)$). The sample comprises $n = 5000$ observations. We use a local polynomial of degree $p = 2$, which delivers estimates of the first and second derivative functions. We conduct cross-validated bandwidth selection and then solve the quadratic program. The unconstrained and constrained estimates are presented in Figure 6.14.

Further illustrations of shape constrained estimation appear in the Practitioner's Corner.

For additional related work, see Noh (2014), who tailors the approach of Du et al. (2013) to frontier estimation. This entails minimization of the area under the frontier via a linear programming procedure. In particular, Noh (2014) minimizes $\int_{x \in \mathbb{R}} \hat{g}(x) \, dx = \sum_{i=1}^n p_i Y_i \int_{x \in \mathbb{R}} H_i(x) \, dx$ rather than

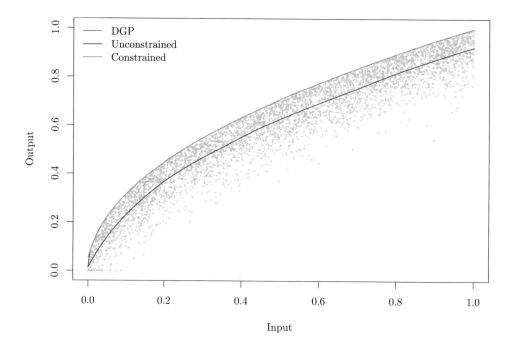

Figure 6.14: Simulated illustration of shape constrained estimation that delivers a deterministic production frontier.

$D(p) = (p_u - p)^{\mathrm{T}}(p_u - p)$. This approach is implemented in the R package npbr (Daouia et al., 2017). For work on shape constrained nonparametric kernel regression in the presence of measurement errors, see Carroll et al. (2011).

6.10 Practitioner's Corner

6.10.1 Kernel Regression Is Weighted Least Squares Estimation

Nonparametric kernel regression is simply locally weighted least squares estimation. This is shown in the following code chunk. Note that for local-linear regression, we can use the convention where the intercept is $\hat{g}(x)$ (i.e., regress Y_i on $x - X_i$), or where the fitted value is $\hat{g}(x)$ (i.e., regress Y_i on X_i). Both of these produce identical results.

```
set.seed(42)
## Simulate some data
n <- 100
x <- sort(runif(n))
dgp <- sin(2*pi*x)
y <- dgp + rnorm(n,sd=0.5*sd(dgp))
## Fit a Nadaraya-Watson (local-constant) model using npreg()
model <- npreg(y~x)
```

```
## Extract the cross-validated bandwidth
h <- model$bws$bw
## Compute the WLS estimate (the default kernel in npreg() is the Gaussian)
## regressing y on a constant (the fitted value is the conditional mean
## estimate)
wls.fit <- numeric()
for(i in 1:n) wls.fit[i] <- fitted(lm(y~1,weights=dnorm((x[i]-x)/h)))[i]
## Compare the output from npreg() and lm(...,weights=)
cbind(fitted(model),wls.fit)[1:5,]
##               wls.fit
## [1,]  0.2132  0.2132
## [2,]  0.2144  0.2144
## [3,]  0.2166  0.2166
## [4,]  0.2199  0.2199
## [5,]  0.2204  0.2204
## Fit a local-linear model using npreg()
model <- npreg(y~x,regtype="ll")
## Extract the cross-validated bandwidth
h <- model$bws$bw
## Compute the WLS estimate (the default kernel in npreg() is the Gaussian)
## regressing y on x (the fitted value is the conditional mean estimate)
wls.fit <- numeric()
for(i in 1:n) wls.fit[i] <- fitted(lm(y~x,weights=dnorm((x[i]-x)/h)))[i]
## Compute the WLS estimate (the default kernel in npreg() is the Gaussian)
## regressing y on x-X_i (the intercept is the conditional mean estimate)
wls.fit.diff <- numeric()
for(i in 1:n) {
    wls.fit.diff[i] <- coef(lm(y~I(x[i]-x),weights=dnorm((x[i]-x)/h)))[1]
}
## Compare the output from npreg(,regtype="ll"), lm(y~x,weights=), and
## lm(y~I(x[i]-x),weights=)
cbind(fitted(model),wls.fit,wls.fit.diff)[1:5,]
##              wls.fit wls.fit.diff
## [1,]  0.1591  0.1591      0.1591
## [2,]  0.1630  0.1630      0.1630
## [3,]  0.1699  0.1699      0.1699
## [4,]  0.1794  0.1794      0.1794
## [5,]  0.1809  0.1809      0.1809
```

6.10.2 Joint Determination of the Polynomial Degree and Bandwidth

Suppose that we would like to use the approach of Hall and Racine (2015) to jointly determine the degree of the local polynomial and the bandwidth. The following code chunk considers four cases where (i) X is irrelevant, (ii) Y is linearly related to X, (iii) the relationship is quadratic, and (iv) the relationship is $\sin(\pi x)$ on $X \in U[-1, 1]$. We make use of the function npglpreg() (*nonparametric generalized local polynomial regression*) in the R package crs (Racine and Nie, 2017; Nie and Racine, 2012).

```
par(mfrow=c(2,2),mar=c(5,4,4,2)+0.1)
set.seed(42)
n <- 250
## No relationship between X and Y, ideally large bandwidth and
## zeroth degree polynomial (local constant)
x <- sort(runif(n,-1,1))
y <- rnorm(n,sd=0.5)
dgp <- rep(0,n)
model <- npglpreg(y~x)
summary(model)
## Call:
## npglpreg.formula(formula = y ~ x)
##
## Generalized Local Polynomial Kernel Regression
##
## Polynomial type: Bernstein
## Using (local) Seifert & Gasser shrinkage for cross-validation
## There is 1 continuous predictor
## Bandwidth type: fixed
## Continuous kernel type: gaussian
## Continuous kernel order: 2
## Bandwidth for x: 202586 (scale factor = 1048577)
## Degree for x: 0
## Training observations: 250
## Multiple R-squared: 0.0005605
## Cross-validation score: 0.21355687
## Number of multistarts: 5
## Estimation time: 2.8 seconds
plot(x,y,ylab="$Y$",xlab="$X$",cex=.25,
     sub=paste("Degree = ",model$degree[1],", $h$ = ",
               formatC(model$bws[1],format="f",digits=2),sep=""))
lines(x,fitted(model),lwd=2)
lines(x,dgp,col=2,lty=2,lwd=2)
## Linear relationship between X and Y, ideally large bandwidth and
## first degree polynomial (local linear)
dgp <- x
y <- dgp + rnorm(n,sd=0.5*sd(dgp))
model <- npglpreg(y~x)
summary(model)
## Call:
## npglpreg.formula(formula = y ~ x)
##
## Generalized Local Polynomial Kernel Regression
##
## Polynomial type: Bernstein
## Using (local) Seifert & Gasser shrinkage for cross-validation
## There is 1 continuous predictor
## Bandwidth type: fixed
## Continuous kernel type: gaussian
## Continuous kernel order: 2
## Bandwidth for x: 410942 (scale factor = 2127018)
## Degree for x: 1
## Training observations: 250
```

```
## Multiple R-squared:. 0.7905
## Cross-validation score: 0.09099957
## Number of multistarts: 5
## Estimation time: 3.1 seconds
plot(x,y,ylab="$Y$",xlab="$X$",cex=.25,
     sub=paste("Degree = ",model$degree[1],", $h$ = ",
               formatC(model$bws[1],format="f",digits=2),sep=""))
lines(x,fitted(model),lwd=2)
lines(x,dgp,col=2,lty=2,lwd=2)
## Quadratic relationship between X and Y, ideally large bandwidth and
## second degree polynomial (local linear)
dgp <- x^2
y <- dgp + rnorm(n,sd=0.5*sd(dgp))
model <- npglpreg(y~x)
summary(model)
## Call:
## npglpreg.formula(formula = y ~ x)
##
## Generalized Local Polynomial Kernel Regression
##
## Polynomial type: Bernstein
## Using (local) Seifert & Gasser shrinkage for cross-validation
## There is 1 continuous predictor
## Bandwidth type: fixed
## Continuous kernel type: gaussian
## Continuous kernel order: 2
## Bandwidth for x: 202586 (scale factor = 1048578)
## Degree for x: 2
## Training observations: 250
## Multiple R-squared: 0.8327
## Cross-validation score: 0.019534235
## Number of multistarts: 5
## Estimation time: 2.0 seconds
plot(x,y,ylab="$Y$",xlab="$X$",cex=.25,
     sub=paste("Degree = ",model$degree[1],", $h$ = ",
               formatC(model$bws[1],format="f",digits=2),sep=""))
lines(x,fitted(model),lwd=2)
lines(x,dgp,col=2,lty=2,lwd=2)
## Analytic relationship between X and Y, ideally large bandwidth and
## moderate degree polynomial
dgp <- sin(pi*x)
y <- dgp + rnorm(n,sd=0.5*sd(dgp))
model <- npglpreg(y~x)
summary(model)
## Call:
## npglpreg.formula(formula = y ~ x)
##
## Generalized Local Polynomial Kernel Regression
##
## Polynomial type: Bernstein
## Using (local) Seifert & Gasser shrinkage for cross-validation
## There is 1 continuous predictor
## Bandwidth type: fixed
```

```
## Continuous kernel type: gaussian
## Continuous kernel order: 2
## Bandwidth for x: 0.6274 (scale factor = 3.247)
## Degree for x: 5
## Training observations: 250
## Multiple R-squared: 0.7609
## Cross-validation score: 0.1499163
## Number of multistarts: 5
## Estimation time: 2.9 seconds
plot(x,y,ylab="$Y$",xlab="$X$",cex=.25,
     sub=paste("Degree = ",model$degree[1],", $h$ = ",
               formatC(model$bws[1],format="f",digits=2),sep=""))
lines(x,fitted(model),lwd=2)
lines(x,dgp,col=2,lty=2,lwd=2)
```

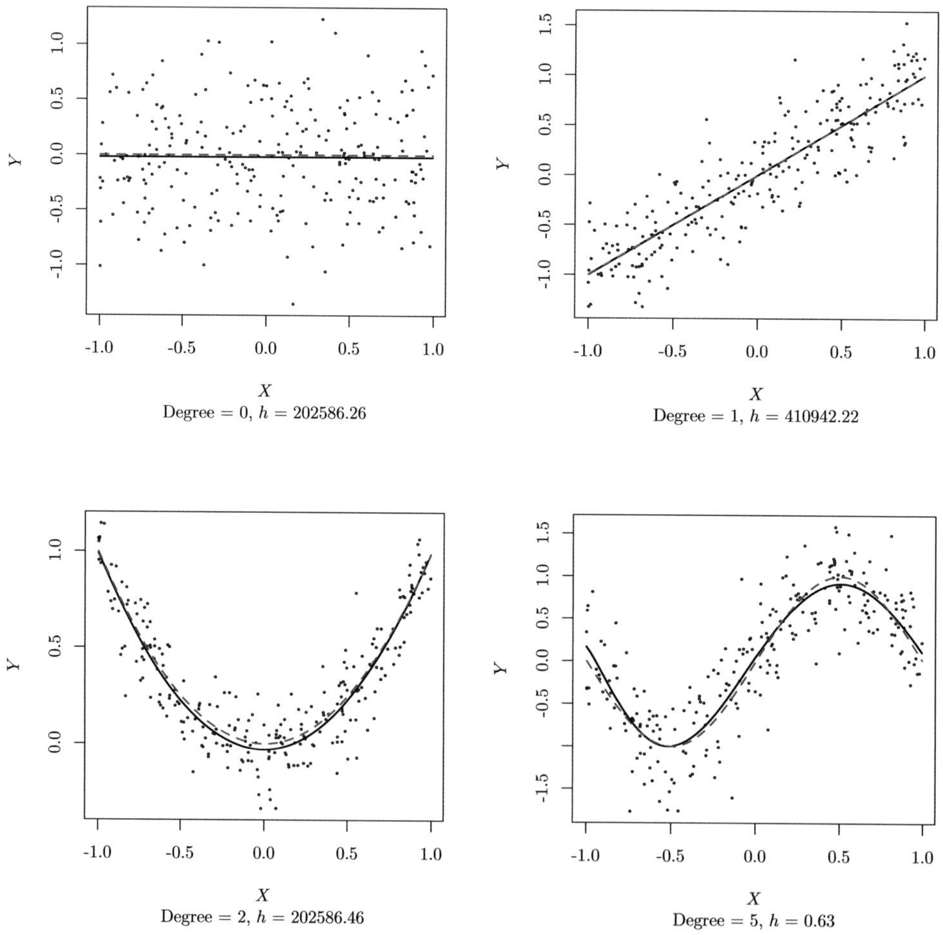

Figure 6.15: Cross-validated joint determination of the polynomial degree and bandwidth.

6.10.3 A Consistent Nonparametric Test for Correct Parametric Specification

The literature on nonparametric kernel-based hypothesis testing is extensive. There exist a variety of nonparametric tests for correct specification of parametric models, equality of distributions, and equality of regression functions, among others.

Parametric tests typically require the analyst to specify the set of parametric alternatives under which the null hypothesis ought to be rejected. However, if the null is false but there exist alternative models that the test is unable to detect, then the test is *inconsistent* insofar as it lacks power in certain directions. Nonparametric methods can be used to construct consistent tests, unlike their parametric counterparts.

Let us now provide a precise definition of a *consistent test*. Let H_0 denote the null hypothesis whose validity we wish to test. A test is said to be *consistent* if

$$P(\text{Reject } H_0 \mid H_0 \text{ is false}) \to 1 \text{ as } n \to \infty.$$

Recall that the power of a test is defined as $P(\text{Reject } H_0 \mid H_0 \text{ is false})$. Therefore, a consistent test has asymptotic power equal to one.

There exist a variety of tests for correct specification of parametric regression models, including those proposed by Härdle and Mammen (1993), Horowitz and Härdle (1994), Horowitz and Spokoiny (2001), Hristache et al. (2001) and Hsiao et al. (2007). We briefly describe the approach of Hsiao et al. (2007) since it admits the mix of continuous and categorical data types that is often encountered in applied settings.

Suppose that one's objective is to determine whether a parametric regression model is correctly specified. The null hypothesis can be stated as follows:

$$H_0 : \mathrm{E}(Y|x) = g(x; \beta_0) \text{ for almost all } x \text{ and for some } \beta_0 \in \mathcal{B} \subset \mathbb{R}^p,$$

where $g(x; \beta)$ is a known function that includes a linear regression model as a special case, β is a $p \times 1$ vector of unknown parameters, and $\mathcal{B}$ is a compact subset of $\mathbb{R}^p$. The alternative hypothesis is the negation of H_0, that is, H_1: $\mathrm{E}(Y|x) = g(x) \neq g(x; \beta)$ for all $\beta \in \mathcal{B}$ on a set of x with positive measure. If we define $u_i = Y_i - g(X_i; \beta_0)$, then the null hypothesis can be equivalently written as

$$\mathrm{E}(u_i|X_i) = 0 \text{ almost surely.} \tag{6.17}$$

One may construct a consistent model specification test that involves nonparametrically estimating (6.17) and averaging over the u_i in a particular manner that we now briefly describe. First, note that $\mathrm{E}(u_i|X_i) = 0$ is equivalent to $(\mathrm{E}(u_i|X_i))^2 = 0$. In addition, given that we would like to test the null that $\mathrm{E}(u_i|X_i) = 0$ for almost all x, we need to consider the expectation $\mathrm{E\,E}(u_i|X_i)$ or equivalently $\mathrm{E}(\mathrm{E}(u_i|X_i))^2$. By the law of iterated expectations, it is the case that $\mathrm{E}(\mathrm{E}(u_i|X_i))^2 = \mathrm{E}\,u_i\,\mathrm{E}(u_i|X_i)$. One may therefore construct a consistent test statistic that is based on a density weighted version of $\mathrm{E}\,u_i\,\mathrm{E}(u_i|X_i)$, namely $\mathrm{E}\,u_i\,\mathrm{E}(u_i|X_i)f(X_i)$, where $f(x)$ is the joint PDF of X. Density weighting is used to avoid a random denominator that would otherwise appear in the kernel estimator.

The sample analogue of $\mathrm{E}\,u_i\,\mathrm{E}(u_i|X_i)f(X_i)$ is given by the formula $n^{-1}\sum_{i=1}^{n} u_i\,\mathrm{E}(u_i|X_i)f(X_i)$. To obtain a feasible test statistic, we replace u_i by $\hat{u}_i$, where $\hat{u}_i = Y_i - g(X_i; \hat{\beta})$ is the residual and $\hat{\beta}$ is a $\sqrt{n}$-consistent estimator of β based on the parametric null model ($\hat{\beta}$ might be, say, the nonlinear least squares estimator of β). We adopt the leave-one-out kernel estimator of $\mathrm{E}(u_i|X_i)f(X_i)$, which is given by $(n-1)^{-1}\sum_{j\neq i}^{n} \hat{u}_j K_\gamma(X_i, X_j)$. If we assume that X_i is a vector of mixed discrete and continuous predictors, then a generalized product kernel is required and the test statistic is based on

$$
\begin{aligned}
I_n &= \frac{1}{n}\sum_{i=1}^{n} \hat{u}_i \left(\frac{1}{n-1}\sum_{j=1, j\neq i}^{n} \hat{u}_j K_\gamma(X_i, X_j) \right) \\
&= \frac{1}{n(n-1)}\sum_{i=1}^{n}\sum_{j=1, j\neq i}^{n} \hat{u}_i \hat{u}_j K_\gamma(X_i, X_j).
\end{aligned}
$$

The studentized version of this test is denoted by J_n. Bootstrap methods can be used to obtain the distribution of I_n (J_n) under the null and to compute a P-value; see Hsiao et al. (2007) for further details.

Example 6.13. Testing Correct Specification of a Naïve Linear Model.

Having estimated, say, a parametric wage model that is linear in predictors, one might use the previously described approach of Hsiao et al. (2007) to test the null hypothesis that the model is correctly specified. Bandwidths are selected by means of cross-validation, and a simple bootstrap method is used to compute the distribution of J_n under the null. The function `npcmstest()` in the R package np implements this approach.

```
data(wage1)
model <- lm(lwage ~
            female +
            married +
            educ +
            exper +
            tenure,
            data = wage1,
            x = TRUE,
            y = TRUE)
X <- with(wage1,data.frame(female,married,educ,exper,tenure))
with(wage1, npcmstest(model = model, xdat = X, ydat = lwage))
##
```

```
## Consistent Model Specification Test
## Parametric null model: lm(formula = lwage ~ female + married + educ + exper +
##                              tenure, data = wage1, x = TRUE, y = TRUE)
## Number of regressors: 5
## IID Bootstrap (399 replications)
##
## Test Statistic 'Jn': 5.542   P Value: <2e-16 ***
## ---
## Signif. codes:  0 '***' 0.001 '**' 0.01 '*' 0.05 '.' 0.1 ' ' 1
## Null of correct specification is rejected at the 0.1% level
```

Unsurprisingly, we reject this naïve linear specification that does not include any interaction terms and that limits the effect of the categorical predictors to a simple shift of the intercept. Note that this parametric model is not being considered as the ideal candidate; rather, it is being used for the purpose of demonstration that the test is able to detect a misspecified parametric model in a finite-sample setting.

Example 6.14. Inconsistent and Consistent Model Specification Tests.

Next, we undertake a comparison of an inconsistent parametric test (Ramsey, 1969) and the consistent nonparametric test under two different scenarios. In the first scenario, the parametric model that is under consideration is incorrectly specified, whereas in the second scenario, it is correctly specified. Interestingly, even though the null is false, the RESET test has no power in the first scenario, no matter how large n may be.

```
library(np)
set.seed(42)
library(lmtest)
## Parametric model is misspecified, it appears there is no
## relationship between x2 and y though indeed there is, which
## confounds the RESET test
n <- 250
x1 <- runif(n,-2,2)
x2 <- runif(n,-2,2)
dgp <- x1 + x2**2
y <- dgp + rnorm(n,sd=0.5*sd(dgp))
model <- lm(y~x1+x2,x=TRUE,y=TRUE)
summary(model)
##
## Call:
## lm(formula = y ~ x1 + x2, x = TRUE, y = TRUE)
##
## Residuals:
##    Min     1Q Median     3Q    Max
## -2.950 -1.138 -0.108  0.958  3.589
##
## Coefficients:
##               Estimate Std. Error t value Pr(>|t|)
## (Intercept)    1.3573     0.0938   14.47   <2e-16 ***
## x1             0.9674     0.0804   12.04   <2e-16 ***
```

```
## x2              -0.0221      0.0797    -0.28      0.78
## ---
## Signif. codes:  0 '***' 0.001 '**' 0.01 '*' 0.05 '.' 0.1 ' ' 1
##
## Residual standard error: 1.47 on 247 degrees of freedom
## Multiple R-squared:  0.372,   Adjusted R-squared:  0.367
## F-statistic: 73.1 on 2 and 247 DF,  p-value: <2e-16
## Inconsistent parametric test for correct specification of the
## conditional mean fails to reject the null of correct specification
reset(model)
##
##  RESET test
##
## data:  model
## RESET = 0.77, df1 = 2, df2 = 240, p-value = 0.5
## Consistent nonparametric test for correct specification correctly
## rejects the null
npcmstest(model=model,xdat=data.frame(x1,x2),ydat=y)
##
## Consistent Model Specification Test
## Parametric null model: lm(formula = y ~ x1 + x2, x = TRUE, y = TRUE)
## Number of regressors: 2
## IID Bootstrap (399 replications)
##
## Test Statistic 'Jn': 26.46   P Value: <2e-16 ***
## ---
## Signif. codes:  0 '***' 0.001 '**' 0.01 '*' 0.05 '.' 0.1 ' ' 1
## Null of correct specification is rejected at the 0.1% level
## Now consider a correctly specified parametric model
dgp <- x1 + x2
y <- dgp + rnorm(n,sd=0.5*sd(dgp))
model <- lm(y~x1+x2,x=TRUE,y=TRUE)
## Both tests correctly fail to reject the null
reset(model)
##
##  RESET test
##
## data:  model
## RESET = 0.44, df1 = 2, df2 = 240, p-value = 0.6
npcmstest(model=model,xdat=data.frame(x1,x2),ydat=y)
##
## Consistent Model Specification Test
## Parametric null model: lm(formula = y ~ x1 + x2, x = TRUE, y = TRUE)
## Number of regressors: 2
## IID Bootstrap (399 replications)
##
## Test Statistic 'Jn': -0.3144 P Value: 0.38
## ---
## Signif. codes:  0 '***' 0.001 '**' 0.01 '*' 0.05 '.' 0.1 ' ' 1
## Fail to reject the null of correct specification at the 10% level
```

6.10.4   Shape Constrained Kernel Regression

The code chunk below illustrates the implementation of shape constrained nonparametric regression. The R packages quadprog (Turlach and Weingessel, 2013), np (Hayfield and Racine, 2008), and crs (Racine and Nie, 2017) must all be installed prior to running the code. Before we proceed, we will briefly review how to solve a quadratic program in R. A quadratic program involves finding a solution to the following problem:

$$\min_{b} \frac{1}{2} b' D b - d' b \text{ subject to } A' b \geq b_0,$$

where D is a matrix and d is a vector that respectively appear in the quadratic function that is to be minimized, A is a matrix and b_0 is a vector that together define the relevant linear constraints, and b is a weight vector. This is illustrated in the following example.

```
require(quadprog)
## Assume we want to minimize: -(0 5 0) %*% b + 1/2 b^T b
## under the constraints:      A^T b >= b0
## with b0 = (-8,2,0)^T
## and        (-4  2  0)
##       A = (-3  1 -2)
##            ( 0  0  1)
## we can use solve.QP as follows:
##
Dmat        <- matrix(0,3,3)
diag(Dmat) <- 1
dvec        <- c(0,5,0)
Amat        <- matrix(c(-4,-3,0,2,1,0,0,-2,1),3,3)
bvec        <- c(-8,2,0)
solve.QP(Dmat,dvec,Amat,bvec)$solution
## [1] 0.4762 1.0476 2.0952
```

Suppose that we would like to conduct shape constrained nonparametric regression. In the following code chunk, there are three constraints that respectively pertain to the level, i.e., $lb \leq \hat{g}(x) \leq ub$, the first derivative, i.e., $lb \leq \hat{g}'(x) \leq ub$, and the second derivative, i.e., $lb \leq \hat{g}''(x) \leq ub$. The illustration that involves the first derivative is presented, while the two examples that remain can be uncommented by the reader who wishes to experiment with the code.

```
set.seed(42)
ckertype <- "epanechnikov"
n <- 500
## Constrain the level of the function
## p <- 1
## lower <- -0.5
## upper <- 0.5
## Constrain the first derivative of the function
p <- 1
gradient <- 1
```

```
lower <- -2
upper <- 2
## Constrain the second derivative of the function
## p <- 2
## gradient <- 2
## lower <- -20
## upper <- 20
x <- sort(runif(n))
dgp <- function(x) {dgp <- sin(2*pi*x)}
y <- dgp(x) + rnorm(n,sd=0.5*sd(dgp(x)))
model <- crs::npglpreg(y~x,
                       ckertype=ckertype,
                       nmulti=2,
                       cv = "bandwidth",
                       degree = p)
bw <- model$bws
W.gradient <- W <- crs:::W.glp(xdat=x,
                               degree=p)
if(gradient>0) {
  W.gradient <- crs:::W.glp(xdat=x,
                            degree=p,
                            gradient = gradient)
}
K <- npksum(txdat=x,
            bws=bw,
            ckertype=ckertype,
            return.kernel.weights=TRUE)$kw
## Uniform weights (unconstrained model)
p.u <- rep(1,n)
A.mean <- A <- sapply(1:n,function(i){
 W.gradient[i,,drop=FALSE]%*%chol2inv(chol(t(W)%*%(K[,i]*W)))%*%t(W)*K[,i]*y})
## Compute the unrestricted model/object being constrained
object.unres <- fitted.unres <- t(A)%*%p.u
if(gradient>0) {
  A.mean <- sapply(1:n,function(i){
      W[i,,drop=FALSE]%*%chol2inv(chol(t(W)%*%(K[,i]*W)))%*%t(W)*K[,i]*y})
  fitted.unres <- t(A.mean)%*%p.u
}
## Solve the quadratic programming problem (you must first install and
## load the R package quadprog). We branch to avoid imposing
## nonbinding constraints (solve.QP will handle these cases but it
## imposes unnecessary (slack) variables).
if(all(object.unres >= lower & object.unres <= upper)) {
  p.hat <- p.u
} else if(all(object.unres >= lower)) {
  QP.output <- solve.QP(Dmat=diag(n),
                        dvec=rep(1,n),
                        Amat=cbind(-A),
                        bvec=c(-rep(upper,n)))
  if(is.nan(QP.output$value)) stop("solve.QP failed.
                        Try larger bandwidth/degree")
  p.hat <- QP.output$solution
} else if(all(object.unres <= upper)) {
```

```r
  QP.output <- solve.QP(Dmat=diag(n),
                        dvec=rep(1,n),
                        Amat=cbind(A),
                        bvec=c(rep(lower,n)))
  if(is.nan(QP.output$value)) stop("solve.QP failed.
                                    Try larger bandwidth/degree")
  p.hat <- QP.output$solution
} else {
  QP.output <- solve.QP(Dmat=diag(n),
                        dvec=rep(1,n),
                        Amat=cbind(A,-A),
                        bvec=c(rep(lower,n),-rep(upper,n)))
  if(is.nan(QP.output$value)) stop("solve.QP failed.
                                    Try larger bandwidth/degree")
  p.hat <- QP.output$solution
}
## Compute the restricted model
fitted.res <- t(A.mean)%*%p.hat
## Plot the data and DGP
plot(x,y,
     cex=0.2,
     col="black",
     ylab="$Y$",
     xlab="$X$",
     sub=paste("Bandwidth = ",format(bw,digits=3,format="f"),
     ", degree = ",p,
     ", $n$ = ",n,
     ", ub = ",formatC(upper,format="f",digits=1),
     ", lb = ",formatC(lower,format="f",digits=1),
     sep=""))
lines(x,dgp(x),lty=1,col=1)
## Plot the unrestricted and restricted models and restricted y
lines(x,fitted.unres,lty=2,col=2,lwd=2)
lines(x,fitted.res,col=4,lty=4,lwd=3)
legend("topright",
       c("DGP","Unconstrained Estimate","Constrained Estimate"),
       col=c(1,2,4,"orange","black"),
       lwd=c(1,2,3,NA,NA),
       lty=c(1,2,4,NA,NA),
       pch=c(NA,NA,NA,1,1),
       bty="n")
```

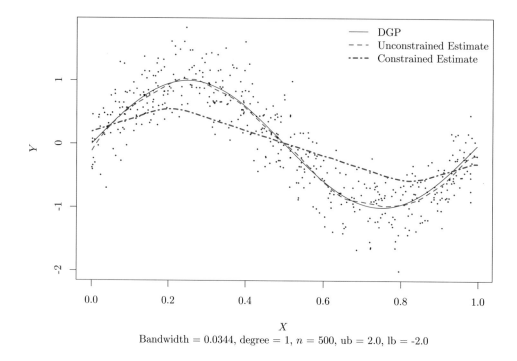

Bandwidth = 0.0344, degree = 1, $n = 500$, ub = 2.0, lb = -2.0

6.10.5   A Multivariate Application of Local Linear Regression

We consider a model whose dependent variable is `lwage` (log hourly wage).
There are three continuous predictors, namely `educ` (years of education),
`exper` (number of years of potential experience), and `tenure` (number of
years with current employer). There are also two qualitative predictors in
the model, namely `female` ("Female", "Male") and `married` ("Married",
"Notmarried"). In this example, there are $n = 526$ observations taken from
the `wage1` data in the R package np. We use the method of Hurvich et al.
(1998) for bandwidth selection.

```
data(wage1)
model <- npreg(lwage~female+
               married+
               educ+
               exper+
               tenure,
               regtype="ll",
               bwmethod="cv.aic",
               data=wage1)
summary(model)
##
## Regression Data: 526 training points, in 5 variable(s)
##               female married   educ exper tenure
## Bandwidth(s): 0.01978   0.1523  7.847 8.433  41.61
##
## Kernel Regression Estimator: Local-Linear
## Bandwidth Type: Fixed
```

```
## Residual standard error: 0.3703
## R-squared: 0.5148
##
## Continuous Kernel Type: Second-Order Gaussian
## No. Continuous Explanatory Vars.: 3
##
## Unordered Categorical Kernel Type: Aitchison and Aitken
## No. Unordered Categorical Explanatory Vars.: 2

## Plot the estimated conditional mean
plot(model,
     plot.errors.method="bootstrap",
     plot.errors.type="quantile",
     plot.errors.style="band")

## Plot the estimated marginal effects
plot(model,
     plot.errors.method="bootstrap",
     plot.errors.type="quantile",
     plot.errors.style="band",
     gradients=TRUE,
     common.scale=FALSE)
```

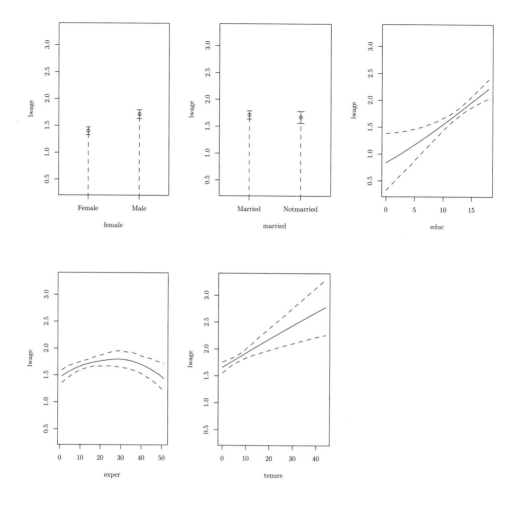

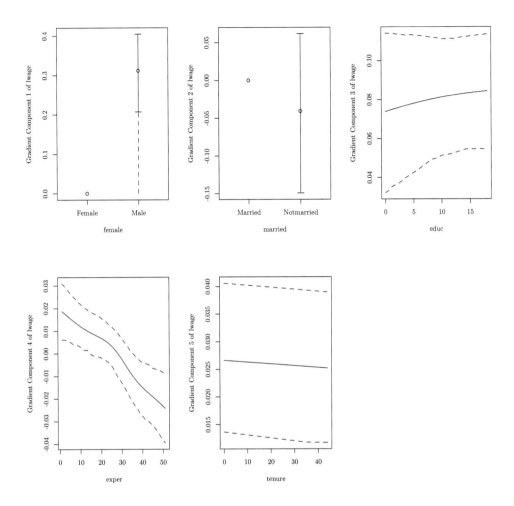

6.10.6   Confidence Bands and Nonparametric Estimation

If no corrective measures are taken, confidence bands that are constructed for nonparametric estimators such as the local linear kernel regression estimator $\hat{g}(x)$ will be centred on $\mathrm{E}\,\hat{g}(x)$ rather than $g(x)$ since $\hat{g}(x)$ is biased in finite sample settings. We can use the bootstrap to bias-correct the confidence bands. Resampling from the estimated model can be carried out by means of, e.g., a wild bootstrap with Rademacher weights.

The following code chunk illustrates the simplicity of this procedure when applied to the local linear estimator.

```
set.seed(42)
n <- 250
neval <- 250
B <- 999
alpha <- 0.05
x <- runif(n)
dgp <- sin(2*pi*x)
y <- dgp + rnorm(n,sd=0.5*sd(dgp))
```

```
## Compute the likelihood cross-validated bandwidth
bw <- npregbw(y~x,regtype="ll")
model <- npreg(bws=bw)
## Compute the kernel estimator on a sequence of points
x.seq <- seq(0,1,length=neval)
dgp.eval <- sin(2*pi*x.seq)
g <- fitted(npreg(tydat=y,txdat=x,exdat=x.seq,bws=bw$bw,regtype="ll"))
## Create matrices to hold the bootstrap replicates
g.boot.kr <- matrix(NA,B,neval)
g.boot <- matrix(NA,B,neval)
for(b in 1:B) {
    ## Resample from the raw data to get estimates of variability
    ii <- sample(n,replace=TRUE)
    g.boot[b,] <- fitted(npreg(tydat=y[ii],txdat=x[ii],exdat=x.seq,
                          bws=bw$bandwidth$x,regtype="ll"))
    ## Wild bootstrap with Rademacher weights
    y.boot <- fitted(model) + residuals(model)*ifelse(rbinom(n,1,.5)==0,-1,1)
    ## Resample from the kernel estimate to bias-correct
    g.boot.kr[b,] <- fitted(npreg(tydat=y.boot,txdat=x,exdat=x.seq,
                          bws=bw$bandwidth$x,regtype="ll"))
}
## Compute the Bootstrap pointwise bias and the true bias
bias <- colMeans(g.boot.kr) - g
true.bias <- -bw$bandwidth$x**2*4*pi**2*sin(2*pi*x.seq)/2
```

We draw $n = 250$ observations from the smooth kernel estimate $\hat{g}(x)$, where $X \sim U[0,1]$ and $g(x) = \sin(2\pi x)$. We repeat this $B = 999$ times and then compute the pointwise bootstrap bias. The bootstrap bias estimate and the true bias are presented in Figure 6.16. The true bias is given by $h^2 g''(x)\kappa_2/2 = -h^2 4\pi^2 \sin(2\pi x)$. The results are based on a Gaussian kernel function and a bandwidth ($h = 0.0536$) selected via likelihood cross-validation. Figure 6.17 presents the uncorrected and the bias-corrected nonparametric confidence bands.

6.10.7   Assessing Model Performance

Below, we consider a simple (paired) test of differences in means for two distributions of expected true ASPEs - one that is based on a parametric regression model (we consider three different specifications) and another that is based on a nonparametric estimator (we consider the local constant and local linear methods, as well as the local polynomial approach of Hall and Racine (2015) that jointly selects the polynomial degree and bandwidth vectors).

We use the wage1 data from the np package. The null hypothesis is that a parametric and a nonparametric model have equal expected true ASPE. The alternative is that the nonparametric model has lower expected true ASPE. Rejection of the null indicates that the nonparametric model performs significantly better than the parametric model on independent data drawn from the same DGP.

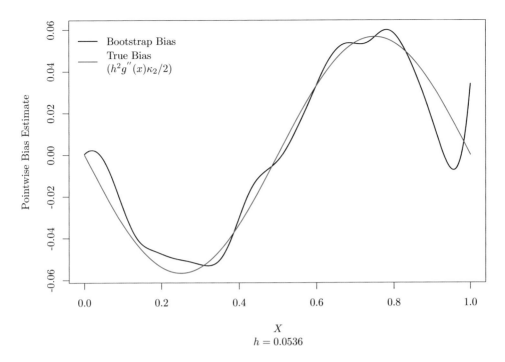

Figure 6.16: Pointwise bootstrap bias estimate.

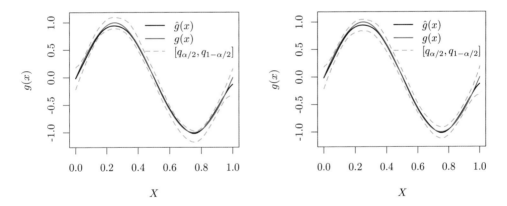

Figure 6.17: Nonparametric confidence bands; bias-corrected on the left, uncorrected on the right.

The three parametric specifications that we consider are (i) the linear-in-predictor model, (ii) the linear-in-predictor quadratic-in-experience model, and (iii) the specification recommended by Murphy and Welch (1990) and studied by Lemieux (2006), among others.

```
## This code chunk illustrates the RP test (Revealed Performance)
## detailed in Racine and Parmeter (2014)
require(crs)
require(np)
```

```
data(wage1)
options(crs.messages=FALSE,np.messages=FALSE)
set.seed(42)
## Set the size of the evaluation data (n.eval) and the training data
## (n.train) and number of train/eval splits (M).
n.eval <- 10
n <- nrow(wage1)
n.train <- n-n.eval
M <- 1000
## Create storage vectors.
aspe.linear <- numeric(M)
aspe.quadint <- numeric(M)
aspe.MW <- numeric(M)
aspe.lc <- numeric(M)
aspe.ll <- numeric(M)
aspe.glp <- numeric(M)
## Copy the full sample into the object train.
train <- wage1
## Fit the parametric and nonparametric models for the full sample.
##
## Linear
lm.linear <- lm(lwage~female+
                married+
                educ+
                exper+
                tenure,
                data=train)
## Linear with interactions and quadratic in experience (common
## specification).
lm.quadint <- lm(lwage~(female+
                        married+
                        educ+
                        exper+
                        I(exper^2)+
                        tenure)^2,
                  data=train)
## Murphy-Welch quartoc specification
lm.MW <- lm(lwage~female+
                married+
                educ+
                exper+
                I(exper^2)+
                I(exper^3)+
                I(exper^4)+
                tenure,
                data=train)
## Local constant
bw.lc <- npregbw(lwage~female+
                married+
                educ+
                exper+
                tenure,
                regtype="lc",
```

```
                        bwmethod="cv.aic",
                        data=train)
model.lc <- npreg(bws=bw.lc)
## Local linear
bw.ll <- npregbw(lwage~female+
                    married+
                    educ+
                    exper+
                    tenure,
                    regtype="ll",
                    bwmethod="cv.aic",
                    data=train)
model.ll <- npreg(bws=bw.ll)
## Generalized local polynomial
ghat <- npglpreg(lwage~female+
                    married+
                    educ+
                    exper+
                    tenure,
                    cv.func="cv.aic",
                    data=train)
model.glp <- npglpreg(ghat$formula,cv="none",degree=ghat$degree,bws=ghat$bws
                        ,data=train)
## Apparent (in-sample) performance
aspe.app.lin <- with(train,mean((lwage-predict(lm.linear,newdata=train))^2))
aspe.app.qint <- with(train,mean((lwage-predict(lm.quadint,newdata=train))^2))
aspe.app.MW <- with(train,mean((lwage-predict(lm.MW,newdata=train))^2))
aspe.app.lc <- with(train,mean((lwage-predict(model.lc,newdata=train))^2))
aspe.app.ll <- with(train,mean((lwage-predict(model.ll,newdata=train))^2))
aspe.app.glp <- with(train,mean((lwage-predict(model.glp,newdata=train))^2))
## Conduct the M train/eval splits
for(m in 1:M) {
    ## We set the seed here to guarantee that the shuffles generated
    ## here and those in the illustration that augments the models
    ## here with semiparametric models are identical
    set.seed(m)
    ## Shuffle the data into independent training and evaluation
    ## samples.
    ii <- sample(1:n,replace=FALSE)
    train <- wage1[ii[1:n.train],]
    eval <- wage1[ii[(n.train+1):n],]
    ## Extract the APSEs for the independent evaluation data where we
    ## know the outcomes (update() refits the lm model on train)
    aspe.linear[m] <- with(eval,mean((lwage-predict(update(lm.linear),
                                            newdata=eval))^2))
    aspe.quadint[m] <- with(eval,mean((lwage-predict(update(lm.quadint),
                                            newdata=eval))^2))
    aspe.MW[m] <- with(eval,mean((lwage-predict(update(lm.MW),
                                        newdata=eval))^2))
    ## Calling npreg with the bandwidth object re-estimates the model
    ## with the updated training data
    model.lc <- npreg(bws=bw.lc)
    aspe.lc[m] <- with(eval,mean((lwage-predict(model.lc,newdata=eval))^2))
```

Table 6.8: Apparent versus expected true model performance (lower values are preferred) and P-values from a test for equality of expected true performance based on (i) the kernel versus linear models, (ii) the kernel versus linear with interaction models, and (iii) the kernel versus MW-optimal models (rejection of the null implies the kernel model has significantly lower mean ASPE on independent data).

	Apparent	Expected	Rank	P-GLP	P-LL	P-LC
Par-Linear	0.1682	0.1741	6	0	0	0.000
Par-Quad-Int	0.1474	0.1639	5	0	0	0.214
Par-MW	0.1561	0.1634	4	0	0	0.326
Nonpar-GLP	0.1419	0.1556	1	NA	NA	NA
Nonpar-LL	0.1372	0.1579	2	NA	NA	NA
Nonpar-LC	0.1319	0.1630	3	NA	NA	NA

```
    model.ll <- npreg(bws=bw.ll)
    aspe.ll[m] <- with(eval,mean((lwage-predict(model.ll,newdata=eval))^2))
    model.glp <- npglpreg(ghat$formula,cv="none",degree=ghat$degree,
                    bws=ghat$bws,data=train)
    aspe.glp[m] <- with(eval,mean((lwage-predict(model.glp,newdata=eval))^2))
}
## Conduct a paired t-test that the mean expected true ASPE for each
## model is equal versus the alternative that the kernel has a
## significantly lower expected true ASPE than the MW-optimal lm
## model.
## LC versus parametric
p.lin <- t.test(aspe.lc,aspe.linear,alternative="less",paired=TRUE)$p.value
p.qint <- t.test(aspe.lc,aspe.quadint,alternative="less",paired=TRUE)$p.value
p.MW <- t.test(aspe.lc,aspe.MW,alternative="less",paired=TRUE)$p.value
p.lc <- c(p.lin,p.qint,p.MW,NA,NA,NA)
## LL versus parametric
p.lin <- t.test(aspe.ll,aspe.linear,alternative="less",paired=TRUE)$p.value
p.qint <- t.test(aspe.ll,aspe.quadint,alternative="less",paired=TRUE)$p.value
p.MW <- t.test(aspe.ll,aspe.MW,alternative="less",paired=TRUE)$p.value
p.ll <- c(p.lin,p.qint,p.MW,NA,NA,NA)
## GLP versus parametric
p.lin<-t.test(aspe.glp,aspe.linear,alternative="less",paired=TRUE)$p.value
p.qint <- t.test(aspe.glp,aspe.quadint,alternative="less",paired=TRUE)$p.value
p.MW <- t.test(aspe.glp,aspe.MW,alternative="less",paired=TRUE)$p.value
p.glp <- c(p.lin,p.qint,p.MW,NA,NA,NA)
## Apparent performance
apparent <- c(aspe.app.lin,aspe.app.qint,aspe.app.MW,
              aspe.app.glp,aspe.app.ll,aspe.app.lc)
## Expected true performance
true <- c(mean(aspe.linear),mean(aspe.quadint),mean(aspe.MW),
          mean(aspe.glp),mean(aspe.ll),mean(aspe.lc))
```

Table 6.8 reveals that all three nonparametric estimators outperform the linear parametric models on independent data and have significantly lower expected square error. In this application, the approach of Hall and Racine (2015) that jointly selects the polynomial degree and bandwidth vectors dominates its peers.

6.10.8   Fixed-Effects Panel Data Models

Data panels are samples formed by drawing observations on N cross-sectional units for T consecutive periods leading to a dataset of the form $\{Y_{it}, X_{it}\}_{i=1,t=1}^{N,T}$. A panel is simply a collection of N individual time series that may be short (*small T*) or long (*large T*). The nonparametric estimation of panel data models has received substantial attention as of late, and a number of surveys are available for the interested practitioner including Ai and Li (2008), Su and Ullah (2011), Henderson and Parmeter (2015), Sun et al. (2015), and Rodriguez-Poo and Soberon (2017), among others.

When T is large and N is small then there exists a lengthy time series for each individual unit and, in such cases, one can avoid estimating a panel data model by simply estimating separate nonparametric models for each individual unit using the T individual time series available for each unit. If this situation applies, we direct the interested reader to Chapter 18 in Li and Racine (2007) for pointers to the literature on nonparametric methods for time series data, though note that all methods and results presented so far are valid for weekly dependent stationary processes and can be applied without modification.

When contemplating the nonparametric estimation of panel data models, one issue that immediately arises is that the standard (parametric) approaches that are often used for panel data models (such as first-differencing to remove the presence of so-called *fixed effects*) are no longer valid unless one is willing to presume additively separable effects, which for many defeats the purpose of using nonparametric methods in the first place.

A variety of approaches have been proposed in the literature, including Wang (2003), who proposed a novel method for estimating nonparametric panel data models that utilizes the information contained in the covariance structure of the model's disturbances, Wang et al. (2005) who proposed a partially linear model with random effects, and Henderson et al. (2008) who consider profile likelihood methods for nonparametric estimation of additive fixed effect models which are removed via first differencing. In what follows, we consider direct nonparametric estimation of fixed effects models using the methods covered previously, while those interested in random effects approaches are directed to Chapter 11 in Henderson and Parmeter (2015) or Chapter 19 in Li and Racine (2007).

Consider the following nonparametric panel data regression model,

$$Y_{it} = g(X_{it}) + u_{it}, \quad i = 1, 2 \ldots, N, \, t = 1, 2, \ldots, T,$$

where $g(\cdot)$ is an unknown smooth function, $X_{it} = (X_{it,1}, \ldots, X_{it,q})$ is of dimension q, all other variables are scalars, and $E(u_{it}|X_{i1}, \ldots, X_{iT}) = 0$.

We say that panel data are *poolable* if one can *pool* the data, by in effect, ignoring the time series dimension, that is, by summing over both i and t without regard to the time dimension thereby effectively putting all data into the same pool then directly applying the methods outlined above. Of course, if the data are not poolable this would obviously not be a wise choice.

However, to allow for the possibility that the data are in fact *potentially* poolable, one can introduce an *unordered* discrete variable, say $\delta_i = i$ for $i = 1, 2, \ldots, N$, and estimate $E(Y_{it}|X_{it}, \delta_i) = g(X_{it}, \delta_i)$ nonparametrically using the generalized product kernel function that we have been exploiting. The δ_i variable is akin to including cross-sectional dummies (as is done, for instance, in the least squares dummy variable approach for linear panel data regression models). Letting $\hat{\lambda}$ denote the cross-validated smoothing parameter associated with δ_i, then if $\hat{\lambda}$ is at its upper bound, one gets $g(X_{it}, \delta_i) = g(X_{it})$ and the data are thereby pooled in the resulting estimate of $g(\cdot)$. If, on the other hand, $\hat{\lambda} = 0$ (or is close to 0), then this effectively estimates each $g_i(\cdot)$ using only the time series for the ith individual unit. Finally, if $\hat{\lambda}$ lies between 0 and its upper bound (say, $(c-1)/c$, where here c denotes the number of units N as outlined in Chapter 3), one might interpret this as a case in which the data are partially poolable.

It bears mentioning that, in addition to the issue of poolability, there is also the issue of correcting inference for potential serial correlation in the u_{it} residuals. That is, even if the data are poolable, you can't blindly apply the asymptotic approach; an appropriate bootstrapping approach is likely best in practice.

We consider a panel of annual observations for six U.S. airlines for the 15–year period 1970 to 1984 taken from the Ecdat R package (Croissant, 2016) as detailed in Table F7.1, page 949 of Greene (2003). The variables in the panel are airline (`airline`), year (`year`), the logarithm of total cost measured in thousands of U.S. dollars (`log(cost)`), the logarithm of an output index in revenue passenger miles (`log(output)`), the logarithm of the price of fuel (`log(pf)`), and load factor (`lf`), i.e., the average capacity utilization of the fleet. We estimate a parametric linear fixed-effects model using the R package `plm` (Croissant and Millo, 2008), then we estimate a nonparametric fixed-effects model where we treat `airline` as an unordered factor and `year` as an ordered factor and use a local linear estimator with bandwidths selected using the approach of Hurvich et al. (1998).

```
library(np)
library(plm)
library(Ecdat)
data(Airline)
## Compute the parametric fixed-effects model
model.plm <- plm(log(cost) ~ log(output) + log(pf) + lf,
```

```
                    model = "within",
                    index=c("airline", "year"),
                    data = Airline)
## Compute the nonparametric fixed-effects model
model.np <- npreg(log(cost)~log(output) +
                    log(pf) +
                    lf +
                    ordered(year) +
                    factor(airline),
                    regtype="ll",
                    bwmethod="cv.aic",
                    gradients=TRUE,
                    data=Airline)
```

The estimated coefficients for `log(output)`, `log(pf)`, and `lf` from the parametric linear model are, respectively, *0.9193, 0.4175* and *-1.07*, while the *average* derivative estimates from the nonparametric model are *1.015, 0.3777* and *-1.214* (the average derivatives for the nonparametric model are computed using the command `colMeans(gradients(model.np)[,1:3])`). The R^2 for the parametric linear model is *0.9926* while that for the nonparametric model is *0.9994*. It is interesting to note that $\hat{\lambda}_{airline} = 0.0006163$ which indicates that the data are *not* poolable across airlines. It is evident that, even with this small sample size and a model having five predictors, the nonparametric approach is delivering sensible estimates that are comparable in magnitude and sign to those obtained from the parametric model.

Problem Set

1. Demonstrate that the Nadaraya-Watson regression estimator given by

$$\hat{g}(x) = \frac{\sum_{i=1}^{n} Y_i K\left(\frac{X_i - x}{h_x}\right)}{\sum_{i=1}^{n} K\left(\frac{X_i - x}{h_x}\right)}$$

can be obtained as the solution to the following locally weighted least squares problem:

$$\hat{g}(x) = \mathrm{argmin}_\alpha \sum_{i=1}^{n} (Y_i - \alpha)^2 K\left(\frac{X_i - x}{h}\right).$$

2. Demonstrate that when $Y \in \mathcal{D} = \{0, 1, \ldots, c-1\}$ is a discrete unordered variable and you model the numerator of $f(y|x) = f(y,x)/f(x)$ with the mixed-data estimator from Chapter 3 that uses Aitchison and Aitken's unordered kernel function, the resulting estimator of the conditional mean, $g(x) = \sum_{y \in \mathcal{D}} y f(y|x) = \sum_{y \in \mathcal{D}} y f(y,x)/f(x)$, can be expressed as

$$\hat{g}(x) = \sum_{y \in \mathcal{D}} y \frac{\hat{f}(y,x)}{\hat{f}(x)}$$

$$= \frac{\sum_i Y_i W\left(\frac{X_i - x}{h}\right)}{\sum_i W\left(\frac{X_i - x}{h}\right)},$$

where

$$\hat{f}(y,x) = \frac{1}{nh} \sum_{i=1}^{n} W\left(\frac{X_i - x}{h}\right) L(Y_i, y, \lambda),$$

and where

$$\hat{f}(x) = \frac{1}{nh} \sum_{i=1}^{n} W\left(\frac{X_i - x}{h}\right),$$

if and only if $\lambda = 0$. In addition, show that when $\lambda = (c-1)/c$, which is the upper bound of λ, the resulting kernel estimator of the conditional mean can be expressed as

$$\hat{g}(x) = \bar{C},$$

where $\mathcal{C} = \sum_{y \in \mathcal{D}} y$ is the sum of the support and $\bar{\mathcal{C}} = \mathcal{C}/c$ is the equally weighted mean of the support, so that $c\bar{\mathcal{C}} = \mathcal{C}$. First derive the general case for the estimator, and then obtain the corner cases above.

3. Consider the nonlinear measure of goodness-of-fit (Doksum and Samarov, 1995) given by

$$R^2 = \frac{\left(\sum_{i=1}^{n}(Y_i - \bar{Y})(\hat{Y}_i - \bar{Y})\right)^2}{\sum_{i=1}^{n}(Y_i - \bar{Y})^2 \sum_{i=1}^{n}(\hat{Y}_i - \bar{Y})^2}$$

$$= \frac{\left(\sum_{i=1}^{n}(Y_i - \bar{Y})(\hat{Y}_i - \bar{Y})\right)^2}{TSS \times ESS},$$

where $TSS = \sum_{i=1}^{n}(Y_i - \bar{Y})^2$ denotes the *total sum of squares* and $ESS = \sum_{i=1}^{n}(\hat{Y}_i - \bar{Y})^2$ denotes the *explained sum of squares*. Demonstrate that this robust measure coincides with the usual (unadjusted) measure $R^2 = ESS/TSS$ for an ordinary least squares estimate of a classical linear regression model with an intercept term (it might be helpful to recall that $Y_i = \hat{Y}_i + \hat{\epsilon}_i$ and to make use of certain properties of the least squares residuals $\hat{\epsilon}_i$).

4. Consider a single predictor regression setting (i.e., $X \in \mathbb{R}^1$). Show that if one uses $h = \infty$, then the local linear estimator $\hat{a} = \hat{g}(x)$ is identical to $\hat{\alpha}_0 + \hat{\alpha}_1 x$, where $\hat{\alpha}_0$ and $\hat{\alpha}_1$ are respectively the ordinary least squares estimators of α_0 and α_1 based on the linear model $Y_i = \alpha_0 + \alpha_1 X_i + \epsilon_i$. You ought to use the $X_i - x$ variant of the local linear estimator in your proof (i.e., you ought to minimize $\sum_{i=1}^{n}(Y_i - a - b(X_i - x))^2 K((X_i - x)/h))$.

Note that the local linear estimators $\hat{a} = \hat{g}(x)$ and $\hat{b} = \hat{\beta}(x)$ are the minimizers of $\sum_{i=1}^{n}(Y_i - a - b(X_i - x))^2 K((X_i - x)/h)$, and that the least squares estimators are given by $\hat{\alpha}_0 = \bar{Y} - \hat{\alpha}_1 \bar{X}$ and $\hat{\alpha}_1 = \sum_{i=1}^{n}(X_i - \bar{X})Y_i / \sum_{i=1}^{n}(X_i - \bar{X})^2$.

Chapter 7

Conditional Mean Function Estimation with Endogenous Predictors

Can I see some identification please? (police officer to vehicle driver)

7.1 Overview

Consider a model given by

$$Y = \varphi(Z) + U.$$

The statistical objects of interest are the unknown function $\varphi(Z)$ and the marginal effects function $\beta(Z) = d\varphi(Z)/dZ$, where $Z \in \mathbb{R}$. For notational convenience, let $\mathrm{E}(U|Z = z) = \mathrm{E}(U|z)$ and recall that $\mathrm{E}(U|z) = 0$ is one of the assumptions outlined in Section 6.2 of Chapter 6 that underlie conditional mean models; that is, Z is *exogenous*. However, this assumption is violated if both Y and Z are endogenous and therefore $\mathrm{E}(U|z) \neq 0$. In this case, the object of interest $\varphi(z)$ is no longer the conditional mean of Y since

$$\mathrm{E}(Y|z) = \varphi(z) + \mathrm{E}(U|z) \neq \varphi(z).$$

When Z is not exogenous, the regression of Y_i on Z_i delivers the estimated conditional mean $\hat{g}(Z_i)$, which does not coincide with $\hat{\varphi}(Z_i)$. That is, as outlined above, $\hat{g}(Z_i)$ is not an estimate of the function of interest since $\hat{g}(Z_i) = \hat{\varphi}(Z_i) + \hat{\mathrm{E}}(U_i|Z_i)$. The assumption that Z and U are uncorrelated is crucial for the consistent estimation of a range of parametric and nonparametric conditional mean models. Without this assumption, the conditional mean is no longer an object that is of much interest. The following example uses a simulated dataset with $n = 1000$ observations to illustrate the divergence between $\varphi(z)$ and $g(z) = E(Y|z)$ when Z is endogenous.

Example 7.1. The Function of Interest $\varphi(z)$, the Conditional Mean Function $\mathrm{E}(Y|z)$, and $\mathrm{E}(U|z)$ when Z Is Endogenous and $\varphi(z)$ Is Nonlinear.

Figure 7.1 presents $\varphi(z)$, $\mathrm{E}(Y|z)$, and $\mathrm{E}(U|z)$ when Z is not exogenous. Endogenous predictors give rise to a divergence between the function of interest $\varphi(z)$ and the conditional mean function $g(z) = E(Y|z)$. Therefore, consistent estimators of $g(z)$ will not be consistent for $\varphi(z)$.

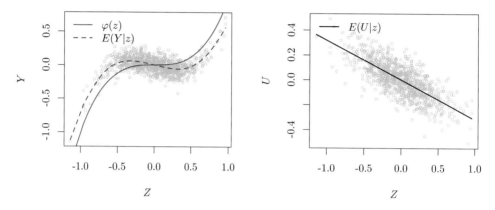

Figure 7.1: The function of interest $\varphi(z)$, the conditional mean function $\mathrm{E}(Y|z)$, and $\mathrm{E}(U|z)$ when Z is not exogenous.

When Z is not exogenous, a popular approach to the estimation of $\varphi(Z)$ makes use of an *instrument* W with the property that $\mathrm{E}(U|W = w) = \mathrm{E}(U|w) = 0$, which is equivalent to $\mathrm{E}(Y - \varphi(Z)|w) = 0$ since $U = Y - \varphi(Z)$. In general, the functional form of neither $\varphi(Z)$ nor $\mathrm{E}(Y|z)$ is known in advance. Fortunately, nonparametric instrumental variables (IV) regression allows for the consistent estimation of $\varphi(Z)$ and its associated marginal effects function. We briefly review identification, continuous/discontinuous identifying mappings, and the notion of *ill-posedness*, and shed light on the role of *regularization* in dealing with *ill-posed* problems. After a brief review of parametric IV models, we then proceed to the topic of nonparametric IV regression.

7.2   Ill-Posed Inverse Problems and Identification

Many of the definitions and some of the example topics in this section are based on those in Horowitz (2014), who provides a comprehensive review of ill-posed inverse problems.

Let φ denote a *parameter* of interest that can be a scalar, vector, or function (i.e., $\varphi = \varphi(Z)$). This parameter is *identified* if it is uniquely determined by the probability distribution from which the available data are sampled. As a simple illustration, consider the population mean $\varphi = \mathrm{E}\,Y =$

$\int_{-\infty}^{\infty} y \, dF(y)$. Provided that this integral exists and is finite, the population mean is identified and can be consistently estimated by its sample counterpart $\widehat{E} Y = n^{-1} \sum_{i=1}^{n} Y_i$, which is obtained by replacing $F(y)$ with the ECDF $F_n(y)$ defined in Chapter 1. Strictly speaking, a parameter φ is identified (overidentified) if there is a one-to-one (or many-to-one) mapping from the population distribution to the parameter.

For many popular parametric estimators (e.g., linear least squares, linear instrumental variables), the parameter of interest is a vector and the *identifying mapping* is *continuous*. By *continuous*, we mean that small changes in the population distribution only produce small changes in the identified parameter. In such cases, the parameter of interest is identified and can be consistently estimated by replacing the unknown population distribution with a consistent sample analog such as the empirical distribution of the data.

However, when the identifying mapping is discontinuous, the parameter of interest φ cannot be consistently estimated by simply replacing the population distribution of the data with a consistent sample analog. This is due to the fact that, even when the sample size is large enough to ensure a negligible difference between the sample and population distributions, the estimated and true values of φ can be very different.

Hadamard (1923) characterizes a problem as *well-posed* if it has a unique solution that depends continuously on the available data (i.e., if the *identifying mapping* is *continuous*). An estimation problem is *ill-posed* if a discontinuous identifying mapping prevents consistent estimation of the parameter of interest via replacement of the population distribution of the data with a consistent sample analog. We say that an estimation problem is an *ill-posed inverse problem* if the discontinuous identifying mapping is obtained by inverting another mapping that is continuous.

We now consider two cases in which ill-posed problems arise, namely consistent estimation of a PDF and least squares parametric regression with a singular design matrix. Endogeneity is not assumed to be an issue in either case.

7.2.1 Kernel Smoothing and Ill-Posedness

It turns out that the smooth nonparametric estimation of a CDF, which we studied in Chapter 2, overcomes an ill-posed inverse problem. Let $F(x) = \int_{-\infty}^{x} f(t) \, dt$ denote a CDF and let $f(x) = dF(x)/dx$ denote the PDF. Recall that the ECDF is given by

$$F_n(x) = \frac{1}{n} \sum_{i=1}^{n} \mathbf{1}(X_i \leq x),$$

where $\mathbf{1}(A)$ is an indicator function whose value is one if A is true and zero otherwise. $F_n(x)$ is a uniformly consistent estimator of $F(x)$, that is,

$\sup_x |F_n(x) - F(x)| = o(1)$ almost surely.

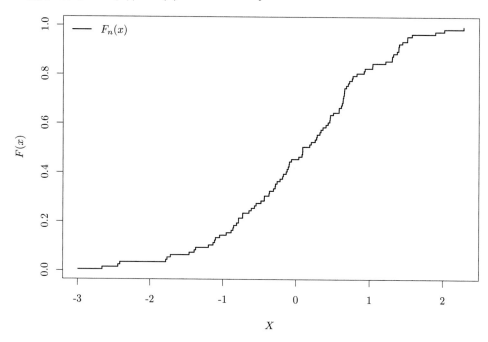

Figure 7.2: The empirical distribution function $F_n(x)$.

Figure 7.2 plots the ECDF $F_n(x)$ for a sample of simulated data. Although $F_n(x)$ is uniformly consistent, it is a step function whose derivative is either 0 or ∞ (when $0 < f(x) < \infty$) *even as $n \to \infty$*. Nonparametric estimation of $f(x)$ is therefore an ill-posed inverse problem. That is, $f(x)$ cannot be consistently estimated by replacing $F(x)$ with a consistent estimator such as $F_n(x)$ in the identifying mapping $f(x) = dF(x)/dx$. For nonparametric density estimation, a *regularization* approach entails modifying (or *regularizing*) the identifying mapping $f(x) = dF(x)/dx$ by *smoothing* the empirical distribution $F_n(x)$ with a *regularization parameter*. Let the regularized (i.e., kernel smoothed) CDF estimator be

$$\hat{F}(x) = \frac{1}{n} \sum_{i=1}^{n} G\left(\frac{x - X_i}{h}\right),$$

where $G(z)$ is a CDF kernel and h is the bandwidth. Recall that we studied $\hat{F}(x)$ in Chapter 2. The regularized (i.e., kernel smoothed) PDF estimator $\hat{f}(x)$ is obtained by differentiating the regularized CDF estimator $\hat{F}(x)$, i.e.,

$$\hat{f}(x) = \frac{d\hat{F}(x)}{dx} = \frac{1}{nh} \sum_{i=1}^{n} K\left(\frac{x - X_i}{h}\right),$$

where $K(z) = G'(z)$. Consistent estimation of $f(x)$ requires that as $n \to \infty$, the bandwidth h must vanish but not too quickly ($nh \to \infty$ as $n \to \infty$);

otherwise, there is not enough regularization to overcome the discontinuity. In this setting, the bandwidth $h > 0$ is the regularization parameter.

Figure 7.3 plots the ECDF, the kernel smoothed CDF, and the first derivative $\hat{f}(x) = d\hat{F}(x)/dx$ of the kernel smoothed CDF for a simulated data sample.

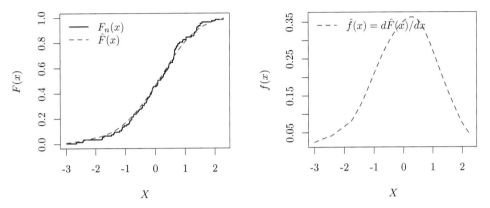

Figure 7.3: The empirical distribution function $F_n(x)$, the kernel smoothed distribution function $\hat{F}(x)$, and the regularized estimate $\hat{f}(x)$.

To summarize and cement ideas, we have the relationship

$$F(x) = \int_{-\infty}^{x} f(t)\, dt.$$

The mapping from $f(x)$ to $F(x)$ is a continuous one, so that small changes in $f(x)$ produce small changes in $F(x)$. However, the converse is not true; the inverse mapping from $F(x)$ to $f(x)$ that is given by $dF(x)/dx$ is not continuous. Hence, we face an *ill-posed inverse problem*. Replacing $F(x)$ with a consistent nonparametric estimator such as $F_n(x)$ and attempting to solve for $f(x)$ can fail. The root of the problem is that the nonparametric model is infinite-dimensional. Regularization can overcome this problem, and in this case, the regularization parameter is a bandwidth.

7.2.2 Singular Design Matrices and Ill-Posedness

Ill-posed problems can surface in parametric regression settings. Consider the model $Y = X\beta + \epsilon$, where $\mathrm{E}\, X'\epsilon = 0$ and hence $\mathrm{E}\, X'Y = \mathrm{E}\, X'X\beta$. If the inverse matrix exists, then

$$\beta = \left(\mathrm{E}\, X'X\right)^{-1} \mathrm{E}\, X'Y.$$

Replacing the unknown expectations with sample moments, we obtain

$$\hat{\beta} = \left(n^{-1} \sum_{i=1}^{n} X_i X_i'\right)^{-1} n^{-1} \sum_{i=1}^{n} X_i Y_i.$$

However, in the presence of multicollinearity, the inverse matrix is singular. *Ridge regression* (Hoerl and Kennard, 1970) is a popular method of overcoming this problem and it entails shrinking $\hat{\beta}$ towards the zero vector. The ridge estimator of β is given by

$$\hat{\beta}_r = \left(n^{-1} \sum_{i=1}^{n} X_i X_i' + h I_k \right)^{-1} n^{-1} \sum_{i=1}^{n} X_i Y_i.$$

Ridge regression is a form of regularization known as *Tikhonov regularization* (Tikhonov, 1943). In this instance, $h > 0$ is the regularization parameter.

In short, regularization procedures can be applied as a solution to ill-posed inverse problems. It turns out that the endogeneity of predictors in a regression model also creates an ill-posed inverse problem, and there are two ways to overcome the discontinuous identifying mapping. The first is to adopt a parametric model that involves a finite number of parameters, but we might worry about the adverse consequences of a potentially misspecified model. The second is to adopt an infinite-dimensional nonparametric approach that can deliver consistent estimates of the objects of interest.

7.3   Parametric Instrumental Regression

Consider the finite-dimensional parametric model in which it is assumed that $\varphi(Z) = Z\beta$, and hence

$$Y = Z\beta + U, \tag{7.1}$$

where Z and U are correlated, $E(Y^2) < \infty$, and $E(Z^2) < \infty$. We assume that there exists an instrument W such that $E(U|W) = 0$, which implies $E(W'U) = E(W'E(U|W)) = 0$ by the law of iterated expectations.

Pre-multiplying Equation (7.1) by W' and taking expectations yields

$$E(W'Y) = E(W'Z)\beta + E(W'U)$$
$$= E(W'Z)\beta.$$

Pre-multiplying $E(W'Y)$ by $E(Z'W)\,(E(W'W))^{-1}$ yields

$$E(Z'W)\,(E(W'W))^{-1}\,E(W'Y) = E(Z'W)\,(E(W'W))^{-1}\,E(W'Z)\beta.$$

If the inverse matrices exist, then

$$\beta = \left(E(Z'W)\,(E(W'W))^{-1}\,E(W'Z) \right)^{-1} E(Z'W)\,(E(W'W))^{-1}\,E(W'Y),$$

which identifies β.

Furthermore, β is a continuous function of the moments and probability distributions of the right-hand-side random variables Z, W, and Y. Replacing unknown expectations with sample averages is equivalent to replacing the unknown distribution of (Y, Z, W) with the empirical distribution of the given data. Hence, the parametric linear IV estimator of β in the model $Y = Z\beta + U$ is given by

$$\hat{\beta}_{IV} = \left(n^{-1} \sum_{i=1}^{n} Z_i W_i' \left(n^{-1} \sum_{i=1}^{n} W_i W_i' \right)^{-1} n^{-1} \sum_{i=1}^{n} W_i Z_i' \right)^{-1} \times$$

$$n^{-1} \sum_{i=1}^{n} Z_i W_i' \left(n^{-1} \sum_{i=1}^{n} W_i W_i' \right)^{-1} n^{-1} \sum_{i=1}^{n} W_i Y_i.$$

$\hat{\beta}_{IV}$ is a consistent estimator of β in the parametric model $Z\beta$. However, $Z\hat{\beta}_{IV}$ is only consistent for $\varphi(Z)$ if the parametric model is correctly specified. Parametric instrumental regression overcomes the ill-posed inverse problem because the linear specification of $\varphi(Z)$ renders $\mathrm{E}(\varphi(Z)|W) = \mathrm{E}(W'Z)\beta$ finite-dimensional. Presuming non-singularity, we can solve a finite set of linear equations to obtain $\hat{\beta}_{IV}$. However, if the parametric model is misspecified, then the resulting estimator of $\varphi(Z)$ is biased and inconsistent, and hence *infinite-dimensional* nonparametric approaches may be preferable. If we treat this as an infinite-dimensional problem, we are in effect trying to solve a set of infinitely many equations in infinitely many unknowns. Roughly speaking, $\mathrm{E}(\varphi(Z)|w)$ is thus a *nearly singular infinite-dimensional matrix*. As a result, in nonparametric settings, we must pursue regularized solutions.

7.4   Nonparametric Instrumental Regression

The approach that we consider recovers $\varphi(Z)$ as the solution to

$$\mathrm{E}(Y - \varphi(Z)|w) = 0.$$

This equation characterizes $\varphi(Z)$ as the solution of a *Fredholm integral equation of the first kind* (Fredholm, 1903). Obtaining a solution for $\varphi(Z)$ is an ill-posed inverse problem and therefore necessitates a *regularization* method. A regularized solution is a sequence of solutions to well-posed problems (called the *regularized problems*) that converges to the desired object, namely $\hat{\varphi}(Z)$.

Let $Y = \varphi(Z) + U$, $r = \mathrm{E}(Y|w)$, and $T\varphi = \mathrm{E}(\varphi(Z)|w)$. T is an operator (specifically, the conditional expectation operator). Using these relationships, $\varphi = \varphi(Z)$ corresponds to any solution of the functional equation

$$T\varphi - r = 0, \tag{7.2}$$

that is,

$$\mathrm{E}(\varphi(Z)|w) - \mathrm{E}(Y|w) = 0.$$

If the joint CDF F is characterized by its density $f(y, z, w)$ with respect to Lebesgue measure, then by the definition of the conditional expectation, Equation (7.2) can be expressed as

$$\int \varphi(z) \frac{f(w, z)}{f(w)} \, dz - \int y \frac{f(y, w)}{f(w)} \, dy = 0.$$

The task at hand is therefore to solve $T\varphi = r$ for φ, which is an ill-posed inverse problem. Let $T\varphi = \mathrm{E}(\varphi(Z)|w)$, $r = \mathrm{E}(Y|w)$, and $T\varphi = r$. First, we take the scalar product with respect to the adjoint operator $T^\dagger$ ($T^\dagger$ is the adjoint of T and is also an expectation operator). Next, we multiply by a constant c and subtract this from φ. Hence, we can write

$$cT^\dagger T\varphi = cT^\dagger r,$$
$$\varphi - cT^\dagger T\varphi = \varphi - cT^\dagger r,$$
$$(I - cT^\dagger T)\varphi = \varphi - cT^\dagger r.$$

We can then express φ as

$$\varphi = (I - cT^\dagger T)\varphi + cT^\dagger r$$
$$= \varphi + cT^\dagger (r - T\varphi).$$

An iterative scheme can be followed to solve this fixed point problem (note that $c < 1$ is required; see Landweber (1951) and Fridman (1956)). The iterative scheme is of the form

$$\varphi_k = \varphi_{k-1} + cT^\dagger_{k-1}(r - T_{k-1}\varphi_{k-1}),$$

and writing this without the simplifying notation yields the expression

$$\varphi_k(z) = \varphi_{k-1}(z) + c\,\mathrm{E}\left(\mathrm{E}(Y - \varphi_{k-1}(Z)|w)|z\right).$$

To solve for $\hat{\varphi}(z)$, we nonparametrically estimate all of the unknown conditional mean objects and iterate for $k = 0, 1, \ldots$ until a stopping condition is met. We need an initial guess for $\varphi(z)$, and the conditional mean estimator $\hat{g}(z) = \widehat{\mathrm{E}}(Y|z)$ from Chapter 6 is a suitable candidate. Hence, we set $\hat{\varphi}_0(z) = \hat{g}(z)$. Next, we compute $\widehat{\mathrm{E}}(Y - \hat{\varphi}_0(Z)|w)$ by means of a kernel regression of $Y - \hat{\varphi}_0(Z)$ on W. Next, we compute $\widehat{\mathrm{E}}\left(\widehat{\mathrm{E}}(Y - \hat{\varphi}_0(Z)|w)|z\right)$ by means of a kernel regression of $\widehat{\mathrm{E}}(Y - \hat{\varphi}_0(Z)|w)$ on Z. This gives us $\hat{\varphi}_1(z)$ since $\hat{\varphi}_1(z) = \hat{\varphi}_o(z) + c\widehat{\mathrm{E}}\left(\widehat{\mathrm{E}}(Y - \hat{\varphi}_0(Z)|w)|z\right)$. We then use $\hat{\varphi}_1(z)$ to compute $\hat{\varphi}_2(z)$ in a similar manner, which delivers a sequence of solutions $\hat{\varphi}_k(z)$, $k = 0, 1, 2, \ldots$, and so on. This process continues until $\|(\widehat{\mathrm{E}}(Y|w) - \widehat{\mathrm{E}}(\hat{\varphi}_k(Z)|w))/\widehat{\mathrm{E}}(Y|w)\|^2$ stabilizes from iteration to iteration; see Morozov (1967).

Note that a *completeness condition* is required for identification; in particular, we must assume that $\mathrm{E}(\varphi(Z)|w) = 0$ almost surely implies $\varphi(Z) = 0$

almost surely. For a more comprehensive discussion of this completeness condition, which is a necessary assumption for identification, see Newey and Powell (2003), Carrasco et al. (2007), Darolles et al. (2011), and Horowitz (2011). Recent work by Freyberger (2017) has established that a consistent nonparametric estimator is obtainable even when completeness fails.

To summarize, we convert an ill-posed inverse problem into one that avoids inversion. Instead, the problem involves an iterative procedure that begins with, say, the conditional mean estimate $\hat{g}(z)$ as an initial guess for $\varphi(z)$ and continues until a stopping criterion is met. To avoid committing a *regularization crime*, we replace all unknown moments with consistent nonparametric estimates. It will be seen that this is a particularly effective method of consistently estimating the object of interest $\varphi(z)$. This is just one of many approaches that have been proposed in the literature; for a comprehensive treatment, see Chapter 17 of Li and Racine (2007) and the references that appear below.

Example 7.2. Illustration of Nonparametric Instrumental Regression.

We make use of the R function `npregiv()` from the np package in a simulated example that involves a sample of size $n = 1000$ based on the DGP that is used by Darolles et al. (2011). It is given by

$$Y = \varphi(Z) + U,$$
$$Z = \rho_{z,w}W + V,$$
$$U = \rho_{u,z}V + \epsilon,$$

where $\rho_{u,z} = -0.5$, $\rho_{z,w} = 0.2$, $\varphi(Z) = Z^3$, and where

$$W \sim N(0,1),$$
$$V \sim N(0, 0.27^2),$$
$$\epsilon \sim N(0, 0.05^2).$$

Figure 7.4 presents the function $\varphi(z)$ and the conditional mean estimate $\hat{g}(z)$. We note that $\hat{g}(z)$ is an inconsistent estimator of $\varphi(z)$, i.e., plim $\hat{g}(z) \neq \varphi(z)$. Figure 7.5 presents the initial guess for $\varphi(z)$, namely $\hat{\varphi}_0(z) = \hat{g}(z)$, as well as the iterated estimates $\hat{\varphi}_1(z)$, $\hat{\varphi}_2(z)$ that converge to $\hat{\varphi}(z)$.

Figure 7.4 reveals that, even when we do not know the functional form of the respective conditional moments that are required for the iterative procedure, we can use nonparametric methods to consistently estimate them. The nonparametric instrumental regression estimate that is delivered by the regularization approach is indeed a useful approximation.

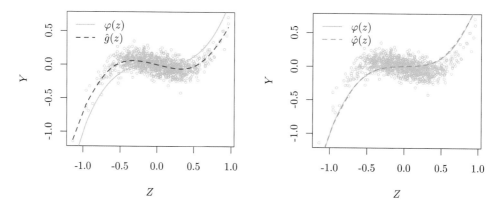

Figure 7.4: The function of interest $\varphi(z)$, the nonparametric conditional mean estimate $\hat{g}(z)$, and the regularized nonparametric instrumental regression estimate $\hat{\varphi}(z)$.

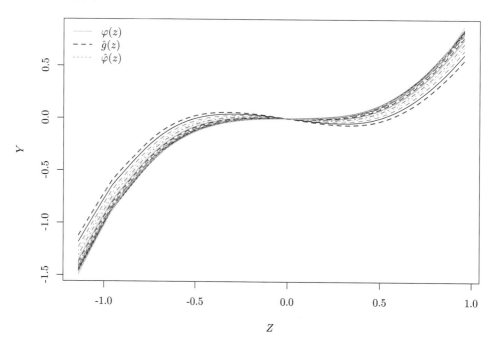

Figure 7.5: The regularized solution path starting from the initial guess $\hat{g}(z)$ and ending with the instrumental regression estimate $\hat{\varphi}(z)$ via the stopping rule.

There is a rich and growing literature on nonparametric IV methods. Theoretical aspects have been considered in Florens (2003), Ai and Chen (2003), Hall and Horowitz (2005), Carrasco et al. (2007), Su and Ullah (2008), Darolles et al. (2011), the special issue of *Econometric Theory* (Florens and Linton, 2011), Chen and Pouzo (2012), Chesher and Rosen (2014), Chen and Pouzo (2015), and Centorrino and Racine (2017). Practical issues surrounding nonparametric IV methods are addressed by Fève and Florens (2010), Horowitz (2011), Shaw et al. (2015), and Centorrino et al. (2017). Asymptotic normality results can be found in Horowitz (2007) and Carrasco et al. (2014). The extension to panel data settings has been addressed by Fève and Florens (2014). For another approach that involves approximation by compact subspaces of the functional parameter space, see Newey and Powell (2003). See also Johannes et al. (2013) for the properties of Landweber-Fridman regularization with projection methods for the estimation of an instrumental regression function $\varphi(Z)$.

7.5 Practitioner's Corner

7.5.1 Estimation of Engel Curves

We consider a random sample from the 1995 British Family Expenditure survey that is used in Blundell et al. (2007) to estimate an Engel curve. If Y is a household's expenditure share on a particular good or service, which in this instance is food, and Z is the household's total expenditure, then $\varphi(Z)$ is an Engel curve. In this setting, Z is endogenous because there are likely omitted factors that affect both the household's total expenditure and its expenditure on food. If wage and salary income is not influenced by household budgeting decisions, then the total wages and/or salary of the head of the household, denoted by W, can be used as an instrument for Z (Blundell et al., 2007). The estimated Engel curve $\hat{\varphi}(z)$ and conditional mean $\hat{g}(z)$ are plotted in Figure 7.6.

Figure 7.6 reveals that the marginal effect function $\hat{\beta}(z) = \hat{\varphi}'(z)$ is negative over its entire support. This indicates that expenditure share on food tends to fall as the log of total expenditure increases. Note also that the IV marginal effect function is smaller in magnitude than the conditional mean marginal effect function that is obtained by regressing Y on Z. This suggests that the marginal effect might be overstated in the event that endogeneity is ignored.

7.5.2 Nonparametric Instrumental Regression with a Linear DGP

In Chapter 6, we noted the interpretation of kernel regression as a shrinkage estimator. Below, we apply a local linear nonparametric IV estimator to a linear DGP that is characterized by endogeneity. This framework is then compared to the linear parametric two-stage least squares IV approach, which is correctly specified by construction. The results are plotted in Figure 7.7. It can be seen that the local linear estimator has shrunk towards the globally linear IV estimator. Furthermore, it coincides with the two-stage least squares estimator when the parametric model is correctly specified.

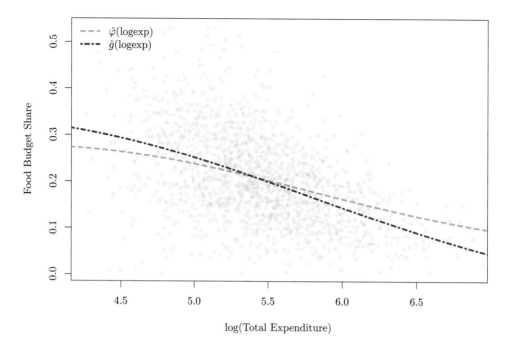

Figure 7.6: The estimated Engel curve for British family expenditure data $\hat{\varphi}(\text{logexp})$ and the conditional mean estimate $\hat{g}(\text{logexp})$.

```
require(sem)
## Credit for this example goes to Samuele Centorrino
set.seed(42)
n <- 1000
nmulti <- 2
rho.zw <- 0.2
rho.uz <- -0.5
sigma.u <- 0.05
dgp <- function(z) { z }
v <- rnorm(n,mean=0,sd=0.27)
eps <- rnorm(n,mean=0,sd=sigma.u)
u <- rho.uz*v + eps
w <- rnorm(n,mean=0,sd=1)
z <- rho.zw*w + v
y <- dgp(z) + u
## Sort on z (for subsequent plotting only)
ivdata <- data.frame(y,z,w,u,v)
rm(y,z,w,u,v)
ivdata <- ivdata[order(ivdata$z),]
attach(ivdata)
model.iv <- npregiv(y=y,z=z,w=w,nmulti=nmulti)
phi.iv <- model.iv$phi
## Now the non-iv local linear estimator of E(Y|z)
ll.mean <- fitted(npreg(y~z,regtype="ll",nmulti=nmulti))
model.2sls <- tsls(formula=y~z,instruments=~w)
model.ols <- lm(y~z)
```

```
par(mfrow=c(1,2))
ylim <- c(min(y,dgp(z),phi.iv,ll.mean,fitted(model.2sls),fitted(model.ols)),
          max(y,dgp(z),phi.iv,ll.mean,fitted(model.2sls),fitted(model.ols)))
## Plot nonparametric estimates
curve(dgp,min(z),max(z),
      ylim=ylim,
      ylab="$Y$",
      xlab="$Z$",
      lwd=2,
      lty=1)
points(z,y,type="p",cex=.25,col="grey")
lines(z,phi.iv,col="blue",lwd=2,lty=2)
lines(z,ll.mean,col="red",lwd=2,lty=4)
legend("topleft",
       c("$\\varphi(z)$",
         "Nonparametric $\\hat\\varphi(z)$",
         "Nonparametric $\\hat g(z)$"),
       lty=c(1,2,4),
       col=c("black","blue","red"),
       lwd=c(2,2,2),
       bty="n")
## Plot parametric estimates
curve(dgp,min(z),max(z),
      ylim=ylim,
      ylab="$Y$",
      xlab="$Z$",
      lwd=2,
      lty=1)
points(z,y,type="p",cex=.25,col="grey")
abline(model.2sls,col="green",lwd=2,lty=5)
abline(model.ols,col="orange",lwd=2,lty=6)
legend("topleft",
       c("$\\varphi(z)$",
         "Parametric $\\hat\\varphi(z)$",
         "Parametric $\\hat E(Y|z)$"),
       lty=c(1,5,6),
       col=c("black","green","orange"),
       lwd=c(2,2,2),
       bty="n")
```

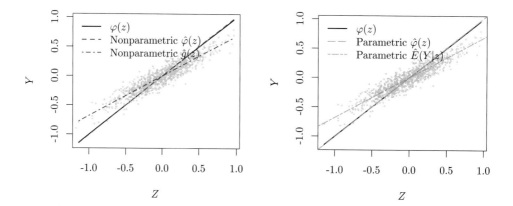

Figure 7.7: Nonparametric local linear instrumental regression with a linear DGP and the linear parametric IV estimate.

Problem Set

1. Consider the random sample from the 1995 British Family Expenditure survey that is used in Blundell et al. (2007) to estimate an Engel curve. If Y is a household's expenditure share on a particular good or service, which in this instance is food, and Z is the household's total expenditure, then $\varphi(Z)$ is an Engel curve. In this setting, Z is endogenous because there are likely omitted factors that affect both the household's total expenditure and its expenditure on food. If wage and salary income is not influenced by household budgeting decisions, then the total wages and/or salary of the head of the household, denoted by W, can be used as an instrument for Z (Blundell et al., 2007). Run the illustration in the help file for the Engel95 data (load the np package in R, see `?Engel95`, and then run the example code that appears near the end of this file).

Chapter 8

Semiparametric Conditional Mean Function Estimation

And in the end we compromised. (Paul Simon, *Think Too Much*)

8.1 Overview

Semiparametric models combine parametric and nonparametric specifications in a manner that achieves a compromise between the two approaches. They are used to reduce the dimension of the nonparametric component in order to attenuate the curse of dimensionality. They have proven to be quite popular in applied settings since they tend to be easier to interpret than fully nonparametric models. However, they still rely on parametric assumptions and can therefore be misspecified and inconsistent, just like their parametric counterparts. We shall restrict our attention to three popular regression-type models, namely the partially linear, single index, and varying coefficient specifications.

8.2 Robinson's Partially Linear Model

The semiparametric partially linear model proposed by Robinson (1988) is given by

$$Y_i = X_i'\beta + g(Z_i) + U_i, \quad i = 1, \ldots, n$$

where X_i is a $p \times 1$ vector of predictors, β is a $p \times 1$ vector of unknown parameters, and $Z_i \in \mathbb{R}^q$. The functional form of $g(\cdot)$ is not specified. The finite-dimensional vector β is the parametric component of the model, while the unknown function $g(\cdot)$ is the nonparametric component.

The goal is to consistently estimate the parameter vector β, which requires that certain identification conditions be satisfied. In particular, X cannot include a constant, or equivalently, β must not contain an intercept term. If there was an intercept, say α, it could not be identified separately from the unknown function $g(\cdot)$. To see this, note that for any constant $c \neq 0$,

$$\alpha + g(Z) = (\alpha + c) + (g(Z) - c) \equiv \alpha_{\text{new}} + g_{\text{new}}(Z).$$

Thus, the sum of the new intercept and the new $g(\cdot)$ function is observationally equivalent to the sum of the old ones. Since the functional form of $g(\cdot)$ is not specified, this implies that an intercept term cannot be identified in a partially linear model.

The basic idea that underlies Robinson's procedure is to eliminate the unknown function $g(\cdot)$ at the outset. Taking expectations conditional on Z_i, we get

$$\mathrm{E}(Y_i | Z_i) = \mathrm{E}(X_i | Z_i)' \beta + g(Z_i).$$

Subtracting this from the partially linear model yields

$$Y_i - \mathrm{E}(Y_i | Z_i) = (X_i - \mathrm{E}(X_i | Z_i))' \beta + U_i.$$

If we adopt the shorthand notation $\tilde{Y}_i = Y_i - \mathrm{E}(Y_i | Z_i)$ and $\tilde{X}_i = X_i - \mathrm{E}(X_i | Z_i)$, and apply the method of least squares, we obtain an estimator of β that is given by

$$\hat{\beta}_{\text{inf}} = \left(\sum_{i=1}^{n} \tilde{X}_i \tilde{X}_i' \right)^{-1} \sum_{i=1}^{n} \tilde{X}_i \tilde{Y}_i.$$

Of course, $\hat{\beta}_{\text{inf}}$ is infeasible because it depends on the unknown moments $\mathrm{E}(Y_i | Z_i)$ and $\mathrm{E}(X_i | Z_i)$. The feasible estimator replaces the unknown moments with their nonparametrically estimated counterparts. Under standard regularity conditions, we have

$$\sqrt{n}(\hat{\beta} - \beta) \xrightarrow{d} N\left(0, \Phi^{-1} \Psi \Phi^{-1} \right),$$

provided that Φ is positive definite. Note that

$$\Phi = \mathrm{E}(\tilde{X}_i \tilde{X}_i'), \Psi = \mathrm{E}(\sigma^2(X_i, Z_i) \tilde{X}_i \tilde{X}_i') \text{ and } \tilde{X}_i = X_i - \mathrm{E}(X_i | Z_i).$$

Joint parameter and bandwidth selection entails minimization of the cross-validation function

$$CV(\beta, \gamma) = \sum_{i=1}^{n} \left(Y_i - X_i' \beta - \hat{g}_{-i}(Z_i) \right)^2,$$

where $\hat{g}_{-i}(Z_i)$ is the delete-one estimator of $g(Z_i)$ that is obtained by non-parametrically regressing $Y_i - X_i' \beta$ on Z_i. See Linton (1995) for further theoretical details.

The original formulation of the model in Robinson (1988) treated Z as continuous; however, the extension proposed by Gao et al. (2015) allows for Z to be continuous, categorical, or a combination of both predictor types. Partially linear models can be estimated using the function npplreg() in the R package np.

Example 8.1. Wooldridge's wage1 Dataset.

This example makes use of Wooldridge's wage1 dataset. We first estimate a linear model that is quadratic in experience and then relax this assumption about the functional specification of the relationship between `exper` and `lwage` by relegating `exper` to the nonparametric part of a semiparametric partially linear model. We first provide a summary of an estimated earnings equation whose simple parametric specification is quadratic in experience.

```
data(wage1)
model.lm <- lm(lwage~female+married+educ+tenure+exper+expersq,
               data=wage1)
foo <- cbind(coef(model.lm))
colnames(foo) <- "Coefficient"
xtable.rmd(foo,digits=7)
```

	Coefficient
(Intercept)	0.1811615
femaleMale	0.2911303
marriedNotmarried	-0.0564494
educ	0.0798322
tenure	0.0160739
exper	0.0300995
expersq	-0.0006012

The R^2 for this model is 0.436. The astute reader who attempts to run this code will realize that the function `xtable.rmd()` will not work in a regular R session (it is a wrapper for the function `xtable()` in the R package by the same name). The function is defined in the beginning of the R code for this document. To run this code in an R session use `xtable()` instead (and don't forget to load the xtable package prior to invoking this function).

Next, we consider the semiparametric partially linear specification. Note that, for identification purposes, there is no intercept term. Moreover, there is no coefficient for `exper` because it has been relegated to the nonparametric component of the model.

```
data(wage1)
model.pl <- npplreg(lwage~female+married+educ+tenure|exper,
                    data=wage1)
foo <- cbind(coef(model.pl))
colnames(foo) <- "Coefficient"
xtable.rmd(foo,digits=7)
```

Interestingly, the in-sample fit of this model ($R^2 = 0.452$) is superior to that of the parametric linear model ($R^2 = 0.436$). Notice that the coefficients that are common to both models are

	Coefficient
female	0.2861456
married	-0.0383323
educ	0.0788131
tenure	0.0161654

of the same sign and order of magnitude. The parametric and partially linear models can be compared by means of the consistent model specification test that is outlined in Chapter 6; this amounts to testing whether $g(Z)$ is linear. See the Practitioner's Corner at the end of this chapter for details. The model assessment exercise in the Practitioner's Corner compares the performance of this approach to that of a variety of parametric and nonparametric methods.

8.3   Varying Coefficient Models

We now consider the varying coefficient (or *smooth coefficient*) model, which is a more general semiparametric regression framework; see Hastie and Tibshirani (1993), Fan and Zhang (1999), Li et al. (2002), and Su et al. (2013). This model is remarkably flexible, and it nests the linear, partially linear, and local linear specifications as special cases. The smooth coefficient model is given by

$$Y_i = \alpha(Z_i) + X_i'\beta(Z_i) + U_i,$$

where $\beta(Z)$ is a vector of unspecified smooth functions of Z. When $\beta(Z) = \beta_0$, it collapses to the partially linear model with $g(Z) = \alpha(Z)$. When $X = Z$ and we use kernel methods, it collapses to the local linear model. We abuse notation slightly and express the model more compactly as

$$Y_i = X_i'\beta(Z_i) + U_i.$$

Now X_i is a $p \times 1$ vector whose first component may be a constant. $\beta(Z)$ is a $p \times 1$ function of Z, while Z is of dimension q. Pre-multiplying by X_i and taking expectations conditional on Z_i leads to $\mathrm{E}(X_iY_i|Z_i) = \mathrm{E}(X_iX_i'|Z_i)\beta(Z_i)$, which yields

$$\beta(z) = \left(\mathrm{E}(X_iX_i'|z)\right)^{-1}\mathrm{E}(X_iY_i|z),$$

where $\mathrm{E}(X_iY_i|z)$ is shorthand notation for $\mathrm{E}(X_iY_i|Z = z)$. This suggests the following local constant least squares estimator for $\beta(z)$:

$$\hat{\beta}(z) = \left(\sum_{j=1}^{n} X_jX_j'K\left(\frac{Z_j - z}{h}\right)\right)^{-1} \sum_{j=1}^{n} X_jY_jK\left(\frac{Z_j - z}{h}\right).$$

Under some regularity conditions (see Li et al. (2002)), and for a fixed value of z with $f_z(z) > 0$ ($f_z(\cdot)$ is the marginal PDF of Z_i), we have

$$\sqrt{n \prod_{j=1}^{q} h_j} \left(\hat{\beta}(z) - \beta(z) - \sum_{s=1}^{q} h_s^2 B_s(z) \right) \xrightarrow{d} N(0, \Omega_z).$$

This follows provided that $M_z \stackrel{\text{def}}{=} f_z(z) \operatorname{E}(X_i X_i' | Z_i = z)$ is positive definite, with

$$B_s(z) = \kappa_2 M_z^{-1} \operatorname{E}(X_i X_i'(\beta_s(z) f_s(X_i, Z_i) / f(X_i | Z_i = z) + f_z(Z_i)\beta_{ss}(Z_i)/2)|z),$$

$\kappa_2 = \int k(v)v^2 dv$, $\beta_s(z) = \partial\beta(z)/\partial z_s$, $\beta_{ss}(z) = \partial^2\beta(z)/\partial z_s^2$, $\Omega_z = M_z^{-1} V_z M_z^{-1}$, $V_z = \kappa^q f_z(z) \operatorname{E}(X_i X_i' \sigma^2(X_i, Z_i)|Z_i = z)$, and $\sigma^2(X_i, Z_i) = \operatorname{E}(U_i^2 | X_i, Z_i)$. Bandwidth selection is carried out via a process known as *backfitting* (Buja et al., 1989). The categorical Z case is treated in Ouyang et al. (2013), while the mixed-data case is treated in Li and Racine (2010). Smooth coefficient models can be estimated using the `npscoef()` function in the R package np. A test for correct specification of a smooth coefficient model is outlined in Li et al. (2002). In addition, Sun et al. (2016) propose a rather general test that covers time series settings in which X is stationary and Z is potentially non-stationary.

Example 8.2. Wooldridge's wage1 Dataset.

Suppose that the researcher believes that the continuous predictors' coefficients might depend on the categorical predictors `female` and `married`.

```
data(wage1)
model.scoef <- npscoef(lwage~educ+tenure+exper+expersq|female+
                       married,
                       data=wage1,
                       betas=TRUE)
summary(model.scoef)
##
## Smooth Coefficient Model
## Regression data: 526 training points, in 2 variable(s)
##
##                 female married
## Bandwidth(s): 0.001824  0.1343
##
## Bandwidth Type: Fixed
##
## Residual standard error: 0.3834
## R-squared: 0.4787
##
## Unordered Categorical Kernel Type: Aitchison and Aitken
## No. Unordered Categorical Explanatory Vars.: 2
```

Consider the average derivatives from the varying coefficient model.

```
foo <- as.matrix(colMeans(coef(model.scoef)))
colnames(foo) <- "Coefficient"
xtable.rmd(foo,digits=7)
```

	Coefficient
Intercept	0.3402132
educ	0.0786505
tenure	0.0142986
exper	0.0300507
expersq	-0.0005951

The average derivatives (ignoring the intercept) are comparable in magnitude to those obtained under the parametric specification; however, the in-sample fit of the smooth coefficient
model ($R^2 = 0.479$) is superior to that of the parametric model
($R^2 = 0.436$). The model assessment exercise in the Practitioner's
Corner compares the performance of this approach to that of a
variety of parametric and nonparametric methods.

8.4   Semiparametric Single Index Models

A semiparametric single index model is of the form

$$Y = g(X'\beta_0) + U,$$

where Y is the dependent variable, $X \in \mathbb{R}^q$ is a vector of predictors, β_0 is a
$q \times 1$ vector of unknown parameters, and U is an error term that satisfies
$E(U|X) = 0$. Even though X is a vector, the term $X'\beta_0$ is called a *single
index* because it is a scalar. The functional form of $g(\cdot)$ is unknown to the
researcher. This model is semiparametric since the functional form of the
linear index is specified, while that of $g(\cdot)$ is not.

In semiparametric single index models, identification of β_0 and $g(\cdot)$ requires
that

- X does not contain a constant (i.e., no intercept)
- X contains at least one continuous variable
- $||\beta_0|| = 1$ or $\beta_{01} = 1$ (i.e., we need some normalization of β)
- $g(\cdot)$ is differentiable and is not a constant function on the support of
  $X'\beta_0$
- Variation in the discrete components of X does not divide the support
  of $X'\beta_0$ into disjoint subsets

Single-index models can be estimated using the `npindex()` function in
the R package np. A test for correct specification of a single index model is
outlined in Stute and Zhu (2005).

8.4.1 Ichimura's Method (Continuous Y)

We compute β via local constant estimation of $g(X'\beta)$ and minimization of the following objective function (Ichimura, 1993; Härdle et al., 1993):

$$S_n(\beta, h) = \sum_{i=1}^{n} \left(Y_i - \hat{g}_{-i}(X_i'\beta)\right)^2 W(X_i) \mathbf{1}(X_i \in A_n).$$

$\hat{g}_{-i}(X_i'\beta)$ is a leave-one-out local constant kernel estimator and h is the scalar bandwidth for the index $X'\beta$. $W(X_i)$ is a non-negative weight function. The indicator $\mathbf{1}(X_i \in A_n)$ is a trimming function that equals one if $X_i \in A_n$ and zero otherwise. Although not required for estimation, the weight and trimming functions are necessary for the derivation of asymptotic results.

It can be shown that

$$\sqrt{n}(\hat{\beta} - \beta_0) \xrightarrow{d} N(0, \Omega_I),$$

where $\Omega_I = V^{-1}\Sigma V^{-1}$ and

$$\Sigma = \mathrm{E}\left(W(X_i)\sigma^2(X_i)\left(g_i^{(1)}\right)^2 (X_i - \mathrm{E}_A(X_i|X_i'\beta_0))\right.$$
$$\left. \times \left(X_i - \mathrm{E}_A(X_i|X_i'\beta_0)\right)'\right).$$

Note that $g_i^{(1)} = (\partial g(v)/\partial v)|_{v=X_i'\beta_0}$, $\mathrm{E}_A(X_i|v) = \mathrm{E}(X_i|x_A'\beta_0 = v)$ where x_A has the distribution of X_i conditional on $X_i \in A_\delta$, and finally,

$$V = \mathrm{E}\left(W(X_i)\left(g_i^{(1)}\right)^2 (X_i - \mathrm{E}_A(X_i|X_i'\beta_0))(X_i - \mathrm{E}_A(X_i|X_i'\beta_0))'\right).$$

Example 8.3. Wooldridge's wage1 Dataset.

```
data(wage1)
model.index <- npindex(lwage~educ+
                       tenure+
                       exper+
                       expersq+
                       female+
                       married,
                       method="ichimura",
                       data=wage1)
summary(model.index)
##
## Single Index Model
## Regression Data: 526 training points, in 6 variable(s)
##
##          educ   tenure    exper    expersq female   married
## Beta:       1 0.004674  0.02085 -0.0004225 0.3692  -0.07438
## Bandwidth: 0.09557
```

```
## Kernel Regression Estimator: Local-Constant
##
## Residual standard error: 0.3751
## R-squared: 0.5047
##
## Continuous Kernel Type: Second-Order Gaussian
## No. Continuous Explanatory Vars.: 1
```

Interestingly, the in-sample fit of the varying coefficient model ($R^2 = 0.479$) is superior to that of the partially linear ($R^2 = 0.452$) and linear parametric ($R^2 = 0.436$) models. The model assessment exercise in the Practitioner's Corner compares the performance of this approach to that of a variety of parametric and nonparametric methods.

8.4.2   Klein and Spady's Method (Binary Y)

For binary outcomes, Klein and Spady (1993) suggest that β be estimated by the method of maximum likelihood, given a local constant estimate of $g(X'\beta)$. The estimated log-likelihood function is given by

$$\mathcal{L}(\beta, h) = \sum_i (1 - Y_i) \ln(1 - \hat{g}_{-i}(X_i'\beta)) + \sum_i Y_i \ln(\hat{g}_{-i}(X_i'\beta)).$$

Maximization with respect to β and h gives rise to the semiparametric maximum likelihood estimator of β, which we denote by $\hat{\beta}_{KS}$ (h is the smoothing parameter for the scalar index). As with Ichimura's estimator, maximization is carried out by numerically solving the necessary first-order conditions.

Klein and Spady (1993) show that $\hat{\beta}_{KS}$ is $\sqrt{n}$-consistent and has an asymptotically normal distribution that is given by

$$\sqrt{n}(\hat{\beta}_{KS} - \beta) \xrightarrow{d} N(0, \Omega_{KS}).$$

Note that

$$\Omega_{KS} = \left(\mathrm{E} \left(\frac{\partial P}{\partial \beta} \left(\frac{\partial P}{\partial \beta} \right)' \left(\frac{1}{P(1 - P)} \right) \right) \right)^{-1}$$

and $P = P(\epsilon \leq X'\beta) = F_\epsilon(X'\beta)$, where $F_\epsilon(X'\beta)$ is the CDF of ϵ_i evaluated at $X'\beta$.

Example 8.4. Low Birth Weight Data.

We estimate a Logit and a semiparametric single index model based on the birthwt data in the MASS package. The dependent variable is a binary indicator of low birthweight. We assess each model's classification ability by means of a comparison of their confusion matrices.

The variables are defined as follows:

- `low` indicator of birth weight less than 2.5kg ($1 = < 2.5$kg)
- `smoke` smoking status during pregnancy ($1 =$ smoker)
- `race` mother's race ($1 =$ white, $2 =$ black, $3 =$ other)
- `ht` history of hypertension ($1 =$ hypertensive)
- `ui` presence of uterine irritability ($1 =$ present)
- `ftv` number of physician visits during the first trimester
- `age` mother's age in years
- `lwt` mother's weight in pounds at last menstrual period

Note that all variables other than `age` and `lwt` are categorical. First, consider the parametric Logit model's confusion matrix.

```
data("birthwt")
model.logit <- glm(low~factor(smoke)+
                   factor(race)+
                   factor(ht)+
                   factor(ui)+
                   ordered(ftv)+
                   age+
                   lwt,
                   family=binomial(link=logit),data=birthwt)
cm.logit <- with(birthwt,table(low,
                   ifelse(fitted(model.logit)>0.5,1,0)))
ccr.logit <- sum(diag(cm.logit))/sum(cm.logit)
```

Table 8.1: Parametric Logit model confusion matrix.

	0	1
0	119	11
1	34	25

The in-sample correct classification ratio is CCR=0.762. It is computed as the sum of the diagonal entries in the confusion matrix divided by the total number of observations.

Next, consider the semiparametric single index model's confusion matrix.

```
data(birthwt)
model.index <- npindex(low~factor(smoke)+
                   factor(race)+
                   factor(ht)+
                   factor(ui)+
                   ordered(ftv)+
                   age+
                   lwt,
                   method="kleinspady",
                   data=birthwt)
cm.index <- with(birthwt,table(low,
```

```
                     ifelse(fitted(model.index)>0.5,1,0)))
ccr.index <- sum(diag(cm.index))/sum(cm.index)
```

Table 8.2: Single index model confusion matrix.

	0	1
0	119	11
1	22	37

The in-sample fit of the semiparametric model (CCR=0.825) is superior to that of the parametric Logit model (CCR=0.762). A comparison of this approach and those considered in Chapter 4 for a binary $Y \in \{0, 1\}$ is left as an exercise.

8.5 Summary

Semiparametric regression models are very popular in applied settings. Their primary benefit is that they attenuate the *curse of dimensionality* of fully nonparametric approaches. They are also popular because they allow for easy interpretation of scalar parameters. However, these models can be misspecified since they are based on assumptions about the functional form of their parametric component. If misspecified, semiparametric estimators of $E(Y|z)$, which is the ultimate object of interest, will be inconsistent. Nonetheless, they are often quite useful and therefore ought to be part of every practitioner's toolkit. In the Practitioner's Corner, it will be seen that they have the potential to outperform popular parametric specifications in applied settings.

8.6 Practitioner's Corner

8.6.1 A Specification Test for the Partially Linear Model

To test a parametric linear specification against the alternative of a semiparametric partially linear model, i.e.,

$$H_0 : Y = X'\beta + Z'\gamma + U$$
$$H_1 : Y = X'\beta + g(Z) + U,$$

one can use the R function npcmstest() in the np package as follows:

```
## Credit for this example goes to Brennan Thompson
set.seed(42)
n <- 100
X <- rnorm(n)
```

```
Z <- runif(n)
## Fully linear specification
dgp <- X+Z
y <- dgp + rnorm(n,sd=0.5*sd(dgp))
model <- lm(y~X+Z,y=TRUE,x=TRUE)
uhat <- resid(model)
npcmstest(xdat=Z,ydat=uhat,model=model)
##
## Consistent Model Specification Test
## Parametric null model: lm(formula = y ~ X + Z, x = TRUE, y = TRUE)
## Number of regressors: 1
## IID Bootstrap (399 replications)
##
## Test Statistic 'Jn': -0.7875 P Value: 0.57
## ---
## Signif. codes:  0 '***' 0.001 '**' 0.01 '*' 0.05 '.' 0.1 ' ' 1
## Fail to reject the null of correct specification at the 10% level
## Partially linear specification
dgp <- X+sin(2*pi*Z)
y <- dgp + rnorm(n,sd=0.5*sd(dgp))
model <- lm(y~X+Z,y=TRUE,x=TRUE)
uhat <- resid(model)
npcmstest(xdat=Z,ydat=uhat,model=model)
##
## Consistent Model Specification Test
## Parametric null model: lm(formula = y ~ X + Z, x = TRUE, y = TRUE)
## Number of regressors: 1
## IID Bootstrap (399 replications)
##
## Test Statistic 'Jn': 5.266   P Value: <2e-16 ***
## ---
## Signif. codes:  0 '***' 0.001 '**' 0.01 '*' 0.05 '.' 0.1 ' ' 1
## Null of correct specification is rejected at the 0.1% level
```

We reject the null hypothesis that the model is linear in Z, and hence preference ought to be given to the semiparametric specification. As discussed in Li and Wang (1998), a slightly better approach would be to use a *mixed* residual $\hat{U}_i = Y_i - X_i'\tilde{\beta} - Z_i'\hat{\gamma}$ in the test, where $\tilde{\beta}$ is the semiparametric estimator of β based on the partially linear specification and $\hat{\gamma}$ is the OLS estimator of γ based on the linear specification. This leads to potential power gains due to the improved efficiency of $\hat{\beta}$ under the alternative.

8.6.2   Assessing Model Performance - Continuous Y

We use the wage1 dataset to undertake a comparison of the performance of various parametric, semiparametric, and nonparametric models. We repeat an earlier model assessment exercise that was based on the wage1 data, but we now add the partially linear (Robinson, 1988), smooth coefficient (Hastie and Tibshirani, 1993), and single index (Ichimura, 1993) estimators to the mix.

```
## This code chunk illustrates the RP test (Revealed Performance)
## detailed in Racine and Parmeter (2014)
require(crs)
require(np)
data(wage1)
options(crs.messages=FALSE,np.messages=FALSE)
set.seed(42)
## Set the size of the evaluation data (n.eval) and the training data
## (n.train), and number of train/eval splits (M).
n.eval <- 10
n <- nrow(wage1)
n.train <- n-n.eval
M <- 1000
## Create storage vectors.
aspe.linear <- numeric(M)
aspe.quadint <- numeric(M)
aspe.mw <- numeric(M)
aspe.vc <- numeric(M)
aspe.pl <- numeric(M)
aspe.si <- numeric(M)
aspe.lc <- numeric(M)
aspe.ll <- numeric(M)
aspe.glp <- numeric(M)
## Copy the full sample into the object train.
train <- wage1
## Fit the parametric, semiparametric, and nonparametric models for
## the full sample.
##
## Linear
lm.linear <- lm(lwage~female+
                married+
                educ+
                exper+
                tenure,
                data=train)
## Linear with interactions and quadratic in experience (common
## specification).
lm.quadint <- lm(lwage~(female+
                        married+
                        educ+
                        exper+
                        I(exper^2)+
                        tenure)^2,
                 data=train)
## Murphy-Welch quartic specification
lm.mw <- lm(lwage~female+
            married+
            educ+
            exper+
            I(exper^2)+
            I(exper^3)+
            I(exper^4)+
            tenure,
```

```
                  data=train)
## Varying coefficient
model.vc <- npscoef(lwage~educ+
                    tenure+
                    exper+
                    expersq|female+married,
                    data=train)
## Partially linear
model.pl <- npplreg(lwage~female+
                    married+
                    educ+
                    tenure|exper,
                    data=train)
## Single-index (Ichimura)
model.si <- npindex(lwage~female+
                    married+
                    educ+
                    tenure+
                    exper+
                    expersq,
                    method="ichimura",
                    data=train)
## Local constant
bw.lc <- npregbw(lwage~female+
                 married+
                 educ+
                 exper+
                 tenure,
                 regtype="lc",
                 bwmethod="cv.aic",
                 data=train)
model.lc <- npreg(bws=bw.lc)
## Local linear
bw.ll <- npregbw(lwage~female+
                 married+
                 educ+
                 exper+
                 tenure,
                 regtype="ll",
                 bwmethod="cv.aic",
                 data=train)
model.ll <- npreg(bws=bw.ll)
## Generalized local polynomial
ghat <- npglpreg(lwage~female+
                 married+
                 educ+
                 exper+
                 tenure,
                 cv.func="cv.aic",
                 data=train)
model.glp <- npglpreg(ghat$formula,cv="none",degree=ghat$degree,bws=ghat$bws,
                      data=train)
## Apparent (in-sample) performance
```

```
aspe.app.lin <- with(train,mean((lwage-predict(lm.linear,newdata=train))^2))
aspe.app.qint <- with(train,mean((lwage-predict(lm.quadint,newdata=train))^2))
aspe.app.mw <- with(train,mean((lwage-predict(lm.mw,newdata=train))^2))
aspe.app.vc <- with(train,mean((lwage-predict(model.vc,newdata=train))^2))
aspe.app.pl <- with(train,mean((lwage-predict(model.pl,newdata=train))^2))
aspe.app.si <- with(train,mean((lwage-predict(model.si,newdata=train))^2))
aspe.app.lc <- with(train,mean((lwage-predict(model.lc,newdata=train))^2))
aspe.app.ll <- with(train,mean((lwage-predict(model.ll,newdata=train))^2))
aspe.app.glp <- with(train,mean((lwage-predict(model.glp,newdata=train))^2))
## Conduct the M train/eval splits
for(m in 1:M) {
    ## We set the seed here to guarantee that the shuffles generated
    ## here and those in the Practitioner's Corner in Chapter 6 are
    ## identical.
    set.seed(m)
    ## Shuffle the data into independent training and evaluation
    ## samples.
    ii <- sample(1:n,replace=FALSE)
    train <- wage1[ii[1:n.train],]
    eval <- wage1[ii[(n.train+1):n],]
    ## Extract the APSEs for the independent evaluation data where we
    ## know the outcomes (update() refits the lm model on train).
    aspe.linear[m] <- with(eval,mean((lwage-predict(update(lm.linear),
                                                newdata=eval))^2))
    aspe.quadint[m] <- with(eval,mean((lwage-predict(update(lm.quadint),
                                                newdata=eval))^2))
    aspe.mw[m]<-with(eval,mean((lwage-predict(update(lm.mw),newdata=eval))^2))
    ## Calling the semi- and nonparametric functions with the existing
    ## bandwidth object re-estimates the model on the updated training data.
    model.vc.boot <- npscoef(bws=model.vc$bws)
    aspe.vc[m]<-with(eval,mean((lwage-predict(model.vc.boot,newdata=eval))^2))
    model.pl.boot <- npplreg(bws=model.pl$bw)
    aspe.pl[m]<-with(eval,mean((lwage-predict(model.pl.boot,newdata=eval))^2))
    model.si.boot <- npindex(bws=model.si$bws)
    aspe.si[m]<-with(eval,mean((lwage-predict(model.si.boot,newdata=eval))^2))
    model.lc <- npreg(bws=bw.lc)
    aspe.lc[m] <- with(eval,mean((lwage-predict(model.lc,newdata=eval))^2))
    model.ll <- npreg(bws=bw.ll)
    aspe.ll[m] <- with(eval,mean((lwage-predict(model.ll,newdata=eval))^2))
    model.glp <- npglpreg(ghat$formula,cv="none",degree=ghat$degree,
                        bws=ghat$bws,data=train)
    aspe.glp[m] <- with(eval,mean((lwage-predict(model.glp,newdata=eval))^2))
}
## Conduct a paired t-test that the mean expected true ASPE for each
## model is equal versus the alternative that the kernel has a
## significantly lower expected true ASPE than the MW-optimal lm
## model.
## LC versus parametric and semiparametric.
p.lin <- t.test(aspe.lc,aspe.linear,alternative="less",paired=TRUE)$p.value
p.qint <- t.test(aspe.lc,aspe.quadint,alternative="less",paired=TRUE)$p.value
p.mw <- t.test(aspe.lc,aspe.mw,alternative="less",paired=TRUE)$p.value
p.vc <- t.test(aspe.lc,aspe.vc,alternative="less",paired=TRUE)$p.value
p.pl <- t.test(aspe.lc,aspe.pl,alternative="less",paired=TRUE)$p.value
```

Table 8.3: Apparent versus expected true model performance (lower values are preferred) and P-values from a test for equality of expected true performance. The cases considered are the kernel versus the parametric model and the kernel versus the semiparametric model. Rejection of the null implies that the kernel model has significantly lower mean ASPE on independent data.

	Apparent	Expected	Rank	P-GLP	P-LL	P-LC
Par-Linear	0.1682	0.1741	9	0	0.0000	0.0000
Par-Quad-Int	0.1474	0.1639	7	0	0.0000	0.2140
Par-MW	0.1561	0.1634	6	0	0.0000	0.3260
Semipar-VC	0.1470	0.1586	3	0	0.1218	1.0000
Semipar-PL	0.1544	0.1650	8	0	0.0000	0.0227
Semipar-SI	0.1540	0.1594	4	0	0.0327	1.0000
Nonpar-GLP	0.1419	0.1556	1	NA	NA	NA
Nonpar-LL	0.1372	0.1579	2	NA	NA	NA
Nonpar-LC	0.1319	0.1630	5	NA	NA	NA

```
p.si <- t.test(aspe.lc,aspe.si,alternative="less",paired=TRUE)$p.value
p.lc <- c(p.lin,p.qint,p.mw,p.vc,p.pl,p.si,NA,NA,NA)
## LL versus parametric and semiparametric.
p.lin <- t.test(aspe.ll,aspe.linear,alternative="less",paired=TRUE)$p.value
p.qint <- t.test(aspe.ll,aspe.quadint,alternative="less",paired=TRUE)$p.value
p.mw <- t.test(aspe.ll,aspe.mw,alternative="less",paired=TRUE)$p.value
p.vc <- t.test(aspe.ll,aspe.vc,alternative="less",paired=TRUE)$p.value
p.pl <- t.test(aspe.ll,aspe.pl,alternative="less",paired=TRUE)$p.value
p.si <- t.test(aspe.ll,aspe.si,alternative="less",paired=TRUE)$p.value
p.ll <- c(p.lin,p.qint,p.mw,p.vc,p.pl,p.si,NA,NA,NA)
## GLP versus parametric and semiparametric.
p.lin <- t.test(aspe.glp,aspe.linear,alternative="less",paired=TRUE)$p.value
p.qint <- t.test(aspe.glp,aspe.quadint,alternative="less",paired=TRUE)$p.value
p.mw <- t.test(aspe.glp,aspe.mw,alternative="less",paired=TRUE)$p.value
p.vc <- t.test(aspe.glp,aspe.vc,alternative="less",paired=TRUE)$p.value
p.pl <- t.test(aspe.glp,aspe.pl,alternative="less",paired=TRUE)$p.value
p.si <- t.test(aspe.glp,aspe.si,alternative="less",paired=TRUE)$p.value
p.glp <- c(p.lin,p.qint,p.mw,p.vc,p.pl,p.si,NA,NA,NA)
## Apparent performance.
apparent <- c(aspe.app.lin,aspe.app.qint,aspe.app.mw,
              aspe.app.vc,aspe.app.pl,aspe.app.si,
              aspe.app.glp,aspe.app.ll,aspe.app.lc)
## Expected true performance.
true <- c(mean(aspe.linear),mean(aspe.quadint),mean(aspe.mw),
          mean(aspe.vc),mean(aspe.pl),mean(aspe.si),
          mean(aspe.glp),mean(aspe.ll),mean(aspe.lc))
```

Table 8.3 reveals that all three nonparametric estimators outperform their parametric counterparts. Two out of the three semiparametric models outperform their parametric counterparts. In this application, the approach of Hall and Racine (2015) that jointly selects the polynomial degree and bandwidth vectors dominates its peers.

Problem Set

1. Consider the illustration in Section 8.2 of Chapter 8 that uses the wage1 data to estimate a partially linear model (Robinson, 1988). As outlined in the Practitioner's Corner, test the null hypothesis of a parametric linear specification against the alternative of a semiparametric partially linear model and comment on the results.

2. Consider the birthwt data that were used in the Practitioner's Corner of Chapter 4 to compare the performance of a parametric Logit model and a nonparametric approach. Re-run this simulation with the semiparametric Klein and Spady (1993) estimator added to the mix. Conduct $M = 10000$ splits of the data using $n_2 = 10$, as per the illustration in the Practitioner's Corner of Chapter 4. Comment on the semiparametric estimator's performance relative to that of its parametric and nonparametric counterparts.

Chapter 9

Conditional Variance Function Estimation

> The information is unavailable to the mortal man. (Paul Simon, *Slip Slidin' Away*)

9.1 Overview

A conditional moment that is particularly popular in time series settings is the *second conditional moment about the conditional mean* or the *conditional variance* function, denoted here by $\sigma^2(x)$. Let (Y_i, X_i) be a strictly stationary process whose marginal distribution is the same as that of (Y, X), and let $g(x) = \mathrm{E}(Y|X = x)$ and $\sigma^2(x) = \mathrm{Var}(Y|X = x)$. We write

$$Y_i = g(X_i) + \sigma(X_i)\varepsilon_i, \quad i = 1, \dots, n,$$

where $\sigma^2(x) > 0$ and $\varepsilon \sim (0, 1)$. For $Y_i = Y_t$ and $X_i = Y_{t-1}$, this is a nonlinear autoregressive conditional heteroskedastic (ARCH) time series model, and $\sigma^2(x)$ is the *volatility function* (Engle, 1982).

9.2 Local Linear Conditional Variance Function Estimation

Fan and Yao (1998) show that estimation of $\sigma^2(x)$ can be carried out by means of a two-stage approach. In the first stage, a local linear regression of Y_i on X_i delivers the (squared) residuals $\hat{r}_i = (Y_i - \hat{g}(X_i))^2$. The bandwidth selection procedure is exactly the same as in Chapter 6. In the second stage, one performs a local linear regression of the squared residuals on X_i (the authors' original consideration was limited to $q = 1$ continuous predictor). Even though $g(x)$ is unknown and must be estimated, with q continuous predictors, the bias of $\hat{g}(x)$ is of order $O(\sum_{s=1}^{q} \hat{h}_s^2)$, whereas its contribution to $\hat{\sigma}^2(x)$ is only of order $o(\sum_{s=1}^{q} \hat{h}_s^2)$.

Fan and Yao (1998) demonstrate that

$$\sqrt{n \prod_{j=1}^{q} h_j} \left(\hat{\sigma}^2(x) - \sigma^2(x) - \frac{\kappa_2}{2} \sum_{s=1}^{q} \frac{\partial^2 \hat{\sigma}^2(x)}{\partial x^2} h_s^2 \right) \rightarrow N(0, \Omega_x),$$

where $\Omega_x = \kappa^q \sigma^4(x) \gamma^2(x)/f(x)$, $\gamma^2(x) = \mathrm{E}\left((\epsilon^2 - 1)^2 | X = x\right)$, and $\epsilon = (Y - g(X))/\sigma(X)$.

Fan and Yao (1998) remark that "the bias and variance expressions given in Theorem 1 are exactly those which arise in the usual nonparametric regression analysis, considering the regression function to be $\sigma^2(x)$. In the bias of $\hat{\sigma}^2(x)$, the contribution from the error caused by estimating $g(x)$ is of smaller order than h^2, namely the order of the bias of $\hat{g}(x)$ itself. This permits us to use the optimal bandwidth to smooth $\hat{g}(x)$; no undersmoothing of $\hat{g}(x)$ is needed."

In the multivariate mixed-data case, the asymptotic distribution becomes

$$\sqrt{n \prod_{j=1}^{q} h_j} \left(\hat{\sigma}^2(x) - \sigma^2(x) - \frac{\kappa_2}{2} \sum_{s=1}^{q} \frac{\partial^2 \hat{\sigma}^2(x)}{\partial x^2} h_s^2 - \sum_{s=1}^{r} \hat{\lambda}_s D_s(x) \right)$$
$$\rightarrow N(0, \Omega_x),$$

where $D_s(x) = \sum_{v^d} (\mathbf{1}_s(v^d, x^d) \sigma^2(x^c, v^d) - \sigma^2(x)) f(x^c, v^d)$.

Given that Fan and Yao (1998) base their approach on the local linear estimator, $\hat{\sigma}^2(x)$ is not guaranteed to be positive (if they used the local constant estimator, it would be, since the local constant weights satisfy $0 \leq K(z)/\sum K(z) \leq 1$ and sum to one; on the other hand, the local linear weights can assume values outside of the range $[0, 1]$). To overcome this limitation, Chen et al. (2009a) propose a variant of the local linear estimator that (a) is guaranteed to be positive and (b) may perform better in the presence of heavy-tailed distributions. However, simulations reveal that in less heavy-tailed settings, this estimator may be less efficient than that of Fan and Yao (1998).

Rewrite $Y_i = g(X_i) + \sigma(X_i)\varepsilon_i$ as $\log r_i = \mathrm{v}(X_i) + \log(\varepsilon_i^2/d)$, where $\varepsilon \sim (0, 1)$, $r_i = (Y_i - g(X_i))^2$, $\mathrm{v}(X_i) = \log(d\sigma^2(x))$, and d satisfies $\mathrm{E}\left(\log(\varepsilon_i^2/d)\right) = 0$. To avoid taking $\log(0)$, Chen et al. (2009a) regress $\log(\hat{r}_i + n^{-1})$ on X_i using a local linear kernel-based method and denote the resulting estimates by $\hat{v}(X_i)$. They estimate d by $\hat{d} = \left(n^{-1} \sum_{i=1}^{n} \hat{r}_i \exp(-\hat{v}(X_i))\right)^{-1}$ and then compute $\tilde{\sigma}^2(X_i) = \exp(\hat{v}(X_i)) / \hat{d}$, $i = 1, \ldots, n$. Applications of both of these estimators appear in the Practitioner's Corner of this chapter.

An alternative would be to use the local linear estimator on the squared residuals $\hat{r}_i$ and impose a non-negativity constraint in the same manner as in Section 6.9 of Chapter 6. When the constraints are binding, this consistent estimator would be more efficient than the unconstrained alternative. This result is left as an exercise for the interested reader.

Related work includes Yu and Jones (2004), who consider a local-likelihood method, and Brown and Levine (2007) and Wang et al. (2008), who consider difference-based approaches. See also Su and Ullah (2013), who propose a nonparametric test for conditional heteroskedasticity based on a measure of nonparametric goodness-of-fit that is obtained from the local polynomial regression of the residuals from a parametric regression on a set of covariates.

9.3 Practitioner's Corner

9.3.1 A Simulated Illustration

We consider a simulated example that involves the estimators proposed by Fan and Yao (1998) and Chen et al. (2009a). Both approaches invoke the function npreg() in the R package np. As outlined above, the latter requires pre and post transformation of the squared residuals $\hat{r}$. The results are plotted in Figure 9.1.

```r
## Fan & Yao's (1998) estimator, trim negative values if they occur
## Chen, Cheng & Peng's (2009) estimator is always positive but my
## Monte Carlo simulations show it is less efficient for this DGP
set.seed(42)
n <- 1000
x <- sort(runif(n))
sigma.var <- 0.1*(.Machine$double.eps+2*pi*x)**2
dgp <- sin(2*pi*x)
y <- dgp + rnorm(n,sd=sqrt(sigma.var))
model <- npreg(y~x,regtype="ll")
r <- residuals(model)**2
## Fan and Yao's (1998) estimator with trimming if needed
var.fy <- fitted(npreg(r~x,regtype="ll"))
var.fy <- ifelse(var.fy<=0,.Machine$double.eps,var.fy)
## Chen, Cheng and Peng's (2009) estimator
log.r <- log(r+1/n) ## Avoids log(0)
V.hat <- fitted(npreg(log.r~x,regtype="ll"))
d.hat <- 1/mean(r*exp(-V.hat))
var.ccp <- exp(V.hat)/d.hat
plot(x,y,cex=.25,col="grey")
lines(x,dgp,col=1,lty=1,lwd=2)
lines(x,fitted(model),col=2,lty=2,lwd=2)
legend("topleft",c("$g(x)=\\sin(2\\pi x)$",
                   "$\\hat g(x)$"),
       col=1:2,
       lty=1:2,
       lwd=c(2,2),
       bty="n")
ylim=c(min(r),quantile(r,0.95))
plot(x,r,ylim=ylim,cex=.25,col="grey")
lines(x,sigma.var,col=1,lty=1,lwd=2)
```

```
lines(x,var.fy,col=2,lty=2,lwd=2)
lines(x,var.ccp,col=3,lty=4,lwd=2)
legend("topleft",c("$\\sigma^2(x)=(2\\pi x)^2/10$",
                    "Fan and Yao (1998)",
                    "Chen et al. (2009)"),
       col=1:3,
       lty=c(1,2,4),
       lwd=c(2,2,2),
       bty="n")
```

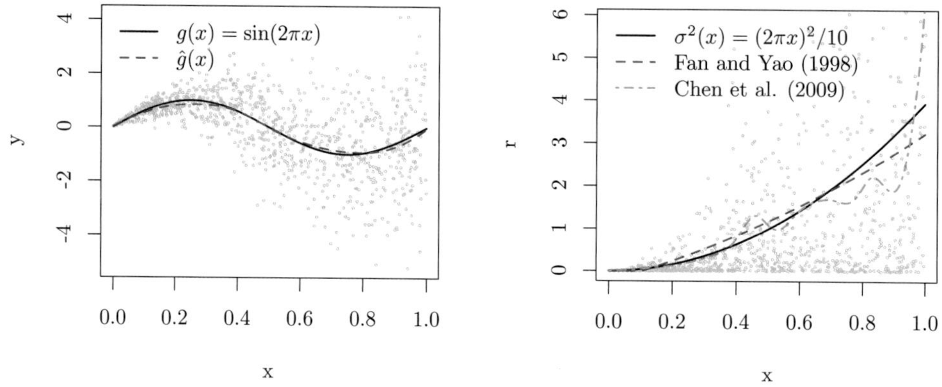

Figure 9.1: Fan and Yao's (1998) and Chen et al.'s (2009) conditional variance function estimators.

Problem Set

1. In Chapter 6, we considered the prediction of weekly percentage changes in US gas prices. Following the approaches of Fan and Yao (1998) and Chen et al. (2009a) that were outlined in the Practitioner's Corner of Chapter 9, model the conditional variance function where the squared residuals $\hat{r}_t$ are based on a local linear regression of Y_t on a single lag of Y_t, i.e., Y_{t-1}.

Part III

Appendices

Appendix A

Large and Small Orders of Magnitude and Probability

Sometimes, we will have to deal with deterministic or stochastic sequences that depend on a positive integer $n = 1, 2, \ldots$ (in our case, n will typically denote the sample size). We will also need to study the leading terms in power series approximations (in our case, Taylor expansions) and characterize the *order of magnitude* (or *order of probability*) of the remaining terms in these approximations. Given assumptions such as $h \to 0$ as $n \to \infty$ and $nh \to \infty$ as $n \to \infty$, certain expressions can then be written in a variety of ways. By way of illustration, we might write Bias $\hat{f}(x) = \frac{h^2}{2} f''(x) \kappa_2 = O(h^2) = o(1)$, which indicates that the bias is deterministic and goes to zero as $n \to \infty$, provided that $h \to 0$ as $n \to \infty$. We might also write $\hat{f}(x) - f(x) = O_p(h^2 + 1/\sqrt{nh}) = o_p(1)$, which establishes that the estimator $\hat{f}(x)$ is stochastic and the random difference $\hat{f}(x) - f(x)$ goes to zero *in probability* as $n \to \infty$, provided that $h \to 0$ as $n \to \infty$ and $nh \to \infty$ as $n \to \infty$.

It is therefore important to know how to interpret this notation, which is simply a shorthand characterization of the behaviour of terms in a power series. These orders convey information about conditions that are required for consistency and so forth, and typically involve parameters such as the bandwidth h that are under our control. We begin with orders that we express as *big O* and *small O* and that pertain to deterministic sequences.

A.1 Big and Small O Notation

Big and *small O notation* is a mathematical convention that conveys the limiting behaviour of a deterministic *function* when its argument tends towards ∞. It is commonly used to describe how closely a *finite series* such as a truncated Taylor expansion approximates a given function.

Definition A.1. Order of Magnitude: Big $O(\cdot)$ and Small $o(\cdot)$.

Let a_n denote a deterministic (i.e., non-stochastic) sequence of scalars that is indexed by the positive integers $n = 1, 2, \ldots$. For instance, the terms in the sequence might be given by $a_n = n + 2$ or $a_n = 1/n^2$.

- We write $a_n = O(1)$ if a_n remains bounded as $n \to \infty$, that is, if there exists some positive constant C and positive integer N such that $|a_n| \leq C$ for all $n \geq N$ (a_n is said to be *a bounded sequence*).

- We write $a_n = o(1)$ if $a_n \to 0$ as $n \to \infty$.

- Similarly, we write $a_n = O(b_n)$ if $a_n/b_n = O(1)$, or equivalently, if there exists some positive constant C and positive integer N such that $|a_n| \leq C|b_n|$ for all $n \geq N$.

- We write $a_n = o(b_n)$ if $a_n/b_n \to 0$ as $n \to \infty$.

In the example below, when we say that something holds for all n, we mean for all $n \in \mathbb{N}$, where $\mathbb{N} = \{1, 2, \ldots\}$ denotes the set of positive integers.

Example A.1.

i. If $a_n = n/(n+1)$, then $a_n = O(1)$ since $a_n \leq 1$ for all n.

ii. If $a_n = 10/(n+1)$, then $a_n = o(1)$ because $a_n \to 0$ as $n \to \infty$.

iii. If $a_n = n + 5$, $b_n = n$, then $a_n = O(b_n)$ because $a_n \leq 2b_n$ for $n \geq 5$, or $a_n \leq 6b_n$ for all n.

iv. If $a_n = 1/n$ and $b_n = 1/n^2$, then $b_n = o(a_n)$ because $b_n/a_n = (1/n) \to 0$ as $n \to \infty$.

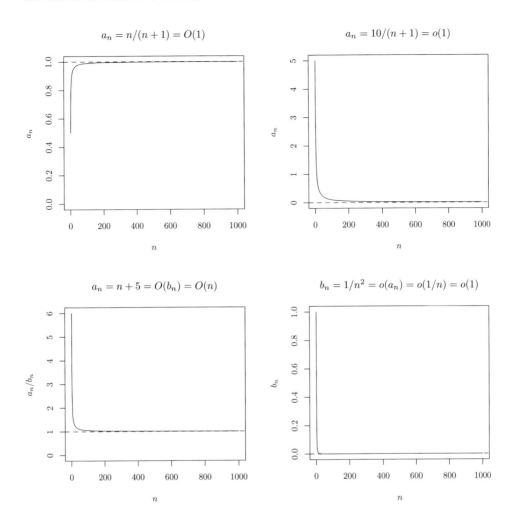

A.2   Big and Small O in Probability Notation

Big and *small O in probability* notation is used in statistics and it parallels the *big* and *small O notation* in mathematics defined above. Whereas *big* and *small O notation* serves to indicate convergence of deterministic sequences, *big* and *small O in probability* notation is used to signify *convergence in probability*,[1] that is, convergence of random variables.

Definition A.2. Order in Probability: Big $O_p(\cdot)$ and Small $o_p(\cdot)$

Let $\mathcal{X}_n$ denote a sequence of real, scalar-valued random variables indexed by the positive integers $n = 1, 2, \ldots$. Then $\mathcal{X}_n$ is said to be *bounded in*

---

[1]The essence of convergence in probability is that the probability of an *unusual* outcome becomes smaller and smaller as the sequence progresses. In statistics, an estimator is *consistent* if it converges in probability to the quantity being estimated. Formally, a sequence $\{\mathcal{X}_n\}$ of random variables converges in probability to X if, for all $\varepsilon > 0$, $\lim_{n \to \infty} \Pr\left(|\mathcal{X}_n - X| > \varepsilon\right) = 0$.

probability if, for every $\epsilon > 0$, there exists a positive constant C and a positive integer N such that

$$\Pr\left(|\mathcal{X}_n| > C\right) \leq \epsilon \qquad \text{(A.1)}$$

for all $n \geq N$, where ϵ is an arbitrarily small positive number.

That is, $\mathcal{X}_n$ is *bounded in probability* if, for any arbitrarily small positive number ϵ, we can always find a positive constant C such that for sufficiently large $n \in \mathbb{N}$, the probability of the absolute value of $\mathcal{X}_n$ being larger than C is less than ϵ.

Equation (A.1) can be equivalently written as

$$\Pr\left(|\mathcal{X}_n| \leq C\right) > 1 - \epsilon$$

for all $n \geq N$.

- We write $\mathcal{X}_n = O_p(1)$ to indicate that $\mathcal{X}_n$ is bounded in probability.
- We write $\mathcal{X}_n = o_p(1)$ if $\mathcal{X}_n \overset{p}{\to} 0$, where $\overset{p}{\to}$ denotes convergence in probability (i.e., $P\left(|\mathcal{X}_n| > \epsilon\right) \to 0$ as $n \to \infty$).
- Similarly, we write $\mathcal{X}_n = O_p(\mathcal{Y}_n)$ if $\mathcal{X}_n/\mathcal{Y}_n = O_p(1)$ and $\mathcal{X}_n = o_p(\mathcal{Y}_n)$ if $\mathcal{X}_n/\mathcal{Y}_n = o_p(1)$.
- Note that if $\mathcal{X}_n = o_p(1)$, then it must be true that $\mathcal{X}_n = O_p(1)$. However, if $\mathcal{X}_n = O_p(1)$, then $\mathcal{X}_n$ may not necessarily be $o_p(1)$. Also, if $\mathcal{X}_n = O(1)$, then $\mathcal{X}_n = O_p(1)$, that is, a bounded sequence is bounded in probability, but the converse is not true.

Example A.2. Let $\mathcal{X}_n = n^{-1}\sum_{i=1}^n X_i$, $n = 1, 2, \ldots$, denote the cumulative mean of a series of i.i.d. draws from the $N(\mu, 1)$ distribution, so that $(\mathcal{X}_1, \mathcal{X}_2, \mathcal{X}_3, \ldots) = (X_1/1, (X_1 + X_2)/2, (X_1 + X_2 + X_3)/3, \ldots)$.
  i. If $X_i \sim N(1, 1)$ and $\mathcal{X}_n = n^{-1}\sum_{i=1}^n X_i$, then $\mathcal{X}_n = O_p(1)$.
 ii. If $X_i \sim N(0, 1)$ and $\mathcal{X}_n = n^{-1}\sum_{i=1}^n X_i$, then $\mathcal{X}_n = o_p(1)$.

$X_i \sim N(1,1),\ \mathcal{X}_n = n^{-1}\sum_{i=1}^n X_i = O_p(1$ $X_i \sim N(0,1),\ \mathcal{X}_n = n^{-1}\sum_{i=1}^n X_i = o_p(1)$

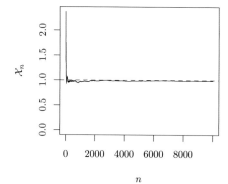
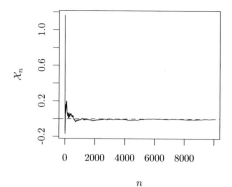

As is the case when we obtain the probability limit of a random variable by computing its limiting MSE (or r^{th} mean), we can also evaluate the order in probability of a random variable by calculating the order of its second moment (or the order of its rth mean).

Theorem A.1. *Let $\{\mathcal{X}_n\}_{n=1}^{\infty}$ be a sequence of real (possibly vector-valued) random variables, and let a_n and b_n be sequences of deterministic, non-negative numbers. Then*

    i. If $\mathrm{E}\,|\mathcal{X}_n| = O(a_n)$, then $\mathcal{X}_n = O_p(a_n)$.

    ii. If $\mathrm{E}(\mathcal{X}_n^2) = O(b_n)$, then $\mathcal{X}_n = O_p\left(b_n^{1/2}\right)$.

Example A.3.

    i. For any sequence of random variables $\{\mathcal{X}_n\}_{n=1}^{\infty}$, if $\mathrm{E}\,|\mathcal{X}_n| \leq C < \infty$ for all n, or if $\mathrm{E}(\mathcal{X}_n^2) \leq C < \infty$ for all n, then $\mathcal{X}_n = O_p(1)$. This follows directly from Theorem A.1.

    ii. Let $\mathcal{X}_n$ be a sequence of random variables with $\mathrm{E}(\mathcal{X}_n) = o(1)$ and $\mathrm{Var}(\mathcal{X}_n) = o(1)$. Then $\mathcal{X}_n = o_p(1)$. This follows from the fact that $\mathrm{E}(\mathcal{X}_n^2) = (\mathrm{E}(\mathcal{X}_n))^2 + \mathrm{Var}(\mathcal{X}_n) = o(1)$ and from Theorem A.1 ii.

Appendix B

R, RStudio, TeX, and Git

B.1 Installation of R and RStudio Desktop

The websites for **R** and **RStudio**, which must be installed separately, are https://www.r-project.org and https://www.rstudio.org, respectively. Successful installation of R and RStudio is the first order of business in order to follow the material that is presented in this textbook. To install these programs, simply click on the links above, navigate to the Download button/link, and follow the installation instructions for your operating system. Note that you will be installing the Desktop version of RStudio.

The underlying statistical engine for the data analysis in this text will be R, and we will be using the R front-end RStudio. RStudio automatically calls R when both are installed, and you will be using it extensively. You can run R in 'stand alone' mode, but RStudio is an integrated development environment that provides a much more intuitive front end for the user. RStudio is also platform independent, so the same menus/options will be available regardless of whether you use Linux, macOS, MS Windows, etc.

B.2 What Is R?

Quoting directly from the R website (https://www.r-project.org),

> R is a language and environment for statistical computing and graphics. It is a GNU project which is similar to the S language and environment which was developed at Bell Laboratories (formerly AT&T, now Lucent Technologies) by John Chambers and colleagues. R can be considered as a different implementation of S. There are some important differences, but much code written for S runs unaltered under R.
>
> R provides a wide variety of statistical (linear and nonlinear modeling, classical statistical tests, time series analysis, classification, clustering, ...) and graphical techniques, and is highly extensi-

ble. The S language is often the vehicle of choice for research in statistical methodology, and R provides an Open Source route to participation in that activity.

One of R's strengths is the ease with which well-designed publication-quality plots can be produced, including mathematical symbols and formulae where needed. Great care has been taken over the defaults for the minor design choices in graphics, but the user retains full control.

R is available as Free Software under the terms of the Free Software Foundation's GNU General Public License in source code form. It compiles and runs on a wide variety of UNIX platforms and similar systems (including FreeBSD and Linux), Windows and macOS.

See "What is R?" on the R website for even more details.

B.2.1   R in the News

There are two *New York Times* articles that provide some background information about R dated January 6, 2009, and January 8, 2009:

http://www.nytimes.com/2009/01/07/technology/business-computing/07program.html?pagewanted=all

http://bits.blogs.nytimes.com/2009/01/08/r-you-ready-for-r

B.2.2   Introduction to R

For an introduction to R, you have a range of options. One popular PDF source that some may find useful is titled "An Introduction to R" (https://cran.r-project.org/doc/manuals/r-release/R-intro.pdf). Or, having installed R, you can browse the help facilities that are available within R itself. You can also see the page Getting Help with R https://www.rstudio.org/docs/help_with_r on the RStudio website.

Here is a link to a set (90+) of *two-minute tutorial* videos that describe "how to do stuff in R in two minutes or less" (http://www.twotorials.com).

The following link is to R *Code School* (http://tryr.codeschool.com).

The following link is to a recent book on using R for data science (http://r4ds.had.co.nz).

The following link is for a Udacity course on exploratory data analysis in R (https://www.udacity.com/course/data-analysis-with-r--ud651).

B.2.3   Econometrics in R

A potentially useful site authored by Franz Mohr can be found at the following link (https://econometricswithr.wordpress.com).

B.3   What Is RStudio Desktop?

RStudio Desktop is an IDE (Integrated Development Environment) for R that you will install after you have installed R on your system. It is a platform-independent front-end for R that is very user-friendly, but recognize that you must **first install R on your system prior to invoking RStudio**. Although RStudio is not necessary in order to use R, it adds features that are unmatched elsewhere and allows the user to interact with the underlying statistical engine in a seamless fashion.

B.3.1   Introduction to RStudio

For a variety of documents that will assist with the use of RStudio, kindly see the RStudio FAQ (https://support.rstudio.com/hc/en-us/articles/200486548-Frequently-Asked-Questions) and the documents section of the RStudio website (https://www.rstudio.org/docs).

B.4   Installation of TeX

What is TeX?   Quoting directly from the link (http://www.ams.org/publications/what-is-tex),

> This powerful typesetting system was created by Donald Knuth of Stanford University. Authors and publishers worldwide use TeX to produce high-quality technical books and papers. TeX does a superior job of formatting complex mathematical expressions. The power of TeX lies in its ability to handle complicated technical text and displayed mathematical formulas. When coupled with a high-quality phototypesetter, TeX produces results equal in quality and appearance to those produced by the finest traditional typesetting systems.

In addition to the above programs, you also need to install TeX on your system. MS Windows users can install TeX from https://miktex.org, macOS users can install it from http://www.tug.org/mactex, and Linux users can install TeXLive from http://www.tug.org/texlive. This allows for sophisticated mathematics formatting via simple commands and enables you to directly generate publication-quality PDF files.

B.5   Installation of Git

What is Git?   Quoting directly from the link (https://git-scm.com/documentation),

> Git is a fast, scalable, distributed revision control system with an unusually rich command set that provides both high-level

operations and full access to internals.

You are encouraged to install Git (see https://git-scm.com), which can be used for version control and source code management from within RStudio.

Appendix C

Computational Considerations

One of the great ironies in this field is that the computationally burdensome nature of kernel methods makes researchers hesitant to apply them to the problems for which they are ideally suited, namely those involving an abundance of data such as large microdata panels, high frequency financial data, and the like.

The computational burden that is associated with kernel methods is rarely an issue when working with small datasets. However, in settings that involve moderate to large datasets, the computations that are required for data-driven bandwidth selection can easily get out of hand. There exist a number of approaches for reducing kernel methods' computational intensity, although at present, we are not aware of any that extend to a general kernel framework that includes unconditional and conditional density estimation, regression, and derivative estimation using a range of kernel functions and bandwidth selection methods that are suitable for both categorical and continuous data. We briefly discuss some of the approaches that currently exist, and draw attention to others that hold promise for a breakthrough in the continuing effort to allow for real-time kernel estimation on a typical personal computer.

C.1 Binning Methods

The use of *binning* has enhanced many estimators' computational appeal. This method entails *pre-binning* data on an equally spaced mesh and then applying a suitably modified estimator to the binned data. For instance, binning methods proposed by Scott (1985) involve the use of averaged shifted histograms (ASH) for smooth nonparametric density estimation. See also Scott and Sheather (1985), who investigate the accuracy of binning methods for kernel density estimation.

C.2   Transforms

Silverman (1986) (Pages 61–66) outlines how efficient computation of univariate density estimates can be carried out by means of fast Fourier transforms (FFT). This approach restricts estimation to a grid of points to further reduce run-time. Elgammal et al. (2003) discuss the use of the fast Gauss transform (FGT) for the efficient computation of kernel density estimates that involve a Gaussian kernel function.

C.3   Parallelism

Racine (2002) exploits both the parallel nature of most nonparametric methods and the availability of multiple processor computing environments to achieve a substantial reduction in run-time.

C.4   Multipole and Tree-Based Methods

Two recent developments in the areas of fast multipole methods and ball-trees hold promise for the enablement of almost real-time computation of kernel estimates. However, a significant amount of work remains to be done in order to extend these recent developments to a general kernel framework that goes beyond unconditional density estimation involving continuous data types only.

Multipole methods are common in potential field settings where a set of n points interact according to a particular potential function. The objective is to compute the field at arbitrary points (Greengard, 1988; Greengard and Strain, 1991). To speed up calculations, these algorithms exploit the fact that all computations must be made to only a certain degree of accuracy.

Trees consist of a set of linked grids that are built at different resolutions and hence they can be thought of as more powerful generalizations of a grid. This technique permits application of *divide-and-conquer* approaches that can integrate local information to obtain a global solution with explicitly defined point-wise precision (Gray and Moore, 2003). While *kd-trees* share the property of grid representations whose complexity grows exponentially with the dimension q, this is not so for *ball-trees*, which have been applied in settings that involve literally thousands of dimensions.

C.5   Computationally Efficient Kernel Estimation in R

The R package np supports a particular type of tree, while its MPI-enabled counterpart npRmpi supports both trees and parallelism. The use of tree *data structures* can lead to substantial reductions in run-time, provided that the optimal bandwidth is less than the range of a covariate's empirical support. The trees used in these packages are data structures that, for a given bandwidth, know which components of a kernel sum will be zero without computing their values. This can lead to large reductions in run-time when computing kernel sums using bounded support kernels.

Tree data structures can be enabled in the R packages np and npRmpi by setting the global option `options(np.tree=TRUE)` and by using bounded support kernels (e.g., by adding the option `ckertype="epanechnikov"` to the function call `npreg()` or `npregbw()`). You can then evaluate cross-validation run-time by wrapping the call to `npregbw()` in `system.time()`, with the routine being invoked both with and without trees. This is illustrated in the following code chunk (the last line of output by `summary(bw)` below also reports run-time).

```
require(np)
set.seed(42)
n <- 10000
x <- runif(n)
dgp <- cos(2*pi*x)
y <- dgp + rnorm(n,sd=0.5*sd(dgp))
options(np.tree=TRUE)
t.tree <- system.time(bw <- npregbw(y~x,ckertype="epanechnikov"))
summary(bw)
##
## Regression Data (10000 observations, 1 variable(s)):
##
## Regression Type: Local-Constant
## Bandwidth Selection Method: Least Squares Cross-Validation
## Formula: y ~ x
## Bandwidth Type: Fixed
## Objective Function Value: 0.1271 (achieved on multistart 1)
##
## Exp. Var. Name: x Bandwidth: 0.01148 Scale Factor: 0.2491
##
## Continuous Kernel Type: Second-Order Epanechnikov
## No. Continuous Explanatory Vars.: 1
## Estimation Time: 5.278 seconds
options(np.tree=FALSE)
t.notree <- system.time(bw <- npregbw(y~x,ckertype="epanechnikov"))
summary(bw)
##
## Regression Data (10000 observations, 1 variable(s)):
##
## Regression Type: Local-Constant
## Bandwidth Selection Method: Least Squares Cross-Validation
## Formula: y ~ x
## Bandwidth Type: Fixed
## Objective Function Value: 0.1271 (achieved on multistart 1)
##
## Exp. Var. Name: x Bandwidth: 0.01148 Scale Factor: 0.2491
```

```
##
## Continuous Kernel Type: Second-Order Epanechnikov
## No. Continuous Explanatory Vars.: 1
## Estimation Time: 49.64 seconds
## Run-time ratio (trees versus no trees)
t.tree[1]/t.notree[1]
## user.self
##      0.1103
```

In this illustration that involves one predictor, run-time is reduced from 49.9 seconds to 5.5 seconds. This represents a 89.0% reduction in run-time. Note that the minor discrepancy between the run-time reported in `summary(bw)` and that from the `system.time()` calls is due to overhead associated with invoking the function `npregbw()`.

It turns out that the curse of dimensionality can morph into a blessing when conducting cross-validation on multivariate objects using bounded support kernels and trees. The multivariate product kernel evaluates to zero when the univariate kernel associated with the *smallest* entry in the bandwidth vector equals zero, taking the scale of the covariate into consideration. In cases where the optimal bandwidths are less than the range of the covariates, the reduction in run-time can improve as the number of covariates increases. This is shown in the following code chunk (compare the run-time ratio below that involves two predictors with that above that involves only one).

```
require(np)
set.seed(42)
n <- 10000
x1 <- runif(n)
x2 <- runif(n)
dgp <- cos(pi*x1)*sin(pi*x2)
y <- dgp + rnorm(n,sd=0.5*sd(dgp))
options(np.tree=TRUE)
t.tree <- system.time(bw <- npregbw(y~x1+x2,ckertype="epanechnikov"))
summary(bw)
##
## Regression Data (10000 observations, 2 variable(s)):
##
## Regression Type: Local-Constant
## Bandwidth Selection Method: Least Squares Cross-Validation
## Formula: y ~ x1 + x2
## Bandwidth Type: Fixed
## Objective Function Value: 0.06449 (achieved on multistart 1)
##
## Exp. Var. Name: x1 Bandwidth: 0.05381 Scale Factor: 0.8591
## Exp. Var. Name: x2 Bandwidth: 0.03181 Scale Factor: 0.5101
##
## Continuous Kernel Type: Second-Order Epanechnikov
## No. Continuous Explanatory Vars.: 2
## Estimation Time: 42.2 seconds
options(np.tree=FALSE)
t.notree <- system.time(bw <- npregbw(y~x1+x2,ckertype="epanechnikov"))
```

```
summary(bw)
##
## Regression Data (10000 observations, 2 variable(s)):
##
## Regression Type: Local-Constant
## Bandwidth Selection Method: Least Squares Cross-Validation
## Formula: y ~ x1 + x2
## Bandwidth Type: Fixed
## Objective Function Value: 0.06449 (achieved on multistart 1)
##
## Exp. Var. Name: x1 Bandwidth: 0.05381 Scale Factor: 0.8591
## Exp. Var. Name: x2 Bandwidth: 0.03181 Scale Factor: 0.5101
##
## Continuous Kernel Type: Second-Order Epanechnikov
## No. Continuous Explanatory Vars.: 2
## Estimation Time: 572.3 seconds
## Run-time ratio (trees versus no trees)
t.tree[1]/t.notree[1]
## user.self
##    0.0741
```

In this illustration that involves two predictors, run-time is reduced from 572.6 seconds to 42.4 seconds, which represents a 92.6% reduction in run-time.

If, in addition to trees, we exploit the existence of multiple processors for coarse grained applications (i.e., those involving a large number of observations), then run-time can be further reduced. With large datasets, run-time is reduced by a factor of roughly $1/(\# \text{ processors})$, modulo overhead. By way of illustration, if we invoke both trees and parallelism, the example above that involves two predictors could be executed in just over 5.3 seconds on an 8-core computer. This is not an uncommon configuration as of the penning of this book, which was compiled using 1 core running on an 8-core Intel Core i7 processor. For the two-predictor example, exploiting the presence of 8 cores could reduce run-time by up to 99.1% relative to the no-tree serial benchmark (i.e., from 9.54 minutes to just over 5.3 seconds).

However, one caveat is in order. The C routines in the R package npRmpi rely on the MPI interface, which is an industry standard. You need to install OpenMPI and be familiar with executing parallel jobs via mpirun. You also need to modify the R code that invokes routines in the np package so that it can be run using the npRmpi package. This is a non-trivial task, and requires you to be fairly proficient in computing. Of course, one can always substitute patience for parallelism.

Appendix D

R Markdown for Assignments

D.1 Source Code (R Markdown) for This Document

Link to R Markdown Code for This Document (https://socialsciences.mcmaster.ca/racinej/768/files/Rmarkdown_assignments.Rmd)

D.2 R, RStudio, TeX, and Git

In this textbook, we will be using R, a language and environment for statistical computing and graphics (see http://r-project.org), and RStudio, an integrated development environment for R (see http://rstudio.com). Both of these programs must be installed on your computer. These powerful, free, and open source programs allow you to work anywhere and anytime you wish, rather than being tethered to a lab running closed, licensed proprietary software. In addition, we will be using TeX (MS Windows (https://miktex.org), macOS (http://www.tug.org/mactex), Linux (http://www.tug.org/texlive)) and optionally Git (https://git-scm.com); TeX allows you to generate PDF files and typeset mathematics, while Git is used for version control.

D.3 What Is R Markdown?

This is an R Markdown document. R Markdown is a simple formatting syntax for authoring HTML, PDF, and MS Word documents in RStudio. For more details on using R Markdown, see http://rmarkdown.rstudio.com.

R Markdown allows you to conduct *reproducible research*; that is, others may readily verify your findings and build upon them since your code and narrative are integrated into a single R Markdown file. For your viewing pleasure, see A reproducibility horror story! (http://blog.revolutionanalytics.com/2016/08/a-reproducibility-horror-story.html)

D.4 Creating a New R Markdown Document in RStudio

From within RStudio, navigate to the menu **File -> New File -> R Markdown**.

D.5 Including R Results in Your R Markdown Document

To include results in your R Markdown document that have been generated from your R commands, click on the **Insert** button within the **Editor** pane (upper left by default) in RStudio and select **R** from the pull-down menu. You may then write your code inside the "chunk" that is inserted. If you want to execute the code inside the chunk, simply click on the **Run** button and select the appropriate run argument.

You can also embed an R code chunk manually. Simply write a code chunk that begins with three backticks followed by an r in braces, and that ends with three backticks, as illustrated in the following:

```
```{r foo}
require(MASS)
```
```

D.6 Reading Data from a URL

R can read data from a URL which, in certain instances, saves you from having to manually download the data:

```
foo <- "https://socialsciences.mcmaster.ca/racinej/768/files/attend.RData"
course <- read.table(foo)
## attach() makes the names of the data `course' known to R functions (scope)
attach(course)
```

You can summarize data in your R Markdown document:

```
summary(course)
##      grade           attend
##  Min.   : 29.0   Min.   :0.00
##  1st Qu.: 57.5   1st Qu.:2.00
##  Median : 68.0   Median :4.00
##  Mean   : 67.8   Mean   :3.51
##  3rd Qu.: 80.5   3rd Qu.:5.00
##  Max.   :105.0   Max.   :6.00
```

D.7 Including Plots

You can also embed plots in your R Markdown document:

```
plot(attend,grade,
    ylab="2B03 Grade, Fall 2013",
    xlab="Number of Times Present in Class When Assignments/Exams Returned",
    main="2B03 Grades and Class Attendance")
```

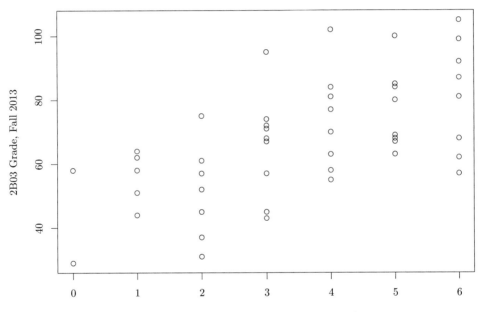

Click on the link for this document (https://socialsciences.mcmaster.ca/racinej/768/files/Rmarkdown_assignments.Rmd) and scroll down to view the code for this plot.

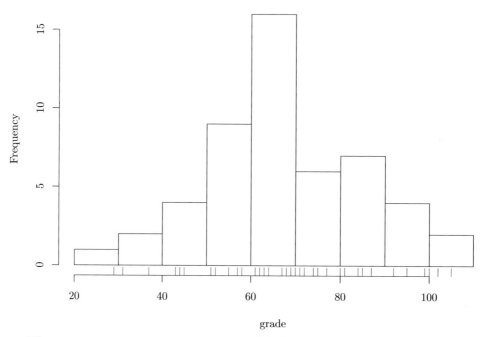

Histogram of grade

The `echo = FALSE` parameter was added to the code chunk to prevent printing of the R code that generated the plot. Note that grades > 100 are possible because bonus marks were awarded to students who used R Markdown to generate their assignments. Click on the link to the R Markdown code for this document (https://socialsciences.mcmaster.ca/racinej/768/files/Rmarkdown_assignments.Rmd) and scroll down to view the code for this plot.

D.8   Including Bulleted and Numbered Lists

Making lists in R Markdown is simple, provided that you pay close attention to the Markdown convention:

- Bulleted lists are created by starting the line with a dash
    - To create sub lists, indent four spaces and then start with a dash
      If you want text to appear below a list item, create a blank line and then indent an *additional* four spaces beyond the spacing of the previous item
- Next item
1. Numbered lists start with a number followed by a period
    (i) Sub items are indented four spaces and start with, e.g., (i) (or (a) if you prefer)
       If you want text to appear below a list item, create a blank line and then indent an *additional* four spaces beyond the spacing of

the previous item

2. Next item

See Troubleshooting and Tips below for further information.

D.9 Including Tables

Creating tables is straightforward, as the following two examples demonstrate:

Table Header	Second Header	Third Header
Table Cell 1	Cell 2	Cell 3
Cell 4	Cell 5	Cell 6

Table D.2: Here's the caption. It, too, may span multiple lines.

Centred D Header	efault Aligned	Right L Aligned	eft Aligned
First	row	12.0	Example of a row that spans multiple lines.
Second	row	5.0	Here's another one. Note the blank line between rows.

For guidance on creating the above table and more sophisticated tables using R Markdown, see the link for creating tables in Markdown (http://pandoc.org/MANUAL.html#tables).

D.10 Including Verbatim (i.e., Freeform) Text

You can include text that appears *exactly* as you type it in your document by enclosing the code chunk with three backticks at the top and bottom:

```
This        is verbatim x1        x2
        x3
```

D.11 Typesetting Mathematics

R Markdown supports mathematics typesetting using TEX/LATEX. It also supports BibTeX for references. You can type math inline using the standard approach, namely by enclosing your TEX equation commands in single dollar signs. For instance, $\hat\beta=(X'X)^{-1}X'y$ will produce $\hat{\beta} = (X'X)^{-1}X'y$ in a paragraph. To have your TEX equation appear

on a separate line, simply enclose it in double dollar signs. For instance,
`$$\hat\beta=(X'X)^{-1}X'y$$` will produce

$$\hat{\beta} = (X'X)^{-1}X'y.$$

Alternatively, you can use `\(` and `\)` to enclose your TeX equation commands instead of single dollar signs. You can also use `\[` and `\]` instead of double dollar signs.

Whether rendering your final document in HTML, PDF, MS Word, etc., the translation of the math that you authored using TeX/LaTeX will be handled transparently when you knit your document via the underlying universal document converter *pandoc* (http://pandoc.org).

For more sophisticated things like cross-referencing, automatic equation numbering, and the like, you can use R bookdown, which is a superset of R Markdown. It extends R Markdown in these and other directions (see https://bookdown.org/yihui/bookdown/).

The following link will give you some helpful pointers for typesetting mathematics using TeX/LaTeX: (https://en.wikibooks.org/wiki/LaTeX/Mathematics).

D.12   Flexible Document Creation

It is worth noting that your document does not have to be related to the R language in order to use Markdown. It can use other computing languages such as C++, SQL, and Python, and it does not even need to involve statistical analysis of any kind. For instance, you could just as easily use R Markdown to write a story, a book, or a collection of poems.

D.13   Knitting Your R Markdown Document

When you click on the **Knit** button within RStudio, which should appear in the top left pane by default, a document will be generated that includes both content and the output of any embedded R code chunks.

D.14   Printing Your Document

- You can **spell-check** your document by navigating the menu **Edit -> Check Spelling**
- The default R Markdown output format is HTML (http://www. simplehtmlguide.com/whatishtml.php). To generate an HTML document, simply click on the **Knit** button (you might need to first select the **Knit to HTML** option on the pull down menu associated with the **Knit** button). Next, click on the **Open in Browser** button in the

viewer that opens, which will open the document in your web browser. Finally, print your document using your web browser's print facilities. The HTML document will remain in your working directory.

- If you have Microsoft Word installed on your system, you can pull down the menu associated with the **Knit** button and select the **Knit to Word** option. If all goes well, you will be presented with a Word document that you can print using Word's print facilities. The Word document will remain in your working directory.

- After you install TEX (http://www.ams.org/publications/what-is-tex) on your system, you can pull down the menu associated with the **Knit** button and select the **Knit to PDF** option. You can then print using your PDF viewer's print facilities. The PDF document will remain in your working directory.

D.15 Troubleshooting and Tips

1. If you are having trouble with TEX, R, RStudio, or Git after you have installed them, one reason for this could be that you did not use the default paths for the installation. If you overrode the defaults and experience trouble, try properly removing and reinstalling, but *this time using the defaults*.

2. Authoring in Markdown can take a bit of getting used to, particularly when making bulleted or numbered lists.

   - You must start a numbered list in column 1 with, e.g., the number 1 followed by a period, i.e., 1.

   - If you want text, an R code chunk, or anything else to line up properly under 1., then everything on the lines that follow *must* be indented 4 spaces (i.e., start in column 5)

   - If you use the tab key to insert spaces, note that a tab takes you only 2 spaces by default. Hence you either will need to tab twice to get 4 spaces or you can change the default by navigating **Tools -> Global Options -> Code -> Tab Width** and substituting 4 for 2.

   - If you have a sublist (e.g., after 1., you wish (a) to be properly indented using Markdown), then your (a) must start in column 5. And again, if you want text, an R code chunk, or anything else to line up properly under (a), then everything *must* be indented another 4 spaces (i.e., start in column 9).

   - Note that you can select multiple lines of code and then hit tab once or twice to indent all of the lines that you have selected

   - If you have an item or subitem (e.g., 1. or (a)) with no text appearing after it, then indented R code chunks that follow on the next line might not display properly (e.g., where you have

indented the entire chunk including the backticks). One simple
solution is to add some descriptive text like 1. `Answer` and `(a)`
`R Code`.

- If you create a list and e.g., `(a)` does not appear, then it could
  be because you have text following `(a)` that has no space, as in
  `(a)my text` - a space is needed
- Spacing and linebreaks are needed for proper formatting of R
  Markdown documents, so if things do not render as you expect,
  try adding e.g., a blank line etc.

3. When knitting HTML code, the default is to open a new window to
   show the output preview. If instead you want the output preview to
   appear in the viewer pane (lower right corner of RStudio by default),
   then select **Tools -> Global Options -> R Markdown -> Show
   Output Preview in Viewer Pane**

4. Sometimes things get messed up (e.g., your code looks fine but is
   producing an error) and you need to clean up intermediate files that
   were generated while knitting. To do so, click on the triangle on the
   knit icon in the editor pane (upper left by default) and clear the knitr
   cache, i.e., **knitr -> Clear Knitr Cache**.

5. Sometimes people have old versions of R and RStudio lingering on their
   system from previous courses and things are not working as expected.
   It never hurts to make sure that you have the latest versions installed.
   You should also update all packages on your system via the update
   button on the **Packages -> Update** tab, which appears in the lower
   right pane by default.

6. Note that if you use some math environments, e.g.,
   `\begin{align}\beta&=1\\ \alpha&=0\end{align}` and so forth,
   you retain HTML and PDF compatibility but you may lose MS Word
   compatibility. To regain MS Word compatibility (and lose PDF but
   still retain HTML compatibility), R Markdown needs a hint. If you enclose your `\begin{align}\beta&=1\\ \alpha&=0\end{align}`
   in double dollar signs, as in `$$\begin{align}\beta&=1\\
   \alpha&=0\end{align}$$`, this appears to be sufficient.

7. Your R Markdown file needs to have the extension `Rmd` (don't create
   arbitrarily named files)

8. If you are having difficulty reading data files that are located in a
   different directory than your R Markdown file, simply place the `Rmd`
   file and the data file in the same directory

   - Alternatively, after changing your working directory (**Session ->
     Set Working Directory**), type `getwd()` within the *console* pane
     (lower left by default). This should reveal the directory where your
     file is located (e.g., `"/foo"`). You can then enter `setwd("/foo")`
     in the line just above your call to `read.table()`.

- Alternatively, append this directory to the call where you read the data; for instance, instead of `read.table("filename")`, use `read.table("/foo/filename")`
- For the hard core among you, you could modify the `root directory` by adding an R code chunk `opts_knit$set(root.dir = "/foo")` at the beginning of your document

9. Chunks of R code begin and end with three backticks, and there *must* be a blank line between two consecutive chunks of R code. That is, you can't have three backticks at the end of one code chunk *touch* the three backticks on the next line.

10. Your R code must reside within an R code chunk in order for it to be appropriately processed. Otherwise, R Markdown will think it is text. See the **Insert** button in the editor pane, which is located in the top left by default.

11. If a hint is provided and is preceded by a question mark, as in `?fivenum`, then this means to enter `?fivenum` in the console, which will pull up help for the R function `fivenum`

12. Typeset mathematics is *not* to be placed inside of R code chunks (it will generate an error since the dollar sign has a special meaning in R), nor are R Markdown tables and other such things

13. The default editor settings are to *insert matching parentheses and quotes*. If you find that this intrudes on your workflow, you can disable it via **Tools -> Global Options -> Code** and by unchecking **Insert matching parens/quotes**.

14. Markdown does not like spaces that immediately follow display math, so you ought to use `$$\alpha$$` rather than `$$ \alpha $$`

Appendix E

Practicum

> In theory, there is no difference between theory and practice. In practice there is. (Yogi Berra)

E.1 Overview

The practicums below are tailored to novice R users who wish to become familiar with nonparametric routines that are part of base R and the R package np (Hayfield and Racine, 2008). These practicums are intended for self-study and, given their applied nature, they stand separate from the problem sets and the Practitioner's Corner examples that appear at the end of each chapter. In what follows, virtually all of the necessary code is provided to the reader, who may pick and choose the topics that best suit their interests. Rather than attempting to provide encyclopedic coverage of the subject matter, we restrict attention to a handful of topics that are likely to be of interest to the majority of readers. We encourage you to work through these practical exercises, study the code and function options, and make any modifications that suit your needs.

There are two main differences between the practicums below and those that appear in the Practitioner's Corner at the end of each chapter. The first is that the results of the code chunks in the Practitioner's Corner are presented alongside the code itself, whereas execution of the code below is left to the reader. The second difference is that some of the subject matter of the practicums in this appendix does not fit neatly into any of the chapters of the main text, yet it should prove to be quite useful for certain tasks (see, e.g., the sections pertaining to the function `npksum()`).

E.2 Getting Started with R

The goal of this practicum is to get you up to speed with certain aspects of working with R. It is not assumed that you are already familiar with R,

RStudio, or nonparametric estimation. These practicums ought to enable you to work with your own data in R almost immediately, regardless of the format in which it is stored.

E.2.1 Reading Datasets Created by Other Software Programs

One of the appealing features of R is its ability to work with data that is stored in binary formats that have been generated by *foreign* software such as Stata, SPSS, SAS, and Minitab. Furthermore, we can read data from a URL and thereby avoid having to download and store the file locally, which can be quite helpful in some cases.

- The functionality for reading data in a variety of formats is contained in the foreign library. After you have installed the foreign package via `install.packages("foreign")` or the RStudio install pane, which you need only do once, load it and see the help file for, e.g., `read.dta` by typing `?read.dta`. You load the foreign library as follows:
  ```
  library(foreign)
  ```

  Having accomplished this, you may type `?read.dta` in the RStudio or R console.

- Let's do two things at once, namely (a) read a binary Stata file into R and (b) do so from a URL:
  ```
  foo <- "http://www.principlesofeconometrics.com/stata/mroz.dta"
  mydat <- read.dta(foo)
  ```

- You can see the names of the variables in the object `mydat` and obtain a summary of one of the variables as follows:
  ```
  names(mydat)
  summary(wage)
  ```

- Oops! You have encountered one of the most common mistakes in R. Scope[1] is important, and in order to access data in the object `mydat`, you must first attach it. Try the following:
  ```
  attach(mydat)
  summary(wage)
  ```

- If you currently work with data that is stored in the binary format of a non-R software platform (e.g., Stata, SPSS, SAS, Minitab, etc.), try to read and attach the data in R under the expectation that it is supported. It would be beneficial for you to do this right away since you

---

[1]Scope refers to the visibility of variables, that is, which parts of your program can see or use a variable. Normally, every variable has a global scope; however, if the variable resides in a data object, it does not. This is useful when working with multiple data objects in the same program that may have variable names in common. To endow it with global scope, you *attach* the data object. Every part of your program will then be able to access variables that reside in the data object.

will be brought up to speed on how to replicate in the R environment something that you are currently doing on another platform.

At this stage, you should be able to read and begin to analyze data in R, which is an open, free, and extensible platform. You have now been freed from the obligation to use a closed, proprietary system for which payment is required (why buy the cow when you can get the milk for free?). If the need arises, you can also write data in the same closed format (see `?write.dta`). Note from `?read.dta` and `?write.dta` that you may only be able to read/write some versions of Stata binary files.[2]

E.2.2 Nonparametric Estimation of Density Functions

The questions below make use of a χ^2 random variable with $\nu = 5$ degrees of freedom.

- What is the mean and variance of a χ^2 random variable with $\nu = 5$ degrees of freedom?
- Simulate a sample X of length 10^6, and compute the mean and variance of this sample using

```
set.seed(42)
x <- rchisq(10^6,df=5)
mean(x)
var(x)
```

  How do the mean and variance of the sample match up with your theoretical mean $E(X)$ and variance $\text{Var}(X)$? If they differ, why is this so?

- Plot the parametric population density function $f(x)$; you must first generate a sequence `x.seq` that ranges from 0 to 25 and then use this to evaluate the parametric density via the R function `dchisq()`.

```
x.seq <- seq(0,25,length=100)
myden <- dchisq(x.seq,df=5)
plot(x.seq,myden,type="l")
```

  Using R's `density()` function, superimpose a nonparametric Rosenblatt-Parzen kernel density estimate on the parametric density above via something like

```
plot(x.seq,myden,xlab="x",ylab="f(x)",type="l")
lines(density(x),col=2,lty=2)
legend("topright",c("Parametric","Nonparametric"),
       col=1:2,lty=1:2,bty="n")
```

- The R function `density()` is very beneficial for Rosenblatt-Parzen kernel density estimation. It is blazingly fast because it relies on a

---

[2] For some bizarre reason, certain closed proprietary systems seem to continuously change the structure of their binary read/write calls. Perhaps this is to encourage (read *force*) users to update? In any event, you should be able to save your data file in an earlier format within Stata and get around such *planned obsolescence*.

Fast Fourier Transform and uses plug-in bandwidth selectors. Note, however, that it is limited to scalar x and does not support categorical kernel functions.

Let's replicate the above using the **non**parametric **u**nconditional **dens**ity function npudens in the R package np. You must first install the np package via `install.packages("np")` or via the RStudio install pane. You may then load the library via `library(np)`. Note that if you don't want screen I/O to be produced by functions in this library, you can disable it with the command `options(np.messages=FALSE)`. This will prevent I/O such as `Multistart 1 of 1 |` from appearing on your screen while routines are executing.

```
require(np)
f <- npudens(tdat=x,edat=x.seq,bws=bw.nrd0(x))
plot(x.seq,myden,xlab="x",ylab="f(x)",type="l")
lines(x.seq,fitted(f),col=2,lty=2)
legend("topright",c("Parametric","Nonparametric"),
       col=1:2,lty=1:2,bty="n")
```

The options `tdat` and `edat` refer to *training* and *evaluation* data. We typically invoke the function via the formula interface that is discussed below. Note that `bw.nrd0` is the default plug-in bandwidth selector that is used by the R function `density()`.

E.3   Introduction to the R Package np: Working with npudens()

Many functions in R, including npudens(), support what is known as the *formula* interface. Furthermore, it is sometimes desirable to separate data-driven bandwidth selection from the task of estimating the density itself. In the np() package, this is accomplished by making available to the user the separate functions npudensbw(), which handles bandwidth selection, and npudens(), which handles density estimation. The authors of the np() package have *overloaded* most functions, that is, they have embedded a lot of the functionality that you may only occasionally use, and they have also tried to guess the intended usage where appropriate.

- Here, we consider the formula interface for least squares cross-validated bandwidth selection, and then feed the resulting bandwidth object bw to the function that computes the density estimate; this is achieved by first invoking npudensbw() and then npudens().

```
set.seed(42)
x <- rchisq(1000,df=10)
bw <- npudensbw(~x,bwmethod="cv.ls")
summary(bw)
f <- npudens(bw)
summary(f)
```

```
plot(f)
```

The tilde ~ is part of the R formula interface. In general, the left-hand-side variables in one's model appear to the left of the tilde, while the right-hand-side variables appear to the right of the tilde. For unconditional density estimation, there are no left-hand-side variables, hence the ~x formula. A univariate or bivariate linear regression model might be estimated via `lm(y~x)` or `lm(y~x1+x2)`, respectively, while nonparametric estimation of a bivariate regression model might be carried out using `npreg(y~x1+x2)`. Note that `lm(y~x1+x2)` imposes a linear additive structure on the model, whereas `npreg(y~x1+x2)` does not. The formula interface in the latter instance merely serves to identify the predictor variables x1 and x2.

- Although in the above example, we invoked two functions, `npudensbw` and `npudens`, we could have performed both of these actions in a single step. That is, if you don't provide a bandwidth in your call to `npudens`, the arguments that you provide to `npudens` will be passed along to `npudensbw`, which is called in the background. Note that, when you call `npudens()` directly, the bandwidth object will be stored as `foo$bws`, where `foo` is the name of your `npudens()` object. As an aside, many R objects contain sub-objects that can be accessed in this manner (i.e., `foo$bws`); to see a list of named sub-objects invoke `names(foo)` which will list all such sub-objects (strictly speaking, you are *extracting elements by name from a named list* via `foo$bws`).

```
f <- npudens(~x,bwmethod="cv.ls")
summary(f$bws)
summary(f)
plot(f)
```

- We might add asymptotic confidence bands to the plot (`plot` calls `npplot` - see `?npplot` for details).

```
plot(f,plot.errors.method="asymptotic",plot.errors.style="band")
```

- We might also change the kernel function from the default Gaussian (`ckertype="gaussian"`) to, say, the Epanechnikov (`ckertype="epanechnikov"`).

```
f <- npudens(~x,ckertype="epanechnikov",bwmethod="cv.ls")
summary(f$bws)
summary(f)
plot(f)
```

- We might wish to change the order of the kernel function from the default 2 (`ckerorder=2`) to, say, 4 (`ckerorder=4`).

```
f <- npudens(~x,ckerorder=4,bwmethod="cv.ls")
summary(f$bws)
summary(f)
plot(f)
```

- We might even try a non-fixed bandwidth by specifying the adaptive nearest neighbour option in the call to `npudens()`.

```
f <- npudens(~x,bwtype="adaptive_nn",bwmethod="cv.ls")
summary(f$bws)
summary(f)
plot(f)
```

As you can see, there are many features of the unconditional density estimation function in the np package that can be modified if the need arises. See `?npudensbw` and `?npudens` for further details. This is also a well-timed opportunity to become familiar with the flow of R's help system.[3]

E.3.1   Introduction to the `npksum()` Function

Sometimes, you may need to compute kernel-weighted sums in order to construct a semiparametric or a nonparametric estimator. The function `npksum()` in the R package np allows you to compute kernel sums of various types. Given that the function makes calls to compiled C code, it has the advantage of being fairly fast. Many functions in the np package make calls either to `npksum()` or to the C code that underlies it. If you wish to implement a novel kernel-based technique that does not exist in any package, this function is of enormous value. By making calls to `npksum()`, you can generate efficient prototypes very quickly and easily.

- You can use `npksum()` to compute the Rosenblatt-Parzen density estimate that was considered above. Let us now do so for the sake of illustration. Recall that the density estimate $\hat{f}(x)$ is given by

$$\hat{f}(x) = \frac{1}{nh} \sum_{i=1}^{n} K((x - X_i)/h).$$

```
set.seed(42)
n <- 1000
x <- sort(rchisq(n,df=10))
h <- bw.nrd0(x)
f.hat <- npksum(~x,bws=h)$ksum/(n*h)
plot(x,f.hat,type="l")
```

Note that plotting the resulting density with a line requires that we first sort the data.

- For comparison purposes, you could superimpose the estimate that is given by the `density()` function in R (the two estimates ought to be identical).

---

[3]The flow of these help pages is **Description, Usage, Arguments, Details, Value, Usage, Issues, Examples**. Thus, you can always view **Examples** at the end of a help page, find out what values a function returns in **Value**, and so on.

```
set.seed(42)
n <- 1000
x <- sort(rchisq(n,df=10))
h <- bw.nrd0(x)
f.hat <- npksum(~x,bws=h)$ksum/(n*h)
plot(x,f.hat,type="l")
lines(density(x),col=2,lty=2)
```

- If you wanted to compute and plot the kernel function, you could do so using `npksum()`.

```
Z <- seq(-sqrt(5),sqrt(5),length=100)
par(mfrow=c(2,2),mar=c(5,4,4,2)+0.1)
plot(Z,ylab="kernel",npksum(txdat=0,exdat=Z,bws=1,ckertype="epanechnikov",
ckerorder=2)$ksum,type="l",main="Epanechnikov [order = 2]")
plot(Z,ylab="kernel",npksum(txdat=0,exdat=Z,bws=1,ckertype="epanechnikov",
ckerorder=4)$ksum,type="l",main="Epanechnikov [order = 4]")
plot(Z,ylab="kernel",npksum(txdat=0,exdat=Z,bws=1,ckertype="epanechnikov",
ckerorder=6)$ksum,type="l",main="Epanechnikov [order = 6]")
plot(Z,ylab="kernel",npksum(txdat=0,exdat=Z,bws=1,ckertype="epanechnikov",
ckerorder=8)$ksum,type="l",main="Epanechnikov [order = 8]")
```

The applications of `npksum()` are essentially unlimited. A diverse range of options have been built into this function to allow for maximum flexibility. Check out `?npksum` for details.

E.3.2   Applied Nonparametric Density Estimation

The goal of this practicum is to carry out kernel density estimation with real-world rather than simulated data, and to introduce you to applications of nonparametric regression models.

We consider a classic dataset (Pagan and Ullah, 1999) that comprises a random sample of $n = 205$ observations from the 1971 Canadian Census Public Use Tapes, involving male individuals with a common level of grade 13 education.

You can load the data and attach the variables `logwage` and `age` as follows:

```
library(np)
data(cps71)
attach(cps71)
## See what is in the dataset
names(cps71)
## For help try ?cps71
```

- Estimate and plot the density of `logwage` under the parametric assumption that it is drawn from a Gaussian distribution. Describe the Shapiro-Wilk test for normality (Shapiro and Wilk, 1965) and apply this test to the assumed parametric distribution of the `logwage` data. Is the data consistent with the parametric Gaussian specification?

```
library(np)
options(np.messages=FALSE)
data(cps71)
attach(cps71)
plot(sort(logwage),
     dnorm(sort(logwage),mean=mean(logwage),sd=sd(logwage)),type="l")
shapiro.test(logwage)
```

- Compute and plot a kernel density estimate for `logwage` using an Epanechnikov kernel and a bandwidth value of 0.1. Next, perform this same task using a bandwidth value of 1.0. The following shows you how to specify a bandwidth of 0.5 and then feed this bandwidth object to the density estimation routine (there are a number of reasons why we might want to keep them separate).

```
bw <- npudensbw(~logwage,ckertype="epanechnikov",bws=0.5,
                bandwidth.compute=FALSE)
fhat <- npudens(bws=bw)
plot(fhat)

bw <- npudensbw(~logwage,ckertype="epanechnikov",bws=0.1,
                bandwidth.compute=FALSE)
fhat <- npudens(bws=bw)
plot(fhat)

bw <- npudensbw(~logwage,ckertype="epanechnikov",bws=1.0,
                bandwidth.compute=FALSE)
fhat <- npudens(bws=bw)
plot(fhat)
```

- Repeat the above using likelihood cross-validation and least squares cross-validation. What are the differences between the cross-validated estimates and those based on the ad-hoc bandwidth values of 0.1 and 1.0?

```
bw <- npudensbw(~logwage,ckertype="epanechnikov",bwmethod="cv.ml")
fhat <- npudens(bws=bw)
plot(fhat)

bw <- npudensbw(~logwage,ckertype="epanechnikov",bwmethod="cv.ls")
fhat <- npudens(bws=bw)
plot(fhat)
```

- Construct and plot the likelihood cross-validated estimate, first with asymptotic and then with bootstrap error bars. See `?npplot` for help. You will use `plot(foo,plot.errors.method=...)`, where `foo` is the name assigned to your model (i.e., fhat in the above example). How do these error bars differ?

```
## Asymptotic
bw <- npudensbw(~logwage,ckertype="epanechnikov",bwmethod="cv.ml")
fhat <- npudens(bws=bw)
plot(fhat,plot.errors.method="asymptotic",plot.errors.style="band")
```

```
## Bootstrap
bw <- npudensbw(~logwage,ckertype="epanechnikov",bwmethod="cv.ml")
fhat <- npudens(bws=bw)
plot(fhat,plot.errors.method="bootstrap",plot.errors.style="band")
```

E.3.3   Introduction to Applied Nonparametric Regression

- Estimate a linear and a quadratic parametric regression model via

  ```
  model.linear <- lm(logwage~age)
  ```

  and

  ```
  model.quadratic <- lm(logwage~age+I(age^2))
  ```

  ```
  library(xtable)
  model.linear <- lm(logwage~age)
  xtable(summary(model.linear))
  model.quadratic <- lm(logwage~age+I(age^2))
  xtable(summary(model.quadratic))
  ```

- Describe the Ramsey (1969) RESET test for functional form. Next, install the lmtest library in R and use `resettest()` to test each model for correct parametric specification. Report the outcome of this procedure. Based on this result, would you be comfortable using either of these models for applied work?

  ```
  library(lmtest)
  resettest(model.linear)
  resettest(model.quadratic)
  ```

- Use the local linear estimator in a regression of `logwage` on `age` (see `?npreg` and `?npregbw` for examples). Plot the resulting estimate and the asymptotic standard errors.

  ```
  bw <- npregbw(logwage~age,regtype="ll")
  model.ll <- npreg(bws=bw)
  plot(model.ll,plot.errors.method="asymptotic",plot.errors.style="band")
  ```

- Plot the resulting gradient estimate and its asymptotic standard errors.

  ```
  bw <- npregbw(logwage~age,regtype="ll")
  model.ll <- npreg(bws=bw)
  plot(model.ll,plot.errors.method="asymptotic",plot.errors.style="band",
       gradients=TRUE)
  ```

- In a plot, compare the fit of the nonparametric local linear model with that of the parametric quadratic model. Note that the generic R function `fitted()` extracts fitted values from a model.

  ```
  plot(age,logwage,main="Quadratic Earnings Profile",
       xlab="Age",ylab="log(Wage)")
  lines(age,fitted(model.quadratic),col=1)
  lines(age,fitted(model.ll),col=2)
  legend("topright",c("Quadratic","Kernel"),col=1:2,bty="n")
  ```

- What is the in-sample fit (R^2) of the parametric and nonparametric models? On the basis of this criterion function, which model would you be most comfortable using? What are the drawbacks of using R^2 as a guide to model selection?

```
summary(model.quadratic)
summary(model.ll)
```

- We often would like to compute predictions or construct *counter-factuals* based on the results of a nonparametric regression. The generic function `predict()` in R allows us to do this. You first create an *evaluation* dataset and then use the option `predict(...,newdata=...)` to generate predictions. Let's load Wooldridge's wage1 dataset and perform a local constant regression with two predictors, one of which is continuous and the other of which is categorical. Note that we must exercise caution when creating the evaluation data, particularly when categorical predictors are involved.

  See also the generic functions `residuals()` and `fitted()`.

```
data(wage1)
attach(wage1)
## Construct the parametric model
model.lm <- lm(lwage~exper+female)
## Construct the nonparametric model
model.lc <- npreg(lwage~exper+female)
## Create an evaluation dataset (counter-factual) for a female
## with 5 years of experience
evaldata.female <- data.frame(exper=5,
                      female=factor("Female",levels=levels(female)))
## Use the generic R function predict(...,newdata=...)
predict(model.lm,newdata=evaldata.female)
predict(model.lc,newdata=evaldata.female)
## Create an evaluation dataset (counter-factual) for a male
## with 5 years of experience
evaldata.male <- data.frame(exper=5,
                      female=factor("Male",levels=levels(female)))
## Use the generic R function predict(...,newdata=...)
predict(model.lm,newdata=evaldata.male)
predict(model.lc,newdata=evaldata.male)
## We could compute Oaxaca-Blinder estimates of wage differentials
## (for Oaxaca-Blinder you would use the e.g., mean values of the
## female predictors which you could implement on your own)
predict(model.lm,newdata=evaldata.female)-
  predict(model.lm,newdata=evaldata.male)
## Nonparametric wage differential
predict(model.lc,newdata=evaldata.female)-
  predict(model.lc,newdata=evaldata.male)
```

E.3.4   Advanced Use of the `npksum()` Function

Sometimes, you may need to compute kernel weighted sums of various objects. The function `npksum()` in the R package np allows you to do this, and given that it makes calls to compiled C code, it is fairly fast. Many functions in the np package make calls either to `npksum()` or directly to the C code that underlies it. Becoming familiar with this function might be of value if you wish to eventually implement a novel kernel-based technique that does not exist in any R package. By making calls to `npksum()`, you can generate efficient prototypes very quickly and easily.

- You could use `npksum()` to compute the Nadaraya-Watson regression estimator that appeared in the previous example.

$$\hat{g}(x) = \frac{\sum_{i=1}^{n} Y_i K_\gamma(X_i, x)}{\sum_{i=1}^{n} K_\gamma(X_i, x)}.$$

Using the `cps71` data, compute the local constant estimator with the `npksum()` function.

```
data(cps71)
attach(cps71)
## Compute the bandwidths using npregbw()
bw <- npregbw(xdat=age, ydat=logwage)
## Compute the fit using npksum
fit.lc <- npksum(txdat=age, tydat=logwage, bws=bw$bw)$ksum/
          npksum(txdat=age, bws=bw$bw)$ksum
## Plot the results
plot(age, logwage, xlab="Age", ylab="log(wage)")
lines(age, fit.lc)
## Compare results with npreg() for the first 10 observations
cbind(fit.lc,fitted(npreg(bws=bw)))[1:10,]
```

- We also often need to implement some form of data-driven bandwidth selection, as in the previous exercise where we used the `npksum` function to construct the local constant estimator. If we wanted to use least squares cross-validation to select a bandwidth for the Nadaraya-Watson estimator, this could be accomplished by including the option `leave.one.out=TRUE` in the call to `npksum()`. Below, we consider a simulated example that involves $q = 3$ continuous predictors. Minimization will be carried out via the R function `nlm()`.

```
## We conduct least squares cross-validation for the local-constant
## regression estimator. We first write an R function `ss' that
## computes the leave-one-out sum of squares using the npksum()
## function, and then feed this function, along with random starting
## values for the bandwidth vector, to the nlm() routine in R (nlm =
## Non-Linear Minimization). Finally, we compare results with the
## function npregbw() that is written solely in C and calls a tightly
## coupled C-level search routine.  Note that we could make repeated
## calls to nlm() using different starting values for h (highly
## recommended in general).
## Increase the number of digits printed out by default in R and avoid
## using scientific notation for this example (we wish to compare
## objective function minima)
options(scipen=100, digits=12)
```

```
## Generate 100 observations from a simple DGP where one explanatory
## variable is irrelevant.
n <- 100
set.seed(42)
x1 <- runif(n)
x2 <- rnorm(n)
x3 <- runif(n)
## Create a data-frame for the predictors
txdat <- data.frame(x1, x2, x3)
## Note - x3 is irrelevant
tydat <- x1 + sin(x2) + rnorm(n)
## Write an R function that returns the average leave-one-out sum of
## squared residuals for the local constant estimator based on
## npksum(). This function accepts one argument and presumes that
## txdat and tydat have been defined already.
ss <- function(h) {
    ## Test for valid (non-negative) bandwidths - return infinite
    ## penalty when this occurs
    if(min(h)<=0) {
      return(.Machine$double.xmax)
    } else {
      mean.loo <-  npksum(txdat,
                          tydat,
                          leave.one.out=TRUE,
                          bws=h)$ksum/
                   npksum(txdat,
                          leave.one.out=TRUE,
                          bws=h)$ksum
    return(mean((tydat-mean.loo)^2))
    }
}
## Now pass this function to R's nlm() routine along with random
## starting values and place results in `nlm.return'.
nlm.return <- nlm(ss, runif(NCOL(txdat)))
## Now compute the bandwidths using the np function
## npregbw.
bw <- npregbw(xdat=txdat, ydat=tydat)
## Bandwidths from nlm()
nlm.return$estimate
## Bandwidths from npregbw()
bw$bw
## least squares objective function value (minimum) from nlm()
nlm.return$minimum
## least squares objective function value (minimum) from npregbw()
bw$fval
```

E.3.5   Consistent Nonparametric Inference

The goal of this practicum is to introduce you to methods of comparing
parametric and nonparametric estimates of regression models. We explore
how to carry out consistent nonparametric inference using the cps71 dataset
that appeared in the previous example.

- First, estimate a parametric regression model that is quadratic in age, and then perform a consistent nonparametric specification test using the function `npcmstest()`.

```
library(np)
data(cps71)
attach(cps71)
model <- lm(logwage~age+I(age^2), x=TRUE, y=TRUE)
npcmstest(model = model, xdat = age, ydat = logwage)
```

Interpret the outcome of this test. How does it compare with the results obtained from `resettest()`?

- Use R's `anova()` function to perform an F-test of significance of the age variable in the above model (see `?anova` for assistance).

```
## Construct the restricted model
model.res <- lm(logwage~1)
## Compute the F-test
anova(model.res,model)
```

- Next, estimate the regression model using the nonparametric local constant method, and use the R function `npsigtest()` to carry out a consistent nonparametric test of significance. How does this result compare to that of the parametric test of significance that was conducted above?

```
model <- npreg(logwage~age)
npsigtest(model)
```

The results obtained under the previous approach agree because the quadratic parametric specification is able to account for much of the variation in the outcome. Now let's simulate some data in which this is not the case.

- Run a Monte Carlo experiment to assess the power of a t-test with nominal size $\alpha = 0.05$ when the parametric model is misspecified. In particular, suppose that the data is generated by $y_i = 1 + x_i^2 + \epsilon_i$, but you estimate the misspecified model $y_i = \beta_1 + \beta_2 x_i + \epsilon_i$. For a sample size of $n = 100$, what fraction of the time does the t-test result in rejection of the null H_0: $\beta_2 = 0$ based on the linear model $y_i = \beta_1 + \beta_2 x_i + \epsilon_i$?

```
set.seed(42)
n <- 100
M <- 1000
t <- numeric()
x <- seq(-2,2,length=n)
for(m in 1:M) {
    y <- 1 + x^2 + rnorm(n,sd=1)
    model <- lm(y~x)
    ## Manually construct the t-statistic
    t[m] <- coef(model)[2]/sqrt(vcov(model)[2,2])
}
## Compute the empirical rejection frequency at the
```

```
## 5% level
reject <- mean(ifelse(abs(t)>qt(0.975,df=n-2),1,0))
reject
## Compute a 95% confidence band for the actual
## rejection frequency (reject is a proportion, so
## construct a CI for a population proportion)
sd.reject <- sqrt(reject*(1-reject)/M)
c(reject - 1.96*sd.reject, reject + 1.96*sd.reject)
```

- Now repeat this exercise with sample sizes $n = 250$ and $n = 500$. Does the power of the t-test increase with n? Why or why not?

- Repeat the above for a correctly specified model; that is, in this case, you will regress y on x^2 via `lm(y~ I(x**2))`.

- As an additional exercise, you could estimate the model using the nonparametric local linear method and use the R function `npsigtest()` to carry out a nonparametric significance test:

```
set.seed(42)
n <- 250
M <- 100
t <- numeric()
P <- numeric()
options(np.messages=FALSE,np.tree=TRUE)
for(m in 1:M) {
    x <- rnorm(n)
    y <- 1 + rnorm(n,sd=1)
    model.lm <- lm(y~x)
    ## Manually construct the t-statistic
    t[m] <- coef(model.lm)[2]/sqrt(vcov(model.lm)[2,2])
    model.ll <- npreg(y~x,ckertype="epanechnikov",regtype="ll")
    P[m] <- npsigtest(model.ll,boot.num=99)$P
}
## Compute the empirical rejection frequency at the
## 5% level for the parametric model
reject.lm <- mean(ifelse(abs(t)>qt(0.975,df=n-2),1,0))
reject.lm
## Compute a 95% confidence band for the actual
## rejection frequency (reject is a proportion, so
## construct a CI for a population proportion)
sd.reject.lm <- sqrt(reject.lm*(1-reject.lm)/M)
c(reject.lm - 1.96*sd.reject.lm, reject.lm + 1.96*sd.reject.lm)
## Compute the empirical rejection frequency at the
## 5% level for the parametric model
reject.ll <- mean(ifelse(P < 0.05, 1, 0))
reject.ll
## Compute a 95% confidence band for the actual
## rejection frequency (reject is a proportion, so
## construct a CI for a population proportion)
sd.reject.ll <- sqrt(reject.ll*(1-reject.ll)/M)
c(reject.ll - 1.96*sd.reject.ll, reject.ll + 1.96*sd.reject.ll)
```

Other variations include (a) assessing the size of both tests when x is irrelevant, that is, when the data generating process is defined by `y<-1+rnorm(n,sd=1)`, and (b) assessing power when the parametric model is correctly specified, that is, when the data generating process is defined by `y<-1+x+rnorm(n,sd=1)`.

E.3.6   Non-nested Model Comparison

- Let us now do some forecasting and model evaluation based on the `cps71` dataset.
  - Split the data into a *training* (estimation) sample of size $n_1 = 175$ and an *evaluation* sample of size $n_2 = 30$. Use the evaluation data to compute the predicted square error of the nonparametric local constant and the parametric least squares estimators, where the latter is applied to a model that is linear in age.

```
library(np)
set.seed(42)
data(cps71)
## Define n1 and n2
n <- nrow(cps71)
n1 <- 175
n2 <- n - n1
## Draw a sample without replacement (i.e., shuffle) from the
## indices 1 to n and use this to create the evaluation and
## training data
ii <- sample(1:n,replace=FALSE)
## data.train uses 175 observations with random indices,
## data.eval uses 30
data.train <- cps71[ii[1:n1],]
data.eval <- cps71[ii[(n1+1):n],]
## Compute the bandwidths for the training data
bw <- npregbw(logwage~age,data=data.train)
## Generate predictions for the evaluation data
model.np <- npreg(bws=bw,data=data.train)
pmse.np <- mean((data.eval$logwage-
    predict(model.np,data=data.train,newdata=data.eval))^2)
## Do the same for the parametric model
model.lm <- lm(logwage~age,data=data.train)
pmse.lm <- mean((data.eval$logwage-
    predict(model.lm,data=data.train,newdata=data.eval))^2)
## Compare... which model is performing better on the
## hold-out data?
pmse.np
pmse.lm
```

  - Repeat the above 1000 times (but do not re-run cross-validation), each time saving the result. The easiest way to do this is to wrap the code from the previous question inside of the loop below, and then to modify the call to pmse.np/pmse.lm as indicated. To avoid re-running cross-validation, you can create a single bandwidth object outside of the loop based on the full sample and then re-use this bandwidth in each iteration (see the comments below). You

should move all lines in the loop that are not indexed by i outside
of the loop (this is a good coding habit). Be sure to also keep
set.seed() outside of the loop, since if you fail to do so, you will
generate the exact same data sample in each of the 1000 iterations.

```
## Create vectors to store the results
pmse.np <- numeric()
pmse.lm <- numeric()
## Compute the bandwidth object by calling npregbw(...)
...
for(i in 1:1000) {
    ## Shuffle data
    ...
    ## Compute the pmse using the bandwidths from the existing
    ## bandwidth object when you call npreg(...)  (e.g.
    ## npreg(..., bws=foo$bw) where foo is the name of your
    ## bandwidth object)
    pmse.np[i] <- ...
    pmse.lm[i] <- ...
}
## Now compare the results... perhaps compare means and
## medians
...
```

– Repeat the above using the local constant, local linear, and parametric least squares estimators, where the parametric specifications
that are considered are linear and quadratic in age. Hence, for
each split of the data, you will be estimating four different models
and comparing the results thereof. How might you assess the *typical* performance of each model? (Hint: you can create a boxplot
of each estimator's predicted square error and/or you can report
their means and medians (see ?boxplot for details on the former)).

• Consider Wooldridge's wage1 dataset. Estimate a linear parametric
model and a nonparametric local linear model with least squares cross-
validated bandwidths.

```
## Linear model
library(np)
data(wage1)
model.lin <- lm(lwage ~ female + married + educ + exper + tenure,
                data=wage1)
## Note - the local linear method will take a few minutes of time
## to optimize the smoothing parameters
model.ll <- npreg(lwage ~ female + married + educ + exper + tenure,
                  regtype="ll",
                  data=wage1)
```

– Compare these two models in terms of their in-sample performance

```
## Linear model
library(np)
data(wage1)
model.lin <- lm(lwage ~ female + married + educ + exper + tenure,
```

```
                         data=wage1)
## Note - the local linear method will take a few minutes of time
## to optimize the smoothing parameters
model.ll <- npreg(lwage ~ female + married + educ + exper + tenure,
                  regtype="ll",
                  data=wage1)
summary(model.lin)
summary(model.ll)
```

E.3.7   Semiparametric Models

The goal of this practicum is to introduce you to applied semiparametric modeling, nonparametric discrete/multinomial choice modeling, and nonparametric quantile modeling.

- Consider Wooldridge's wage1 dataset. First, fit a linear model that is quadratic in experience, and then fit a partially linear model whose nonparametric component is a function of `exper`. Compare and contrast the resulting estimates. Note that the generic R function `coef()` will extract the coefficients from both the parametric model and the linear component of the semiparametric model.

```
data(wage1)
model.lm <- lm(lwage~female+
               married+
               educ+
               tenure+
               exper+
               I(exper^2),
               data=wage1)
model.pl <- npplreg(lwage~female+
                    married+
                    educ+
                    tenure|
                    exper,
                    data=wage1)
```

- Consider Wooldridge's wage1 dataset. Fit a linear model that is quadratic in experience, a smooth coefficient model whose coefficients are functions of the categorical predictors `female` and `married`, and a semiparametric single index model using Ichimura's method for continuous Y. Compare and contrast the resulting estimates.

```
data(wage1)
model.lm <- lm(lwage~female+
               married+
               educ+
               tenure+
               exper+
               I(exper^2),
               data=wage1)
model.scoef <- npscoef(lwage~educ+
```

```
                              tenure+
                              exper+
                              expersq|
                              female+
                              married,
                              data=wage1,
                              betas=TRUE)
model.index <- npindex(lwage~educ+
                              tenure+
                              exper+
                              expersq+
                              female+
                              married,
                              method="ichimura",
                              data=wage1)
```

- Consider the birthwt data from the MASS package. Estimate a Logit model and a semiparametric single-index model using Klein and Spady's method for binary Y. Compare and contrast the models' in-sample classification ability by means of a confusion matrix.

```
library(MASS)
data(birthwt)
model.logit <- glm(low~factor(smoke)+
                        factor(race)+
                        factor(ht)+
                        factor(ui)+
                        ordered(ftv)+
                        age+
                        lwt,
                        family=binomial(link=logit),
                        data=birthwt)
cm.logit <- with(birthwt,table(low,ifelse(fitted(model.logit)>0.5,1,0)))
ccr.logit <- sum(diag(cm.logit))/sum(cm.logit)
model.index <- npindex(low~factor(smoke)+
                        factor(race)+
                        factor(ht)+
                        factor(ui)+
                        ordered(ftv)+
                        age+
                        lwt,
                        method="kleinspady",
                        data=birthwt)
cm.index <- with(birthwt,table(low,ifelse(fitted(model.index)>0.5,1,0)))
ccr.index <- sum(diag(cm.index))/sum(cm.index)
```

E.3.8   Nonparametric Discrete Choice Models

- Consider the birthwt data from the MASS package. Estimate a parametric Logit model, construct a confusion matrix, and report the correct classification ratio.

```
library(MASS)
data(birthwt)
model.logit <- glm(low~factor(smoke)+
                   factor(race)+
                   factor(ht)+
                   factor(ui)+
                   ordered(ftv)+
                   age+
                   lwt,
                   family=binomial(link=logit),
                   data=birthwt)
cm.logit <- with(birthwt,table(low,ifelse(fitted(model.logit)>0.5,1,0)))
ccr.logit <- sum(diag(cm.logit))/sum(cm.logit)
```

- Now estimate a nonparametric discrete choice model using the same dataset. Compare and contrast your results with those of the Logit model (i.e., use `summary(model.np)`).

```
bw <- npcdensbw(factor(low)~
                factor(smoke)+
                factor(race)+
                factor(ht)+
                factor(ui)+
                ordered(ftv)+
                age+
                lwt,
                data=birthwt)
model.np <- npconmode(bws=bw)
```

How do these models compare in terms of their in-sample performance?

- Consider the `Italy` data, which is a GDP panel that covers 21 different regions of Italy over a period of 48 years. Estimate the conditional PDF $f(gdp|year)$ and conditional CDF $F(gdp|year)$ for this panel of data. Make sure that `year` is treated as an `ordered` factor.

```
data(Italy)
attach(Italy)
fhat <- npcdens(gdp~year)
Fhat <- npcdist(gdp~year)
```

Let us now explore the structure of the data. When you call `plot` in R, the appropriate plotting routine is determined by first checking the object's `class`. If the object is detected as having been created by the `np` package, the function `npplot` is automatically invoked (see `?npplot` for details). When using a *perspective plot* of 3D objects, you may indicate whether you would like the plotted object to rotate (default) or to be held fixed (`view="fixed"`). You may also fix the azimuthal angle (`theta=`) and the zenith angle (`phi=`) of the perspective plot, where `theta` and `phi` are expressed in integer-valued degrees. By experimenting with these values, you often get a better sense of what is revealed by the nonparametric estimates. Modifying `theta` and `phi` in different ways also helps determine which values of these angles allow you to best convey the conditional PDF and CDF estimates in a visual representation. The following example might be useful.

```
plot(fhat, view="fixed", main="", theta=300, phi=50)
```

- Next, let us estimate conditional quantiles of the `Italy` data. The *nonsmooth* conditional median, lower quartile, and upper quartile can be shown in *boxplots* (`?boxplot`) of the data. Note that because `year` is an ordered factor, `boxplot` is automatically invoked by the `plot` function.

```
plot(ordered(year), gdp,
    main="Annual Boxplots for the Italian Income Panel",
    xlab="Year",
    ylab="GDP")
```

Next, compute the smooth nonparametric conditional median, lower quartile, and upper quartile, and plot them on the same figure as above.

```
data("Italy")
attach(Italy)
## First, compute the cross-validated bandwidths (default).
## Note - this may take a few minutes depending on the speed of your
## computer...
bw <- npcdistbw(gdp~ordered(year))
## Note - numerical search for computing the quantiles will take a
## minute or so...
model.q0.25 <- npqreg(bws=bw, tau=0.25)
model.q0.50 <- npqreg(bws=bw, tau=0.50)
model.q0.75 <- npqreg(bws=bw, tau=0.75)
## Plot the resulting quantiles manually...
plot(ordered(year), gdp,
    main="CDF Quantile Estimates for the Italian Income Panel",
    xlab="Year",
    ylab="GDP Quantiles")
lines(ordered(year), model.q0.25$quantile, col="red", lty=2, lwd=2)
lines(ordered(year), model.q0.50$quantile, col="blue", lty=3, lwd=2)
lines(ordered(year), model.q0.75$quantile, col="red", lty=2, lwd=2)
legend("topleft", c("tau = 0.25", "tau = 0.50", "tau = 0.75"),
        lty=c(2, 3, 2), col=c("red", "blue", "red"), lwd=c(2, 2, 2),
        bty="n")
```

E.3.9   Shape Constrained Nonparametric Regression

The goal of this practicum is to introduce you to shape constrained nonparametric estimation. In particular, in what follows, we consider shape constrained local polynomial regression. Study the code carefully, and note that you must first install the `quadprog` package before proceeding with this example.

- Run the code and interpret the plot.
- Set the constraints so that they are nonbinding, i.e., modify the lines

```
lower <- rep(-0.5,n+n.eval)
upper <- rep(100,n+n.eval)
```

to read

```
lower <- rep(-100,n+n.eval)
upper <- rep(100,n+n.eval)
```

and then re-run the code. Are the constrained and the unconstrained estimates the same? Why or why not?

```
## We illustrate constrained kernel estimation using the local
## polynomial estimator where the constraints are l(x) <= \hat
## g^(s)(x) <= u(x) (see Du, P. and C. Parmeter and J.S. Racine
## (2013), "Nonparametric Kernel Regression with Multiple Predictors
## and Multiple Shape Constraints," Statistica Sinica, Volume 23,
## Number 3, 1343-1372).
## Load required packages, set options.
library(np)
library(quadprog)
library(crs)
options(np.tree=TRUE)
## Set the kernel function.
ckertype <- "epanechnikov"
## Set the order of the local polynomial. Setting p < 0 will determine
## the appropriate order via cross-validation a la Hall & Racine
## (2013). Note - for large n cross-validation for p and h can be
## slow.
p <- 1
## By default constraints are on the function (g^(s=0)(x|p)). Setting
## this to 1 imposes constraints on the first derivative, 2 the second
## and so forth. Here we have one predictor, but for > 1 predictor set
## e.g., c(0,1) to place a restriction on the first derivative of the
## second predictor. Note that the order of the polynomial p above
## must be >= the order of the derivative.
gradient.vec <- c(0)
## If n.eval > 0 then the constraints are set to hold on a grid of
## equally spaced points of length n.eval in addition to holding at
## the sample observations. n is the number of sample
## observations. n.eval can be quite large, it is n that binds as the
## weight vector being determined is of length n.
n.eval <- 0
n <- 2500
## Set up bounds for the quadratic program. We are going to require
## the lower and upper constraints l(x) and u(x) for g(x). Here they
## are constant, but in general can depend on x.
lower <- rep(-0.5,n+n.eval)
upper <- rep(100,n+n.eval)
## Simulate a sample of data. We can control signal/noise ratio by
## scaling the errors by sd(dgp), so rnorm(n,sd=...) can be set to
## sd=(.25,.5,1,2) which would yield an R-squared for the Oracle model
## of (.95,.8,.5,and .2).
x <- sort(runif(n))
dgp <- sin(2*pi*x)
y <- dgp + rnorm(n,sd=0.5*sd(dgp))
```

```
## X (data frame of predictors) and y are passed below, so if you add
## extra predictors simply add them to X (and x.eval if n.eval > 0)
## here and be done.
X <- data.frame(x)
## Generate the cross-validated bandwidths optimal for the order of
## the local polynomial at hand.
formula.glp <- formula(y~x)
model.glp <- npglpreg(formula=formula.glp,
                      cv=ifelse(p>=0,"bandwidth","degree-bandwidth"),
                      degree=ifelse(p>=0,rep(p,NCOL(X)),rep(0,NCOL(X))),
                      ckertype=ckertype,
                      nmulti=min(NCOL(X),5))
bws <- model.glp$bws
p <- model.glp$degree
if(any(gradient.vec > p)) stop(" gradient order exceeds poly degree")
## The function W.glp is the generalized polynomial (i.e., Taylor
## series with potentially different degrees for each predictor, using
## the Bernstein polynomial), and formula.glp is the formula fed to
## npglpreg() to obtain cross-validated local polynomial bandwidths.
W <- crs:::W.glp(xdat=X,
                 degree=rep(p,NCOL(X)))
if(any(gradient.vec>0)) {
  W.gradient <- crs:::W.glp(xdat=X,
                            degree=rep(p,NCOL(X)),
                            gradient.vec = gradient.vec)
} else {
  W.gradient <- W ## can we avoid copy?
}
if(n.eval>0) {
  x.eval <- seq(min(x),max(x),length=n.eval)
  X.eval <- data.frame(x=x.eval)
  if(any(gradient.vec>0)) {
    W.eval <- crs:::W.glp(xdat=X,
                          exdat=X.eval,
                          degree=rep(p,NCOL(X)),
                          gradient.vec = gradient.vec)
  } else {
    W.eval <- crs:::W.glp(xdat=X,
                          exdat=X.eval,
                          degree=rep(p,NCOL(X)))
  }
}
## Generate the matrix of kernel weights using data-driven bandwidths
## that are optimal for the unconstrained model.
K <- npksum(txdat=X,
            bws=bws,
            ckertype=ckertype,
            return.kernel.weights=TRUE)$kw
A <- sapply(1:n,function(i){
            W.gradient[i,,drop=FALSE]%*%
            chol2inv(chol(t(W)%*%(K[,i]*W)))%*%t(W)*y*K[,i]})
## Create the uniform weights p.u and matrix A for which t(A)%*%p is
## the constrained local polynomial estimator \hat g(x|p).
```

```
p.u <- rep(1,n)
## If n.eval > 0 compute the evaluation kernel weights and
## associated matrix for the fit on the evaluation data.
if(n.eval>0) {
  K.eval <- npksum(txdat=X,
                   exdat=X.eval,
                   bws=bws,
                   ckertype=ckertype,
                   return.kernel.weights=TRUE)$kw
  A.eval <- sapply(1:n.eval,function(i){
            W.eval[i,,drop=FALSE]%*%
            chol2inv(chol(t(W)%*%(K.eval[,i]*W)))%*%t(W)*y*K.eval[,i]})
}
## Solve the quadratic program. The function solve.QP in the quadprog
## package solves the problem min (p-p.u)^T(p-p.u) subject to the
## constraints Amat^T p >= bvec. Note that we construct Amat to
## contain the constraints (a) A^Tp >= lower, and (b) -A^Tp >= -upper
## (here A^Tp = \hat g(x/p)).
if(n.eval==0) {
  output.QP <- solve.QP(Dmat=diag(n),
                        dvec=p.u,
                        Amat=cbind(A,-A),
                        bvec=c(lower,-upper))
} else {
  output.QP <- solve.QP(Dmat=diag(n),
                        dvec=p.u,
                        Amat=cbind(A,A.eval,-A,-A.eval),
                        bvec=c(lower,-upper))
}
if(is.nan(output.QP$value)) stop(" solve.QP failed. Try larger bw/deg")
p.hat <- output.QP$solution
if(!is.na(as.logical(all.equal(p.u,p.hat)))) warning(" not binding")
## Compute the unconstrained and constrained estimators.
if(any(gradient.vec>0)) {
  A <- sapply(1:n,function(i){
            W[i,,drop=FALSE]%*%
            chol2inv(chol(t(W)%*%(K[,i]*W)))%*%t(W)*y*K[,i]})
}
fit.unres <- t(A)%*%p.u
fit.res <- t(A)%*%p.hat
## Plot the DGP, unrestricted, and restricted fits along with the
## constraints and data. We plot the y*p.hat (translated data) in
## orange
ylim <- c(min(dgp,fit.unres,fit.res,y),
          max(dgp,fit.unres,fit.res,y))
subtext <- paste("n = ",n,", local polynomial order = ",p,
                 ", derivative order s = ",gradient.vec,sep="")
plot(x,y,cex=.2,ylab="g(x)",ylim=ylim,col="black",sub=subtext)
points(x,y*p.hat,col="orange",cex=0.35)
lines(x,dgp,col=1,lty=1)
lines(x,fit.unres,col=2,lty=1,lwd=2)
lines(x,fit.res,col=3,lty=1,lwd=2)
lines(x,lower[1:n],lty=1,col="lightgrey")
```

```
lines(x,upper[1:n],lty=1,col="lightgrey")
legend("bottomleft",
       c("DGP","Unconstrained Estimate","Constrained Estimate",
         "Weighted Y","Actual Y"),
       col=c(1:3,"orange","black"),
       lwd=c(1,1,1,NA,NA),
       lty=c(1,1,1,NA,NA),
       pch=c(NA,NA,NA,1,1),
       cex=0.75,
       bty="n")
plot(x,y,cex=.25,ylab="g(x)",ylim=ylim,col="grey",sub=subtext)
lines(x,dgp,col=1,lty=1)
lines(x,fit.unres,col=2,lty=1,lwd=2)
lines(x,fit.res,col=3,lty=1,lwd=2)
lines(x,lower[1:n],lty=1,col="lightgrey")
lines(x,upper[1:n],lty=1,col="lightgrey")
legend("bottomleft",
       c("DGP","Unconstrained","Constrained"),
       lty=rep(1,3),
       col=1:3,
       bty="n",
       cex=0.75)
```

Bibliography

Abramson, M. A., Audet, C., Couture, G., Dennis Jr., J. E., and Le Digabel, S. (2011). The NOMAD project. Technical report, GERAD (Groupe D'Études et de Recherche en Analyse des Décisions).

Ahamada, I. and Flachaire, E. (2010). *Non-Parametric Econometrics*. Oxford University Press, Oxford.

Ahmad, I. A. and Li, Q. (1997). Testing independence by nonparametric kernel method. *Statistics and Probability Letters*, 34:201–210.

Ahmad, I. A. and van Belle, G. (1974). Measuring affinity of distributions. In Proschan and Serfling, R., editors, *Reliability and Biometry, Statistical Analysis of Life Testing*, Philadelphia. SIAM.

Ai, C. and Chen, X. (2003). Efficient estimation of models with conditional moment restrictions containing unknown functions. *Econometrica*, 71(6):1795–1843.

Ai, C. and Li, Q. (2008). Semi-parametric and non-parametric methods in panel data models. In Matyas, L. and Sevestra, P., editors, *The Econometrics of Panel Data: Fundamentals and Recent Developments in Theory and Practice*, pages 451–478. Springer, New York.

Aitchison, J. and Aitken, C. G. G. (1976). Multivariate binary discrimination by the kernel method. *Biometrika*, 63(3):413–420.

Aldrich, J. H. and Nelson, F. D. (1995). *Linear Probability, Logit, and Probit Models*. SAGE, Thousand Oaks, CA.

Altonji, J. G. and Matzkin, R. L. (2005). Cross section and panel data estimators for nonseparable models with endogenous regressors. *Econometrica*, 73(4):1053–1102.

Bai, J. and Ng, S. (2001). A consistent test for conditional symmetry in time series models. *Journal of Econometrics*, 103:225–258.

Bai, J. and Ng, S. (2005). Test for skewness, kurtosis and normality for time series data. *Journal of Business and Economics Statistics*, 23:49–60.

Bashtannyk, D. M. and Hyndman, R. J. (2001). Bandwidth selection for kernel conditional density estimation. *Computational Statistics and Data Analysis*, 36:279–298.

Bauwens, L., Laurent, S., and Rombouts, J. V. K. (2006). Multivariate GARCH models: A survey. *Journal of Applied Econometrics*, 21(1):79–109.

Becker, G. S. (1993). *Human Capital: A Theoretical and Empirical Analysis, with Special Reference to Education*. The University of Chicago Press, Chicago, 3rd edition.

Belaire-Franch, J. and Peiro, A. (2003). Conditional and unconditional asymmetry in U.S. macroeconomic time series. *Studies in Nonlinear Dynamics and Econometrics*, 7. Article 4.

Beresteanu, A. (2005). Nonparametric estimation of regression functions under restrictions on partial derivatives. *RAND Journal of Economics*.

Berry, D. A. and Lindgren, B. W. (1990). *Statistics: Theory and Methods*. Brooks/Cole, Pacific Grove, CA.

Blomqvist, N. (1950). On a measure of dependence between two random variables. *Annals of Mathematical Statistics*, 21(4):593–600.

Blundell, R., Chen, X., and Kristensen, D. (2007). Semi-nonparametric IV estimation of shape invariant Engel curves. *Econometrica*, 75:1613–1669.

Boneva, L. I., Kendall, D., and Stefanov, I. (1971). Spline transformations: Three new diagnostic aids for the statistical data- analyst. *Journal of the Royal Statistical Society. Series B*, 33(1):1–71.

Bosq, D. (1998). *Nonparametric Statistics for Stochastic Processes*. Springer-Verlag, New York.

Bouezmarni, T. and Rolin, J. (2003). Consistency of the beta kernel density function estimator. *Canadian Journal of Statistics / La Revue Canadienne de Statistique*, 31(1):89–98.

Bouezmarni, T. and Rombouts, J. V. K. (2010). Nonparametric density estimation for multivariate bounded data. *Journal of Statistical Planning and Inference*, 140(1):139–152.

Bowman, A. W. (1984). An alternative method of cross-validation for the smoothing of density estimates. *Biometrika*, 71:353–360.

Bowman, A. W. and Azzalini, A. (1997). *Applied Smoothing Techniques for Data Analysis: The Kernel Approach with S-Plus Illustrations*. Oxford, Clarendon.

Bowman, A. W., Hall, P. G., and Prvan, T. (1998). Bandwidth selection for the smoothing of distribution functions. *Biometrika*, 85:799–808.

Box, G. E. P. (1976). Science and statistics. *Journal of the American Statistical Association*, 71:791–799.

Brown, L. D. and Levine, M. (2007). Variance estimation in nonparametric regression via the difference sequence method. *Annals of Statistics*, 35(5):2219–2232.

Buja, A., Hastie, T., and Tibshirani, R. (1989). Linear smoothers and additive models. *Annals of Statistics*, 17:453–555.

Calonico, S., Cattaneo, M. D., and Farrell, M. H. (2017). *nprobust: Nonparametric Robust Estimation and Inference Methods using Local Polynomial Regression and Kernel Density Estimation.* R package version 0.1.1.

Calonico, S., Cattaneo, M. D., and Farrell, M. H. (2018). On the effect of bias estimation on coverage accuracy in nonparametric inference. *Journal of the American Statistical Association*, 113(522):767–779.

Cameron, A. C. and Trivedi, P. K. (1998). *Regression Analysis of Count Data.* Cambridge University Press, New York.

Cantoni, E. and Ronchetti, E. (2001). Resistant selection of the smoothing parameter for smoothing splines. *Statistics and Computing*, 11:141–146.

Carrasco, M., Florens, J., and Renault, E. (2007). Linear inverse problems in structural econometrics: Estimation based on spectral decomposition and regularization. In Heckman, J. J. and Leamer, E. E., editors, *Handbook of Econometrics*, pages 733–751, Amsterdam. North Holland.

Carrasco, M., Florens, J., and Renault, E. (2014). Asymptotic normal inference in linear inverse problems. In Racine, J. S., Su, L., and Ullah, A., editors, *Oxford Handbook of Applied Nonparametric and Semiparametric Econometrics and Statistics*, pages 65–96, Oxford. Oxford University Press.

Carroll, R. J., Delaigle, A., and Hall, P. G. (2011). Testing and estimating shape-constrained nonparametric density and regression in the presence of measurement error. *Journal of the American Statistical Association*, 106(493):191–202.

Centorrino, S., Fève, F., and Florens, J. (2017). Additive nonparametric instrumental regressions: A guide to implementation. *Journal of Econometric Methods*, 6(1).

Centorrino, S. and Racine, J. S. (2017). Semiparametric varying coefficient models with endogenous covariates. *Annals of Economics and Statistics*, 127-128.

Chen, L.-H., Cheng, M.-Y., and Peng, L. (2009a). Conditional variance estimation in heteroscedastic regression models. *Journal of Statistical Planning and Inference*, 139(2):236–245.

Chen, S. X. (1999). Beta kernel estimators for density functions. *Computational Statistics & Data Analysis*, 31(2):131–145.

Chen, S. X. (2000). Probability density function estimation using gamma kernels. *Annals of the Institute of Statistical Mathematics*, 52(3):471–480.

Chen, X. and Fan, Y. (1999). Consistent hypothesis testing in semiparametric and nonparametric models for econometric time series. *Journal of Econometrics*, 91:373–401.

Chen, X., Fan, Y., and Tsyrennikov, V. (2006). Efficient estimation of semiparametric multivariate copula models. *Journal of the American Statistical Association*, 101:1228–1240.

Chen, X. and Pouzo, D. (2012). Estimation of nonparametric conditional moment models with possibly nonsmooth generalized residuals. *Econometrica*, 80:277–321.

Chen, X. and Pouzo, D. (2015). Sieve Wald and QLR inferences on semi/nonparametric conditional moment models. *Econometrica*, 83(3):1013–1079.

Chen, X., Wu, W., and Yi, Y. (2009b). Efficient estimation of copula-based semiparametric Markov models. *Annals of Statistics*, 37:4214–4253.

Cheng, M., Hall, P. G., and Titterington, D. M. (1997). On the shrinkage of local linear curve estimators. *Statistics and Computing*, 7:11–17.

Cheng, M.-Y. and Sun, S. (2006). Bandwidth selection for kernel quantile estimation. *Journal of the Chinese Statistical Association*, 44:271–295.

Chernozhukov, V., Fernández-Val, I., and Galichon, A. (2010). Quantile and probability curves without crossing. *Econometrica*, 78(3):1093–1125.

Chesher, A. and Rosen, A. M. (2014). An instrumental variable random-coefficients model for binary outcomes. *The Econometrics Journal*, 17(2):S1–S19.

Chu, C. I. and Marron, J. S. (1991). Choosing a kernel regression estimator (with discussions). *Statistical Science*, 6:404–436.

Chu, C.-Y., Henderson, D. J., and Parmeter, C. F. (2017). On discrete Epanechnikov kernel functions. *Computational Statistics and Data Analysis*, 116(Supplement C):79–105.

Čížek, P. and Härdle, W. (2006). Robust estimation of dimension reduction space. *Computational Statistics & Data Analysis*, 51:545–555.

Cleveland, W. S. (1979). Robust locally weighted regression and smoothing scatterplots. *Journal of the American Statistical Association*, 74:829–836.

Cline, D. B. H. and Hart, J. D. (1991). Kernel estimation of densities with discontinuities or discontinuous derivatives. *Statistics*, 22(1):69–84.

Connors, A. F., Speroff, T., and Dawson, N. V. (1996). The effectiveness of right heart catheterization in the initial care of critically iii patients. *Journal of the American Medical Association*, 276(11):889–897.

Copas, J. B. and Fryer, M. J. (1980). Density estimation and suicide risks in psychiatric treatment. *Journal of the Royal Statistical Society. Series A (General)*, 143(2):167–176.

Corradi, V. and Swanson, N. R. (2002). A consistent test for nonlinear out of sample predictive accuracy. *Journal of Econometrics*, 110:353–381.

Corradi, V. and Swanson, N. R. (2007). Nonparametric bootstrap procedures for predictive inference based on recursive estimation schemes. *International Economic Review*, 48(1):67–109.

Cowling, A. and Hall, P. G. (1996). On pseudodata methods for removing boundary effects in kernel density estimation. *Journal of the Royal Statistical Society. Series B*, 58(3):551–563.

Craven, P. and Wahba, G. (1979). Smoothing noisy data with spline functions. *Numerische Mathematik*, 13:377–403.

Cressie, N. A. C. and Read, T. R. C. (1984). Multinomial goodness-of-fit tests. *Journal of the Royal Statistical Society, Series B*, 46:440–464.

Croissant, Y. (2016). *Ecdat: Data Sets for Econometrics*. R package version 0.3-1.

Croissant, Y. and Millo, G. (2008). Panel data econometrics in R: The plm package. *Journal of Statistical Software*, 27(2):1–43.

Crum, W. L. (1923). Cycles of rates on commercial paper. *Review of Economics and Statistics*, 5:17–29.

Daouia, A., Laurent, T., and Noh, H. (2017). npbr: A package for nonparametric boundary regression in R. *Journal of Statistical Software*, 79(9):1–43.

Darolles, S., Fan, Y., Florens, J., and Renault, E. (2011). Nonparametric instrumental regression. *Econometrica*, 79(5):1541–1565.

de Boor, C. (2001). *A Practical Guide to Splines*. Springer, New York.

Dehejia, R. H. and Wahba, S. (1999). Causal effects in nonexperimental studies: Reevaluating the evaluation of training programs. *Journal of the American Statistical Association*, 94:1053–1062.

Delgado, M. A. and Manteiga, W. G. (2001). Significance testing in nonparametric regression based on the bootstrap. *Annals of Statistics*, 29:1469–1507.

Denuit, M. and Scaillet, O. (2004). Nonparametric tests for positive quadrant dependence. *Journal of Financial Econometrics*, 2(3):422–450.

Devroye, L. and Györfi, L. (1985). *Nonparametric Density Estimation: The L^1 View*. Wiley, New York.

Diebold, F. X. and Mariano, R. S. (1995). Comparing predictive accuracy. *Journal of Business & Economic Statistics*, 13(3):253–265.

Diggle, P. (1985). A kernel method for smoothing point process data. *Journal of the Royal Statistical Society. Series C (Applied Statistics)*, 34(2):138–147.

Doksum, K. and Samarov, A. (1995). Nonparametric estimation of global functionals and a measure of the explanatory power of covariates in regression. *Annals of Statistics*, 23(5):1443–1473.

Du, P., Parmeter, C. F., and Racine, J. S. (2013). Nonparametric kernel regression with multiple predictors and multiple shape constraints. *Statistica Sinica*, 23(3):1343–1372.

Duin, R. P. W. (1976). On the choice of smoothing parameters for Parzen estimators of probability density functions. *IEEE Transactions in Computing*, C-25:1175–1179.

Efron, B. (1979). Bootstrap methods: Another look at the jackknife. *Annals of Statistics*, 7(1):1–26.

Efron, B. (1982). *The Jackknife, the Bootstrap, and Other Resampling Plans*. Society for Industrial and Applied Mathematics, Philadelphia.

Elgammal, A., Duraiswami, R., and Davis, L. (2003). The fast gauss transform for efficient kernel density evaluation with applications in computer vision. *IEEE Transactions on Pattern Analysis and Machine Intelligence*.

Engle, R. F. (1982). Autoregressive conditional heteroscedasticity with estimates of the variance of UK inflation. *Econometrica*, 50:987–1008.

Epanechnikov, V. A. (1969). Nonparametric estimation of a multidimensional probability density. *Theory of Applied Probability*, 14:153–158.

Fan, J. (1992). Design-adaptive nonparametric regression. *Journal of the American Statistical Association*, 87:998–1004.

Fan, J. and Gijbels, I. (1996). *Local Polynomial Modelling and Its Applications.* Chapman and Hall, London.

Fan, J. and Jiang, J. (2000). Variable bandwidth and one-step local m-estimator. *Science in China (Series A)*, 43:65–81.

Fan, J. and Yao, Q. W. (1998). Efficient estimation of conditional variance functions in stochastic regression. *Biometrika*, 85:645–660.

Fan, J. and Yao, Q. W. (2003). *Nonlinear Time Series: Nonparametric and Parametric Methods.* Springer-Verlag, New York.

Fan, J. and Zhang, W. (1999). Statistical estimation in varying coefficient models. *Annals of Statistics*, 27(5):1491–1518.

Fan, Y. and Gencay, R. (1993). Hypothesis testing based on modified nonparametric estimation of an affinity measure between two distributions. *Journal of Nonparametric Statistics*, 4:389–403.

Fan, Y. and Li, Q. (1996). Consistent model specification tests: Omitted variables and semiparametric functional forms. *Econometrica*, 64:865–890.

Fan, Y. and Ullah, A. (1999). On goodness-of-fit tests for weakly dependent processes using kernel method. *Journal of Nonparametric Statistics*, 11:337–360.

Faraway, J. J. and Jhun, M. (1990). Bootstrap choice of bandwidth for density estimation. *Journal of the American Statistical Association*, 85:1119–1122.

Fermanian, J.-D. and Scaillet, O. (2003). Nonparametric estimation of copulas for time series. *Journal of Risk*, 5:847–860.

Fève, F. and Florens, J. (2010). The practice of non-parametric estimation by solving inverse problems: The example of transformation models. *Econometrics Journal*, 13:S1–S27.

Fève, F. and Florens, J. (2014). Non parametric analysis of panel data models with endogenous variables. *Journal of Econometrics*, 181(2):151–164.

Fix, E. and Hodges, J. L. (1951). Discriminatory analysis, nonparametric estimation: Consistency properties. Technical Report No. 4, Project No. 2149-Oo4, USAF School of Aviation Medicine, Randolph Field, TX.

Florens, J. (2003). Inverse problems and structural econometrics: The example of instrumental variables. In *Advances in Economics and Econometrics: Theory and Applications - Eight World Congress*, pages 284–311. Cambridge University Press.

Florens, J. and Linton, O., editors (2011). *Special Issue on Inverse Problems in Econometrics*, volume 27 (3). Cambridge University Press.

Fox, J. and Weisberg, S. (2011). *An R Companion to Applied Regression*. Sage, Thousand Oaks CA, 2nd edition.

Fredholm, E. I. (1903). Sur une classe d'equations fonctionnelles. *Acta Mathematica*, 27:365–390.

Freyberger, J. (2017). On completeness and consistency in nonparametric instrumental variable models. *Econometrica*, 85(5):1629–1644.

Fridman, V. M. (1956). A method of successive approximations for Fredholm integral equations of the first kind. *Uspeskhi, Math. Nauk.*, 11:233–334.

Fubini, G. (1907). Sugli integrali multipli. *Rom. Acc. L. Rend.*, 16(1):608–614.

Gallant, A. R. (1981). On the bias in flexible functional forms and an essential unbiased form: The Fourier flexible form. *Journal of Econometrics*, 15:211–245.

Gallant, A. R. (1987). *Nonlinear Statistical Models*. Wiley, New York.

Gao, Q., Liu, L., and Racine, J. S. (2015). A partially linear kernel estimator for categorical data. *Econometric Reviews*, 34(6–10):958–977.

Gasser, T. and Müller, H.-G. (1979). Kernel estimation of regression functions. In *Smoothing Techniques for Curve Estimation*, pages 23–68. Springer-Verlag, New York.

Gasser, T., Müller, H.-G., and Mammitzsch, V. (1985). Kernels for nonparametric curve estimation. *Journal of the Royal Statistical Society. Series B*, 47(2):238–252.

Geary, R. C. (1947). Testing for normality. *Biometrika*, 34(3/4):209–242.

Geisser, S. (1975). A predictive sample reuse method with application. *Journal of the American Statistical Association*, 70:320–328.

Gençay, R., Selçuk, F., and Whitcher, B., editors (2002). *An Introduction to Wavelets and Other Filtering Methods in Finance and Economics*. Academic Press, San Diego.

Gilli, M., Maringer, D., and Schumann, E. (2011). *Numerical Methods and Optimization in Finance*. Academic Press, San Diego.

Gini, C. (1914). *L'Ammontare e la Composizione della Ricchezza delle Nazione*. Torino, Bocca.

Golan, A. (2017). *Foundations of Info-Metrics: Modeling, Inference, and Imperfect Information.* Oxford University Press, Oxford.

Granger, C. W. and Lin, J. L. (1994). Using the mutual information coefficient to identify lags in nonlinear models. *Journal of Time Series Analysis*, 15(4):371–384.

Granger, C. W., Maasoumi, E., and Racine, J. S. (2004). A dependence metric for possibly nonlinear time series. *Journal of Time Series Analysis*, 25(5):649–669.

Gray, A. and Moore, A. W. (2003). Very fast multivariate kernel density estimation via computational geometry. In *Proceedings of the Joint Statistical Meetings of the American Statistical Association.*

Greene, W. H. (2003). *Econometric Analysis.* Prentice Hall, Upper Saddle River, NJ, 5th edition.

Greengard, L. (1988). *The Rapid Evaluation of Potential Fields in Particle Systems.* MIT Press, Cambridge, MA.

Greengard, L. and Strain, J. (1991). The fast gauss transform. *Society for Industrial and Applied Mathematics: Journal of Science and Computation*, 12(1):79–94.

Hadamard, J. (1923). *Lectures on Cauchy's Problem in Linear Partial Differential Equations.* Yale University Press, New Haven.

Hahn, J. (1998). On the role of the propensity score in efficient semiparametric estimation of average treatment effects. *Econometrica*, 66:315–331.

Hall, P. G. and Horowitz, J. L. (2005). Nonparametric methods for inference in the presence of instrumental variables. *Annals of Statistics*, 33(6):2904–2929.

Hall, P. G. and Huang, H. (2001). Nonparametric kernel regression subject to monotonicity constraints. *Annals of Statistics*, 29(3):624–647.

Hall, P. G., Huang, H., Gifford, J., and Gijbels, I. (2001). Nonparametric estimation of hazard rate under the constraint of monotonicity. *Journal of Computational and Graphical Statistics*, 10(3):592–614.

Hall, P. G., Li, Q., and Racine, J. S. (2007). Nonparametric estimation of regression functions in the presence of irrelevant regressors. *The Review of Economics and Statistics*, 89:784–789.

Hall, P. G. and Racine, J. S. (2015). Infinite order cross-validated local polynomial regression. *Journal of Econometrics*, 185(2):510–525.

Hall, P. G., Racine, J. S., and Li, Q. (2004). Cross-validation and the estimation of conditional probability densities. *Journal of the American Statistical Association*, 99(468):1015–1026.

Hall, P. G. and Wehrly, T. E. (1991). A geometrical method for removing edge effects from kernel-type nonparametric regression estimators. *Journal of the American Statistical Association*, 86(415):665–672.

Hansen, B. (2018). *Econometrics*. Online PDF available from the author's website (www.ssc.wisc.edu/~bhansen/econometrics/Econometrics.pdf).

Härdle, W. (1990). *Applied Nonparametric Regression*. Cambridge University Press, New Rochelle.

Härdle, W., Hall, P. G., and Ichimura, H. (1993). Optimal smoothing in single index models. *Annals of Statistics*, 21:157–178.

Härdle, W. and Mammen, E. (1993). Comparing nonparametric versus parametric regression fits. *Annals of Statistics*, 21:1926–1947.

Härdle, W., Müller, M., Sperlich, S., and Werwatz, A. (2004). *Nonparametric and Semiparametric Models*. Springer Series in Statistics, Germany.

Harfouche, L., Adjabi, S., Zougab, N., and Funke, B. (2017). Multiplicative bias correction for discrete kernels. *Statistical Methods & Applications*, pages 253–276.

Hart, J. D. (1997). *Nonparametric Smoothing and Lack-of-Fit Tests*. Springer Verlag, New York.

Hartley, R. V. L. (1928). Transmission of information. *Bell System Technical Journal*, 7:535.

Hastie, T. and Tibshirani, R. (1993). Varying-coefficient models. *Journal of the Royal Statistical Society. Series B*, 55:757–796.

Hausman, J. and McFadden, D. (1984). Specification tests for the multinomial Logit model. *Econometrica*, 52(5):1219–1240.

Hayfield, T. and Racine, J. S. (2008). Nonparametric econometrics: The np package. *Journal of Statistical Software*, 27(5):1–32.

Heckman, J. J., Ichimura, H., and Todd, P. (1997). Matching as an econometric evaluation estimator: Evidence from evaluating a job training programme. *Review of Economic Studies*, 64:605–654.

Heckman, J. J., Ichimura, H., and Todd, P. (1998). Matching as an econometric evaluation estimator. *Review of Economic Studies*, 65:261–294.

Henderson, D. J., Carroll, R. J., and Li, Q. (2008). Nonparametric estimation and testing of fixed effects panel data models. *Journal of Econometrics*, 144(1):257–275.

Henderson, D. J., Li, Q., Parmeter, C. F., and Yao, S. (2015). Gradient-based smoothing parameter selection for nonparametric regression estimation. *Journal of Econometrics*, 184(2):233–241.

Henderson, D. J. and Parmeter, C. F. (2015). *Applied Nonparametric Econometrics*. Cambridge University Press, New York.

Hirano, K., Imbens, G. W., and Ridder, G. (2003). Efficient estimation of average treatment effects using the estimated propensity score. *Econometrica*, 71(4):1161–1189.

Hodges, J. L. and Lehmann, E. L. (1956). The efficiency of some nonparametric competitors of the *t*-test. *Annals of Mathematical Statistics*, 27:324–335.

Hoerl, A. E. and Kennard, R. W. (1970). Ridge regression: Biased estimation for nonorthogonal problems. *Technometrics*, 12:55–67.

Hong, Y. M. and White, H. L. (2005). Asymptotic distribution theory for nonparametric entropy measures of serial dependence. *Econometrica*, 73(3):837–902.

Horowitz, J. L. (1998). *Semiparametric Methods in Econometrics*. Lecture Notes in Statistics: Springer-Verlag, New York.

Horowitz, J. L. (2007). Asymptotic normality of a nonparametric instrumental variables estimator. *International Economic Review*, 48(4):1329–1349.

Horowitz, J. L. (2011). Applied nonparametric instrumental variables estimation. *Econometrica*, 79:347–394.

Horowitz, J. L. (2014). Ill-posed inverse problems in economics. *Annual Review of Economics*, 6:21–51.

Horowitz, J. L. and Härdle, W. (1994). Testing a parametric model against a semiparametric alternative. *Econometric Theory*, 10:821–848.

Horowitz, J. L. and Spokoiny, V. G. (2001). An adaptive, rate-optimal test of a parametric mean-regression model against a nonparametric alternative. *Econometrica*, 69(3):599–631.

Hosmer, D. W. and Lemeshow, S. (2013). *Applied Logistic Regression*. Wiley, New York.

Hristache, M., Juditsky, A., and Spokoiny, V. G. (2001). Direct estimation of the index coefficient in a single-index model. *Annals of Statistics*, 29:595–623.

Hsiao, C., Li, Q., and Racine, J. S. (2007). A consistent model specification test with mixed categorical and continuous data. *Journal of Econometrics*, 140:802–826.

Huber, P. J. (1964). Robust estimation of a location parameter. *Annals of Statistics*, 35:73–101.

Hurvich, C. M., Simonoff, J. S., and Tsai, C. L. (1998). Smoothing parameter selection in nonparametric regression using an improved Akaike information criterion. *Journal of the Royal Statistical Society. Series B*, 60:271–293.

Hyndman, R. J. and Khandakar, Y. (2008). Automatic time series forecasting: the forecast package for R. *Journal of Statistical Software*, 26(3):1–22.

Ichimura, H. (1993). Semiparametric least squares (SLS) and weighted SLS estimation of single-index models. *Journal of Econometrics*, 58:71–120.

Ichino, A. and Winter-Ebmer, R. (1998). The long-run educational cost of world war II: An example of local average treatment effect estimation. CEPR publication DP1895, Center for Economic Policy Research.

Igarashi, G. (2015). Bias corrections for some asymmetric kernel estimators. *Journal of Statistical Planning and Inference*, 159:37–63.

Igarashi, G. and Kakizawa, Y. (2018). Limiting bias-reduced amoroso kernel density estimators for non-negative data. *Communications in Statistics - Theory and Methods*, 47(20):4905–4937.

Inoue, A. and Kilian, L. (2004). In-sample and out-of-sample tests of predictability: Which one should we use? *Econometric Reviews*, 23:371–402.

Joe, H. (1989). Relative entropy measures of multivariate dependence. *Journal of the American Statistical Association*, 84:157–164.

Johannes, J., van Bellegem, S., and Vanhems, A. (2013). Iterative regularization in nonparametric instrumental regression. *Journal of Statistical Planning and Inference*, 143(1):24–39.

Jones, M. C. (1993). Simple boundary correction for kernel density estimation. *Statistics and Computing*, 3(3):135–146.

Jones, M. C. and Foster, P. J. (1996). A simple nonnegative boundary correction method for kernel density estimation. *Statistica Sinica*, 6:1005–1013.

Karunamunia, R. J. and Zhang, S. (2008). Some improvements on a boundary corrected kernel density estimator. *Statistics and Probability Letters*, 78:499–507.

Kendall, M. G. (1938). A new measure of rank correlation. *Biometrika*, 30(1/2):81–93.

Keynes, J. M. (1936). *The General Theory of Employment, Interest, and Money*. Macmillan Cambridge University Press, London.

Kiefer, N. M. and Racine, J. S. (2009). The smooth colonel meets the reverend. *Journal of Nonparametric Statistics*, 21:521–533.

Kiefer, N. M. and Racine, J. S. (2017). The smooth colonel and the reverend find common ground. *Econometric Reviews*, 36(1–3):241–256.

Klein, R. W. and Spady, R. H. (1993). An efficient semiparametric estimator for binary response models. *Econometrica*, 61:387–421.

Koch, S. F. (2017). User fee abolition and the demand for public health care. *South African Journal of Economics*, 85(2):242–258.

Koenker, R. and Bassett, G. (1978). Regression quantiles. *Econometrica*, 46:33–50.

Kullback, S. (1959). *Information Theory and Statistics*. Wiley, New York.

Landweber, L. (1951). An iterative formula for Fredholm integral equations of the first kind. *American Journal of Mathematics*, 73:615–624.

Lavergne, P. (2001). An equality test across nonparametric regressions. *Journal of Econometrics*, 103:307–344.

Lavergne, P. and Vuong, Q. (2000). Nonparametric significance testing. *Econometric Theory*, 16:576–601.

Le Digabel, S. (2011). Algorithm 909: NOMAD: Nonlinear optimization with the MADS algorithm. *ACM Transactions on Mathematical Software*, 37(4):44:1–44:15.

Lechner, M. (1999). Earnings and employment effects of continuous off-the-job training in East Germany after unification. *Journal of Business and Economic Statistics*, 17:74–90.

Lehmann, E. L. (1966). Some concepts of dependence. *Annals of Mathematical Statistics*, 37:1137–1153.

Lemieux, T. (2006). The mincer equation thirty years after schooling, experience, and earnings. In Grossbard-Shechtman, S., editor, *Jacob Mincer, A Pioneer of Modern Labor Economics*, chapter 2. Springer Verlag.

Leung, D. (2005). Cross-validation in nonparametric regression with outliers. *Annals of Statistics*, 33:2291–2310.

Li, C., Li, H., and Racine, J. S. (2017). Cross-validated mixed datatype bandwidth selection for nonparametric cumulative distribution/survivor functions. *Econometric Reviews*, 36:970–987.

Li, C. and Racine, J. S. (2013). A smooth nonparametric conditional density test for categorical responses. *Econometric Theory*, 29:629–641.

Li, Q. (1996). Nonparametric testing of closeness between two unknown distributions. *Econometric Reviews*, 15:261–274.

Li, Q., Huang, C. J., Li, D., and Fu, T. T. (2002). Semiparametric smooth coefficient models. *Journal of Business and Economics Statistics*, 20:412–422.

Li, Q., Lin, J., and Racine, J. S. (2013). Optimal bandwidth selection for nonparametric conditional distribution and quantile functions. *Journal of Business and Economic Statistics*, 31(1):57–65.

Li, Q., Maasoumi, E., and Racine, J. S. (2009a). A nonparametric test for equality of distributions with mixed categorical and continuous data. *Journal of Econometrics*, 148:186–200.

Li, Q. and Racine, J. S. (2003). Nonparametric estimation of distributions with categorical and continuous data. *Journal of Multivariate Analysis*, 86:266–292.

Li, Q. and Racine, J. S. (2004). Cross-validated local linear nonparametric regression. *Statistica Sinica*, 14(2):485–512.

Li, Q. and Racine, J. S. (2007). *Nonparametric Econometrics: Theory and Practice*. Princeton University Press, Princeton.

Li, Q. and Racine, J. S. (2008). Nonparametric estimation of conditional CDF and quantile functions with mixed categorical and continuous data. *Journal of Business and Economic Statistics*, 26(4):423–434.

Li, Q. and Racine, J. S. (2010). Smooth varying-coefficient estimation and inference for qualitative and quantitative data. *Econometric Theory*, 26:1607–1637.

Li, Q., Racine, J. S., and Wooldridge, J. M. (2008). Estimating average treatment effects with continuous and discrete covariates: The case of Swan-Ganz catherization. *American Economic Review*, 98(2):357–362.

Li, Q., Racine, J. S., and Wooldridge, J. M. (2009b). Efficient estimation of average treatment effects with mixed categorical and continuous data. *Journal of Business and Economic Statistics*, 27:206–223.

Li, Q. and Wang, S. (1998). A simple consistent bootstrap test for a parametric regression functional form. *Journal of Econometrics*, 87:145–165.

Lin, D. Y., Psaty, B. M., and Kronmal, R. A. (1998). Assessing the sensitivity of regression results to unmeasured confounders in observational studies. *Biometrics*, 54:948–963.

Linton, O. B. (1995). Second order approximation in the partially linear regression model. *Econometrica*, 63(5):1079–1112.

Liu, R. and Yang, L. (2008). Kernel estimation of multivariate cumulative distribution function. *Journal of Nonparametric Statistics*, 20(8):661–677.

Loader, C. R. (1999). Bandwidth selection: Classical or plug-in? *Annals of Statistics*, 27(2):415–438.

Maasoumi, E. and Racine, J. S. (2002). Entropy and predictability of stock market returns. *Journal of Econometrics*, 107(2):291–312.

Maasoumi, E. and Racine, J. S. (2009). A robust entropy-based test of asymmetry for discrete and continuous processes. *Econometric Reviews*, 28:246–261.

Mammen, E. (1992). *When Does Bootstrap Work? Asymptotic Results and Simulations*. Springer-Verlag, New York.

Maronna, A., Martin, R. D., and Yohai, V. J. (2006). *Robust Statistics: Theory and Methods*. Wiley, New York.

Marron, J. S. and Ruppert, D. (1994). Transformations to reduce boundary bias in kernel density estimation. *Journal of the Royal Statistical Society. Series B*, 56(4):653–671.

Maslow, A. (1966). *The Psychology of Science - A Reconnaissance*. Harper & Row, New York.

Masry, E. (1996a). Multivariate local polynomial regression for time series: uniform strong consistency and rates. *Journal of Time Series Analysis*, 17:571–599.

Masry, E. (1996b). Multivariate regression estimation: local polynomial fitting for time series. *Stochastic Processes and Their Applications*, 65:81–101.

Matzkin, R. L. (1991). Semiparametric estimation of monotone and concave utility functions for polychotomous choice models. *Econometrica*, 59:1315–1327.

McCracken, M. W. (2000). Robust out-of-sample prediction. *Journal of Econometrics*, 99(2):195–223.

Medeiros, M. C., Teräsvirta, T., and Rech, G. (2006). Building neural network models for time series: a statistical approach. *Journal of Forecasting*, 25:49–75.

Mitchell, W. C. (1927). *Business Cycles: The Problem and Its Setting*. National Bureau of Economic Research, New York.

Mora, J. and Moro-Egido, A. I. (2008). On specification testing of ordered discrete choice models. *Journal of Econometrics*, 143:191–205.

Morozov, V. A. (1967). Choice of a parameter for the solution of functional equations by the regularization method. *Sov. Math. Doklady*, 8:1000–1003.

Murphy, K. M. and Welch, F. (1990). Empirical age-earnings profiles. *Journal of Labor Economics*, 8(2):202–229.

Müller, H.-G. (1991). Smooth optimum kernel estimators near endpoints. *Biometrika*, 78(3):521–530.

Nadaraya, E. A. (1964). Some new estimates for distribution functions. *Theory of Probability and Its Applications*, 9:497–500.

Nadaraya, E. A. (1965). On nonparametric estimates of density functions and regression curves. *Theory of Applied Probability*, 10:186–190.

Nelsen, R. B. (2006). *An Introduction to Copulas*. Springer-Verlag, 2nd edition.

Newey, W. K. and Powell, J. L. (2003). Instrumental variables estimation of nonparametric models. *Econometrica*, 71(5):1565–1578.

Nie, Z. and Racine, J. S. (2012). The crs package: Nonparametric regression splines for continuous and categorical predictors. *R Journal*, 4(2):48–56.

Noh, H. (2014). Frontier estimation using kernel smoothing estimators with data transformation. *Journal of the Korean Statistical Society*, 43(4):503–512.

Otsu, T. (2009). RESET for quantile regression. *Test*, 18:381–391.

Ouyang, D., Li, Q., and Racine, J. S. (2006). Cross-validation and the estimation of probability distributions with categorical data. *Journal of Nonparametric Statistics*, 18(1):69–100.

Ouyang, D., Li, Q., and Racine, J. S. (2009). Nonparametric regression with weakly dependent data: The discrete and continuous regressor case. *Journal of Nonparametric Statistics*, 21(6):697–711.

Ouyang, D., Li, Q., and Racine, J. S. (2013). Categorical semiparametric varying coefficient models. *Journal of Applied Econometrics*, 28(3):551–579.

Pagan, A. and Ullah, A. (1999). *Nonparametric Econometrics*. Cambridge University Press, Cambridge.

Parzen, E. (1962). On estimation of a probability density function and mode. *The Annals of Mathematical Statistics*, 33:1065–1076.

Patton, A., Politis, D. N., and White, H. L. (2009). Correction to "Automatic block-length selection for the dependent bootstrap" by D. Politis and H. White. *Econometric Reviews*, 28(4):372–375.

Pearson, K. (1895). Contributions to the mathematical theory of evolution II. Skew variation in homogeneous material. *Philosophical Transactions of the Royal Society of London. A*, 186:343–414.

Polansky, A. M. and Baker, E. R. (2000). Multistage plug-in bandwidth selection for kernel distribution function estimates. *Journal of Statistical Computation and Simulation*, 65:63–80.

Politis, D. N. (2015). *Model-Free Prediction and Regression*. Springer, New York.

Politis, D. N. and Romano, J. P. (1994). Limit theorems for weakly dependent Hilbert space valued random variables with applications to the stationary bootstrap. *Statistica Sinica*, 4:461–476.

Politis, D. N. and White, H. L. (2004). Automatic block-length selection for the dependent bootstrap. *Econometric Reviews*, 23:53–70.

Prakasa Rao, B. L. S. (1983). *Nonparametric Functional Estimation*. Academic Press, San Diego, 1st edition.

Prakasa Rao, B. L. S. (2014). *Nonparametric Functional Estimation*. Academic Press, San Diego, 2nd edition.

Premaratne, G. and Bera, A. (2005). A test for symmetry with leptokurtic financial data. *Journal of Financial Econometrics*, 3:169–187.

Press, W. H., Flanery, B. P., Teukolsky, S. A., and Vetterling, W. T. (1990). *Numerical recipes in C*. Cambridge University Press, New York.

Priestley, M. B. and Chao, M. T. (1972). Nonparametric function fitting. *Journal of the Royal Statistical Society*, 34:385–392.

Qu, Z. and Yoon, J. (2015). Nonparametric estimation and inference on conditional quantile processes. *Journal of Econometrics*, 185:1–19.

R Core Team (2018). *R: A Language and Environment for Statistical Computing*. R Foundation for Statistical Computing, Vienna.

Racine, J. S. (1997). Consistent significance testing for nonparametric regression. *Journal of Business and Economic Statistics*, 15(3):369–379.

Racine, J. S. (2001). On the nonlinear predictability of stock returns using financial and economic variables. *Journal of Business and Economic Statistics*, 19(3):380–382.

Racine, J. S. (2002). Parallel distributed kernel estimation. *Computational Statistics and Data Analysis*, 40:293–302.

Racine, J. S. (2016). Local polynomial derivative estimation: Analytic or Taylor? *Advances in Econometrics*, 36:617–633.

Racine, J. S., Hart, J. D., and Li, Q. (2006). Testing the significance of categorical predictor variables in nonparametric regression models. *Econometric Reviews*, 25:523–544.

Racine, J. S. and Li, K. (2017). Nonparametric conditional quantile estimation: A locally weighted quantile kernel approach. *Journal of Econometrics*, 201:72–94.

Racine, J. S. and Li, Q. (2004). Nonparametric estimation of regression functions with both categorical and continuous data. *Journal of Econometrics*, 119(1):99–130.

Racine, J. S., Li, Q., and Yan, K. X. (2017). Kernel smoothed probability mass functions for ordered datatypes. Technical Report Department of Economics Working Paper 2017-14, McMaster University, Hamilton, Ontario, Canada.

Racine, J. S. and Nie, Z. (2017). *crs: Categorical Regression Splines*. R package version 0.15-28.

Racine, J. S. and Parmeter, C. F. (2014). Data-driven model evaluation: A test for revealed performance. In Ullah, A., Racine, J. S., and Su, L., editors, *Handbook of Applied Nonparametric and Semiparametric Econometrics and Statistics*, pages 308–345, New York. Oxford University Press.

Ramsey, J. B. (1969). Tests for specification error in classical linear least squares regression analysis. *Journal of the Royal Statistical Society. Series B*, 31:350–371.

Rényi, A. (1961). On measures of entropy and information. In *Proceedings of the 4th Berkeley Symposium on Mathematical Statistics and Probability*, volume 1, pages 547–561. Berkeley: University of California Press.

Rilstone, P. and Ullah, A. (1989). Nonparametric estimation of response coefficients. *Communications in Statistics - Theory and Methods*, 18(7):2615–2627.

Robinson, P. M. (1983). Nonparametric estimators for time series. *Journal of Time Series Analysis*, 4:185–207.

Robinson, P. M. (1988). Root-n consistent semiparametric regression. *Econometrica*, 56:931–954.

Robinson, P. M. (1991). Consistent nonparametric entropy-based testing. *Review of Economic Studies*, 58:437–453.

Rodriguez-Poo, J. M. and Soberon, A. (2017). Nonparametric and semiparametric panel data models: Recent developments. *Journal of Economic Surveys*, 31(4):923–960.

Rosenbaum, P. and Rubin, D. (1983). The central role of the propensity score in observational studies for causal effects. *Biometrika*, 70:41–55.

Rosenblatt, M. (1956). Remarks on some nonparametric estimates of a density function. *The Annals of Mathematical Statistics*, 27:832–837.

Rudemo, M. (1982). Empirical choice of histograms and kernel density estimators. *Scandinavian Journal of Statistics*, 9:65–78.

Ruppert, D., Sheather, S. J., and Wand, M. P. (1995). An effective bandwidth selector for local least squares regression. *Journal of the American Statistical Association*, 90:1257–1270.

Ruppert, D. and Wand, M. P. (1994). Multivariate locally weighted least squares regression. *Annals of Statistics*, 22:1346–1370.

Ruppert, D., Wand, M. P., and Carroll, R. J. (2003). *Semiparametric Regression*. Cambridge University Press, Cambridge.

Santafe, G., Calvo, B., Perez, A., and Lozano, J. A. (2015). *bde: Bounded Density Estimation*. R package version 1.0.1.

Scaillet, O. (2004). Density estimation using inverse and reciprocal inverse gaussian kernels. *Journal of Nonparametric Statistics*, 16(1–2):217–226.

Scaillet, O. (2005). A Kolmogorov-Smirnov type test for positive quadrant dependence. *Canadian Journal of Statistics*, 33:415–427.

Scott, D. W. (1985). Averaged shifted histograms: Effective nonparametric density estimators in several dimensions. *Annals of Statistics*, 13:1024–1040.

Scott, D. W. (1992). *Multivariate Density Estimation: Theory, Practice, and Visualization*. Wiley, New York.

Scott, D. W. and Sheather, S. J. (1985). Kernel density estimation with binned data. *Communication in Statistics: Theory and Methods*, 14:1353–1359.

Seifert, B. and Gasser, T. (2000). Data adaptive ridging in local polynomial regression. *Journal of Computational and Graphical Statistics*, 9:338–360.

Shannon, C. E. (1948). A mathematical theory of communication. *Bell System Technical Journal*, 27:379–423, 625–656.

Shapiro, S. S. and Wilk, M. B. (1965). An analysis of variance test for normality (complete samples). *Biometrika*, 52(3–4):591–611.

Shaw, P., Cohen, M., and Chen, T. (2015). Nonparametric instrumental variable estimation in practice. *Journal of Econometric Methods*, 1(5):153–177.

Sheather, S. J. and Jones, M. C. (1991). A reliable data-based bandwidth selection method for kernel density estimation. *Journal of the Royal Statistical Society. Series B*, 53:683–690.

Shen, X. and Ye, J. (2002). Model selection. *Journal of the American Statistical Association*, 97(457):210–221.

Silverman, B. W. (1986). *Density Estimation for Statistics and Data Analysis*. Chapman and Hall, New York.

Silverman, B. W. and Young, G. A. (1987). The bootstrap: To smooth or not to smooth? *Biometrika*, 74(3):469–479.

Simonoff, J. S. (1996). *Smoothing Methods in Statistics*. Springer Series in Statistics, New York.

Skaug, H. J. and Tjøstheim, D. (1996). Testing for serial independence using measures of distance between densities. In Robinson, P. and Rosenblatt, M., editors, *Athens Conference on Applied Probability and Time Series*, New York. Springer.

Smith, M. S. and Khaled, M. A. (2012). Estimation of copula models with discrete margins via Bayesian data augmentation. *Journal of the American Statistical Association*, 107(497):290–303.

Spearman, C. (1904). The proof and measurement of association between two things. *American Journal of Psychology*, 15(1):72–101.

Statistics South Africa (1995). *October Household Survey (South Africa), 1995*. Statistics South Africa (producer) and South African Data Archive (distributor), Pretoria.

Stein, C. (1956). Inadmissibility of the usual estimator for the mean of a multivariate distribution. *Proceedings of the Third Berkeley Symposium on Mathematical Statistics and Probability*, 1:197–206.

Stone, C. J. (1974). Cross-validatory choice and assessment of statistical predictions (with discussion). *Journal of the Royal Statistical Society*, 36:111–147.

Stone, C. J. (1977). Consistent nonparametric regression. *Annals of Statistics*, 5:595–645.

Stute, W. and Zhu, L.-X. (2005). Nonparametric checks for single-index models. *Annals of Statistics*, 33(3):1048–1083.

Su, L., Murtazashvili, I., and Ullah, A. (2013). Local linear GMM estimation of functional coefficient IV models with application to the estimation of rate of return to schooling. *Journal of Business and Economic Statistics*, 31(2):184–207.

Su, L. and Ullah, A. (2008). Local polynomial estimation of nonparametric simultaneous equations models. *Journal of Econometrics*, 144:193–218.

Su, L. and Ullah, A. (2011). Nonparametric and semiparametric panel econometric models: Estimation and testing. In Giles, D. E. A. and Ullah, A., editors, *Handbook of Empirical Economics and Finance*, pages 455–497. Chapman & Hall/CRC, Boca Raton, FL.

Su, L. and Ullah, A. (2013). A nonparametric goodness-of-fit-based test for conditional heteroskedasticity. *Econometric Theory*, 29(1):187–212.

Sun, J. and Loader, C. R. (1994). Simultaneous confidence bands for linear regression and smoothing. *Annals of Statistics*, 22(3):1328–1345.

Sun, Y., Cai, Z., and Li, Q. (2016). A consistent nonparametric test on semiparametric smooth coefficient models with integrated time series. *Econometric Theory*, 32(4):988–1022.

Sun, Y. and Li, Q. (2011). Data-driven bandwidth selection for nonstationary semiparametric models. *Journal of Business and Economic Statistics*, 29(4):541–551.

Sun, Y., Zhang, Y. Y., and Li, Q. (2015). Nonparametric panel data regression models. In Baltagi, B. H., editor, *The Oxford Handbook of Panel Data*, pages 285–324. Oxford University Press, Oxford.

Tikhonov, A. N. (1943). On the stability of inverse problems. *Doklady Akademii Nauk SSSR*, 39(5):195–198.

Timmermann, A. and Perez-Quiros, G. (2001). Business cycle asymmetries in stock returns: Evidence from higher order moments and conditional densities. *Journal of Econometrics*, 103:259–306.

Tonelli, L. (1909). Sull'integrazione per parti. *Atti della Accademia Nazionale dei Lincei*, 18(2):246–253.

Trivedi, P. K. and Zimmer, D. (2007). *Copula Modeling: An Introduction for Practitioners*. NOW, Boston.

Tsukahara, H. (2005). Semiparametric estimation in copula models. *The Canadian Journal of Statistics / La Revue Canadienne de Statistique*, 33(3):357–375.

Tsybakov, A. B. (2009). *Introduction to Nonparametric Estimation*. Springer, New York.

Turlach, B. A. and Weingessel, A. (2013). *quadprog: Functions to solve Quadratic Programming Problems*. R package version 1.5-5.

Venables, W. N. and Ripley, B. D. (2002). *Modern Applied Statistics with S*. Springer, New York, 4th edition.

Vinod, R. and Ullah, A. (1988). Flexible production function estimation by nonparametric kernel estimators. *Advances in Econometrics*, 7:139–160.

Wahba, G. (1990). *Spline Models for Observational Data*. Society for Industrial and Applied Mathematics.

Wand, M. P. (2015). *KernSmooth: Functions for Kernel Smoothing Supporting Wand & Jones (1995)*. R package version 2.23-15.

Wand, M. P. and Jones, M. C. (1995). *Kernel Smoothing*. Chapman and Hall, London.

Wang, F. T. and Scott, D. W. (1994). The L_1 method for robust nonparametric regression. *Journal of the American Statistical Association*, 89:65–76.

Wang, L., Brown, L. D., Cai, T. T., and Levine, M. (2008). Effect of mean on variance function estimation in nonparametric regression. *Annals of Statistics*, 36(2):646–664.

Wang, M. C. and van Ryzin, J. (1981). A class of smooth estimators for discrete distributions. *Biometrika*, 68:301–309.

Wang, N. (2003). Marginal nonparametric kernel regression accounting for within-subject correlation. *Biometrika*, 90:43–52.

Wang, N., Carroll, R. J., and Lin, X. (2005). Efficient semiparametric marginal estimation for longitudinal/clustered data. *Journal of the American Statistical Association*, 100:147–157.

Wang, Q. and Phillips, P. C. B. (2009). Asymptotic theory for local time density estimation and nonparametric cointegrating regression. *Econometric Theory*, 25:710–738.

Wang, Y. (2011). *Smoothing Splines: Methods and Applications*. Chapman & Hall/CRC, New York.

Wasserman, L. (2006). *All of Nonparametric Statistics*. Springer-Verlag, New York.

Watson, G. S. (1964). Smooth regression analysis. *Sankhya*, 26(15):175–184.

West, K. D. and McCracken, M. W. (1998). Regression-based tests of predictive ability. *International Economic Review*, 39(3):817–840.

White, H. L. (1984). *Asymptotic Theory for Econometricians*. Academic Press, Orlando, FL.

White, H. L. (2000). A reality check for data snooping. *Econometrica*, 68(5):1097–1126.

Wikipedia (2017). Analytic function.

Wooldridge, J. M. (2002). *Econometric Analysis of Cross Section and Panel Data*. MIT Press, Cambridge, MA.

Xie, Y. (2017). *bookdown: Authoring Books and Technical Documents with R Markdown*. R package version 0.5.10.

Yang, L. and Tschernig, R. (1999). Multivariate bandwidth selection for local linear regression. *Journal of the Royal Statistical Society, Series B*, 61(4):793–815.

Yang, S.-S. (1985). A smooth nonparametric estimator of a quantile function. *Journal of the American Statistical Association*, 80(392):1004–1011.

Yatchew, A. (2003). *Semiparametric Regression for the Applied Econometrician*. Cambridge University Press, Cambridge.

Yatchew, A. and Bos, L. (1997). Nonparametric regression and testing in economic models. *Journal of Quantitative Economics*, 13:81–131.

Ye, J. (1998). On measuring and correcting the effects of data mining and data selection. *Journal of the American Statistical Association*, 93(441):120–131.

Yu, K. and Jones, M. C. (2004). Likelihood-based local linear estimation of the conditional variance function. *Journal of the American Statistical Association*, 99:139–144.

Author Index

Subject Index